ADVANCE PRAISE

"Your writing is superb; I feel each word, keenly. Another excellent piece from you, my friend. I feel your hunger, your pervasive thirst and it fills me up."

—Deborah Rachel "Deb" Filler. Internationally acclaimed writer, actor, musician, and comedian. She has toured the world with her one-woman shows *Punch Me in the Stomach.*

"*The Cello Still Sings* is a memoir that captures both the enduring trauma of the second generation of Holocaust survivors and the enduring healing power of music. It is a powerful, intergenerational narrative mix that reveals and illumines."

—Lawrence Sutin. Professor Emeritus, Creative Writing and Liberal Studies Programs at Hamline University, Saint Paul, MN, and professor of a low-residency program at the Vermont College.

"[Leonard Bernstein] came face to face with the remnants of the unspeakable in the spring of 1948 when, as a 29-year-old on the cusp of world-wide adulation, he conducted an ensemble in Landsberg, Germany. Janet's father Gyuri (George) played the cello... in the very orchestra conducted by Bernstein... The consequences of that emotional music-making serve as brackets to the remarkable tale told in this powerful book by cellist Janet Horvath."

—Martin Goldsmith. NPR Classical Music Host and author of *The Inextinguishable Symphony: A True Story of Music and Love in Nazi Germany*.

"*The Cello Still Sings* is a riveting memoir that captures Janet Horvath's personal quest that led to uncovering her parents' story and trauma during the Nazi occupation of Hungary. In this beautifully written story, Horvath weaves contemporary life and her search for family truth, with ancestral richness alongside the horrific history of the Jews during WWII. She illuminates the healing power of music and how it was a thread that connected generations over time. My heart opened as I read this memoir. I cried and I stood in awe of the courage of this family."

—Ilana (Nancy) Rowe. Professor of Transpersonal Psychology, Sofia University.

"Part memoir and part biography, Janet Horvath's *The Cello Still Sings* is an inspiring chronicle of her journey to unearth the story of how her father and 16 other Holocaust survivors formed an orchestra shortly after their liberation. Readers will be left breathless as Horvath retraces her father's footsteps and reclaims his legacy—one of music, loss, and ultimately redemption."

—James A. Grymes. National Jewish Book Award winning author of *Violins of Hope: Violins of the Holocaust—Instruments of Hope and Liberation in Mankind's Darkest Hour*.

"Janet's memories are a beautiful remembrance of her father and a living testament to the indelible power of music to transcend and unite. Her view of music from the inside out gives the reader a genuine sense of what it feels like to be a professional musician."

—Maestro Marin Alsop. Chief Conductor of the ORF Vienna Radio Symphony Orchestra.

THE CELLO STILL SINGS

A GENERATIONAL STORY OF THE HOLOCAUST
AND OF THE TRANSFORMATIVE POWER
OF MUSIC

JANET HORVATH

CONTENTS

ISBN 9789493276826 (ebook)

ISBN 9789493276802 (paperback)

ISBN 9789493276819 (hardcover)

Publisher: Amsterdam Publishers, The Netherlands

info@amsterdampublishers.com

The Cello Still Sings is part of the series **Holocaust Heritage**

Cover design: Denise Tsui

Editors: Jean Blomquist, Malin Lonnberg

Cover photo of Janet Horvath: Ann Marsden

The Essay "A Musician Afraid of Sound" first appeared in *The Atlantic*, October 20, 2015; excerpts reprinted with permission

Libretto excerpt from the oratorio: *To Be Certain of the Dawn* by Michael Dennis Browne, music by Stephen Paulus, is reprinted with permission of the author.

To My Family
and All Who Carry Burdens of the Past

FOREWORD

The irrepressible and inspirational conductor, composer, pianist, and unconsecrated rabbi Leonard Bernstein declared in one of his captivating books that "Music can name the unnameable and communicate the unknowable." To which he might well have added, "And redeem the unspeakable."

Lenny, as he was known far and wide, came face to face with the remnants of the unspeakable in the spring of 1948 when, as a 29-year-old on the cusp of worldwide adulation, he conducted an ensemble in Landsberg, Germany, known—with a dollop of understated irony —as The Ex-Concentration Camp Orchestra. The performances took place within the confines of a Displaced Persons camp, its inmates/musicians still considered stateless and unrooted three years after the end of the war that had consigned them all for months within the hellish walls of Auschwitz and Dachau, Belsen and Theresienstadt and Mauthausen and all the other facilities in Eastern Europe whose names continue to sound as heavy, tolling bells of the heart. In a letter home, Lenny relates that he was presented with a concentration camp uniform as a gift. "[I was] received by parades of kids with flowers," then "conducted a 20-piece orchestra ... and cried my eyes out."

The consequences of that emotional music-making serve as

brackets to the remarkable tale told in this book by cellist Janet Horvath. Her father Gyuri also played the cello in his native Hungary before enduring slave labor in Yugoslavia. His post-war wanderings led him eventually to that Landsberg DP camp and a place in the very orchestra conducted by Bernstein in 1948. Seventy years later his daughter was among the musicians who memorialized the Ex-Concentration Camp Orchestra with a concert in Landsberg in which she performed the haunting setting by Max Bruch of the *Kol Nidrei*, the solemn prayer that begins the holy service of Yom Kippur every year.

For Janet Horvath, that performance offered—and ultimately provided—a deep emotional catharsis, just the sort of purification and cleansing of a soul seared and scorched by tragedy envisioned by Aristotle when he coined the term 2,300 years ago. For most, if not all, of her adult life she has been wrestling with the ramifications of being a member of the Second Generation: a child of survivors of The Holocaust. It's a condition that I recognize immediately within the first pages of her story.

My parents escaped Nazi Germany relatively unscathed, having survived until the spring of 1941 performing with an all-Jewish performing arts organization that was maintained by Joseph Goebbels as a key cog in the machinery of his Ministry of Public Enlightenment and Propaganda. But their families remained behind in the Old World to be murdered in Auschwitz, in Theresienstadt, in Riga, in Trawniki, leaving my parents George and Rosemary to come to terms with their losses via silence and guilt and occasional bouts of rage.

How familiar do Janet's memories of her father's need for punctuality, his obsessive concern with order, ring true for me! When I read about Janet's "deep-seated, lifelong disquiet about revealing myself as a Jew," how quickly does a clearly etched memory arise within me. My father by this time was in his 90s and suffering from dementia. That summer morning when dressing I had thrown on the T-shirt that lay at the top of the pile, not paying attention to the fact that the shirt clearly bore the words "Pasadena Jewish Book Festival." When I visited my father at his elder-care facility, his first words, uttered in a conspiratorial whisper, were, "You didn't actually wear that out on the street, did you?"

Janet's declaration that "as the living, breathing embodiment of survival, I tried not to cause [my parents] further pain" rings true for every member of the Second Generation. One of my friends, a daughter of survivors, recalls the time when, at age seven, she fell off her bicycle and badly skinned her knee. But rather than limp home crying to her parents, she sneaked up the stairs to the bathroom to tend to her injury herself. "Even at that young age," she recalls, "I knew that something bad had happened to them and that I shouldn't trouble them with something as piddling as a skinned knee."

But to be a 2G, as the shorthand has it, is also to revel in the discoveries of a religious and cultural tradition that our parents may have feared to explore with us, as was the case in my secular household growing up. Even the humble pomegranate, Janet writes, can bear symbolic weight. According to Jewish tradition there are 613 seeds in a single pomegranate, each one representing a commandment one must honor in order to live a righteous life. "The Jewish people, in spite of centuries of persecution," she continues, "have achieved the fertility and renewal promised by the pomegranate. From its seeds has grown a generation—my generation—raised by Holocaust survivors, who continue to pursue good and righteous behavior." In my own rambling pursuit of my 2G identity, I underwent a 20-month program of study, discussion, and learning that culminated in the spring of 2008 with my becoming a Son of the Commandment, a Bar Mitzvah Boy, at the age of 55.

Ultimately, though, what our generation has come to know, and as this book reveals, is the importance of providing comfort, love, and understanding to the rapidly disappearing members of that First Generation of sufferers and survivors, in an echo of the Duke of Albany's words at the end of "King Lear": The oldest hath borne most; we that are young, shall never see so much, nor live so long.

—Martin Goldsmith

AUTHOR'S NOTE

We children of Holocaust survivors have needed a lifetime to process the genetic trauma passed down upon us. Quite aware we're alive today by virtue of our parents' unlikely survival, our internal gauge makes it visceral, as if we'd been there ourselves experiencing the horrors. We have relived the experiences throughout our lives if only in our imaginations. Hence, I have chosen to write the text in the entr'actes, the reflection and musings of my childhood, in the present tense, as it is perennially present for me.

Hungarian is a complex language. Several entries include the translations. The letters *ka* added to the end of a name mean "little." Janetka becomes little Janet; Robika becomes little Robert.

The letters kém (pronounced came) added to the end of a name mean "my little." Janetkém becomes my little Janet.

My father also called me mucikám (pronounced mootsi-calm), a Hungarian endearment which can be translated to my little sweetheart.

Hungary is a small landlocked country of about 36,000 square miles wedged into Central Europe. It was formerly part of the Austro-Hungarian Empire ruled by the Hapsburg dynasty. That powerful empire collapsed after World War I and Hungary's current borders were established.

Map of Hungary. Hungary's capital city Budapest is often called the "Paris of the East" because of its rich history, gastronomic pleasures, and scenic vistas overlooking the Danube River. Shutterstock_144077101 R1.

PROLOGUE

THE SPIRIT OF ANCESTORS IN GERMANY (MAY 2018)

There are no bodies here, only names engraved on barren slabs and forlorn pillars. There's a railcar, which locks from the outside, and a crumbling plaque with a dedication: *Unbekannter*; "Grave of thousands unknown." I climb further, on an overgrown path, wondering what or who I have tread upon. In the distance, a lone memorial, surrounded in stones from a son in memory of his father. Feeling unnerved, with pinpricks of doubt, I retrace my steps to the medieval city on the lake—Landsberg am Lech. Decorative multicolored façades line the cobblestone streets. Scattered throughout the town square, orange, blue, and green umbrellas shelter tables overflowing with Wiener Schnitzel, marzipan cookies, apple strudel, and mugs of dark beer. I hear laughter. For the townspeople, the decades-old memorials must fade into the background.

They are expecting me. I hurry back to the hotel, slip on my gown, and make my way to the theater where a woman ushers me to a bare-bones cubicle. Gray walls, gray floor, a clothes rack without hangers. Even though there's no room for more than three steps in either direction I start to pace. Perhaps the light-headedness will dissipate. The anticipation before making an entrance is always daunting but this is no ordinary concert. After months of planning, I am about to play one of the most hallowed works of Jewish liturgy, *Kol Nidrei*, in Germany, in the very spot my father performed with a group of Holocaust survivors in 1948, 70 years ago to the day.

Mustering the courage to open the door, I peer down bleak cement stairs. A din of voices drift upward from the stalls. The opening gala is in full swing, and laughter and applause can be heard coming from the stage. The babble rouses me. It's time to warm up. Pressing the strings, oscillating slowly between notes, I feel the familiar sensation in my fingertips, the skin softening as the metal meets the ebony fingerboard, each finger curved and firm. A glorious resonance emanates. I try to focus on setting the tone for the evening, confident music might clear the haze of distrust, but I can't help thinking about my father, remembering that for most of my life, he suppressed his story. How mistaken I had been. The volatility, paranoia, and the delicate beauty of his music were not signs of weakness, but belied resilience.

In a state of suspension, I adjust the tautness of my bow and invoke his performance of the lament, shaping the opening motif—D' D-D-C#' C#-C#-A'. Dark sounds fill my every pore, like the keening of an aimless soul. I'm interrupted by a knock on the door—my summons. Clutching the cello, I stand up, then carefully maneuver down the narrow half-lit stairway. Emerging from behind the sapphire velvet curtain, I take the stage—the strong spirit of ancestors beside me.

PART I

UNEXPECTED REVELATIONS
GEORGE'S (GYURI'S) STORY

Music expresses that which cannot be said
and on which it is impossible to be silent.

—Victor Hugo (1802–1885)

1

A CONCERT WITH LEONARD BERNSTEIN IN MAY 1948

He'd already called three times that morning. "Janetkém. When you are coming?" With a firm grip on the steering wheel, I slalomed the car forward on black, ice-covered roads toward my father's high-rise. The dense traffic and the treacherous surfaces hindered my progress. I chose a circuitous route, unplowed but easier to negotiate. With shoulders raised to my ears, I slid into a parking spot and braced myself for the cold trek to the front door. My elevated pulse didn't surprise me. The dusky sky threatened more sleet, and I was nearly late.

The elevator door opened onto the 14th floor, and there stood my father, clean-shaven, waiting in his camel hair coat and jaunty black chapeau. Underneath, as always for any outing, he was dressed in a suit—the gray pinstriped one with a crisp tailored shirt, multicolored matching silk tie, leather shoes tied just so.

Raising his unruly eyebrows, now speckled with gray, he said with a twinkle in his eyes, "Janetkém, where were you so long?"

We embraced and made our way painstakingly into the elevator.

My father at 87 was still sharp, critical, astute; his old-world European elegance and high standards of behavior were unchanged; his taste in fashion, art, and cuisine uncompromised; and his thick

Hungarian accent undiminished. Still, the least slight could set him aflame. He leaned precariously on his walker. When had his posture become so stooped, his physique so frail? He would often forget about his unsteadiness, which had resulted in sudden falls.

As we left the building buffeted in the subzero wind tunnel, I was grateful I hadn't chosen this location for my parents, because I would never have heard the end of it. My father loved all things beautiful. He selected this building because of the striking gold fixtures in the bathroom and contemporary marble tiled floors. The lobby of the multistory condominium located on Yonge Street, the main north-south corridor of Toronto, exudes refinement with its leather furniture, floor to ceiling mirrors, and luxuriant plants—a monolith above the bustling street. But the steep incline between the parking lot and the entryway is difficult even for young people to negotiate. The first week my parents lived there, my father fell flat on his face, breaking his nose. A superstitious man, he decided the place was cursed.

Leaning into the wind, I tightened my hold on him. We lumbered to the car, then I reminded him to place his behind in first and to lower his head so he wouldn't bump it on the way in. I bent down to grab his legs and hoisted them into the car. Success. No bruises or breaks this time. Once I had heaved the walker into the trunk, I settled into the driver's side, sighing audibly in anticipation of the tedious drive to yet another doctor's appointment, this time the neurologist, for his Parkinson's disease symptoms.

"Watch how you are driving, Janetkém."

Still uneasy, I focused on the rugged inflection of his voice, the sound of his fingers tapping on the center console. Cello-playing fingers need to be supple. He was always practicing even without the instrument, even on an armrest, even now that he no longer played. This life-long mannerism temporarily impeded the oscillating tremor in his limbs.

I considered harmless subjects for conversation and settled on music. He loved to talk shop. My orchestra was preparing a festival to honor Leonard Bernstein—the legendary maestro, educator, and pianist, bad boy and superstar—the genius who composed *West Side*

Story; who for nearly half a century conducted the New York Philharmonic.

Despite more than three decades of cello playing, I never crossed paths with Bernstein. But my father, a wonderful cellist in his day, performed under the batons of the greatest conductors as a member of first the Budapest Symphony and then the Toronto Symphony.

He was quite hard of hearing by then, so I hollered, "Papa. Did you ever play with Leonard Bernstein?"

The tapping stopped. His skin paled. He shifted in his seat, rubbed his rheumy eyes, and placed the palm of his hand on his cheek. Several moments passed. Should I pull over? I decided to remain quiet, concentrating on the road, when a whoosh of air escaped from his lungs.

"Yes," he said. "It was very hot day. He came. To conduct Jewish Orchestra in DP camps. In 1948. After war. He played George Gershwin *Rhapsody in Blue* on piano. He was just a kid and was just fan-tas-tic! 'Gentlemen,' he said, 'let's take off our jackets and roll up our sleeves. We are just *schvitzing*!'" My father laughed. "I talked to him... in German. I said, 'I want come to America.' So warm Bernstein was. He said I am great Jewish musician. I should go to Palestine."

Perspiration oozed down my neck. Resisting the urge to brake, I considered what to do. He'd never told me this story before, or others. Ice pellets strafed the car and my father, a defiantly taciturn man, had just disclosed a long-held secret. Hoping for more, hoping not to intrude, I kept driving.

He always remembered the music—a Weber overture preceded *Rhapsody in Blue*, and a beautiful young girl named Henia thrilled the audience with Yiddish and Hebrew songs.

"Chaim Arbeitman, fan-tas-tic violinist, played solo. What a tone! Younger than me—maybe 18 he was? He changed his name when he came to America—to Arben? David Arben? He was accepted by Philadelphia Orchestra," my father said proudly, as if it was his own accomplishment. "We played for 5,000 people. Everybody needed music, needed to hear Bernstein."

My father's face glowed as he evoked Bernstein, his luxuriant hair tumbling down his brow, his vivid personality, his exuberant gestures. And during the passion-infused piano-playing of *Rhapsody in Blue*, his body swaying for emphasis, he led the ensemble with a mere nod of his head, a swivel of his hips, a shrug of his shoulders. My father recalled the healing power of the music, not the hardship and the deprivation of the times.

Like other Holocaust survivors, Papa rarely, if ever, alluded to his experiences during or after the war. What had my question unleashed?

Thoughts sprinted through my mind. How and when did he go to Germany, of all places? Was my mother there, too? Were they displaced persons? Why had he never before boasted about the encounter with Bernstein?

"But Papa. How did you—?"

My father shrank in his seat and huddled closer to the passenger door. He shook his head; his eyes turned grave. Tapping, and staring straight ahead, he reverted to silence.

As a child, I knew not to ask questions. After the ravages of the war, my parents buried the memories of who and what they were before, silencing the past in order to live. My younger brother, Robert, and I grew up in Toronto in the 1960s, bewildered by the constant intensity of our parents' emotions. When they spoke, we listened. It never occurred to us not to. We tried to be the most well-behaved children. Still, my father's displeasure could churn and foam in his throat, and bubble over into earsplitting screams. We often wondered what we'd done to trigger such anger.

My father's English was different, hesitant, and strongly accented —the "th" and "wh" sounds unpronounceable. "Long time not seen"; "How you keeping"; and "Vat taking so long?" he'd say. By age ten, I was the official translator. My parents depended on me to make telephone calls, read and write letters, and explain American idioms like "necking" and "nincompoop."

Papa didn't play baseball or watch football like most Canadian dads. He practiced the cello all day long. He played concerts at night and performed at weddings and funerals on the weekends. We often heard choking sounds at night. I knew other dads didn't cry like he did.

Mama's sudden intake of breath conjured steely control. "*Never* tell anyone you're Jewish," she'd say. Not allowed to play outside alone or to attend a sleepover, I wondered, why couldn't I be like other Canadian kids? Why couldn't I have peanut butter sandwiches on white bread for lunch? Hang out at the mall? Go sailing? Date boys... even Jewish ones? I didn't want to be different.

Even as an adult I was fearful of what I might hear, fearful of emotions I might unleash. Whenever I thought about what my parents experienced, even for a moment, dread, obsession, and guilt simmered in a thick goulash. Grousing about being cold or tired, hungry or impatient, incensed or disappointed brought self-recrimination. *What are you complaining about? You're not in a concentration camp.* My parents never spoke about it. Yet nebulous memories, sinister visions, and stifled emotions infused the air.

I remember a knock at our front door as my brother and I were drifting to sleep. We heard our parents' agitated voices in a flurry of Hungarian. Leaping out of bed we rushed into our mother's arms. I started to cry. A knock on the door late at night could only mean catastrophe.

My father sidled to the door. "Who is that?"

"It's Phil," a voice said. "Your neighbor."

My dad cracked the door open, squinting into the darkness.

"Your headlights are on. I didn't mean to startle you!" Phil apologized, although I could tell he wasn't sure why.

My brother and I were mystified. Innocent as the encounter seemed, our parents' dread sucked us into the mire. I spent most of my life inhaling, rarely exhaling.

After the conversation about Leonard Bernstein, and after I settled my father in his apartment that January evening, I rushed to my computer. Surely there must be some documentation for this notable event. My mind whirled. I wondered who the musicians were. How did they meet? Where did they get instruments, clothing, sheet music, and the strength to perform? And, as preposterous as it sounds now, when my father indicated he played in an orchestra of survivors, I envisioned a full symphony orchestra with 100 musicians.

The information practically leapt out at me from Leonard Bernstein's website: On May 10, 1948, Bernstein conducted at the Landsberg and Feldafing displaced persons (DP) camps in Bavaria, Germany, in the American zone, for thousands of Holocaust survivors, spectators, and American military personnel. Bernstein described the experience, noting the bedraggled appearance of the handful of musicians. My father was one of only 17 musicians, all survivors, who performed with Bernstein that day.

Late into the night, I pursued further details, hoping for more leads. I came across a newspaper article—March 14, 2008:

"Leonard Bernstein: A Musical Tribute. The Israel Philharmonic and Tony Bennett applaud Leonard Bernstein.

Several luminaries attended the event, among them Rita Lerner, a trustee of the Museum of Jewish Heritage in New York City. She is quoted as saying, "My mother Henny Durmashkin Gerko, [sic] had been accompanied by Leonard Bernstein in Munich in 1948. My mother sang Hebrew songs from the ghetto [with the Ex-Concentration Camp Orchestra.] ... Years later, she donated the printed program autographed by Bernstein ... to the Holocaust museum."[1] Despite the late hour, my fingers pummeled the keyboard. I emailed the museum. "My father participated in a program with Leonard Bernstein in 1948. Might I come to see the signed program you have in your collection?"

The response arrived the next day: "Yes, we have the autographed program. You can make an appointment to see it the next time you are in New York. But don't you want to see the eyewitness testimony of Mrs. Gurko on videotape and the photographs?" My husband was downstairs. "Howie," I shrieked, "they have photographs!"

My first opportunity to travel to New York in 2009 would occur four months later, in May. I'd be on tour with the Minnesota Orchestra. In the meantime, the Museum of Jewish Heritage sent a licensing agreement for me to sign, which allowed me to procure a copy of the program. It faithfully represented the age and fragility of the original document complete with folds, frayed edges, and cracks. My father had recalled the entire program exactly.

The musical works performed were all familiar to me, but I needed the help of a German-speaking friend to translate the words. Scrutinizing carefully, he exclaimed, "This isn't German."

Of course. Yiddish. How else would the survivors from so many countries communicate? Impatiently, I waited for the trip to New York, to play in Carnegie Hall and, more importantly, to see the photographs.

Central Committee of Liberated Jews, Jewish Agency for Palestine
AMERICAN JOINT DISTRIBUTION COMMITTEE
IN THE U.S. ZONE OF OCCUPATION

Direktorjum far Kultur un Dercijung
in der U.S. Zone

Montik, dem 10. V. 1948 13 a zejger in Lager Feldafing
Montik, dem 10. V. 1948 20 a zejger in Lager Landsberg

LEONARD BERNSTEIN

tret ojf far der Szeerit Hapleitah mit dem
Reprezentanc Orkester fun der Szeerit Hapleitah
un kinstler fun der Szeerit Hapleitah:
FOLKSZINGERIN H. DURMASZKIN / TENOR M. GOLDSZTEIN
FIDLER CH. ARBEITMAN

PROGRAM

1. Ouverture fun der oper „Freischütz" . . . Carl Maria von Weber
2. Menuet un Farandol fun Suite L'Arlesienne . . . . G. Bizet
Reprezentanc Orkester unter lejtung fun Gast-Dirigent *Leonard Bernstein*
3. Sonate G-Moll . . . . Tartini *Ch. Arbeitman*
4. „Jeruszalaim" . . . . . Erec-Jisroel Lid
5. „Kalanijot" . . . . Erec-Jisroel Lid *Ch Dormaszkin*
6. Arje fun der oper „Rigoletto" . G. Verdi
7. Arje fun der oper „Tosca" . . G. Puccini *M. Goldsztein*
8. „Rapsody in Blue" . . . . . G. Gershwin *Leonard Bernstein*

Papa sometimes called me *mucikám*—my little sweetheart—after my mother. I am strikingly like her—just shy of five feet tall, with hazel eyes, an aquiline nose, and a feisty personality. It is her face I see when I catch a glimpse of my own reflection. Vivacious, loquacious, astute, she brimmed with life: the antithesis of my despondent father whose fury at the world would flare up and consume him.

It was my mother who overcame the disruption in their lives, who struggled for more than subsistence. With formidable strength, she propelled my father into success in this new land, while she yearned to replace those she had lost.

Their circle of friends, all Hungarian survivors, were an insular assembly of the few among the many, who hadn't experienced a normal life free of fear, persecution, and death. Who lived for the moment, who had to figure out a human way to live, in a world more just and fair, who sought above all, beauty—in painting, literature, fine clothing, gastronomy, music, and love.

They eagerly anticipated my birth. Wringing adaptation from distress, transcending all hardships, the newcomers without English language skills, without kin, and virtually no belongings except a cello, conceived a Canadian child when only 30 percent of Hungarian Jews had survived the Holocaust. Their longing for continuity trumped their aversion to bringing another Jew into a hostile world. No two parents could have welcomed their child with more joy—a birth unforeseen, the first positive thing to happen to them in years. They named me Janet—intentionally English, not Hungarian, and not Jewish. Later I learn that Janet, a medieval diminutive of Jane, in Hebrew means "God has been merciful."

My earliest memories are sweet. Hungarian lullabies, warm embraces, and tender strains of the cello. Rage had been momentarily mollified by my presence, the chasm of the past submerged so deeply; only the overnight whispers and sporadic sighs suggested pervasive distress.

The highly charged atmosphere in our home shaped our uneasy relationship. Ultimately, I learned how to sidestep conflict—through the cello, and music.

Entr'acte 2007

"A corned beef sandwich on rye please, no seeds, hold the mustard, a pickle, and a side of matzo ball soup," I order breathlessly. I check my watch. My father, I know, is salivating, fantasizing about his favorite sandwich. For several years, he's been homebound with my invalid mother and her live-in health-care provider, Ian. It is up to me to deliver the savory goods. Lunchtime is promptly at noon.

I've spent the morning dashing from errand to errand in a rented Ford Focus on a wretched, bitterly cold, Toronto day. I migrate upstream in traffic, dodging gridlock wherever possible, my long list of tasks accomplished: purchase provisions, check; pick up prescriptions, check; buy a couple of new outfits and nightgowns for my mom, check; do the banking and pay some bills, check; stock up on adult diapers and liquid thickening agents, check; get a box of rubber gloves for the caregiver, check; buy some delectable desserts for my father's incurable sweet tooth, check—all tasks that I've squeezed into a few days, tasks familiar to any caregiver of aging parents. My frequent visits from Minnesota entail, subconsciously perhaps, making up for not being the in-town and ever-present daughter.

Each stoplight turns red as I approach the intersection. *Damn!* It always takes me much longer than I think it will in this big, busy city. I pass designer boutiques and elegant women, kiosks with unidentifiable vegetables and raw chickens suspended in storefronts, bearded men braced against the wind in wide-brimmed hats and long black coats, European pastry shops, and neon signs in myriad tongues: French, Italian, Chinese, Creole, Punjabi, Filipino.

For my neurotically punctual father, even corned beef sandwiches must be on time. Early for every occasion, during my childhood, when my father told us we were to leave at six, he'd be in the car by five with the engine running, blaring the horn every few minutes. As a kid, I scuttled; as a teenager, I stalled; as an adult, I speed.

Undeterred by the icy roads, I careen in and out of lanes, cursing here and there, but I arrive promptly with the treasures.

The load of bags is heavy as I ascend from the parking lot up to the door of the high-rise. Carefully cradling the box containing the corned beef sandwich, I'm nearly toppled over by the impetuous wind. The doorman—kind-hearted, older—buzzes me in with a greeting. "Back again?" He smiles. "You are a dedicated daughter." I don't see myself as a dutiful daughter, but the daughter who's moved away, who doesn't do enough, can't be enough, never stays long enough, who leaves her husband and little boy behind in Minnesota. Clearly not a good daughter, not a good mother, not a good wife. "Mommy," my son says, "do you love Grandma and Grandpa more than me?"

I take the elevator to my parents' 14th-floor apartment, trying to fix my disheveled appearance, expecting my father to be waiting at his door. Sure enough, there he is, as always nattily dressed, this time in a cashmere V-necked sweater, a crisp white starched shirt, tweed pants, and freshly polished leather shoes, with a few lonely strands of hair aligned across his bald head. "Janetkém. Such a long time you took."

Fashionable clothing fails to conceal the fragile and hunched figure standing in the doorway. He leans toward me, letting go of his walker. I manage to steady him without dropping all of the grocery bags and the longed-for lunch while he coats my face and ears with moist, noisy little smooches.

The apartment is stifling. I hurry in and greet the immobile figure in the wheelchair who is my mother, as I unload the valuable cargo—only Hungarian specialties will do: cabbage rolls, *Gulyás* soup, *Pick* salami, *dobos* torte, apple strudel, and the ingredients for several meals I plan to cook, some of which I will freeze for later.

I sit my father down at noon for his lunch. He unwraps the corned beef sandwich almost lovingly, anticipating the rich smells and flavor. "Give some to Mummy," he says as he removes the top piece of rye bread, pulling several layers of meat from his sandwich. He brandishes the fork. I take the corned beef and put it in the blender with some broth and vegetables, add a tablespoon of the thickening agent I have bought, and whir it into a purée. It has to be a certain texture so Mama can swallow it.

My father wolfs the sandwich down in a flash, one thick eyebrow rising with each swallow. Cooing sounds emanate. After I spoon-feed my mother, I sit down too and pick at a few pieces of cheese and berries. "Janetkém, eat more! You don't eat bread? Have a toast. Strudel." He takes it as a personal insult when I decline dessert.

I divert his attention by proffering the oversized outfits I've purchased for my mother. The clothing has to be brightly colored, sequined, ornately tailored but easy to get on—loose fitting with wide scoop necks, zippers or buttons, and ample sleeves. My father insists that she look stylish and impeccable, as she always has.

"Is not these bee-you-ti-ful?" he exclaims to my silent, inert mother as he lifts each piece toward her vacant eyes. He seems pleased with the reception. Then he turns to me and frowns. "You are tired. *You are tired*. Lie down," he says. I had planned to practice. I'll have to jump back into my cello skin immediately upon landing back home.

My father gestures toward the living room. Dutifully, I collapse onto the cushion-laden couch. It will soon be time to begin preparations for dinner, to be served promptly at six.

What I know now, I didn't know when I was growing up. Through the 1930s and much of World War II, Jews had been relatively safe while Hungary was allied with Germany, despite pervasive antisemitism. The Nazis invaded, on March 19, 1944, when most of the world thought the war was ending. Thousands of Hungarian Jewish men were deported, and forced to work in the mines, to dig trenches, to build railways, and later, to burn and bury corpses.

My parents married on May 26, 1944, with the knowledge my father would be seized for slave labor the next morning, destination —the copper mines of Bor, Yugoslavia (now eastern Serbia). A death sentence, or so my father thought. My 18-year-old mother vanished. By July—in less than two months—440,000 Jews would be sent to the gas chambers at Auschwitz. An eerie silence surrounded the experiences of aunts and uncles shot into graves, of friends chained and blasted into the Danube, of hundreds of thousands deported, scattered, slaughtered. Somehow my parents, grandparents, aunt, and uncle survived.

Music preserved our family, gave us solace from the nightmare of repression. Although my father played with the Toronto Symphony and my mother gave piano lessons, neither of them attained their dreams. My father had wanted to become an engineer, but by 1920 in Hungary, Jews were not allowed to attend university. He turned to the cello, and imagined becoming a soloist, or at least the principal cello of an orchestra of stature. My mother fantasized about her budding singing and acting career. But the war erupted.

Afterward, my parents yearned for a fresh start, away from blood-soaked Europe. Without a penny to their name, they sailed away from the living hell, bidding their fervent farewell—to parents, siblings, friends, and everything familiar. In Canada they took any work, menial work—as a sweatshop seamstress; a late-night sweeper; an office cleaner.

When we were born, even though my brother was talented and loved to play the French horn, my parents insisted that he, the longed-for son, would attend medical school to become a doctor—a Jewish boy was expected to be no less. Excelling as a musician would be up to me.

The cello sound, before conscious memory, permeated my very being—its lush, golden tones the closest sound to the human voice. My earliest memories are of lying on the floor next to my father as he practiced the cello, the metronome marking the music's pulse, the tones resonant. He practiced for hours, the repertoire embedded even before I took up the instrument. When I did, my parents insisted on discipline, dedication, and persistence—cello before school and piano in the living room after dinner while my mother did the dishes. They never considered that my petite stature and tiny hands were not ideal for playing the cello or carrying the bulky beast in and out of vehicles and up staircases. Nonetheless, engulfing the instrument with my body in an embrace, determined to muster the strength required to play the instrument, I endeavored to produce the seductive sounds my father coaxed out of his cello.

My parents' tremendous sacrifices allowed me to study at the great music schools in the US and Europe. After years of practice, in 1980, I won the associate principal cello position of the Minnesota Orchestra. When I called with the news, elated squeals could be heard all the way from Toronto to Minneapolis. But their delight soon gave way to distress. My career would take me to a city far away.

After a short stint with the Indianapolis Symphony in the late 1970s, I settled in the Twin Cities. When I married in 1993, my husband, Howard, and I juggled our demanding careers and our growing family. We continued to travel to Toronto as often as we could especially after our son, Harris, was born.

Although my parents remained devoted to making this a more beautiful world through music, their past remained shrouded in silence. When I was older I convinced myself the feverish pace of my life precluded interrogations. Wasn't caring for my aging parents a further encumbrance? Why coax them for information after all these decades?

And yet, I couldn't let the enigma endure. Over the years, I grew more obsessed with the Holocaust, reading everything I could on the subject. I tried to imagine, then tried *not* to imagine, what my parents might have gone through. My core harbored the unspeakable, at times crushed by the repulsive burden. Breaking free was futile. I had been genetically stamped. In order to make sense of my parents, my upbringing, and ultimately my own baffling anxieties and behaviors, I resolved to pursue truths about the past.

Entr'acte 1964

Papa's throat noises are really gross—gargling, blowing his nose, hawking up, and spitting phlegm. The guttural expectorations, often at night, emanate from the bathroom and they make me cringe.

I hear my father weeping. This time I get up out of bed and open the bathroom door a crack. "What's wrong, Papa?"

The scene before me: a whimpering, keening figure held partially upright by my mother, clinging to him for dear life. His nose is red.

"Mama. Is Papa sick?" Her fierce exhalation makes me scurry back to bed.

In the morning, I scrutinize my parents, but they act as if nothing happened. "Papa, were you sick last night?"

"*Na*, Janetkém. Eat breakfast. I make an omelet just like you like it." Mama wields the frying pan with extra verve, a strained smile on her face.

"I thought I heard something... crying...."

"What you mean?" My mother looks curiously at me, as if she recognizes my budding adolescence for the first time. "Hurry up. Eat, already. You'll be late for school."

But I can't let it go. "What were you sad about, Papa?"

At first, he avoids my eyes. The silence prickles my skin. When he looks at me, it's with revulsion. "Lesson to me. Lesson now. Not your business. Nothing happened, *never*."

Consider a time when hell was on earth, when hands accustomed to a musician's bow, a writer's pen, a doctor's scalpel, a painter's brush, a tailor's needle, wielded shovelfuls of rocks, limestone, or human remains; when the air smelled of smoke, ashes, and grief; when the foundations of existence and the illusions that sustain us crumbled. My father, a young man confident of his future, wrenched from society, a celebrated artist turned slave-laborer. The swollen and bloody knuckles, the backbreaking effort, the swirling musical phrases stilled. Depleted by the shame of helplessness, the shock of nakedness, the dread of men in uniform stomping by, he could never again tolerate being alone. A whiff of boiling cabbage or rusted copper or dripping blood triggered distress. In our family trust was never regained.

After the years of grief and imposed silence, my father's hands tingled to fill the stillness, and the hunger to create gnawed. His playing blossomed with a vitality, profundity, and spirituality I can only marvel at now. It must have been unnerving to learn how to feel again, when survival entailed learning how not to feel. At least while he was playing, music imparted peace of mind; his cello wept, his music-making stirred those who were equally scarred.

A strange sensation would ripple in my throat when he played. The generous vibrato warmed the sound and conveyed a deeply moving story, expressed not in words or thoughts, but in emotions illuminating a path to rebirth.

I know now that beauty and inspiration ignites the best of the human spirit. The untenable pulsating, the tactile sensation of hugging the instruments, and breathing the music as one, creates a current that transforms us, elevates us, unites us, and propels us in ways we cannot explain.

My parents attempted to spare us the pain of reliving those terrifying years. Survival carries a heavy burden and forever changed them. Today, the aftereffects of their psychological ordeal—degradation, paranoia, post-traumatic stress disorder (PTSD), and the subsequent guilt and apprehension—are more understood. But as a child, these feelings were submerged with stoicism.

According to the relatively new field of epigenetics, change in genetic expression is a natural occurrence, which varies according to one's lifestyle and environment. Recent studies indicate that trauma can be passed on to the next generation. Children of parents who survived massacres, who grew up with alcoholic or abusive parents, and children of Holocaust survivors carry toxic stress, which scars and chemically sears their DNA, leaving a molecular residue. Psychological and behavioral tendencies can be inherited. Affected by the tragedy of the epoch, I feel vulnerable. I feel as if I carry their grief.

From my mother, I inherited my eye and hair color, my height and skin tone. I inherited my intelligence and musical ability from them both. But my hypervigilance, and the tendency to conjure up a monstrous array of dreadful disasters, is from my father.

Still prisoners of the past, afraid of what lay ahead, my parents braced themselves to meet a world that might capsize at any moment. This, I discover, is the legacy, the marker that has genetically stamped my soul.

There were futile attempts to glean information, to understand the past—their past and mine. Even as he aged, my father's Hungarian temper blazed at the slightest insult. After an eruption, a punishing silence could follow, even for months, with the telephone ignored, callers scorned, and family shunned. "Papa. Remember *Schindler's List*, the movie you watched? I went to see it too. Powerful, wasn't it? Directed by Steven Spielberg? He's been videotaping the experiences of survivors, um, like you. They have told their stories, as eyewitnesses..."

Between 1994 and 1999, the USC Shoah Foundation, founded by filmmaker Steven Spielberg, collected testimony from thousands of Holocaust survivors. If the Shoah Foundation showed an interest in my father's story, perhaps, I thought, he'd be willing to be interviewed.

But his scowl caused me to shrivel in my seat. I averted my eyes, my voice making a sudden diminuendo. Did I have wax in my throat? Swallowing hard, I pressed on, "It's really courageous—"

"You think I gonna talk to stranger? In Front. Of. A. Ca-me-ra?"

He struggled to get up from his chair. Then he fled, the atmosphere in the room thick with indignation.

Entr'acte 1957

The ground is swaddled in iridescent yellows and reds—brilliant hues of garnet, citrine, and amber. My brother Robert and I roll in the cloak of leaves until the heaps cover us. When my mother calls us in to dinner, we emerge from the golden sanctuary and race to the front door of our modest suburban Toronto bungalow. I brush the stems from my coat just as Mama comes to the door to greet us. A stray yellow leaf is affixed to my chest. Ashen, she flicks it off and pulls me into the house.

"Quickly children," my mother exclaims. "Your daddy is coming home. Pick up your toys!" All three of us scurry like squirrels collecting nuts. Nothing should be out of place. Everything must be in order: plastic covering the sofa; toys in our room in a toy box; laundry, utensils, and clothing put away; beds made, and shoes perfectly aligned in the closet. Mama swipes at a spot on the front window. My father might come home from his orchestra rehearsal humming Beethoven or furious at some slight—real or imagined. The door opens and first we see the cello. We search our father's face and hold our breath.

"Goddamn antisemitic bastards!"

"Gyurikám, the children," my mother murmurs.

"*Baszdmeg* fuck."

Robert and I scuttle to our room, taking turns to observe the scene. My mother touches my father's arm, but he jerks away with a bellow. Her attempts to mollify him infuriate, causing total combustion. "Always you take their side! Don't protect them, sonofabitch bastards!" He stomps to their bedroom and slams the door. We hear plaster crumbling.

I whimper as Mama creeps into our room and sweeps us into a three-way hug. "Your daddy is angry. Don't worry darlings. Everything is fine." I try to ignore my father's convulsive moans.

At the time, I suppose I thought all dads behaved like this after a hard day at work. Later, I understood. Paranoid. Suspicious. Unpredictable. After hours, or days, repressed emotions held in a delicate balance would splinter, triggering caustic eruptions.

After an hour or two, my father comes out of the bedroom. He kneels down to embrace me and buries his wet nose in my neck. My body stiffens. Meekly I pull away.

Days later, conscience-stricken, he tries in vain to recognize himself. "My life was a miserable torture, not worth a penny. I am cursed, a failure... Everybody turning against me, arrogant bastards... They talking to me like animal. Always behind my back they talk about me." His diatribes make no sense to us.

Usually the tenacious one, my mother stands motionless, listening, a tormented expression in her eyes.

George Horvath, cellist, 1940s. *Papa cut quite a figure dressed in tails, posing for this publicity shot, unaware his world would soon be upturned.*

The overnight wedding. *In a borrowed dress, Katolina and Gyuri married in a hasty civil ceremony the evening before Gyuri was deported.*

Conductor Leonard Bernstein in 1948. Credit: Courtesy of The American Jewish Joint Distribution Committee archives (JDC), New York, NY.

---

1. *The Forward* by Masha Leon.

2

FROM ARTIST TO SLAVE LABORER

Dreary Minnesota winters often pass in an agonizing adagio, but that year, in anticipation of the spring Carnegie Hall concert in New York, the season seemed interminable. A muddy residue eventually supplanted towers of melted snow, but I was too edgy to celebrate the arrival of luxuriant trees and aromatic blossoms. The orchestra trip would be a tight run-out—a flight to New York late in the evening, an overnight in a hotel directly across the street from the famous hall at West 57th and Seventh, a 90-minute rehearsal the following day, time for a quick bite, play the concert, immediately load buses to drive to the airport, and fly home. Would a mere two-hour window in the morning, before the rehearsal at Carnegie Hall, be sufficient to get to the museum, see the Bernstein mementos, and make the rehearsal on time?

I'm typically a fitful sleeper, but that night in New York I checked my watch every five minutes, all night. Finally, very early, I got up, dressed hurriedly, bypassed breakfast and coffee, and summoned a cab. "The Museum of Jewish Heritage down by Battery Park and quickly please," I said.

The cab deposited me at the museum just as the custodians unlocked the main doors for the day. After an obligatory security check, I was escorted upstairs to the offices. The head archivist,

Esther Brumberg, a diminutive woman with beautifully coiffed silver hair, sensed my anticipation. While she retrieved the archived and numbered box, I reminded myself to breathe. Esther returned with a black shoebox-sized container. She sat down, donned white calf-skinned gloves and gently, almost tenderly, opened the lid, lifting four tiny, 60-year-old, black-and-white photos out of the box, each encased in a protective sleeve.

She laid them side by side onto the small table in front of me. "That's him! That's my father!" I squealed. There was no doubt. Debonair, with a mustache and a full head of hair, he stood among the 16 other musicians with Leonard Bernstein. On an accompanying photocopy, notes could be written and a few of the musicians were identified. There were no marks written above my father's face. The archivist grabbed a pencil and, with a firm stroke, drew an arrow pointing to the center of the image. She wrote his name: "George Horvath, Hungarian, Toronto, Canada."

Euphoria and distress at this irrefutable proof made me tingly all over. I lingered over the snapshots, then asked, "May I have a copy of these photos?"

Showing the prints to my father might jog his memory. Perhaps he'll recognize and identify some of the other members of the orchestra.

Once Esther put the photos back into the box, she led me to a cluttered little cubicle where heaps of papers covered every surface and the floor. Esther shoved a pile of folders aside and hoisted an old black-and-white television onto a shelf. Placing a tape into the VCR, she pressed the start button and left the room.

The speakers crackled as the camera zoomed in on Henia. Statuesque, with high cheekbones and crimson-tinged lips, her eyes held a quiet grief. Before the war, one of the most talented students at the Vilna Conservatory, her singing, during the concert with Leonard Bernstein, as my father remembered, was utterly captivating. The film, made only a few years before Henia's death, is imbued with power and dignity. She appeared to search for words to describe the untenable: "Music, culture—give the people a lift. You can't live with this pain." There are hardly any Yiddish singers left, she said, and very few remember the words to village and ghetto songs. Then, with her hands clasped near her throat, she closed her eyes and sang. I heard a gentle whirr of sound as if anguish surged from within:

> Ghetto! / We're standing by the walls / With heartache, lost, defenseless / With hands that hang and fall. / Just like the weeping willow branches.

The descending intervals, like sorrowful mourning doves, accompanied Vilna Jews on their final destination to extermination camps.

My reflections were interrupted as the tape came to a close. The archivist poked her head around the doorway of the cubbyhole. "Henia's daughter Rita lives here in New York. I called her, 'Some lady all the way from Minnesota is watching your mother's video!' Rita is curious. Her mother's been gone for seven years. Would you call her?"

Rita. Sounded familiar. Then it dawned on me. She was quoted in the newspaper, which led to my discovery of the program with Leonard Bernstein and presence here at the museum. I nodded. "Of course."

The hours had passed. I looked at the time. Mustn't miss the rehearsal. Through throngs of people and dense traffic, I made it to Carnegie Hall, with just enough time to locate the instrument trunks in the labyrinth backstage, take my cello out of the tall black shipping trunk—coffins, we call them—and get on the stage. Carnegie is the most famous concert hall in the country. It was not my first time performing here, yet it was difficult for me to concentrate on the music in front of me. During a break, I hurried backstage to call Rita. Within a few moments, she and I realized that my father played in the small Jewish orchestra with her mother and aunt. She mentioned a documentary film about the survivors' Ex-Concentration Camp Orchestra—*Creating Harmony: The Displaced Persons' Orchestra from Saint Ottilien* by John Michalczyk, a veteran filmmaker, professor of fine arts at Boston College—inspired by the book by her cousin Sonia Beker, *Symphony on Fire*, in which she recounts their family story. I could hardly wait to meet Rita and Sonia in person, but it would have to be on another trip to New York.

After our rehearsal, I called my father. "Papa. Remember when you told me about the concert with Leonard Bernstein—in 1948? I saw the program at the museum. There are pictures and you're in them! You look so young and handsome."

"Pictures? I don't remember. You saw Bernstein? Did you see Arbeitman?"

The prolonged war caused the displacement of hundreds of thousands. The Jewish inmates of concentration camps and slave labor presented thorny issues. Repatriation seemed like the logical solution to the American liberators but the Jews had nowhere to go. They couldn't return to desolation, to looted and destroyed homes. Survivors were leery of neighbors who had turned them in, of hoodlums who had helped themselves to their belongings and their dwellings, who had willingly participated in the carnage. Searching for family members who might have survived the years of brutality, they posted notes on whatever was left standing. They grilled other concentration camp inmates: "Have you seen my brother, my mother, my son?" Infirmaries and makeshift camps were set up haphazardly. They moved on, if they could, searching for loved ones.

Those who survived were barely alive. Dying by the dozens of typhus, the Jewish DPs urgently needed medical care, nutritious food, clean clothing, and delousing. Heartbreaking photos from the time leave no doubt—emaciated bodies clothed in striped pajamas, the tattered lice-infested garb of the concentration camps; an elderly man so severely malnourished his yellowed skin just covers his bones; a young girl with blood on her slack-swollen lips, her unblinking eyes vacant; a mother huddling over her long-dead child.

During the war, the Nazis had commandeered the St. Ottilien Benedictine Archabbey near Munich as a hospital for German soldiers. After the war, it took some convincing by the Americans to move the Jews in and the Germans out. St. Ottilien became an understaffed, miserable haven for the gravely ill, cadaverous survivors of the Holocaust. A handful of musicians ended up there. Some of them had been forced to entertain the Nazis in the camps after long hours of toil. At age 15, shivering in terror, Henia had to sing for Nazi officers.

More than once, Chaim Arbeitman, as he later told me, was pulled out of the line from the day's "selection"—that is, given a reprieve from being sent to the gas chambers, because "the little violinist," a "privileged prisoner", played Beethoven and Mozart so beautifully.

And my father? A cello-loving Nazi guard gave him a pair of gloves to protect his hands.

The captive Jews used music to keep their communities intact and their spirits up. They reminisced about better days. They felt somewhat human when singing ghetto songs, humming melodies from their childhoods, chanting bitterly facetious ballads: "Blockhouse Resort" or "Transport" or "Theresienstadt—the Best Town in the World."

Nazi oppressors used music to mobilize their soldiers and taunt their victims. Photos of talented prisoners who appeared in theater troupes, and jazz, cabaret, and classical ensembles, circulated to the media and used for propaganda, proved how well-treated the prisoners were. In truth, the Nazis coerced the musicians to perform even at the doors to the gas chambers of Auschwitz. They played while slave laborers marched to and from their daily toil; they played at executions and at meetings of Nazi officers. Had my father been subject to this torment?

I know now that many artists taken to Terezin (Theresienstadt), the "model" camp, were forced to stage productions of Felix Mendelssohn's oratorio *Elijah*, Giuseppe Verdi's massive *Requiem*, a musical setting of the Catholic Mass, and even jazz banned elsewhere in the Reich. The children's opera *Brundibár*, composed by Hans Krása and written by Adolf Hoffmeister in 1938, was performed approximately 55 times in Terezin with a constantly changing cast. New arrivals to the camp replaced the children who had been sent to the crematoriums. The International Red Cross came to inspect the "model" ghetto in 1944 and found a hastily beautified camp. They were duped. Even the grass was painted green.

Poets continued to write, musicians continued to compose, until moments before they were shipped to Auschwitz in 1944. The Nazis could torment them physically, but nothing could prevent the lyrics and the harmonies germinating within.

Artists found each other on the grounds of the St. Ottilien Benedictine monastery. Liberated musicians understood the desperate need for hope, for the inspiration of music. What better way to soothe and comfort and attest to their triumph? They would play a concert: a liberation concert. Taking the name Ex-Concentration Camp Orchestra, their first program took place on May 27, 1945, at St. Ottilien.

DP inmates and staff put a stage together on the lawn with whatever wood boards could be found. Parachute remnants stitched together partially covered the stage. A few rows of seats were set up, but most of the attendees lay on the grass, too limp, too numb, too infirm to sit. They no longer remembered their names—hardly dared believe that they were free. Three or four violinists sat hunched over their instruments on low, rickety chairs. A skeleton of a man, a singer, with his withered fingers clasped, took center stage. Sheet music on wire music stands flapped in the chilly wind, and a motley group of instrumentalists—a drummer, an accordionist, a clarinetist, a double bass player who struggled to stay upright with his heavy instrument —huddled beside a beat-up piano. Large Stars of David dominated the scene, imprinted with the word *JUDE*—JEW, the hateful insignia that singled out every man, woman, and child, for "special treatment," worn as required by the Nazi regime throughout the war —now an emblem of survival. Yellow stars hung from the hastily erected back wall behind the orchestra, a wall symbolically embedded with barbed wire. The small group performed in their malodorous striped pajamas behind the banner "*Am Yisroel Chai*" —*The People of Israel Live!* The musicians somehow stirred their rusty fingers. Then, with a ritardando, a gentle slowing, the music whispered: heal and be transformed. Breathe. Restore your hope for a world where decency and beauty prevail.

Sonia Beker's parents, Fanny and Max Beker, were in the orchestra, as was Henia, Fanny's sister. A mere month before, in April 1945, Fanny and Henia were on a death march to Dachau, freed when American tanks disrupted the slow advance.

In *Symphony on Fire*, Robert Hilliard, a World War II veteran and eyewitness to the concert, described:

> A liberation concert at which the liberated people were too weak to stand. A liberation concert at which most of the people could not believe they were free... The musicians played Mahler and Mendelssohn and others whose music had been forbidden by the Nazis—a concert of life.

The music penetrated through a shroud of darkness, revealing a glimpse of distant homelands, and veiled memories—songs of home and the synagogue, especially the soulful *Kol Nidrei* chant, a work of immense symbolism and importance, which opens the Day of Atonement service each year. On the Holy Day of Yom Kippur, the sacred Torah scrolls are removed from the ark. Two Rabbis stand on either side of the cantor, and the plaintive lament begins and gently restores ailing spirits:

> May all the people of Israel be forgiven, including all the strangers who live in their midst, for all the people are at fault in their ignorance. (Numbers 15:26)

The Jewish group renamed the Ex-Concentration Camp Orchestra and later *Shearith HaPleitah* (surviving remnant) Orchestra, soon gained fame and international attention, and performed at sanatoriums, army bases, and DP camps, even at the Nuremberg Opera House during the Nuremberg trials in 1945.

Other musicians who had survived made their way to St. Ottilien to share in the orchestra's mission. My father was not yet a member of the orchestra. The bloody siege of Budapest had ended February 13, 1945 and the city lay in ruins, with hundreds of thousands of citizens dead. He was still making his way back to Hungary on foot after his liberation from slave labor.

Responsible for seven million displaced persons in Europe, the American Joint Distribution Committee (JDC or The Joint) and the United Nations Relief and Rehabilitation Administration (UNRRA) sponsored the orchestra. The organizations provided clothing, musical instruments, and canned American food to the musicians. At the time, my father was hallucinating about having a little bread to eat, a piece of soap, and an overcoat to protect him from the gusty winter winds.

Bread signified liberty. When we were growing up my father insisted on at least two slices of thick Jewish rye at each meal, toasted. On Fridays and holidays, he'd inhale the slightly sweet, moist challah, in one sitting. Many Jewish foods represent important tenets; the egg-bread symbolizes the separation of the mundane week from the spirituality of the Sabbath. During the year challah is braided to form a long loaf. Six strands of dough tightly wound together represent six days of the week, and symbolize unity on the day of Shabbat. Challah is baked in a round shape on the High Holy Days to indicate the cycle of a year—one strand of dough kneaded until the edges are smoothed as we hope our imperfections will be.

Similar to brioche bread, whatever the shape, challah is scrumptious: slightly sweet with a pillow-soft texture. The following morning Mama would make challah French toast, frying thick slices soaked in a rich, spiced custard of eggs, milk, honey, vanilla, and cinnamon. The aroma emanating from the kitchen enticed the whole neighborhood from their beds.

Our family never missed the High Holy Days, which fall each year on the first and second day of the Jewish calendar—in September or October. The Days of Awe, or Days of Repentance, date back from the third century BCE, and offers us the opportunity to reform ourselves and to improve the world. A vitally important time of thoughtful introspection, during the service on the day of Rosh Hashanah, the mournful cry of the ram's horn, the shofar, is sounded, shattering complacency, calling us to action. Between the New Year, Rosh Hashanah, and the Day of Atonement, Yom Kippur, we are commanded to scrutinize our behavior, and to firmly commit ourselves to *teshuvah*, *tefilah*, and *tzedakah*—repentance, prayers, and good deeds.

As children, we were taught that God has a book in which He writes the names of those who will live and those who will pass on.

To mitigate the stern decree, we must atone for our sins by promising to do better next year. Asking God to pardon us is not enough, my mother explained. To satisfy God, it's our obligation to apologize in person for any hurt we might have inflicted upon our parents, our siblings, our neighbors, our friends, our coworkers—whether we meant harm or not—and to excuse anyone who seeks forgiveness for hurting us. Pursuing reconciliation, and a greater understanding and acceptance of others is a mitzvah.

The *Kol Nidrei* prayer sets the tone for meditation on Yom Kippur. My father performed the ancient chant, arranged for cello and piano by composer Max Bruch, every year when we were growing up. He practiced day and night for weeks, lovingly sculpting each note and thrilling the congregation with his passionate rendition. The sonorous cello sound whispers, then intensifies with an entreaty:

> Listen well and sincerely. Remember our ancestors who were not free to worship. Transform your fear of others, your distrust of those who are different, and acquire reverence for all of creation.

Entr'acte 1967

Our family prepares for the High Holy Days months in advance. In Toronto, the days shorten, and September temperatures can be cool. "Mama," I ask, "Can I wear a pant suit this year? I have that really nice navy-blue p—"

"Pants? A mother lets her daughter to wear pants in the synagogue? It is not proper." She chooses a wool pleated skirt, matching jacket, tights, and patent leather Mary Janes for me, and a dark suit, white shirt, and bow tie for Rob.

It's a tight squeeze in the car. My parents in the front seat and Rob and I on either side of the irreplaceable cello, too old and valuable to put in the trunk of the car. Still practicing the piece, my father's fingers tap on the steering wheel. Rob and I, and even my mother, sit silently all the way to Temple Sinai.

When he enters the sanctuary and sits down to play the first D of *Kol Nidrei*, I know his performance will be beautiful. I hear not only the music sobbing in supplication. I have a glimpse of his imprisoned heart laid bare.

The next morning, we are up early for the Day of Atonement service. My father, already downstairs in his suit and tie, shouts, "Janetkém, *mucikám*. Why aren't you ready?"

Mama, I know, is breaking into a sweat. "*Yay Istenem* (Oh my God). I am putting on makeup! *Jaaannaaattte!* Are you ready?"

"No, Mama. It's only 9:30." Styling my long tresses, I handle the hot comb with finesse.

"Hurry up. You know your daddy."

"I *am* hurrying. Why do we always have to leave so early?"

"Robika is ready! Aren't you, my darling?"

My father sits in the car with the ignition on, then he lays on the horn. I thrust my arms into the sleeves of my blouse, force the jacket on over it, shove my pumps on, and, when I tumble down the stairs, my mother panting behind me, I hear an insistent, *vooRRR, varoom* of the gas pedal. My father scowls as I climb into the backseat. Muttering something incomprehensible, he pulls out of the driveway with a jolt. While I strain to sit back it occurs to me that maybe I haven't pulled out the plug of the hot comb. Maybe it's scorching my dresser. I envision a dark crusty hole igniting with a burst of flames, burning the house down, but my heart thumps at the thought of asking my father to turn back. I swallow hard. My voice cracks and my words come out pianissimo.

"Papa. I think ... I left the hot comb plugged in."

"Vat? Vat?!"

"I said, I think, um," then *molto prestissimo*, "the hot comb is still plugged in!"

"Always you don't think. You should shame yourself. Thank you very much. You had shortened our life!"

Yanking the steering wheel, he turns the car around, then pulls back into our driveway, stopping the car with a lurch and a few choice Hungarian swear words. I sprint to the front door, taking the stairs to my room two at a time. I had not left the hot comb plugged in after all, but the relief is short-lived. My father's eyes burn as I fumble with the keys. I jump back into the car, knowing it's futile to defend myself, to point out it's still well before the service.

My father explodes at the first red light. "*Baszdmeg!* Dirty rotten sonofabitch bastards!"

A strange feeling in my throat meanders down into my groin expanding along the way.

"*Na*, Gyurikám, slow down. Too fast. Turn here!" Mama says. "Take side streets."

A sudden turn screeches the brakes.

"*Baszdmeg, a szar*. Shit!"

"Gyuri. It's *next* street. Not here! Watch. What you doing? Gyuri, let me drive!"

My saliva turns sour. When we pull into the parking lot at the temple another volley of swear words whack us. "Sonofabitch. *Seggfej*. No places. Always we leave late!"

"It was your turn make us late!" Mama interjects.

"KATO. What you saying? YOU are so slow. Janet so awful thoughtless."

"Dad. Stop it. Stop yelling. Stop it!"

Rob nudges me. "Janet. Keep quiet."

"Why? I can't listen to this!"

"You're making it worse."

"Am not!"

"Are too!"

"*Jaaannaaattte.* Why you talking back?" Mama's face is red, her mouth compressed.

"For God's sake, Dad. It's just parking!"

Rob elbows me again.

"Who you talking? Your own father you are yelling?" He turns around in his seat to glare at me. "What you think? You can talk like that to me? Do you?"

Momentarily cowed, I wheeze, "No. Well, you—"

"Like your mother. Always talking. Always lectures."

The bellows tremor through my body. "Stop! I can't stand—"

"What you are doing just unbearable. You did it again. As you had for 15 years..."

Although the car is moving a little, I throw the door open and leap out.

"*Jaaannaaattte*! Come back."

I stumble away—away from the car, from them, from the tumult of our lives.

Landsberg concentration camp—63 kilometers [39 miles] west of Munich and 55 kilometers [34 miles] southwest of the parent camp Dachau—liberated April 28, 1945, subsequently housed more than 5,000 Holocaust survivors. After suffering the loss of precious family members, and living through the death camps, the survivors were branded with a new label: "stateless." Liberated without an identity, without a history, without a country, without proof of what happened to family members. Liberated but still confined—in barracks surrounded by barbed wire, in pitiful living conditions, and embedded among 150 Nazi war criminals who were interned and later executed in Landsberg.

The survivors waited, many of them for years. *Were my parents among them?* They waited in endless lines for food, for medical care, for news of living relatives or friends. They waited for the right paperwork to emigrate to other countries in horrible conditions. Finally, in September of 1945, two American soldiers, Robert Hilliard and Edward Herman, began a letter-writing campaign, which highlighted the DPs' plight. When the news reached President Truman and the *New York Times*, the President ordered General Eisenhower to end the continued abuse of survivors. Much-needed supplies started to arrive. Even so, countries promulgated strict quotas for Jews.

By 1948, Leonard Bernstein had heard about the daring musicians of the Ex-Concentration Camp Orchestra. During a tour of Europe, he sought them out. The first of two emblematic concerts with Bernstein took place at the Landsberg DP camp in May 1948, the program I heard about from my father in 2009. Bernstein described his experience in a letter to Helen Coates dated May 11, 1948, 2:30 a.m., from his memoir, *Findings – Fifty Years of Meditations on Music*:

> The Munich concert was the greatest success to date. Especially because I had three obstacles to overcome—youth, Americanism, and Jewishness. And what a riotous success! There's nothing more satisfying than an opera house full of Germans screaming with excitement... Almost more exciting were the two concerts in DP camps yesterday (Monday). I was received by parades of kids with flowers, and the greatest honors. I conducted a 20-piece concentration-camp orchestra (Freischütz, of all things!) and cried my heart out... It's all amazing and horrible and beautiful and ugly and messy and inspiring.

Der Freischütz, the opera based on a German legend by Carl Maria von Weber, embodies foreboding: "Am I then by heaven forsaken?"

In addition to the bouquets, the musicians presented a gift to Bernstein—a concentration camp uniform. Eventually he had to give it away because the smell couldn't be eradicated.

Toronto, July 2009

Two months after the Minnesota Orchestra's Carnegie Hall concert, in July, Sonia Beker's *Symphony on Fire* arrived in the mail. The book cover is all in black, the white-edged snapshot of Sonia's parents superimposed on rust-colored barbed wire. Pictured below are musicians performing in striped concentration camp attire: Sonia's father, Max Beker, one of the violinists, Sonia's mother, Fania, at the piano, and a conductor with his back to the camera. Sonia's family, at the cultural epicenter of Vilna (Vilnius), Lithuania, represented just a handful of the 100,000 people shot and buried near the railway station at Ponary, a suburb of Vilna, among them 80,000 Jews, many thousands of Poles, and Russian POWs. The subtitle, *A Story of Music and Spiritual Resistance During the Holocaust*, perfectly encapsulates what we believe sustained our parents.

Sonia inscribed the inside cover:

Dear Janet,

How rare and wonderful to meet and connect with a sister of the soul, a branch from the same tree. It's beautiful to share common sensibilities and memories as well as the strong desire to make the world a better place by sharing our stories and legacy! Thank God, we found each other. The music goes on!

Love, Sonia

I hesitated to leaf through the book. Perhaps I should wait. Perhaps it was premature to rifle through my father's memories, which he hadn't yet shared with me.

In preparation for another visit to my father, I had the miniature black-and-white photos blown up to poster size, rolled them up, and stuffed them into a tube to carry onto the plane. With the poster tube firmly under my arm, I took my seat, plagued by anxious questions—could I find the right moment to show the photos to my father? Will he revisit these haunting times? Recall any other details of that memorable day? Would he castigate me or praise me? Once I landed, I hurried through customs hearing his voice in my imagination, "When you coming, Janetkém?"

With a sigh, I stepped into the elevator at my father's building. When the heavy doors opened, there he was, propped up against the wall.

"Janetkém, *mucikám*, long time not seen! Such a long trip." After a feeble embrace, he leaned to pick up my bag but I snatched it away in an awkward tango, nearly dropping the poster tube. So much for keeping it somewhat out of view.

"What you have there in that thing? Show me. Show me already!" he said as we wobbled into his apartment.

"Now? Okay, Papa. Let's go to the dining room where there's more space."

I crossed the living room to the other end of the apartment where the table stood covered in tchotchkes—huge vases with artificial flowers, framed family photos, a sculpted salver filled with artificial fruit, a Lladro figurine exquisitely shaped, an ecru candle still in cellophane wrapping and tied with a gold ribbon, and a hand crocheted tablecloth with quilted wadding underneath. A mirage appeared—magnificent multicourse meals, Mama cooking in our family home.

I tried to clear the table. My father searched for his black-rimmed bifocals and a magnifying glass, as well as his thick, worn, corduroy seat cushion for his old bones, which were sore from prolonged sitting.

While I removed and carefully unfurled the enlarged photos, he took his place at the head of the table. He paused for a moment and looked at me, rather than down at them. My heart fluttered. Would he change his mind? But then he leaned over, a few inches from the first photo, and peered at each face before him. For several minutes, he was silent.

"That is Hofmekler. He conducted, sometimes played violin. Stupel. Here. *Here*. Stupel the concertmaster. Polish. He was very good violinist. Older than me. I was very friendly with him. And another cellist. What his name was?" He looked up at me and pointed to a bald older man with distinguished features. I realized that I was holding my breath. He remembered.

"I told you. About Chaim Arbeitman—youngest violinist. Here. Here he is. Must be 18. All the time we sat together on bus."

"This is amazing, Papa, amazing. All the time? What do you mean —all the time?"

My father winced, removed his glasses and leaned further back in the chair.

"We played two concerts every week, sometimes more. They took us on bus... I played 200 concerts. Maybe in 100 DP camps? Sometimes more than once. Late at night we would get back." He paused. "For survivors, for American soldiers, for people in sanitariums. Jewish Orchestra saved us after we left Hungary."

A somber air chilled the room. My father tried to push himself up out of his chair, but he slumped backwards.

I gently enfolded his hands in mine as his fingers started their tap-dance on the table. His expression betrayed the inner turmoil between apprehensions of the past and realities of the present. During the rest of my stay, we talked about and listened to music, comforting topics—conductors, composers, concert halls. "Wasn't that just bee-you-ti-ful?" But we avoided discussing the past. The glimmer of information, although fleeting, gave me hope for more details.

Back in St. Paul, I continued my detective work. I Googled, rifled through papers, and waited impatiently for the orchestra documentary to come in the mail. I'd left the book in Toronto with my father. In the meantime, Sonia's website had to suffice. I typed in the address. A photo appeared on my computer screen—the St. Ottilien Orchestra. This time, they are seated in two rows. Five musicians stand along the back wall, and there, in the middle, is my father.

Credit: From the archive of Sonia P. Beker, author of
Symphony on Fire: A Story of Music and Spiritual Resistance During the Holocaust

Entr'acte 1978

The couple enters New York's famed Russian Tea Room, arm in arm. The older gentleman looks snazzy in a camel hair jacket and suit and tie. His classic homburg is tilted at a rakish angle, which covers his graying hair. The young lady beams. Earlier in the day the gentleman purchased the outfit she wears—a silk sheer blouse, lightly tinged with taupe blossoms, and a sinuous tea-length skirt. Her edgy updo is held by a faux pearl hairpin. The maître d', with a collusive smile and a wink full of innuendo, promises to escort them to a private table in the back.

We are on a date, my father and I, purely by chance. I have landed a position with the Indianapolis Symphony, as associate principal cello—an impressive beginning—and my father couldn't be more proud. He still plays in the Toronto Symphony. Their performance in Carnegie Hall took place the previous evening and mine will occur tomorrow. A rare day off coincides in the Big Apple.

We indulge in our father-daughter day: shopping; our dinner out of savory red cabbage, blini with a spoonful of black caviar and sour cream, shashlik, lamb kabobs, and Russian cherry teacakes; and a ballet performance at Lincoln Center.

I remember every detail—one of very few occasions my father and I spent together, just the two of us. Previous moments with my father have been strained, but this outing—two adults, two professional cellists, and a day of choice activities in an exciting city—brings out the best in both of us.

There is a soft breeze and quiet sunshine. Our high spirits mellow the sharp edges of the city as we sashay past high-end shops.

The next evening, my first concert in the famous auditorium, I tiptoe onto the stage. The bright and buttery glow takes my breath away—the balcony edged in lavish crimson velvet matches the seats; the creamy, curved walls are embellished in gold and whimsically carved bas-relief, and the sound blooms like a garden of chrysanthemums in an astonishing palette of colors. Exquisitely attuned to the vibrations of performers and composers who came before us, who graced this very stage: Pyotr Ilyich Tchaikovsky, composer of *The Nutcracker* and *1812 Overture*, conducted the first concert on opening night; Igor Stravinsky, Sergei Rachmaninoff, Benny Goodman, Itzhak Perlman, Philip Glass, as well as Dr. Martin Luther King Jr. We musicians never forget that our goal is to make mystical, meditative, and revelatory experiences come alive, through great music. My father participates from his seat in the audience tapping the cello part with his left-hand fingers on his armrest, playing every note with me.

Our exceptional day together prompts me to confide in my father. I had just ended a long-term relationship. He escorts me to the steps of the orchestra bus. "Many people love you, Janetkém. Very soon I am sure, someone special will love you and deserve your love, my darling."

He waves and puts on a bashful smile as the bus pulls away from the curb. The Brahms *Symphony No. 1* in C minor still resounds. Its throbbing, relentless timpani pulse and the pleading strings—intense and lush, *un poco sostenuto*—is the cord which more firmly connects me to him.

Leonard Bernstein poses with the Ex-Concentration Camp Orchestra. *Bernstein (far right, in a white shirt), Fania Durmashkin (to his left), Max Beker (fourth from the right), Henia Durmashkin (seventh from the right), and my father (ninth from the right, second row behind the trumpet player in a gray suit).* Credit: From the archive of Sonia P. Beker, author of *Symphony on Fire: A Story of Music and Spiritual Resistance During the Holocaust.*

Dad sees photos from 1948. *My father leaned into his past, hurtling not only back six decades but into the morass of fraught memories.*

Ex-Concentration Camp Orchestra (St. Ottilien) performing in 1945. Credit: From the archive of Sonia P. Beker, author of *Symphony on Fire: A Story of Music and Spiritual Resistance During the Holocaust.*

3

A DOCUMENTARY TAKES US BACK IN TIME

A few weeks later, the documentary, *Creating Harmony: The Displaced Persons' Orchestra from St. Ottilien* arrived.

I tore the package open. Like the cover of the book, it's all in black except for the yellow Jewish star. A lone violinist with hollowed out cheeks and a somber expression is pictured, playing in his shabby striped concentration camp uniform.

Handling the DVD with sweaty palms, half expecting it to come alive, I read and reread the cover: "A remarkable documentary about renewal, resistance, and resilience." World Premiere, June 10, 2007, at the Museum of Jewish Heritage—A Living Memorial to the Holocaust, co-producers John J. Michalczyk and Ronald A. Marsh.

Was I ready for what I might see? Uncertain of my father's reaction to the revelations—or perhaps my own faintheartedness—I decided to wait to watch the film with him during my upcoming summer trip to Toronto.

But Rob called the next day with troubling news. Our father had a sudden bout of chest pain. "He's okay now. Dad took a puff of nitroglycerine," he said, adopting his reassuring doctoral manner.

"What were his symptoms?" I asked.

"It's angina. Typical indicators. Probably heart disease."

"But on top of Parkinson's? What do you think?"

“Not unusual in someone his age. He’s 87. No need to overreact. We’ll have it thoroughly checked out this week.”

Could this be more serious than he was letting on? Self-reproach consumed me. Preoccupied by my own guilt, Rob’s hidden distress slipped by unnoticed.

We juggled caregivers for four years until finally, in 2004, Ian came into our lives. Herman Ian Barçon, stocky and strong, with obsidian eyes and a gentle demeanor, had first studied banking and finance in college. He changed course when he heard about a Canadian government policy offering Filipino nursing school graduates caregiving positions with elderly Canadians, with the option to apply for landed immigrant status. It was a way to a better life. Ian entered the competitive school and studied hard. His application and one interview convinced me.

Ian’s unfailing composure and captivating smile calmed us all. He cared for our mother as if she were his, with ears attuned to the slightest stir from the bedroom any hour of the day or night. He washed and diapered her, dressed and undressed her, lifted her out of bed, and settled her back. He puréed her food, fed her spoonful by spoonful, and perhaps most challenging of all, Ian humored my father. But Papa felt alone. He needed my company, and my annual vacation in August was several weeks away.

Trying not to think his health might be failing, I focused on the significance of sharing the video. I couldn’t squander the time I had left with my father. I needed him to share more of his experiences. A quick glance at my schedule indicated a four-day break, soon, in July, before our summer season. I booked a flight to Toronto.

The plane arrived on schedule. Even so, my father had already called my cell phone—anxiously bracing himself for any calamity—a fabric of life in our family. I called him immediately, to assure him I was on the way, and to remind him that, with traffic, it might take me 45 minutes to get to his apartment.

"You have good car? Watch how you driving, Janetkém. Slow. Go slow."

As quickly as I could, I collected my luggage, found the rental car, and maneuvered out of the bustling airport.

"Touch wood, Janetkém. Thanks God, you arrived," my father said, rapping his temple with his knuckles when I walked in. Carefully taking his aim, he bent forward to kiss me but the smooches landed on my ear.

I'd arrived after dinnertime, and, although eating always took precedence, my father had waited with the delectables laid out for me, chocolate *babka* for dessert, my agenda on hold.

Humming appreciative noises, my father gulped his food as if it might disappear at any moment. "Wonderful. This soup. Fan-tas-tic. Try it! You like the chicken? Eat more. Mummy always made it for you."

The kitchen table barely accommodated us all: my father, Ian, me, and my mama in her wheelchair. It didn't help that profusely blooming orchids in lavender and white surrounded the table. A memory came to mind. My father's garden. Plants lovingly coddled. They were transferred into the house during harsh Toronto winters and placed all around the family dining room table. His year-round nurturing triggered an acrimonious accompaniment from Mama. "How can I make supper with these all over the place? We can' even move! I have to step on them? All day you dig outside. You gonna fall. Don' lift those heavy pots! Wear a hat in the sun... Your hands!"

My father interjected upon the memory, "Have cake. Don't you want *babka*?"

"Papa. I've eaten plenty and—"

"What you talking. So fresh. Eat." He looked disgruntled.

Unexpectedly, I reverted to the frightened adolescent haunted by the menacing power of my father's rage. I took a small piece.

In a flash, he consumed three pieces of cake, leaving not a morsel, and just as quickly he was up to tidy the dishes as he always had. Ian took the plates from his hands, "Don't worry Lolo George, I can do it. It's okay. Go sit with Janet."

I was edgy. *Now, can we proceed?* I asked my father if he felt able to walk over to the chairs in front of the television set. Ian and I gently assisted. My father's body, rigid and unyielding, tired easily. With a deep audible breath, he sat heavily into one of the chairs and fumbled for his glasses. I pulled the video out of its case. The clock seemed to tick loudly. While I loaded the tape, my father leafed through pages of *Symphony on Fire*. He peered closely. Several moments passed, but I didn't interrupt. Once in a while, I thought I heard him mumble. My throat was parched.

"Are you ready, Papa?"

We sat close together and held hands, bracing ourselves, silently suspended as the music started. A lone, melancholy violin played Jules Massenet's *Médiation* from the opera *Thaïs*: *Andante religioso*. The camera spanned the barbed wire surrounding Auschwitz. A bird floated across the screen.

In an instant he blurted, "It's me!"

My father pointed to his handsome, young face. "There. There I am. There I am again. I had so much hair!"

I leapt out of my chair, touched the TV screen as if I needed to be part of the scene, and shouted, "Here you are, Papa!"

The camera panned over the musicians huddled together on a bus just like any group of young people on an outing. Then it zeroed in on my father. He looked classy with a neatly draped scarf tucked into a dark wool coat, a tie evident on his formal shirt. The musicians, with an obvious camaraderie and warmth for each other, were not heading out for adventure but on their way to one of the DP camp performances on a mission of hope. The camera moved to his seatmate.

"There. There is Chaim Arbeitman. He was fan-tas-tic young violinist I told you about," he said, as he pointed to a young man with a mischievous smile sitting next to him. "And there is conductor Hofmekler! Isn't this Stupel? A very good violinist, older, middle-aged, I think."

I rewound the tape so we could see the close-up of my father again. When I sat down, I scribbled the names and details as quickly as I could—memories might flutter away. My father stared at the television set, shaking his head. Then he turned toward me hesitantly, eyebrows upturned, puzzled to see his grown-up daughter beside him.

"Who made this film? Where they get the pictures?"

He sighed again, trying without success to recover his composure. Boundaries blurred. Who was this shy young man on the television screen? After a moment, he looked at me again.

"Unbelievable, Janetkém. How you found these, *kicsi* (little) Janetkém, *mucikám!*"

Dad and I smiled through our tears.

The grainy black and gray film panned over a large crowd which included military personnel and the wan and cadaverous group. The carcasses looked alike, men, women, and children with shaven skulls, sickly hollow cheeks, and grainy faces—yet they were living beings. The scenes seemed to reek of carrion. Bloody ravaged feet and fingers were wrapped haphazardly in strips of dirty pieces of cloth. Steam rose from a huge simmering pot. An emaciated little boy waited patiently for a piece of bread. I sensed a frozen stillness. Some of the survivors had been carried on stretchers to a large open field for the performances. Others, swaddled in blankets, stood shoulder to shoulder. Bereft of all sensation, they wept and grieved as the music transported them beyond comprehension, beyond what they endured to a place of sanctity.

Archival footage had been interpolated with present-day interviews. The narrators included Rita Lerner and her mother, Henia Durmashkin Gurko, the vocalist on the original program; Sonia and her father, Max Beker, and Chaim Arbeitman, two violinists who played on the program; and the American soldiers Robert Hilliard and Edward Herman. Where there was no filmed record, performance scenes were reenacted with actors or depicted using still photos. The musicians began in silence, then with a unifying breath they delved deeply into their inner worlds, compelling the newly liberated prisoners to lift up their spirits. The concerts allowed them to lament their losses, offered sustenance and hope, enchanted them with long-forgotten serenity: music as essential for their spirits, as food and medicine for their bodies. The survivors, still clothed in tattered striped pajamas, languished, awaited news of loved ones, and prayed for priceless documents that would allow them to leave Europe.

Had the filmmaker been aware that my father was still with us, he would have been in this documentary. No matter. I had another piece of the puzzle. We rewound the film several times, so my father could absorb the memories. Was he feeling distress? Torment? Pride? "Papa," I interrupted, "aren't you tired? Maybe we should stop. We can watch more tomorrow, okay?"

"What? What time it is? Already ten o'clock? It's late. Iy-awn (Ian), I want go to sleep."

Ian helped my father shuffle ever so slowly to his bedroom to prepare for bed. I leapt to my feet, my ribcage ready to burst—the sudden silence, oppressive, the saga too much to grasp in one sitting. How could the musicians even move their fingers, let alone hold their instruments to play? Overcome by a wave of nausea, I moved to the balcony, slid the door open a crack, and took several cool gulps of air. And what of the miseries prior to the concert? I needed to know. Asking made me weak with anxiety.

When the evening ablutions had been accomplished, Ian invited me to come into the bedroom to kiss my father goodnight. I circled Mama's hospital bed and exhaled at last.

That night, images haunted. When I stirred, Rob's purple guest room confused me. My belly seized. Like a child, I pulled the covers over my head. Between dreaming and wakefulness, I tried to revel in the amazing discoveries of the last few months and enjoy the soft down quilt on the bed, but I couldn't keep the horrors at bay. The images eclipsed all other sensations. I even dozed through my father's very early phone call.

"Janetkém, when you coming already?"

Dressing without any thought to my appearance—unusual for me—I did grab my red sweater (the one my father really liked), and I jumped into the car to drive over, concerned that something was amiss. The sound of the television, even more piercing than usual, could be heard from the elevator. *Here it comes! From the Bob Barker studios at CBS in Hollywood, it's* The Price is Right! *Come on down!* My father barely greeted me. He was guarded; spoke little, his arms crossed over his chest. We sat together all day in front of the TV, no hint of our journey back in time. All he wanted was my company.

The bus ride—The St. Ottilien musicians on their way to offer spiritual sustenance to DPs. *My father, with a full head of hair and wearing a tie, sits by the window of the bus.* Credit: From the archive of Sonia P. Beker, author of *Symphony on Fire: A Story of Music and Spiritual Resistance During the Holocaust.*

Bernstein and the St. Ottilien Orchestra take a bow, Feldafing. *Leonard Bernstein center on the podium, my father standing to his left (facing forward).* Credit: Courtesy of The American Jewish Joint Distribution Committee archives (JDC), New York, NY, who sponsored the concerts and provided the musicians with food and supplies.

The St. Ottilien Orchestra poised for the downbeat. *Bernstein is standing, my father sits far left.* Credit: Courtesy of The American Jewish Joint Distribution Committee archives (JDC), New York, NY.

Bernstein receives flowers, Feldafing. *Sponsored by the American Jewish Joint Distribution Committee on May 10, 1948, near Munich.* Credit: Courtesy of The American Jewish Joint Distribution Committee archives (JDC), New York, NY.

PART II

BACH, BEETHOVEN, AND BRUTALITY
KATHERINE'S (KATO'S) STORY

When I hear music, I fear no danger. I am invulnerable.
I see no foe. I am related to the earliest times and to the latest.

—Henry David Thoreau (1817–1862)

4

PAPRIKA, PRAYER, AND PERSECUTION

"Peanut butter? They give their children peanut butter for lunch?" My mother was outraged. And these were purported to be good Toronto families? How inadequate. Abusive, almost. To my Hungarian mother, lunch was an ingenious enterprise. Rob and I carried paper bags stuffed with a thick slice of Wiener schnitzel on a poppy seed roll eight inches long, a succulent peach when in season, Hungarian pastry—perhaps cherry strudel or several *rugelach* filled with walnuts, cinnamon, or chocolate—and a mammoth slice of fresh green pepper. How could I hide this hideously large bag lunch and smuggle it into my locker without being seen? Kids at Willowdale Middle School could be mean. I cringed at the remarks.

"Eew! Yuck! What is that stuff?"

Nonetheless, my friends loved to come over to the Horvath household. My father's accent and European manner were pleasing, exotic. Before the doorbell rang, I'd try to forestall the inevitable. Every visitor was their visitor. It was simply unacceptable not to formally greet guests at the door. After quickly pulling off the plastic coverings on the furniture, my parents ushered my friends to the living room as I skulked behind. While my father made small talk, Mama would prepare an array of hors d'oeuvres and a selection of Jewish and Hungarian pastries—filled with marzipan or poppy seeds

—cheese blintzes, and layered cream tortes served on platters, large enough for the whole neighborhood. It was unthinkable to have guests without offering them hospitality. They shouldn't starve! Already seduced by magical American foods—donuts, hot dogs, spaghetti and meatballs, M&Ms—I would beg my mother to leave off the green pepper.

My mother grilled them, "What does your daddy do? Where you live? You should wear the makeup. Why you don' wear the makeup? You would be much prettier." Tact was not her strongest suit. I couldn't get a word in.

While impatience and resentment burned, I fantasized. A designated eater. That's what I needed—a designated eater so my best friend could be squirreled away to privacy in my bedroom.

Our family ate like Austro-Hungarian royalty. A consummate culinary virtuoso, my mother whipped up masterpieces each night. She'd dash up the stairs from her piano teaching studio, leaving her student sitting there, while she assembled some cabbage rolls. Then, barely missing a beat, she'd return to her student, whose stomach, no doubt, grumbled from the heavenly smells wafting from the kitchen.

Chicken *paprikás*, thick cauliflower soup with dumplings, *Rizsi Bizsi* (just the name made us giggle)—a concoction of peas and rice with a sauce piquant—and, of course, goulash, generously saturated with sweet paprika, served with her mouth-watering mashed potatoes and thick slices of rye bread, or new potatoes and onions fried to a golden brown. The aroma was simply intoxicating. My father had an aberrant sweet tooth. Tour de force finales followed—paper-thin melt-in-your-mouth *palacsinta*: famous Hungarian-style crepes, filled with ground walnuts and sugar, or chocolate and apricot jam, or a ricotta-like cheese with lemon and sugar (my favorite), or cherry *pité*, oozing fresh sour cherries. My father delighted in *dobos*: a creamy chocolate-layered torte with a hard topping of caramel. Ignoring the risk of prodigious circumferences, no other food would do. Anything non-Hungarian was sadly inferior.

Mama's grandest performances took place when guests were invited, timing her magnum opus just as guests arrived at the door. They were ushered directly to the dining room without chatting, drinking, or munching, certainly no television. My mother considered such activities out of the question. Guests were invited for one thing: to eat. My mother waited on high alert. It shouldn't get cold!

She was breathless, beads of sweat on her brow, poised and ready to dole out heaping ladles of her famous Hungarian bean soup, *bab leves*. The task at hand, an overflowing colossal bowl of thick soup teeming with meat, kidney beans, and vegetables, with perfectly shaped little dumplings. A meal in itself. Beyond what I could manage. But the spoonfuls kept coming until I'd protest, "No! I don't want any more!" and literally pull my plate out of her reach. Offended, with a flushed countenance, my mother would retort, "*Na*, Janetkém, you are too thin. You eat like bird!"

"Sit down and eat with us, Mama."

"Have more!" she'd cajole.

My mother considered the repast warily. What if someone didn't like the main course? Problem solved: two main dishes. She'd watch as I picked at a small piece of roast veal. "What? You don' like the cabbage rolls?"

Much later I realized that her talent in the kitchen was not merely a Jewish mother's penchant for food. After the deprivation in her youth, feeding us well defined her—proof that those days were behind her. And my parents' obsession with crisp shirts, and fashionable outfits, dispelled the dark memories of filth, lice, clothing in tatters, and soleless shoes.

My vivacious mother, always in vogue with head-to-toe stylish outfits—scooped necklines, sequined blouses, ruched skirts, and tastefully matching shoes and purses—never went out before she was put-together, requiring hours of preparation: eye shadow over her beautiful hazel eyes, powder on her blemish-free complexion (*Never let anyone see you witout makeup*), and proper corsets to pull in some unsightly bulges. Her home-dyed hair flattened against her scalp, held securely with pin curls, would be transformed after two hours in the bathroom into a voluminous bouffant. Once the coif was erected she'd spray prodigious amounts of VO5 hair spray, which wafted through the house, choking us with its syrupy fragrance. No sense throwing away hard-earned money at beauty salons—Mama styled her raven hair beautifully.

No one else's hair satisfied her. My father's scalp was virtually bald with just wisps of long hairs around the sides of his head. He would submit to my mother's daily charge—a comb-over—teased and sprayed (*super-hold!*) into a hardened mass to cover the unsightly patina.

My hairstyle and choice of clothing drew stinging criticisms. She would look at me with distaste, vigorously shake her head, and say, "*Jaaannaaattte!* Fluff up your bangs!"

No miniskirts for me. I played the cello. You can't spread your legs in that kind of skirt. And jeans? They were simply unacceptable, unfeminine, common.

Entr'acte 1956

Carefully preserved behind cellophane, in an old blue family album, is a photo. It's summer and I am perhaps four years old. Peeking through dense foliage, the sun beams on the neatly arranged rock garden. We are standing in front of our five-room bungalow at 958 Castlefield Avenue. My mother and I hold hands, and, although she appears elusive or perhaps reserved, her head slightly cocked, I am smiling broadly. Posing in fancy, black strapped Mary Janes, white ankle socks, and a belted crinoline dress, I clutch the strap of a white handbag and a pair of gloves in my left hand.

My mother looks regal in a formfitting dark suit—a satin skirt, a matching short-sleeved buttoned-down chemise, and elbow-length gloves. Her shoes are black with a strap too, but open at the toe. Like me, my mother is holding her purse by the strap in her left hand. Its oblong shape resembles mine, however hers is dark to match her outfit, of course. But our hats are striking—both white, trimmed with a flower or two, very soft, of felt perhaps, and oddly shaped, the half-hat, the latest fashion in millinery at the time—close fitting and stiffened to seem like a halo extending just beyond the crown of our heads (worn also by Queen Elizabeth II in the 1950s and very popular with brides of the day). I am Mama's reflection in miniature.

My mother reigned over the appearance empire. Even years later, as a teenager, I would endure wearing matching attire. Suitable outfits could only be found as a duo—an unhappy version of follow the leader. She and I would hunt for clothing with made-in-Canada labels, first at the department stores. Sometimes my father would be allowed to come along with us. His eyes sparkled. Papa adored beautiful things: jewelry, art, music, and stylish clothing. He liked nothing better than to see us model the priciest designer outfits even though we couldn't afford them. But his presence disrupted my mother's agenda—to dress me properly. My parents bickered. "*Gyurikám.* Here we are not buying!" my mother would say. I'd disappear to the back of the store to rifle through the displays, unhindered. Maybe, I thought, I could pretend I didn't know them.

Every few minutes my father found something. "Janetkém, look. Look here!"

I'd tear myself away from an outfit that had caught my eye and trudge to the front of the store where my father waved a garish treasure he had found in a size that would fit a buxom woman of a certain age.

"Papa, that's so ugly! It's way too fancy. None of my friends wear anything like that!"

"Try it."

Turning my back on him I'd careen through the displays back to the other side of the store. Undeterred, a moment later I would hear, "Janetké, is not these bee-you-ti-ful? Buy it!!"

Heads turned as they witnessed the scene. I hid among the racks in the plus-sized collection, hoping my parents wouldn't think to look for me there.

Mama, exasperated, vexed, excelled in speed shopping. With armloads of clothing, my parents rushed the dressing rooms. She would ignore my reticence and squeeze into the tiny cubicle with me. I didn't want to undress in front of her. She'd hover too close; look me over, size up my body. According to my mother, we were exactly alike, especially our tendencies to add girth to our compact figures. Weren't we both *zaftig*?

"Mama, I love this sweater. Can't we buy this? And the skirt. It's the latest fashion."

"*Jaaannaaattte!* You don' see yourself from the back!"

We both knew she would prevail—nothing too tight, low-cut, or short. She made the selections, scrutinized the tags, and stealthily wrote the garment code numbers down before we made a hasty exit.

Then she'd drag me downtown to the factory district, where they manufactured the outfits, in search of the chosen ensembles. Trying on clothing wasn't possible there.

In the crowded, smoky hallways, my mother haggled in fierce whispers. I stood off to the side, gazing at the floor. After several minutes, the supervisor would concede. She always bought her clothes this way—never paying retail. My mother proffered cash, counting each dollar, for two identical outfits, albeit in vastly different sizes—one in 12 and one in 4. It didn't seem odd to her. She had impeccable taste, and wasn't it the same as mine? The tailored emerald green skirt with black velvet accents, the purple wool one-piece dress, and the trendy sweater that I had my heart set on were not available there. I would entreat my mother to return to the department store. Inevitably, the outfits had been sold by then.

Soon after my birth in 1952, my mother's home piano-teaching studio flourished. Instilling a love of music was her passion. She constantly harangued her young students, including my brother and me, about the many benefits of playing a musical instrument—discipline, motivation, perseverance, concentration, coordination, dexterity, and creativity, let alone improving memory, comprehension, and listening and reading skills. A formidable teacher, both feared and adored by her students.

On Saturday mornings, I could hear her all the way upstairs in my bedroom, "You don' know how to build a major scale?? Two-whole, one-half—Three-whole, one-half." She'd demonstrate the alternating tones on the piano. "Play with ex-pre-ssion! One an' da, two an' da," she'd croon, her student's tinkles unable to compete. Pulling the sheets over my head, I would grumble, "Is this a piano lesson or a singing lesson? How can that poor kid even hear himself think, let alone play?"

Rob and I visited the art gallery nearly every weekend with my father. Cultural activities always took precedence. My mother ensured our knowledge of all the European literary classics. But music was primary. Mozart, Beethoven, Bach, Brahms, Stravinsky, and, of course, the great Hungarian composer, Béla Bartók, resonated in our home most hours of the day—a veritable conservatory. Music lessons and daily practice were compulsory, and often the simultaneous sounds of two cellos, a horn, the piano, and my mother's warbling could be heard down the block. Even as youngsters, we went to concerts often, my parents proud that we could sit without fidgeting. An elderly woman noticed and felt compelled to say, "Madam, you are to be congratulated. Your children are so well behaved."

"Well, they better," my mother replied. "Their daddy is playing."

Mama envisioned me flamboyantly striding onstage in a long diaphanous dress clutching my cello. They eavesdropped on my practice and barked criticisms. "Janetkém. Play it SL-O-WER... That is so out of tune."

"*Na, Jaaannaaattte.* Play it *again*. Count!"

Never missing an opportunity to show me off, whenever we had visitors or any captive audience, there would be a command performance, "Janetkém, play the new piece. Look how musical she is!" And they'd push me toward the piano in our living room to play no matter how squirmy the guests seemed.

But the alluring tones of the cello beckoned. I craved to learn the secrets behind its fantastic range of expression—the deep lamenting baritone, the silken tenor, the dazzling soprano.

I persisted, at times with bumps in the road. When I was ready for my first solo recital my father allowed me to play his beautiful 18th-century Italian cello, the instrument he had brought from Europe, a *Panormo*: hand-carved, with a spruce top, a striking flamed maple back, and a deeply textured varnish. The concert, held in the Art Gallery of Ontario in 1970—a prestigious location for a 17-year-old to play—tested the performer with conditions that were far from ideal. The cavernous space was open to museum browsers, and the pock-marked, white, marble walls created a reverberant acoustic. Audience members, who had to peer around Greek style pillars, ranged from curious museum attendees, to music enthusiasts hoping to hear the latest wunderkind, and mothers with fussy children who just wanted a chance to sit down.

Warming up in a backstage room, my jitters took over. Why had I chosen to start with such a taxing work, the Bach *Solo Suite No. 3* in C Major? —a challenging masterpiece even for a seasoned performer. I forced myself to focus mentally, to inhale and exhale deeply. At the appropriate time, with a firm hold on my cello, I took one more breath, remembered to hitch up my dress so as not to trip, smiled with my teeth (as my mother would insist), and waltzed across the stage exuding confidence. Jamming my endpin, the metal spike that holds the cello, into the unyielding wooden floor, I launched into the first C of the music. Then came a cellist's nightmare: my cello careened forward out of my hands and I only just caught it with my knees. I shoved it back into the floor with my torso, somehow not missing a beat of the music, but I didn't dare look up. My father had lurched forward in his seat, moaning audibly. My breathing eventually calmed, but he turned ashen.

After the Bach, when I retired to the back room, the stage manager wheeled the piano out for the next piece. My father jumped out of his seat to canvass the audience. "Anyone have pocketknife?" he demanded.

Someone did, on his keychain. Clutching the knife, my father scaled the stage, got down on all fours, and dug a hole in the floor.

Satisfied that he had prevented further equipment disasters, he returned to his seat. When I sashayed onto the stage for my second number I didn't see the newly gouged rut. Then, just as I was about to thrust the cello into the floor, I saw my mother flailing. "*Jaaannaaattte*!" she said to my complete mortification, "Your daddy made a hole! Your daddy made a *hole!*"

Entr'acte 1961

Autumn—the season lovely for its golden yellows and reds, the harvest moon, fading siphoned light and the frivolity of Halloween: when you who yearn to become someone else (if only for an evening) partake in the ultimate masquerade party—of disguises, costumes, creepy effigies, spooky cobwebs—eliciting horror and dread, demanding a trick or a treat, and sprinting from house to house.

My mother finds Halloween abhorrent. Not until my twenties did I understand it reminds her of attacks aimed at Jews, pogroms, especially the Night of Broken Glass—*Kristallnacht*, November 9, 1938 —the night Nazi dogma emerged as an execrable apparition. When organized massacres wreaked havoc, and ghetto inhabitants were terrorized. When doleful cries went unheeded, and rampaging mobs violently plundered shops and homes, and freely attacked synagogues. The menfolk beaten (or murdered), rounded up, sent to Dachau—30,000 of them—while the police turned a blind eye. The night when everything: law and order, a place in society, citizenship, civility, community, justice, honor, and humanity, was called into question.

Mama explains why we don't celebrate October 31 or Christmas either; why we wouldn't be getting presents, why we are the only house on the block without lights and decorations. I think Rob and I understand. We still sing in our school pageants and know all the holiday carols. I remember *Away in a Manger*. I'd leave out two words, humming through the melody. "No crib for a bed, the little—hm *hm* hm—lay down his sweet head."

We think it's a beautiful holiday and smile politely when people wish us a merry Christmas, even when we know they know we are Jewish.

Each morning in school we stand and say the *Lord's Prayer*, which I can still recite: "Our Father who art in heaven; Hallowed be thy name; Thy kingdom come; Thy will be done..." *Thy will be done*? Considering all that has been perpetrated during and prior to the 20th century, I wonder how often this line has been distorted for nefarious ends.

Do my parents pray? I don't know, but they teach me the *Sh'ma* (*Shema*). Meaning listen, the *Sh'ma* is the centerpiece of Jewish prayer, a prayer specifically commanded in the Torah. I can recite the first two lines in Hebrew by heart, and we hear the words and the melody every time we attend synagogue; in fact, the refrain is the same in synagogues everywhere.

A declaration of faith, the *Sh'ma* is considered the most important of all Jewish prayers, to be recited daily, morning and evening, at the conclusion of the Holy Day of Atonement, Yom Kippur, and before death. The emphasis is given to the famous six initial words, with a six-word response.

> *Sh'ma Yisrael, Adonai Eloheinu, Adonai Echad!*
> *Baruch shem kavod malchuto l'olam va'ed.*

> Hear O Israel: The Lord our God, the Lord is One. Praised be His name and glorious kingdom forever and ever.

It continues:

> You shall love the Lord your God with all your heart, with all your soul, and with all your might. And these words, which I command you this day shall be upon your heart. And you shall teach them diligently unto your children, speak of them when you sit in your house, when you walk by the way, when you lie down and when you rise up...

These words invoke strong sensations in me. During the Spanish

Inquisition, anyone who dared utter even the word *Sh'ma* was severely punished. Later, I would discover that these two lines recited in Hebrew saved my father's life during the Holocaust.

A dusky memory wafts through the air. A bedtime prayer, but it's not the *Sh'ma*. It's in Hungarian. I'm snuggling under the covers, tucked in, and my Mama is sitting on the bed. Together we say... What did we say? Struggling to recall the words, I manage to conjure fragments,

Én Istenem, Jó Istenem, Lecsukódik már a szemem.
De a tiéd nyitva Atyám, amig alszom, vigyázz reám!

I've probably mispronounced the words for decades, but with persistence, I find the prayer on a Catholic Church website. "My God, Good God. My eyes have already closed. But Yours remain open. Please watch over me while I sleep." And then we add our own family entreaty, "watch over my kind parents, and my little brother; so that when the day again arises, we can kiss each other in the morning."

Why did they teach me to recite a Christian prayer? Somehow, even as a child, I sensed ambivalence. My parents came to Canada after all that had happened, resolute. With the intention to forget they were Jewish. But they're unable to relinquish their heritage, especially after Rob and I are born. Our unlikely births signify triumph over the Nazis. I've learned my mother carried false ID papers during the Holocaust, identifying her as Roman Catholic. Perhaps she memorized Christian prayers. Perhaps she felt compelled to teach us Christian rituals to prepare us, in case we, too, have to hide our religion. It could mean the difference between life and death.

Entr'acte, April 1961

An altered awareness begins to descend upon me. I am nine years old. My parents huddle around our newly acquired black-and-white television. They watch with intense apprehension. I remember watching too, agitated, unable to grasp their flurry of Hungarian, "*Na*

Gyurikám. Nem! No. Change station! *Itt van Janetke és Robika.* (Janet and Robert are here.) *Kapcsold ki* (turn it off)."

"*Baszdmeg. Az a szar* (that shit), Eichmann."

They wrench the dials to find world news. Eichmann. Trials. The Bay of Pigs. What did these mean for us? In Canada? Usually we watch *The Ed Sullivan Show* on television Sunday evenings, harmless and entertaining. But this week, world attention is fixated on the trial of German Nazi Adolph Eichmann, one of the most notorious war criminals in history.

Adolf Eichmann's trial brings Nazi atrocities to the forefront of world news, chilling people's homes. It is the first televised trial in the history of television. One hundred and sixteen Holocaust survivors recount their traumatic experiences for the first time since the war ended. Eichmann, responsible for the Final Solution, transported millions of Jews to death camps all over Europe.

I recall watching television, but it's not a trial. I see maps of a little island called Cuba, an assault on someone named Castro, US-backed insurgents, and a few months later in 1962, hearing about missiles and a dramatic face-off between people named President Kennedy and a Russian, Nikita Khrushchev.

My parents are distressed. In muted whimpers, they discuss digging a bomb shelter in our backyard, hiding, hoarding water and food, burying jewelry, and stocking provisions.

It takes me decades to gather the courage to watch a portion of the Eichmann trial. It's on YouTube. Physically wrenched, I observe the accused sitting calmly in a specially built shatterproof-glass cage, black-rimmed glasses dominating his pinched face. Eichmann personally supervised the deportation and murder of Hungary's Jews. Each day, 12,000 men, women, and children were transported against their will, to Auschwitz, to the crematoriums. The mastermind? A meek little man with a penchant for Bach, Beethoven, and brutality.

Entr'acte 1962

In the summer, we often picnic at Rouge Hill, a public beach and park with a view of Lake Ontario. A group of Hungarians including

Ada, my mother's best friend, and her husband Tibor, would rendezvous with their lidded metal containers, stuffed full: *körözött* (a cream cheese spread, liberally dosed with paprika and green onions); *Halászlé* (fisherman's soup), which when chilled with a clove of garlic jellifies and is delicious served cold; *kifli* (dense croissant-like rolls) heaped with meats and cheeses; slices of bell peppers; and for dessert, watermelon and *begli* (a spiral-shaped log roll filled with sweet ground walnuts or poppy seeds). But just like other kids, Rob and I beg for ice cream cones, and if there is any money to spare, we happily scamper to the ice cream stand.

My hair sticks to the gobs of suntan lotion Mama applies all over my skin. It feels icky. She invites me to sit cross-legged on a blanket and unpacks the wide-toothed wooden brush. Kneeling behind me, she smooths my tresses. I can feel her soft breath on my neck.

"Mama, why don't Ada and Tibi have any kids?"

She hesitates. "They not able to have children."

"Why, Mama?"

A pause. She stops brushing. "Well. Something happened during war."

"What, Mama?"

Another pause. "Ada was in bad place, a camp. The Germans... She can' have kids because of camp."

Mama resumes twirling my curls, a little too firmly, into a tight bun. I don't turn around. I know about a war. I know for some reason Jews were targeted. I know by then I'm not supposed to talk about being Jewish. But I have friends who go to camps for summer fun.

"Mama. Why does she have that number on her arm?" The tattooed number makes me shudder, and manages somehow to impart uninvited grief.

A very long pause. Her breath quickens. "*Na!* Janetkém. Ada was in very bad place. Germans took Jews there. Jewish prisoners got number on their arm."

I turn around. Mama's eyes widen and she pulls away from me. "*Yay Istenem* (Oh my God)," she sputters. "Many, many, people died. Your daddy... We were lucky. I didn' get caught. We didn' get sent to... It was—"

Abruptly she gets up, and wades into the water. Although the sun is shining and the billed pelicans soar overhead, I feel a cold haze. Jewish prisoners? At a terrible camp? They didn't get caught? A sudden disquiet washes over me. I have asked questions I'm not supposed to ask.

Elegant mama. *Austro-Hungarian Royalty? Who would think this beauty had suffered through hiding, deprivation, and terror?*

Mother-daughter duo in hats, May 1957. *At five years old, I'm the mirror image of Mama.*

Janet and Robert slurp ice cream cones, Rouge Hill.

Rouge Hill updo and Day of Revelation. *Mama attended to hair, as if styling couldn't be a more serious affair. She was impeccable even when we picnicked.*

5

FINDING THE CELLO (AND THE MAN) OF MY DREAMS

My parents would consider entrusting my future to only the best teacher—the brilliant Hungarian cellist and pedagogue, János Starker. Like my parents, Starker studied at the famed Franz Liszt Academy of Music in Budapest. Emerging from the cinders of World War II, he immigrated to the US in 1948 and became principal cello of first the Dallas Symphony, then the Metropolitan Opera, and finally the Chicago Symphony. When his solo career took off, he became one of the revered professors at the Indiana University Jacobs School of Music in Bloomington, teaching countless cellists, inspiring hundreds if not thousands of musicians. Much later, I learned Starker's two older brothers, both violinists, were massacred during the Holocaust.

My mother never forgot hearing Starker perform in Budapest before the war, a prodigy in short pants and suspenders, playing the cello with such virtuosity. He became the darling of Budapest's arts community. As a young teenager, my lovely mother vied for a date with the wunderkind. He had hair then—dark, cut in a squarish "Buster Brown" style covering his ears but revealing thick eyebrows and piercing eyes. Decades later, Starker would tease his wife about his rendezvous with my mother.

My graduation from the University of Toronto's music program approached. Time for advanced study on the world stage. Juilliard attracted me. The teacher there, Leonard Rose, a genial man, played the cello with a lustrous, dazzling sound. Starker's uncompromising standards circulated among prospective students, his acerbic, accented speech full of vitriolic condemnations. "I wish I could chop off your hands and give them to someone more deserving." Still, Starker had the crème de la crème of students to pick from.

There were heated discussions in our household.

"Janetkém. *Mucikám*. Wait. When he hears you, he will love your gorgeous tone. Best students from around world go to Starker. A fan-tas-tic cellist."

"*Na, Jaaannaaattte!* You don' know what kinda teacher Rose is. Go to New York? Such a dangerous city? Enough talking already. We know Starker. He is Hungarian."

Despite my protestations, when Starker next performed with the Toronto Symphony, my father approached him, to ask if he would consider accepting me as his student; that is, if he thought I had a future as a cellist. Starker agreed to give me a few moments of his time.

The next day, my father and I, white-faced, took the elevator up to Starker's hotel room. After a terse greeting, Starker invited me to unpack my cello. Did I imagine him scanning my small hands?

While I fumbled to set up, he loaded a glass with ice and plenty of scotch, lit a cigarette, took a deep drag, and lowered himself into a chair. Starker's angular features, searing eyes, and completely bald head emerged from the haze of smoke. A scene from Bram Stoker's *Dracula* came to mind. I hurtled back to my nine-year-old self squeaking out a sound from a half-sized cello.

Tightening my bow, feigning confidence, I launched into Tchaikovsky's *Rococo Variations*, a piece of music that demonstrates every challenge on the instrument, full of pyrotechnics, a work I'd performed often. Descending into vibrato-hell, my limp fingers slowed to a mere wobble, the pitches on the fingerboard increasingly tenuous.

Starker crossed his arms and legs, and leaned well back into the leather chair, his eyes boring through me. He stopped me, mid-phrase. "You," he said, spitting out each consonant, "have a lot of physical development to do."

I drooped in my seat, hiding behind the cello. What did he mean? Run around the track? Push-ups? Something more strenuous, like rock climbing? Or was I impossibly tiny to play the cello?

Summarily dismissed, my father and I took the bus home in silence.

My mother peered out the front window, waiting for good news. We hauled ourselves and the *Panormo* cello, which was newly mine, into the house. I ran up the stairs, shut the door to my room, and plugged my ears to escape cross-examination, and my father's postmortem.

Days after the humiliating audition in Starker's hotel room, I made a vow. *I'll practice intensely for a year. Seven hours a day. More if I need to. Then he'll see. I will be ready. I know I can do it.*

Entr'acte 1972

It's my first concerto competition and I'm driving to the school of music in my parents' car—downtown Toronto. They don't want me to drag the cello on the bus and tire myself out before the final round. I pull up to the front drive of the building to drop the cello off before parking the car. Leaving the flashers on, I run the cello inside. When I come back out, the front half of the car is flattened under an enormous truck. The apologetic driver pulls ahead with a horrendous scraping sound. I don't dare look at the squashed remains, the metal exposed and streaked with flakes of red and green paint. Quaking at the thought of calling home, I'm no longer thinking about the competition but my father's reaction. He blows up for even the slightest offenses. Trudging to the pay phone, unable to control my sobs, my mother can barely understand what I'm trying to say. But when she realizes I'm unhurt, she takes charge, "Janetkém. Leave it now. You play. Play good."

Despite the car disaster, when I appear for the audition, I'm prepared to immerse myself in the sounds of the cello. It's my first time performing Tchaikovsky's *Rococo Variations*, the lyrical opening, sweet, lilting, Mozart-like, but dangerously exposed. Bows mustn't tremble. I try not to think about the challenging variations coming up, in the upper stratosphere of the instrument, fast and virtuosic. The slow, sinuous movements are my forte. Using ample vibrato, I coax a velvety sound out of the cello, the aura enveloping me. The judges sit stone-faced but I think the performance goes well.

Once we've played, each contestant joins the others and we sit in a row on the corridor floor, waiting for the deliberations of the panel of judges. When at the end of the day the jury posts the results, we crowd around the notice. My name is at the top of the list.

Even the dented, offending car, doesn't curb my delight. I can hardly wait to get home to tell my mother. As soon as she opens the door to our house, Mama throws her arms around me. Her cagey grin gives me pause.

"You know?" I ask.

With an awkward chuckle she says, "Wellll... I make just little phone call to judges of competition. I tell them you had bad accident! You can play much better than today after accident! But they tell me, 'Mrs. Horvath, Janet has already won the competition.'"

A flush crept up into my face. Fumbling to slip my boots back on, unzipped, running into the street, into the winter slush, I'm trailed by her voice, "*Jaaannaaattte! Don' run. Come back! I'm your mother. Can' I say anytink?*"

Privacy was a foreign notion to my parents—a closed door and a room of one's own an American luxury. Jewish families of my parents' generation were tight-knit figuratively, literally, and of necessity. Everyone knew everyone's business. Why not? What secrets would you want to keep from your own parents? My mother eavesdropped when I made telephone calls, questioned my whereabouts, insisted on complete details about my relationships, and required me to report in immediately when I arrived and left from wherever I went (even after I moved to the US). On top of that, a musician's art is audible. My playing was under constant scrutiny.

Never knocking before entering my room, not even the bathroom, nothing could be hidden from prying eyes. Obsessive about order, first thing in the morning, my father, while grumbling about how messy I was, would put away my clothes and homework I'd laid out the evening before for school. Forget about hiding the pill—impossible. He practically made my bed with me in it. My mother would pump my friends for information about me, and never restrained herself from giving unsolicited opinions.

Their constant prying made me itch to move away—away from the claustrophobic atmosphere. It would take me decades to understand that for my parents, staying together was paramount. When they were ghettoized by the Nazi regime, separation meant deportation, to unknown destinations and fates too terrible to contemplate. Being alone, a symbol of statelessness and loss, exemplified the ultimate punishment rather than an illicit fantasy.

Nonetheless, remaining together didn't guarantee safety. When the Nazis marched into Budapest, my mother's cousin, Arpád, someone I heard about only years afterward, had been visiting her family.

"What should I do, Uncle Nándor?" he'd asked.

When my grandfather told him, "Your place is with your parents," Arpád left Budapest immediately. My grandfather never forgave himself. Arpád and his family all perished in Auschwitz.

By 1975, after a year of intensive "physical development," Starker accepted me to join his exclusive class of students. I was 22 years old. An ambitious and driven musician, I thought I'd discovered my true calling; in reality, pursuing a life in music afforded the escape I yearned for. The only way I could become independent, away from the smothering possessiveness, interference, and the weight of the past, would be to move away. To another country.

Prickling doubts tiptoed in. Could I gain Starker's approval? Live up to the standards of students coming to study with him from all over the world? Fulfill my own expectations? I'd never been away from home except for summer camp. How would I manage? Well aware of what it would take to become the musician I wanted to be, my keen aspirations silenced my qualms.

The irony is not lost on me now. I chose to leave—a luxury my parents never had. My father at age 22 was wrenched from his home, his family, his cello, and sent for slave labor. My parents later embarked on a desperate journey to an unknown future, to somewhere utterly foreign, without the support of family, without knowing the language, without resources, and after unimaginable hardships. But I didn't want to think about that then, or to consider my decision to settle so far away from them would engender such heartache. In hindsight, I see how my absence was magnified. They never got over it. I suppose I didn't either.

Letting me go was but one concern. My parents understood the fierce competition. To reach my full potential as one of a dozen talented cellists in János Starker's elite class at Indiana University meant I needed a better instrument. With trepidation, they agreed to send me to New York to visit with dealers who might have an appropriate instrument. My father researched the fine musical instrument shops and individuals who were selling cellos privately. My parents considered the idea only because my aunt Magda lived in New York. I would stay with her.

Like most 22-year-olds, I felt very sure of myself—my first trip to New York, the adventure of my life. The famed dealership *Jacques Français*, known to have the best selection of quality instruments, beckoned. Why not start at the top? I took the slow elevator to the upper floor. When the doors opened, a vast carpeted showroom appeared before me. Several potential buyers hovered alongside the walls lined with stringed instruments. All the rooms to try instruments were filled to overflowing, and the echoes of the Mendelssohn *Violin Concerto* clashed with the Elgar *Cello Concerto*. From another room, I could hear scales, arpeggios, and octaves, the sounds of agreeable cacophony. Français, tall, elegant, impeccably dressed, and haughty, greeted his distinguished-looking clients. But that didn't stop me. I introduced myself to Mr. Français and told him I wanted to try cellos, in a price range higher than my parents intended.

Français selected several cellos and brought them to where I was standing. Since the place was packed, I grabbed a chair, opened a cello case, parked myself in the enormous anteroom, and started to play. From the first moment, I was smitten—an Italian, honey-colored instrument with an exquisite burnished tone to match. I knew it was the one. Finding an instrument is like finding your soul mate—you know it instantly.

Lost in the cello, I hadn't noticed an older man listening intently to my playing. He asked who I studied with. Starker's name prompted the man to counsel me. I sounded excellent on this cello, and he thought we were well matched. A few moments later a younger (and handsome) man came over; he also praised my sound. But even after two compliments I doubted myself. *You've fallen in love with the first cello you've tried. What are you thinking? You don't have a clue what you're doing.*

Despite the interior chatterbox I followed my instincts and signed the instrument out, taking it with me to my aunt's apartment, to spend more time getting to know the cello.

Carefully loading it onto the backseat of a cab right next to me, and against the wishes of the driver, (he couldn't understand why I wouldn't put my new love in the trunk), we made our way across town to my aunt's place. She greeted me with a surprise—a ticket to the Boston Symphony concert at Lincoln Center. I'd never heard the orchestra, one of the top ensembles in the country. That evening my aunt put me in a cab and sent me to the performance by myself. (My parents would've been appalled.)

Nestling into the comfy seats in the Alice Tully Hall at Lincoln Center, I studied the program notes. It would be a thrilling evening of Beethoven, and Prokofiev's *Romeo and Juliet,* Op.64 a compilation of music from his *Three Suites* from the ballet score, some of my favorite music. I watched as the orchestra members started to file in, then instantly sank lower in my seat. The older man who'd spoken to me earlier at Français's shop? He was the *principal cellist* of the Boston Symphony. And the younger man? Also a cellist with the BSO. Mortified, I realized how innocent and cocky I must've seemed earlier that day, without regard for the illustrious company surrounding me.

But the music calmed me. After the performance, I thought, I would wait at the stage door to greet and perhaps apologize to whomever came out first.

The younger (and handsome) man came out first. He invited me for an after-concert aperitif (I could sense my parents' disquiet), and over drinks he suggested we meet at the hall the next morning. He'd bring his cello along so I could try it—an invaluable opportunity for someone with very little experience playing great cellos. He also offered to play the instrument I had tentatively chosen, onstage, so I could hear it from a different vantage point. Playing his valuable instrument reassured me. Mine (or what I hoped would be mine) sounded better. My parents were speechless when I called them. How could I have found an instrument so quickly? How would they be able to afford the price? How could they trust my judgement?

By the next day I was hopelessly in love—with the cello I mean. The young (and handsome) man who'd taken an interest in me advised, "Don't let on you know the information I'm about to tell you or where you heard it." He leaned in closer. "The cello is being sold on *consignment* by Français. The person who entrusted the cello to Français happens to be another cellist with the Boston Symphony. He doesn't have to sell this cello in order to be able to afford a better instrument." In other words, Français would earn only a commission, a small percentage of the selling price.

Too naive to know one didn't haggle with Jacques Français, my mind was made up—I couldn't do this to my parents. Put them in the poor house, I mean. Either Français would reduce his price or I'd give up the cello.

The next day the elegant showroom was once again packed with people. I settled in a corner of the room, trying to look inconspicuous, with my arms wrapped tightly around the cello while I summoned the courage to speak to Français. He dashed from customer to customer, carrying violins, violas, and cellos this way and that. After a few moments, he sauntered over to where I was standing. As bravely as I could, gripping the cello more tightly, I said, "Mr. Français. I love this cello. It's the one for me, but I can't do this to my parents. Please give it to me for ..." Français yanked the cello from my arms, spun around, and, not missing a beat, said to another client, "You mademoiselle, must try also Zeesss shello." Much to my chagrin, hot tears started streaming down my face. *What are you doing? At a time like this, when you need your wits about you? Pull yourself together.* Despite my best intentions, I knew I couldn't leave without the cello.

Français bustled around for a few more minutes. Then, unable to ignore the weeping young lady in his showroom, he grabbed me by the arm and guided me into his office. Français fumbled for Kleenex. "But my dear. My dear! Zeeesss ees not my shello! Take zee shello. Don't worry. I will talk to zee owner." And with that I walked out of the shop with my new love.

After brief negotiations Français agreed to take one of my father's bows in trade to help defray the cost of the cello, and he gave my parents an entire year to pay him. My father had his doubts about my decision, but I knew: the cello would become my constant companion for the next several decades, the cello I would play throughout my career.

Entr'acte 1975

Packing went slowly. It's difficult to travel light with a cello and piles of music, and I couldn't leave my cherished books behind, nor my beautifully carved menorah bookends. I sealed them carefully in a box, which my father promised to send to me, and without a further thought, away we flew, my cello and I, to Indiana, leaving Canada forever—although I didn't know that then.

My apprehensions about where I would spend the next two years were not unfounded. As the cab pulled into the parking lot of the university dormitory, I noted a white high-rise—square, utilitarian, unfriendly. The sterile room, no more than a cubicle and devoid of charm, had just a narrow bed, a dresser, a doorless closet, a small desk, and a glaring overhead fluorescent light. I waited. My books, I thought, would make the hovel feel a bit homier.

When the box arrived, I slit it open and cradled my treasures. But the menorah bookends were gone. I hurried down the hallway to the pay telephone—one per floor—to call my father.

"Papa. Where are my menorah bookends? I'm sure I put them in the box with my other things but they're not in there."

"*Mucikám*. Janetkém. What you thinking? Why they should know you are Jewish?"

My extraordinary experience at IU with Starker, among elite students from across the globe, is difficult to articulate. Intense, inspiring, enriching, and rigorous, my studies prepared me for a career not only as a cellist, but a musician with purpose, who would "spread the word," Starker's mantra. For the first time, the responsibility and privilege to contribute to healing the world would fall on my shoulders. For the first time, I saw music as life bringing and soul enriching, and I realized, however subconsciously at the time, my father had committed his life to the pursuit of these aspirations through his music making. I did not yet know his art had been "culture food" for Holocaust survivors after the war, and I had only a vague notion of his belief in the moral power of music and its importance to humanity.

After graduation, in 1977, I spent the summer at the Aspen Music Festival, determined to make as many contacts as possible with the great artists who performed there. I'd won the coveted spot—principal cello of the Aspen Chamber Symphony—and hoped for a job, preferably in the US. That summer, the summer I turned 25, I was offered several attractive propositions. I turned down a marriage proposal but said yes to the conductor of the Indianapolis Symphony when he said, "I want you."

My first job! I conveyed the wonderful news to my parents. I'd been offered the associate principal cello position of the Indianapolis Symphony, but their reaction was unsettling.

"Janetkém, you have contract?" my father asked.

"*Yay Istenem*. In the States? So far," my mother added.

"What about auditions? No job until you sign contract."

Such a pessimist. I thought. He always looks at the dark side.

That summer, I'd been preparing for the prestigious Munich International Cello Competition, which would take place in the fall. I practiced every spare moment between rehearsals and concerts, ignoring sore fingers and aching muscles. Before I knew it, several weeks had passed without news from Indianapolis. Puzzled, I called the orchestra's manager. "Hello. This is Janet Horvath and, uh—"

A long pause indicated no sign of recognition. Dismayed, I mumbled on slightly more *sotto voce*, "The conductor offered me the cello position? The associate principal cello—"

The manager interjected, "Auditions for associate principal cello are being held on September 12." He continued in a disapproving tone, "Do you want the audition repertoire list? Please send an application with the 25-dollar fee."

Barely managing to keep my thoughts to myself, I replied, "Yes. Please send the list and, uh... could you please ask the conductor to call me?"

Less than an hour later, the conductor telephoned. "What exactly did you tell the manager? Because if *he* thinks *you* think you have the job, it will work against you. We'll go ahead with auditions. If you win a prize at the competition, it will be a feather in your cap. We can then arrange for you to play for the current principal cello as, you know, a formality."

Telling my father was the worst part. He'd been right. What if the audition committee chose someone else? Everyone in Aspen had congratulated me on winning the position. Copious tears ran down my cheeks when Papa advised me to skip the Munich competition. I cancelled my flight. Instead, I stayed home, practiced hard, learned the orchestral excerpts, and traveled instead to Indianapolis to audition, to win the job, determined to play whatever they asked for, and however they wanted it—faster or slower, shorter or longer, more legato or more staccato, or even standing on my head. Following the audition, the principal cellist congratulated me, "Beautiful playing. Thank you and good luck."

Good luck? Didn't I play a perfect audition? I even sight-read a cello solo I'd never seen before, using her fingerings and bowings written in the part in bright red, green, and blue markings.

The conductor sauntered in an agonizing 30 minutes later. "Oh, there was never any doubt you'd have the job."

My mother and Rob drove from Toronto to Indianapolis to help me find a suitable and safe apartment, move in, and purchase necessities. I don't think Mama had ever been in a Zayre discount store. After Rob muscled the larger pieces upstairs to the flat, we went out to grab some food. My mother surprised me by agreeing to White Castle, her first time eating cheese sliders with fries, but there really weren't any fine-dining choices in those days in Indianapolis, certainly no Hungarian establishments. "Not so bad these: how you call it?"

Mama rarely missed any of my solo performances. She'd often travel from Canada without my father, who could not always get time off from his orchestra schedule. Wherever I played, at festivals, in recital, for competitions, in Canada or in the US, invariably, Mama's "*Bravo-oh-OH!*" could be heard above the audience's applause.

I prepared cautiously for my initial concert with the Indianapolis Symphony, aware that I looked too young for my new leadership role. Would I make a good impression? Perhaps even more crucial for me, I hoped the orchestra's standards would compare to the venerable Toronto Symphony, an orchestra my father had been playing with for 27 years by then.

The women of the orchestra had to don a mandatory long black gown, custom-designed to be uniform, but proportionately unflattering. My mother waited backstage for me while I changed. And change I did. I admit the billowy sleeves made me look like a prehistoric flying reptile. When I came back upstairs from the dressing room wearing the dress, she exclaimed, "What's *DAT*?" loud enough to be heard by the entire orchestra.

Indianapolis was but a stepping-stone. I won the Minnesota Orchestra associate principal cello position in 1980, against fierce competition. My mother travelled this time to Minneapolis to help me settle into a miniature downtown apartment. I couldn't wait to show her around. Every language can be heard on the bustling streets of Toronto, a dense, culturally rich, dynamic city with soaring skyscrapers. In contrast, the cities of Minneapolis and St. Paul are much less hectic. Enchanting parks, extensive greenery, and 10,000 lakes as well as two excellent orchestras, and a thriving theater scene, more than compensates.

Mama quietly took in the scenery, though her feet ached from the long walk around Lake Harriet, the wind already brisk with the promise of frigid temperatures to come. Years of wearing spiked heels to add height to her four-foot, ten-inch frame had taken a toll.

We strolled arm in arm along Nicollet Mall, the pedestrian outdoor mall where the city's upscale shops are located. When we neared Orchestra Hall we ran into a colleague and her boyfriend.

My mother pulled me aside and grimaced, "She is really so ugly. How can such *ugly* girl get such a handsome man?"

My jaw tightened. "Mama! What are you saying? How can you say that about a colleague of mine?"

We both understood her implication. My failure to attract anyone disrupted her life.

In 1992, finally, at the much-too-mature age of 40—almost matronly, as far as my mother was concerned—I met my future husband on a blind date set up by his mother, Adelyne, and a mutual friend.

Howard drove up to my charming, stone Cape Cod house in a snappy Mercedes. As he alighted and came to the door, shivers rippled down my arms into my hands. I fumbled with the doorknob. His inscrutable mystique radiated from the first moment—an abundance of jet-black hair, a rugged build, and a distinctive cleft chin—his white, short-sleeved shirt and gray dress pants offset my gold-buttoned red dress and strappy sandals. Overdressed again. It's my mother in me.

His choice for our first date was a jazz club on the other side of town. Howie took the scenic route along Minnehaha Creek, which traverses The Cities for 22 miles, a tributary of the Mississippi River surrounded by walking and bike paths, lush foliage, and fields of yellow-green grass, mown like a soft carpet. Howie rolled the windows down, relishing the soft summer breeze, and talked the entire way. I couldn't help staring at his shapely, impeccably groomed fingers.

Clearly, I enjoyed hearing about his interests and accomplishments, and thought it was a good sign when he alluded to being a classical music devotee, but by the time we arrived at the restaurant, I must admit I wondered when he'd express an interest in me. After we ordered wine, he said, "Janet. This is the last time you'll hear me talk about myself." It proved true. Howie is a man of few words.

Sleep eluded me that night. My excitement and the sleeplessness continued for three months as we spent more time together. In hindsight, we both knew after the second date we would marry.

Not a doctor, but almost as good, a lawyer. Virtually my mother's dream for me. Of course, Howie had to get her approval first. I nervously planned a visit to Toronto for his debut.

Fashion is not Howie's forte. I drilled him on a long list of do's and don'ts. Despite all my instructions, he wore the same jersey two days in a row—a plaid, *flannel* jersey. My mother was appalled. Already downstairs, my father, an early riser, sat perched on the living room sofa in a shirt and tie—a *silk* tie.

"That Howvard. He's lawyer? That's good. Good. But. Why he wears shirt like that? So *ugly*. When are you having a baby already?"

"Mama. He's relaxing. Most people wear comfortable clothes at home on the weekend."

"*Na*, Janetkém. Why he's sleeping in afternoon all-a time? You're not getting any younger. Get pregnant."

We'd been dating only six months when Howard and I took a trip to Hawaii, a place I'd never been. As soon as we boarded the plane, Howie promptly fell asleep. Unconscious most of the way, I wondered if I really was so boring, or had I made a huge mistake? My family never slept. We were too busy practicing.

Howie and I had a beautiful retreat, but, despite serene and mystical moonlit walks on the seashore, the riveting stillness, the sound of the surf, and hot embraces, he remained quiet. He didn't pop the question.

His silence baffled me. My garrulous mother rarely took a breath between words. If she stiffened, if she turned uncommunicative, it meant trouble—frustration, even rage. And after my father's explosive tantrums, he'd retreat aggrieved and wounded into silence. Howie's peculiar reticence meant contentment, his propensity to sleep, serenity.

In retrospect, after 25 years of marriage, Howie continues to do expensive napping with a remarkable ability to stay upright—in the theater, during movies, in classes, and at concerts (even those I'm performing). I, the consummate worrier, churn all night and can't sleep even prone, in darkness.

A few months after our Hawaiian vacation, when we dozed in tangled sheets one morning, Howie mumbled, "I want you as my spouse." I wasn't sure I'd heard him right. What about kneeling? The ring? The champagne and elegant dining room? Not until I heard him tell his ex-wife he would be getting married again did I know for certain he'd proposed. We planned a summer wedding, a few months later, in 1993. A good match, even if he did wear the same plaid flannel shirt two days in a row.

"A lawyer, tanks God. *Na*! When you goin' to get pregnant?"

My mother already had four grandchildren. Rob and his first wife, Ziporah, a daughter of survivors, had spawned a large family—tangible evidence the Nazis hadn't succeeded. Immediately after the war, survivors yearned to have children as soon as possible. To give life. Grandchildren symbolized even more continuity. My clock was ticking, and I knew it. Still my mother's diatribes made my innards burn.

And there was another issue. When Howie and I first met he'd been clear. "No kids, Janet." He was 50 years old and already had a 12-year-old daughter, Alexandra. No more kids? A distressing revelation. I called in sick, which I rarely did, and lay in bed my fists clenched, the blankets over my head, and pondered: *I've met the guy. I could break up with him and not meet anyone else. Or maybe I won't even be able to get pregnant at my age.*

Before our wedding—one night of unprotected sex, and much more quickly than would be expected—I was pregnant. It took four Clearblue Digital Pregnancy Tests for it to sink in.

I waited to divulge my news except, of course, to Howie.

Sitting him down, I felt like a guilty teenager. "Howie, I have something to tell you." He noticed my hesitancy as I told him the news.

For a moment or two, or more, he didn't say anything, expressionless as usual. Then he said, "Well, we can get one of those baby chair swingy things and take it with us, still go on trips, go to restaurants, take the little critter with us. It shouldn't slow us down much."

Two weeks before our wedding day, Mama had to be rushed to the hospital. An unconfirmed diagnosis. Her white blood-cell count tumbled to dangerously low levels. When I called the hospital, my mother sounded completely unlike herself. Her spirit quelled. To bolster her morale, I revealed my secret over the phone. "Mama, I'm pregnant! In March, you'll have a grandchild."

No delighted screams. No exclamation. No reaction. For several days, it seemed my mother would not be able to make the wedding. Unthinkable. She had been impatiently waiting years for my nuptials. No other successes I had achieved so far compensated.

We held our breaths, and, miraculously, my mother recovered enough to be present for our Minneapolis wedding, although she had to travel with assistance. Other family members arrived safely from Canada—Rob, Ziporah, and their four small children, my aunt Eva and uncle Tibi, and cousins Peter and Susie. Colleagues offered to perform Franz Schubert's *Trout Quintet*, a glorious piece of music for violin, viola, cello, double bass, and piano; Alexandra, my step-daughter, played a tune on the flute; and a chef prepared a sumptuous fish repast. Even the weather obliged with an indigo sky and a moderate breeze—just enough to keep the guests cool, yet not topple the chuppah—the canopy held by four poles beneath which the Jewish ceremony is performed. The traditional covering represents the bride and groom's new home. One side of the chuppah is left uncovered to symbolize the home should always be open and hospitable. The marble whiteness of my skin matched my dress, which, now that I was showing, had to be let out three times. I threw up in the shower on our wedding day but prevailed over my nausea at least during the marriage rites.

On August 20, 1993, Howie and I were married in the garden of friends surrounded by profuse blossoms of daffodils, zinnias, and dazzling purple irises.

We'd decided against a traditional wedding cake—only European sweets would do—apple strudel; a yeasted cake filled with currants, cloves, and marzipan; and Hungarian caramel-topped chocolate butter cream-filled *dobos* torte to please my father. I was unable to eat a thing but he devoured several slices of each when he thought my mother wasn't watching. Hugging me close during the first dance, and, as usual, burying his nose in my neck, he murmured how much he loved me, how happy I'd made him.

My mother seemed content. Finally, I was married and expecting, fulfilling my daughterly duty.

Mama in a tailored white suit looked classy as always, her skin smooth, her makeup flawless. After the meal, she reapplied lipstick with a slightly shaky hand. None of us discussed her health. We ignored how tired she looked, how quiet she was. Denial seemed an easier reality. *Not my Mama. No, no.* She had always been the pillar, bolstering the rest of us.

Entr'acte 1957

As I dig through old albums, I come across a black-and-white photo. I must be four or five years old, and Rob no more than two. The expression on our father's face is one I don't remember ever seeing. He's beaming.

Rob and I sit on his lap, and all three of us are looking off camera, to the right. Dad's collapsed fingers suggest a firm grip on us. His arm encircles my chest, and Rob's little arm is clasped securely by my father's right hand. His mouth is wide open, his teeth and tongue visible, and beneath luxuriant black eyebrows his eyes sparkle. Yet he still looks formal—a trace of a mustache, a full head of thick dark hair, and, as usual, he is wearing a tie, and a white, plain but trim shirt.

I'm leaning forward, obviously charmed, but Rob has a look of consternation. His eyebrows are raised, and his little forehead is slightly furrowed as if he's not sure quite what to make of what he sees.

It must be an occasion, as we two are stylishly gussied up. Rob looks adorable in a clip-on polka dot bow tie and white buttoned-down shirt, and his pants appear to be a dark tweed weave. Under a black jumper, I'm wearing a short-sleeved white blouse with a high scoop neckline and puffy shoulders. The dress seems a creamy texture, like velvet. Even though Mama is not in the photo, our hair has her touch. She's gone to some trouble to cut my bangs short, and to align my profuse curls around a straight part. Rob's hair shines as if a liberal dose of Brylcreem has been applied.

Just to the left of our trio, there's a mere suggestion of a piece of furniture. Since it's light in color it must be our upright piano with the unusual blond finish. It has a place of honor in the living room. We don't own much else.

I turn the photo over. The scrawl is my father's, in Hungarian. I stare at the compressed cursive trying to make it out. *Dear good sweet mother with lots of love: Robertke, Janetke, and your son, 12 Apr. 1957.*

I deduce it's the evening my uncle Tibor, my mother's older brother, arrived safely to Toronto from Budapest—the first of my parents' family members to escape communist Hungary after the 1956 uprising. I can only imagine my mother's joy at finally being reunited with her adored sibling.

The scene that night is still vivid: Tibi's almost completely and prematurely bald scalp glistens, and his eyes glimmer with warmth. I dance for him, kicking as high as I can to impress him. As soon as I finish my performance and join Rob on my father's lap, Tibi grabs the spotlight. Although he speaks no English, we're immediately under his spell. His fantastic, rubbery face droops into a long, teasing shape. Then he puffs out his cheeks, pulls his ears out to the side, and sticks out his tongue, something I'd never seen a grown-up do. But as soon as we burst out laughing, his expression transforms. Tibi reaches up to his bare scalp and pulls up on non-existent hair like the comedian Stan Laurel, the slender, silly member of the Laurel and Hardy duo. With eyebrows arched and a crumpled mouth, he sinks into clownish despair. Rob's sudden concern makes us giggle even harder, but most of all it's the sight of my father chuckling that inspires such hilarity.

Tibi was the only person in my family who could make our father laugh. I stare at the picture for several minutes to take in this side of him—a side we rarely saw—not a scorched soul in turmoil but a happy, relaxed, and momentarily untroubled being.

I never saw my uncle again. Six months after our wedding, Tibi died suddenly. He was only 72. My aunt Eva immediately called her son, Peter, and her daughter, Susie, then she tracked down Rob, who was skiing with his young family, about two hours north of Toronto. Rob, the doctor, with his gentle and compassionate approach, would know how to relay this terrible news to my mother and to me. I was more than eight months pregnant at the time and devastated at the loss, devastated that I could not be with my family in Toronto for the funeral and shiva.

Less than one month later, I gave birth to our son Harris. My father and my mother, always the resilient one, were by my side within a week of his birth. That Tibi and Harris would never meet chafes. The new life before us blurred the edges of deep mourning.

When my water broke in the middle of that frigid night in March 1994, I was already in the hospital. While I swam in the hospital bed, Howie rested comfortably at home. I called him. "That's nice, dear," he said, promptly falling back asleep. The following day, each time I had a contraction, Howie glanced uneasily at the monitor, then buried his face in a book. Labor went on all day into the evening. I know now he felt helpless watching my agonizing spasms. By 11:00 p.m., my parents had started to panic. At last, with a final push, the tiny being with light, fuzzy hair emerged. When Harris was placed on my chest, Howie and I fell instantly in love with him. "Here's your new boss," Howie said.

Harris was born just in time for Passover, narrowly missing Saint Patrick's Day. I wonder if my parents found it baffling that their grandchild's bris, the Jewish circumcision ceremony, was held in a remote corner of the world, in a Minneapolis synagogue. The ritual, which takes place on the eighth day of life, links Harris to generations of our people. "Blessed is the one who has arrived... this child has entered into Abraham's covenant and a life of Torah and good deeds."

It was a poignant morning for me. In the mix: the recent loss of my uncle, the traumas my own parents had suffered, and the fraught relationship they had with their religion. Looking upon Harris's precious face, moved by an epiphany, I made a pledge to raise my son in the faith, as a Jew, despite my own uncertainties of what the future might hold. For so long, I'd been exposed only to the negatives of being Jewish. That day I was suffused by the beauty.

A bris during Passover meant no bagels, coffee cakes, breads, or Hungarian pastries. Only unleavened foods were permitted for the celebration that followed. But the hardship was more than offset a few hours later. Howie's lifelong friends invited us to join 30 other guests for their Passover Seder. I couldn't remember the last time I had Passover with my parents, and Harris must have been their first eight-day-old participant. As a brand-new mother, I gaped, unable to enjoy the lavish repast, while Harris, swaddled in a sapphire onesie, was passed around the table for everyone to dote, and breathe, upon.

The next day my mother took action. "What is Huggies? You don' use cloth diapers? I boiled your diapers. On stove in big pot, to make them very clean. Every two hours you feed him? Too much."

The changing-table layout, not up to her standards, needed to be reorganized. She moved the wipes, diapers, ointments, and clothing, muttering all the while. My father, uncomfortable with my breast-feeding, left the room.

I was apprehensive enough about handling my tiny son. It had been decades since I'd even changed a diaper. Give the slippery fellow a bath? In front of my mother? Out of the question.

"Mama. Why don't you go downstairs and start the chicken paprikás for dinner?"

"You don' need me?"

"I'm famished and it's been a long time since we were treated to your cooking."

"Okay. Okay. You have sweet paprika? Green pepper? Onion and tomato? Where's the big pot? You want I should make *nokedli* too?"

My mother could whip up the most delicious Hungarian dumplings. When the smell of caramelized, golden onions wafted upstairs from the kitchen, I sighed. A reprieve. Soon Howie's mother, Adelyne, would arrive, and she never interrupted with her opinions. It took some time to get used to her calm, quiet, presence. Alexandra, thrilled to hold her baby brother, lived with us during the week, and she helped too—a full house and a convincing excuse to have my parents stay down the street at a local bed and breakfast.

*Tanks God, a **lawyer!** Howie and I pose for our wedding portrait, August 20, 1993.*

Janet with Uncle Tibi.

Untroubled being—Papa, Rob, and Janet in 1957 or '58. *What I remember most was that life was a serious affair. And yet here's a mystifying snapshot, proof my father could indulge for a moment in laughter.*

Janet begins the cello, 1961. *Playing on a half-sized cello, I remember the sticky black tights I had to wear for modesty's sake. My hair in an updo, (Mama's touch), I'm impressed with my exemplary hand position and bow-hold (Papa's touch)!*

Harris and me, 1998. *Overwhelmed to have given birth to a son at age 41, I couldn't have predicted I would see my mother's face in his.*

6

LOSING EVERYTHING AGAIN

With some hesitation, the summer of 1998, I invited my parents to come to St. Paul to stay with us. During a previous visit, my mother rearranged my kitchen. But this time her deference suggested passivity. She had recently suffered a stroke. We pretended not to notice how vulnerable, unsteady, and dispirited she seemed. It would be my parents' last visit.

Early in the morning, I tiptoed into Harris's room. My four-year-old son opened his eyes, and my mother's face peered back at me, the resemblance even more striking than when he was younger—full, high cheekbones, a plump little face, and perpetually raised eyebrows promising mischief or mayhem. I bent down to run my fingers through his blond ringlets, lingering a few moments, breathing in his scent. "Honey-bunny, time to get up. Shall we see what Grandma and Grandpa are up to?"

When he was scrubbed and dressed we went downstairs. We found my mother in the kitchen wrapped in her fleece robe, her pin-curls unfurled, rummaging through the cabinets. I made a quick breakfast for Harris, showed my mother where to find the cereal and coffee, and said I'd be back in a few minutes after I had a shower. More sensible breakfast fare—lox and other smoked fish, Hungarian salami, blintzes, cream cheese, tomato and onion slices, fruit and bagels, of course—were ready to be placed onto the dining room table.

My mother, determined to make coffee while I undressed upstairs, placed the glass Pyrex coffee carafe with its plastic handle directly on the gas burner. Turned it on. I'd just soaped up when Harris banged on the bathroom door. "Mommy. Grandma made a fire. Grandma made a *fire*."

Lunging out of the shower, I threw a towel around my body, and careened down the stairs. The acrid odor of burning plastic filled the stairwell. Just in time. Shattered glass everywhere. While my mother twirled round and round muttering, "*Yay Istenem! Yay*—" I grasped an oven mitt and tossed the melting, stinking, smoking remains into the sink.

Crisis averted, glass dust-busted, and blood pressure more or less back to normal, my mother, I noticed, had seated herself at the table in front of a plateful of cereal. She grappled with the half-gallon carton, seconds away from pouring milk onto the flat surface. Harris giggled when I snatched it out of her hands. "Grandma is so funny."

"Yes, she is, isn't she honey?" I replied, stifling my tears.

One year later, in the spring of 1999, the air was still brisk. I lingered at the Starbucks near my parents' home sipping a cappuccino and dreading the conversation ahead. With a final mouthful, I tossed the empty cup, got in my car, and drove to the brick split level house where my brother and I had grown up. The façade appeared before me unchanged. Despite pools of mud and soggy leavings from the winter's prodigious snowfall, over the last few days my father had been busy puttering in the garden, clearing spindly bushes and debris, lovingly undressing the plants that had been covered for the winter.

I took a deep, audible breath, then got out of the car. My father greeted me at the front door. Although it was early morning, he'd already donned a silk shirt and tie, his teased comb-over congealed with VO5 hair spray.

"Janetkém. How you keeping? You must be terrible tired. Mummy just made *palacsinta*, your favorite," he said, as he helped me with my coat and hung it up in the closet.

My mother's Hungarian crepes dusted with powdered sugar were irresistible: light, fluffy works of art—but I had a weighty mission. I ascended to the living room overflowing with tchotchkes impulsively purchased by my father. An enormous Persian carpet lay over the wall-to-wall jade broadloom to highlight the centerpiece of the room —a grand piano, black with an ivory interior, nobly sitting at the opposite end of the room next to the stone fireplace. Suspended above the mantel, one of my father's impressive oil paintings, this one a seascape.

In the studio, stacked floor to ceiling, and crammed on shelves, their tremendous collection of sheet music—piano and cello works, chamber music and orchestral parts, my mother's piano music and student pieces, and a cabinet full of my father's solo cello performances on video and audio tapes. I thought about the closets full of my parents' clothing, the separate shelving unit just for my mother's collection of purses.

My innards dissolved when I invited my parents to sit down. Taking my mother's hand in mine, I hesitated for several moments. Then I soft-pedaled. "Mama, Papa, it's time. Mama's had a, well... a *mild* stroke, and how many times have you both tumbled down these hardwood stairs? It's time—"

"What you mean, time?" My father said, an edge to his voice. Mama looked confused. I stared down at the carpet. Affronted, with an intentional exhale, my father left the room.

Jettisoning hoarded treasures required tough decisions, and I dreaded the wounded feelings that might follow. The overriding principle in our household, to ease my parents' distress, was to circumvent confrontation with my father. But the time had come. Paring down the contents of the house, downsizing as we euphemistically put it, would fall on my shoulders. For the last several years, on and off, my father, consumed by resentments, had seethed and raged, and had become estranged from my brother.

Entr'acte 1984

During medical school, Robert brought home several nice Jewish girls to introduce to Mama. Rob and I, inured to her strongly accented English and freely voiced opinions, didn't always grasp how caustic her judgements seemed to outsiders. When Rob finally met Ziporah, a daughter of survivors whose parents had fled to Israel, he proposed, and they married in 1984. Soon after, their first child, a son, was born. Perhaps that's when the trouble started. Perhaps my parents' first grandchild, Aaron, stirred a welter of emotions—elation, expectation, apprehension. Looking back, it's difficult to see how the discord emerged.

Our mother offered liberal and unsolicited advice. Her chin trembled in confusion when her comments backfired. Tempers flared. Both Zippy and my father were quick to anger and easily insulted. Rob found himself in an impossible situation, in the middle. Accusations flew back and forth,

"Why you are never on time! Always you are late."

"You think I never had children and don' know how to change diaper? I'm your mother. Can' I say anytink?"

Three more children, Ilana, Danielle, and Jesse, were born in close proximity.

"You never call us."

"Zippy is with the kids all day! I had my office hours and then an emerg shift. We're totally exhausted and can't stop over this week."

"What? You can' drive 15 minutes to see your own parents? Eat some nice food? You have to eat."

Somehow, it all escalated. Screaming phone calls, offensive letters, long silences.

"Yes, I always had been terrible father. You did it again as you had for 35 years. What you did to us just unbearable, without any love to your parents. Vishes [vicious]. Evil. You forgetting that you never gave anything to your mother, or to me. I gave you everything. You should shame yourself! Thank you very much. Do not phone us. Do not come here. My life not worth a penny—"

Rob would forward the emails to me.

Hi Dad.

I hope you and mom are OK. I know it's been a long time since I was there. I am angry. We made a peace gesture and you refused. I have asked you to stop being angry and to put everything behind you, but you can't and you won't. There is only so much we can do. I would, the kids would, and even Zippy says she would. Believe me I am guilty that you are there alone and we don't see you, but it is hard going there, seeing your anger, seeing your sadness. I want to go visit but do not want a scene again...

We were all heartbroken. Months would go by without a glimpse of Rob or their grandchildren, and I lived hundreds of miles away.

Three trips to Toronto over several weeks barely sufficed to manage my parents' collectibles. Frequently consulting my to-do lists, I packed 20 boxes to transport to a secondhand shop: loads of clothing and shoes, towels and bedding, videotapes and tablecloths. I loaded and secured their art into crates wrapped in layers of bubble wrap.

One day, while running in and out with boxes, I noticed my father stuffing something into the garbage bin at the far side of the house. His demeanor puzzled me. After he moved stealthily back into the house I reached into the trash bin and dug out a crumpled, brittle, and yellowed document. Gently, I flattened what I saw was a poster advertising an impressive concert program:

Internationales Konzert-Tournee-Büro München

Regina-Palast-Hotel/ Sontag 18. Januar 1948/18:30 hr

Cello-Konzert—Georg Horváth
Vitali: *Chaconne*
J. Haydn: *Konzert D-dur*

Rich. Strauss: *Sonata F-dur*
Ravel: *Habanera*
Moussorgsky: *Gopak*
Davidoff: *Am Springbrunnen*
D. Popper: *Konzert-Polonaise*

Not until I noticed the very small print at the bottom of the placard did the place and date sink in. "Produced under Licensenumber 1092 of Military Government."

Why did my father discard such a noteworthy souvenir? A solo program in Munich, in 1948? After I retrieved the poster from the trash, between trips up and down the stairs to fetch bubble wrap or packing tape, I remember asking him about the recital.

"Papa, I found a poster in the garbage. What an amazing program! How did you manage the endurance to play all the octaves at the end of the Popper after the other virtuoso works? I'd love to frame it. Why did you throw—?"

"What for?" He dismissed me with a brusque gesture. "Leave it. Leave it now."

The poster hangs in my music studio in St. Paul in its gilded frame. When I glance at it, I realize it's a memento of my father's crushed aspirations.

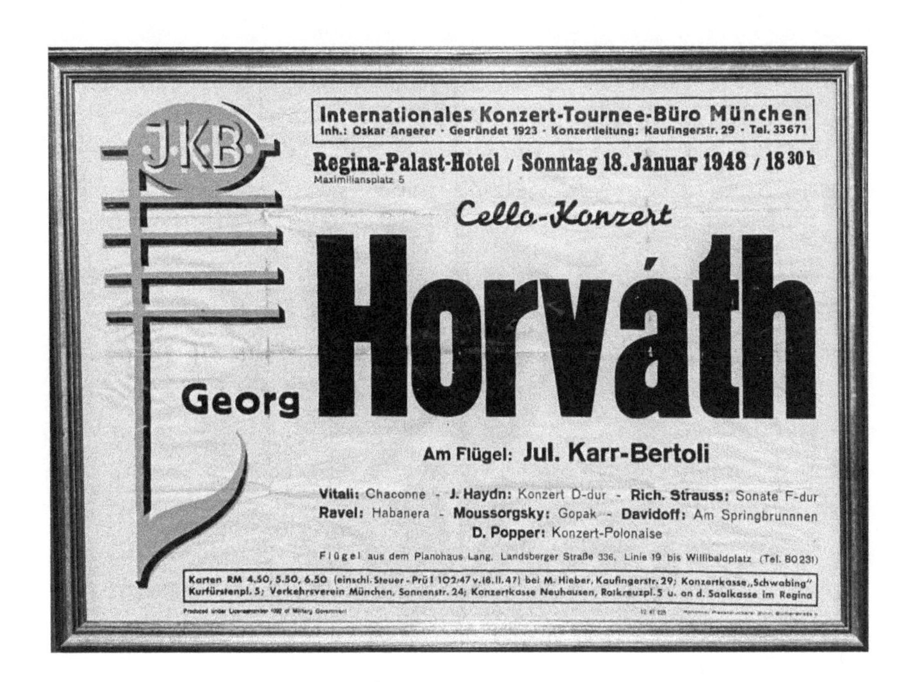

Moving day loomed. My parents barely participated, and not only because of their fragile health. To see their home dismantled in front of their eyes was agonizing and I blamed myself for bringing this upon them. I pretended to be upbeat, although I've never been adept at suppressing my feelings. Caught in an act of appropriation of the very accouterments that gave them joy, each sealed box contributed to their pain. But my brooding or second-guessing distracted me from the task at hand. I had to keep packing. However, when my parents weren't looking, in sanctification, I snapped several photos.

The human condition forces us all to accept life's limitations. For my parents, something deeper seethed under the surface. Finery painstakingly acquired over the years could never replace all they'd lost during the Holocaust. Every item became laden with significance, and to give them up negated proof of survival.

Fallout in the kitchen. Debating with Mama intensified after I hinted she wouldn't need or have room for three sets of bone china. "Mama. When would you have 36 people over? You've never even used—"

"I don' know. I might need it. We need them."

"But Mama you won't have room for—"

"And that. We need it," she said, pointing to the tall, slender wine glasses in the vitrine—octagonal shaped stems topped with blue, green, or ruby glass and enveloped by ornately carved gold lacquer.

Feeling helpless, in no shape to make thornier decisions, I decided to tackle the "crawl space." The house has no attic. Instead, downstairs next to untouched liquor bottles from my childhood, stands a legitimate-looking bookcase. It did hold books, but it could be pulled out to reveal a storage space barely four feet high running the entire length of the house—a great hiding spot for us as kids. I took a framed photo of my parents off one of the shelves. What a handsome couple, looking relaxed on a rare vacation: my father in a sapphire sport coat and snappy tie; my mother, made-up and bejeweled, with perfectly coiffed hair dyed blonde to hide the gray.

No time for reminiscing, I thought. Maybe I could quickly dispose of the stuff behind the bookcase. Within moments of pulling the bookshelf out, I felt chilled, imagining with a tinge of horror, in another era, in another country, my parents or others forced to hide in a place like this.

Placing something under my knees to protect myself from the cold cement floor, I slithered in to reach the paraphernalia untouched for decades. It was dark and musty smelling, and the lone light bulb I turned on shed little light. I reached for the closest boxes. They'd saved everything: boxes full of letters, old photos, and years of birthday cards; containers of childhood toys; a beat-up luggage set; and bags of out-of-fashion clothing "too good" to just give away. I ventured farther, thinking I'd pull out one more load and call it a day.

My hands, back, wrists, and knees started to protest—my body no longer able to withstand pretzelization—but a strangely shaped wicker basket caught my eye. Ghoulish spider web clusters dangled ahead and the dank gloom increased the deeper I went. I crept closer. After a several-minute struggle, I managed to drag the heavy almond-colored container, about six feet wide by three feet tall, out into daylight. It was coated with dust. Who knew how long this padlocked crate had been here? Uncontorting myself and stepping back from the dirty old thing, I noticed the luggage tags, and realized I'd unearthed a rattan steamer trunk. Dealing with this would take more energy than I could muster. People from the local Appraisers Association of Canada were coming over the next day. They could decide what to do with it and the other collectibles.

The ladies arrived in the morning with their notepads and businesslike demeanor. They began to catalogue the items; noting what should be given away, what ought to be tossed, and what could potentially be of interest to them. I pointed to the trunk shoved into a corner of the room. The ladies insisted it was against the rules to take anything that is locked. A key, if it ever existed, must surely be hidden or lost. I attempted to pry it open.

After a great deal of commotion, and likely a curse or two, I heard my mother come stomping down the stairs. "*Na!* Janetkém. What you doing? Don' open that! No, no, no. We are not opening that."

"The ladies won't take the trunk unopened, Mama. It's been locked here in the crawl space for such a long—"

"Leave it now. Leave it. We take it just like is. Put it back."

"But Mama. Do you need—"

"Are you craaazy? No, No, No." She scuttled out of the room.

Baffled, I let the subject go. It really wasn't worth a shouting match when there were still so many other issues to tackle.

Howie and Harris accompanied me to Toronto in August. My husband's calm, soothing attitude, and my son's mischief-making, I hoped, might dispel some of the melancholy on moving day. My father waited impatiently, pacing at the front door. We arrived late, disheveled. Not my style—to be late or disheveled. Before climbing into the car, my father walked around the house to the backyard. I imagined a silent prayer of farewell to his magnificent garden. My mother's lips quivered slightly. An unnerving hush descended as we drove to the condominium. My every breath tamped, I inhaled imperceptibly and let the air out one tiny puff at a time.

When we pulled up to the condo, the movers had already

unloaded the larger pieces of furniture and every shape and size of crate had been crammed into the small apartment. Harris found the maze the best hide-n-seek game ever. But my mother wobbled between the piles of boxes, her hands clasped, moaning, "*Yay Istenem. Yay.*" My spirits plummeted. Gritting my teeth, I unpacked at warp speed, fashioning harmony out of the disorder. The sets of bone china did fit after all, I stacked piles of photo albums in a back closet, and the ancient rattan trunk, delivered unopened to the storage lockers in the garage, was soon forgotten.

Nine months later, Mama suffered a massive stroke. My voluble Mama, always the strong one—incapacitated, aphasic, helpless. While I tried to cope with the catastrophe, my mother's care loomed. The one-level condominium apartment made it at least theoretically possible to keep her at home. Not much comfort. I knew nothing about interviewing and hiring live-in caregivers or the equipment and supplies that would be needed. Even with Rob's connections in the medical world it was an overwhelming proposition. My father, inconsolable, wouldn't leave my mother's side, not for a moment. Did he speculate upon what the future held, or whether their latest quarrel had in some way instigated the seizure? I imagine so.

Despite his grief, my father made some things clear. He didn't want her in a nursing home, relegated to living "in a box" (his euphemism for a retirement facility); he didn't want a man touching her, or a stranger living with them. But what alternative did I have? I knew keeping them together eclipsed other considerations.

My mother had been robbed of her stories, her essence. Her heart still beat. She ate, she slept. She heard, she saw. For eight years, our loquacious mother was consigned to a wheelchair, immobile and silent, installed in the living room and turned to face the booming television.

My father sat all day, every day, by my mother's side. He frequently kissed her—long, smoldering kisses (I wondered how she could breathe)—and poured his heart out to this silent being who had been his wife and partner for more than 50 years, convinced she understood every word.

"What a wonderful woman. She never complains."

My father was afraid to go out. He was afraid to leave her side. He was even afraid to sleep. My mother, unable to make a sound even to cry out in pain, smiled at him.

I called from St. Paul, "Hi Papa, how are—?"

"Talk to Mummy!" My father demanded. He'd hold the phone by her ear.

"Mommyka! How are you? It is so cold here!"

"Pa-pa-pa-pa-pa. Mmm-mm pa-pa."

My enthusiastic tone sometimes elicited a reaction. Or did she truly recognize my voice? More often, I spoke to silence on the other end.

Determined to keep our mother at home, Rob and I hired caregivers, purchased the necessary equipment—a hospital bed, a Hoyer lift, a wheelchair with a tall back and head grip, nightgowns that slipped on and fastened with Velcro in the back, gadgets to purée food—and I negotiated with government bureaucracies about services we hoped she might be entitled to. I resolved conflicts. My father, frequently paranoid, suspected ill intentions; his caregivers didn't do what he wanted; he imagined my mother was angry at him, accused me of wanting to put him in a nursing home. And more distressing, his high expectations of Rob resulted in ever increasing high-voltage arguments.

To break the monotony day after day, week after week, and perhaps to assuage my pain, I bought not only necessities, but also special items. I ordered meals from restaurants and had them delivered to their door (not Indian, not Italian, only Hungarian). I wrote voluminous letters and cards, and sent whatever I could, anything of interest—photos, the latest Minnesota Orchestra programs, reviews of my solo performances, my son's nascent drawings. Ian and Cristy, and Juliana, the caregiver relief person sent by the government, celebrated every holiday and birthday with my parents in the airless apartment.

My visits to Toronto entailed speed. I shopped and cooked

Hungarian food, packed the meals into individual containers, and carefully labeled them as to their contents. I picked up provisions in large quantities—diapers, thickening agents, cans of Ensure, oxygen, and condom catheters for my father (this would forestall waking Ian during the night to help my father pee). Organized their apartment, filed papers, filled out forms. Hired a full-time caregiver during the week and another for weekends. Sometimes my father would offend the person hired for the weekend. I'd get an angry call from him.

"Goddamn sonofabitch bastard abandon us!" And, reaching out to the extended Filipino caregiving community, I'd somehow fill the void.

To enable outings—to the mall, to gardens, to art galleries—I hired transportation services. My father would never go out without Mama. We even wheeled her across the busy street for celebrations. It wasn't fine dining, not Hungarian, but Red Lobster was right across the intersection.

Harris would often come to Toronto with me. He played on the Hoyer lift—the large chrome contraption with a cradle that lifted my mother—and he tinkered with my computer. Such a patient little boy. We sat from early morning until Mama was put to bed. Occasionally the oppressive atmosphere emboldened me. "Papa," I'd say, "I think we'll go out for a while. Harris needs some fresh air. He needs a little fun." But the look on my father's face said it all. We had to stay. All day. One misstep could engender his wrath.

After a particularly interminable day, I noticed a deserted field on the way back to my brother's home. I pulled over. The sky was clear and full of twinkling stars. Peaceful. "Harris, honey," I said, "let's get out of the car for a minute." When we were both standing in the dirt, I started to scream as loud as I could. Harris joined me. We shrieked until we were hoarse and snorting with laughter.

During those eight, long, wrenching years we grieved. I'd either leave my young son and husband, or I'd leave my aging and frail parents. Perpetually split in two, torn asunder. Each time I left Toronto I lamented—would this be my last farewell? And more disconcerting—did she know what she had become?

My father's eyes narrowed with rage. "Don't call me again. Never!" The ongoing rift between Rob and my father made the situation much more challenging. I strained to act as the mediator, eliciting ire from them both. My brother, the doctor with the kind bedside manner. My brother, whose four kids called for their father in the middle of the night when they had a bad dream. My brother, who would attend to anyone who asked. Rob could never live up to the expectations my father had of a good and dutiful son. The wrangling was interminable. Altercations and recriminations led to constant distress. I imagine my mother knew.

Rob struggled to break through my father's anger and the firmly entrenched delusions that everyone conspired against him. Seemingly out of the blue, he would attack. My father who loved us intensely couldn't see beyond his own demons.

I have no doubt that had I lived in Toronto subject to my father's daily demands, I too would have fallen short. Rob had to get away, stay away. Behind the scenes, he continued to do what he could to manage their medical care, intervening when a specialist was needed, and rushing over when medications ran out.

Even I didn't know that before my parents' move, Rob had combed the city to find the perfect apartment for them, one with a main floor grocery store, only to have it rejected by my father.

One night, after a particularly long day at work, I realized I hadn't called my father for a few days.

"Hi Papa? I know it's late but I wanted to say a quick—"

"I did not hear nothing from Robert, my dear son, for two weeks. I did not slept. I have terrible headaches. Then I called him. I do not want any more lectures, insults. Oh yes, we had been very bad parents! Lessen to me now. You both never lessened to me in your life!"

"Dad. I don't—"

"I am alone here. He and his wife, Zippy, never did anyting for us. What he and his wife did to us for 20 years just unbearable! I will not go to nursery or old age home. *NOWAY* and you and Robert won't force me. Rotten lies. My life a waste."

Oh, God. Swallowing hard, I tried to shout over him. "No, no. Dad. What are you saying? Stop. They are busy with four kids, and his patients, overnight shifts... of course he cares about you. Doesn't he always—?"

My lungs felt bruised. Defending Rob only increased his rage. "You NEVER cared about us, about what we feel, about what bothering us! You never wanted to hear our miseries. You are exactly like your brother. Not interested in me. You and Robert behavior is just too much! I had a lot of aggervation from you. Just leave me. I am not interested to see you again ever!! I will live rest of my life *alone* with my darling wife. Do not bother me. Do not phone me!"

Stunned by the diatribes, I held the telephone at arm's length, gasping to regain my breath. But I couldn't take it anymore either. Smashing the phone receiver down with all my might, I shrieked to no one in particular, "I can't stand this anymore! For God's sake! Why do I have to deal with this?"

Was Harris just as dazed by my behavior as I had been by my father's when I was his age? A distressing notion. I had to extricate myself from the triangle.

He didn't speak to me for six months. My father refused my calls and didn't answer my emails. I hesitated to fly to Toronto even though I had a few days off from the orchestra. What if he wouldn't let me into the apartment? I knew the only way to break the ice would be in person. But the specter ahead filled me with dread.

When I arrived at the security door to the condominium, I dithered for a full minute before pressing the entry code numbers. Then I held my breath. Within a few moments my reprieve—*bzzz, bzzz, bzzz*—the door opening. When I arrived at the 14th floor, I found the apartment door ajar but he didn't acknowledge me or speak to me. My father spurned reconciliation. Constrained by his bitterness, he was his own miserable companion. My father stayed in his bedroom with the door closed tight while I sat beside the wheelchair, my mother silent, asleep, listing slightly left.

Ian busied himself in the kitchen with the production of lunch preparations: puréeing veggies, meats, pasta. My father came out for the meal promptly at noon. I noticed worn slippers, his unshaven face, a T-shirt. He didn't make eye contact. Not a word was said at the kitchen table.

After spooning the mush into my mother's mouth, Ian removed the bib, cleaned her off, and wheeled her to the bedroom for her afternoon nap. Dad shuffled along behind them, leaving me marooned in the living room.

At the time, I struggled to understand. I'd come all this way, had left my family in Minneapolis, and for the infraction of taking my brother's side in their ongoing strife, I was banished.

There were other horrible battles over the years, when I was a teenager, and after I had moved away. Perplexing. Acrimonious. Occasionally, when I visited Toronto, I dared take a break from sitting all day in the stagnant condominium. On a winter visit a few months after my parents' move, I'd set up a quick coffee date with a friend. When I appeared later in the afternoon, my father was vexed, his neck throbbed, his face flushed. "You always come see your friends, not Mummy and me."

"Papa, no. That's not. I—"

"Leave me! Go way."

He rushed toward the door. When I tried to grab his arm to keep him from running out, as he had done countless times, his eyes widened in rage. He pulled free and bolted to the elevator, peppering the hallway with choice Hungarian swear words. My mother stood there helplessly, it seemed to me, trying to pacify me, taking the verbal abuse foisted upon her. Although he was elderly by this time, his anger fueled him. He pushed past me out of the building on foot into the gusts outside. Reeling from the tirade, I huddled in the corner against the wall. Mama wailed, "Janetkém, *yay Istenem*. My God. Why you always talk back? Gyurikám. Gyuri!"

Then a crushing guilt rushed in. I hurried to my car and slowly combed the neighborhood searching for him. *How far could he go on foot? What if he were to fall, as he so often did?* (A few years later, he would tumble forward in the marble-tiled bathroom. He hit his head and fractured his neck.) I kept driving. The wind harangued, in concert with our quarrel. Saturated by the icy gusts and quivering with outrage, still, I was apprehensive, unable to recall during the argument whether my father had donned gloves or a hat.

I searched unsuccessfully for hours, hoping I wouldn't find him face down in the snow. I didn't find him. I doubled back to the apartment, shivering convulsively, trying to calm myself, trying to calm my mother. All we could do was wait.

Several hours later, my father came home safe and contrite. We were so relieved we forgot what had triggered this implosion. Subsequently, an old childhood friend told me she saw my father at Yorkdale, the nearby mall, sitting with a forlorn look all alone on a bench. I believe now he needed to run away from himself.

During the difficult years after the onset of my mother's illness, I'd stood by my father and now that he, too, was ailing, he'd shut me out. The daily ablutions had become more problematic. With my father, now incapable of even menial tasks, we needed two people round-the-clock for the myriad daily concerns. My scheme to hire Ian's girlfriend and wife-to-be, Cristy, had to be deferred, until he would talk to me, until I could persuade him, until I could redeem myself.

Time ceased in a spiral of self-recrimination. My father must have sensed me standing in the kitchen in anguish. He could never endure my tears. After all, I am his *mucika*, his sweetheart. He shuffled out of his room and over to me, and began to rub my shoulders, squeezing as hard as his feeble Parkinsonian fingers would allow, his expression intent. Ill-at-ease, ill-equipped, confused by the grudge he held, my father mumbled what may have been an apology. Did he know that with or without his rationalizations, I would nonetheless always cleave to him? Perhaps. Did I grasp the depths of his despair? Not entirely. Not until a few months later, when I did want to hear about his miseries, and he wanted to tell me.

7

KATHERINE'S LAST RECITAL

Late May 2007: Morbid thoughts flickered despite the lyrical tones of a vireo warbling outside. It happened to be my parents' wedding anniversary and under normal circumstances a reason to celebrate, the date 63 years ago, almost to the day, my father had been deported from Budapest to the copper mines of Bor, Yugoslavia, for slave labor.

Life was tenuous. I knew my parents would never again hear me play the cello, their greatest pleasure, unless I brought my professional life to Toronto.

An idea for a recital program came to me—a unique format, soirée style, featuring appealing virtuoso and dance pieces, preceded by a few informal anecdotes. I designed the program to enchant anyone who might attend but have special significance to my parents. A few weeks after contacting a church in Toronto with my offer to perform, an official invitation came in the mail. *Would Friday, November 21, 2008, be possible?* I quickly called my accompanist to confirm her availability.

A few months before the concert, my mother's health took a downturn. Barely able to swallow, each mouthful of mush triggered convulsive choking. My father became more tortured, more fearful. Helplessly he embraced my mother while Ian administered forceful blows between her shoulder blades. She turned crimson from the effort to breathe.

We consulted my brother who confirmed the prognosis. Rob, who'd been divorced from his first wife, planned to remarry the following spring. He and his fiancée, Sara, had a lovely venue picked out, but it became obvious: if they wanted both of our parents present they'd have to marry sooner, in 2008, the day after my November concert. Instead of the charming bed and breakfast inn, it would be held in the party room of my parents' condominium building. Sara, a petite blonde with gentle warmth, and astonishing empathy, won our hearts, even my father's, and with special alchemy, she fashioned the rapprochement between my brother and father.

A few days ahead of the concert, Howie and Harris, my pianist and I and my cello arrived in Toronto—each of us with our own seat on the airplane, including the cello. My father was already uneasy, his complexion ashen, his stomach topsy-turvy. Anyone else would have resorted to taking Valium—his turmoil never in proportion to the many successes we'd both survived.

Right on cue, the day before the recital, my father made a strategic retreat. "Janetkém. I stay home. I will spoil it for you!" My parents' complicated needs, especially the many arrangements and transportation required to move my mother, might distract me from my performance. It took no small measure of persuasion and finesse to convince him. "Papa. The planning is all done. This is what I *do*. The playing is the easy part!" He'd attended so many of my performances, yet he foresaw failure.

I attempted to settle my father's apprehensions, not an easy task, while Ian turned his attention to my mother. Gently he dressed her, styling her hair as she used to, curling, back-combing, and then misting the creation with hair spray. He powdered her nose, lined her lips with red lipstick, and, using the Filipino endearment for Mama, said, "Lola. You look lovely."

The Metro-Mobility van pulled up right on time. Ian rode with my parents, and our party of four and the cello squeezed into a rental car. We actually made it to the concert venue on time—family members, caregivers, fans, friends, and even teachers from high school.

Backstage, wrapped in a heavy sweater and mittens to keep my fretful fingers warm and limber enough to play, I wobbled unsteadily (those darned stilettos). The sound of my heels clicking on the parquet floor mingled with animated chitchat drifting through the paper-thin walls.

When I made my entrance, my heart plummeted at the sight of Mama's wheelchair placed in the center aisle, near and in front of me —my once-elegant mother slumped over and drooling. Always impassioned about music, and the cello above all, I had to believe my playing would reach her.

The recital opened with Ludwig van Beethoven, the immortal German composer with whom my parents, and hence I, had a deep affinity. Trusting in the life-bringing power of music, who better to represent music's intangible and deeply emotional force? Beethoven's *Seven Variations* in E flat major from Mozart's opera, *The Magic Flute*, is based on the flirtatious duet sung by mythical characters Papagena and Papageno. As I lay bow to string shaping the sound of the andante, an ode to love, my butterflies whispered away.

I caught a glimpse of my father's head bobbing to the uninhibited rhythms of Béla Bartók's *Romanian Folk Dances*, a piece I grew up with. Picture the villagers dancing—the men dressed in flowing white pantaloons, orange buttoned-down high-collar vests, matching leather boots, and jaunty fur and feathered caps. None stray from their heads despite the spirited low squats, deep lunges, and whirling spins.

Immersing myself in the rhapsodic cadences of the music, my fingers flew over the fingerboard producing singular effects—harmonics (whistling sounds), wild pizzicatos (plucking), enticing melodies in modal harmonies—and the culminating 'A' of the piece, a swooping upbow, never fails to garner enthusiasm from the audience.

Après un Rêve (*After a Dream*), the profound lamentation by

Gabriel Fauré expires with a hush—*Alas! Alas, sad awakening from dreams! ... Return, return with your radiance ...* Through the murmur of the final diminuendo, I willed vibrations toward my mother but her posture remained stooped, motionless.

A blazing Argentinian dance ended our program. Entwined around the cello, I simulated the syncopated, pulsing stamps of the dancers' footwork, the close embraces, locked horns, and swooning back-bending poses of Astor Piazzolla's *Le Grand Tango*. The tempo accelerated to an impossible presto. After the breathless finish the audience leapt to their feet. My father clapped as loudly as he could —the unrestrained "*Bravo-oh-OH!*" from my mother conspicuously absent.

I'd planned a special encore: *Pièce en forme de Habanera* by French composer Maurice Ravel. My father performed this piece after the war in Munich, in January 1948; it appears on the crumpled poster I found in the garbage when my parents moved.

Throughout the entire recital Mama had remained slumped in her wheelchair with her eyes closed. Just as I began the encore, the Metro-Mobility transportation service arrived to pick up my mother. Ian started to wheel her backwards down the aisle toward the exit as quietly and unobtrusively as possible. Mama's eyes fluttered open in surprise. She lifted her head, as if to say, *Why are we leaving? It's not over yet!* While my mother disappeared through the back door of the church, I completed the program with tears streaming down my face.

We arose early and drove over to the condominium the next morning to decorate the party room with flowers and ribbon, see to the catering, arrange chairs, and prepare the chuppah. The boys—Rob's two sons Aaron and Jesse, Sara's son Zach, and Harris—adorned four poles with blue and silver sparkling paper and then draped Sara's father's *tallis*, his prayer shawl, over the top.

Later we all descended from the 14th floor to the party room and took our seats for the happy occasion. As Aaron, Jesse, Zach, and

Sara's nephew Josh marched in, each holding a pole of the chuppah, I played the cello, this time traditional Jewish wedding songs. *L'dor Vador* (From Generation to Generation), which refers to continuity. *Grateful for all who've come before, the circle of life goes on.*

Pictures were taken, vows exchanged, kisses and hugs given and received. Everyone looked smart, especially Harris in his first tuxedo, and the bride, radiant, in a deep violet gown. We adored Sara; were thrilled Rob had remarried. Even Mama smiled—because she sensed Rob's happiness? His reconciliation with our father? Or that my tipsy father could barely suppress his chuckles? Our family squeezed into the adjoining room for dinner and we ate our fill of kosher Jewish and Hungarian delicacies—ladlefuls of soup with plenty of bread for my father, and cabbage rolls (not as good as my mother used to make), wine-braised brisket, veal paprikás with *nokedli* (dumplings), followed by, as always, decadent sweets—*dios torta* (walnut torte, my favorite), chocolate *babka*, and a non-dairy wedding cake. The following morning, the four of us tumbled sleepily out of beds, caught a taxi to the airport, and flew back to Minnesota, content that the weekend festivities had been such a success.

One week after the concert and the wedding, my mother passed away.

Rob called and related simply, "She's gone." Within days of the wedding, a fever had developed. As we'd feared, my mother aspirated and developed pneumonia. While my father held her hand, she inhaled one last deep breath and left this world.

The three of us flew back to Toronto. Our family gathered for the funeral and shiva, the eight days of ritual mourning, an observance that keeps the mourners in touch with reality, and accompanies them through those first harrowing days of loss. Family members and friends, acquaintances and students, came to express their condolences. And visitors brought every fattening delicacy imaginable, comfort food extraordinaire. "What a wonderful, colorful person she was... Always noticed the instant she entered a room." "Nobody made the delicious specialty rakott káposzta like Kato." "She loved her students, but your performances were the highlight of her life."

I agonized over the questions never asked. Plenty of time, I'd thought. Like any young person, my own life dominated, and I'd had little genuine interest in my parents' lives as people until I had my own family. Conversations that might have occurred instead of the bickering didn't happen, and the taboo subjects, the pain borne by the people we loved most, lingered unexplored. Had I been afraid of what I might hear? Or more interested in protecting my own sensibilities?

A few days after Mama's death, during day three of the shiva, I heard a knock at the door. My cousin, Peter, had come to pay his respects, but he seemed eager to pull me aside. We excused ourselves. Why the urgency to retreat to the back bedroom?

Peter insisted I sit down. "Janet, I have something to show you. I forgot about it. I'm sorry. I've moved so many times, and um—during my dad's shiva, so many years ago now—could it really have been more than a decade ago? I taped a conversation with Auntie Kato."

Momentarily stunned, I remembered the sense of desolation I'd felt around my Uncle Tibi's death. I couldn't attend the funeral because I was eight months pregnant. There was a tape from those painful days?

"Your mother talked about her youth. I don't know what made me think of it, probably the funeral, and, uh, I spent all day yesterday digging through drawers and boxes in the attic, and I found it. I found the tape."

He reached into his pocket and handed the precious artifact to me. Through the rest of the day my attention meandered, diverted from the crowd in the apartment. All I could think about was the tape.

That evening, after all the visitors left, my father and I heard my mother's voice, after eight years of silence. Too overcome, I couldn't absorb what she was actually saying. Some days later, once I returned home to St. Paul, I replayed the tape. My mother had revealed her story of surviving the Holocaust for the first time.

Harris, the mischief-maker, with unflappable Howie.

***Elegant pair on a rare vacation.** How relaxed and content they look in this photo.*

Papa and his magnificent garden.

Dad and Janet after one of her solo performances.

PAYR Toronto recital.

A birthday celebration with our angels. *Did she know what she had become? Left to right Cristy, Papa, Juliana, Mama, and Ian. Cristy baked a magnificent cake for my mother's birthday on June 8, 2008, her last.*

Rob and Sara, November 22, 2008. *The lovely bride wore purple. My mother, I think, understood we were together finally reconciled, Rob a happier man.*

8

EICHMANN IN BUDAPEST, A TALE OF MONSTERS AS MEN

The audiotape beckoned. In February, I cast aside my qualms. I was ready; at least I hoped I was. Easing out of bed so as not to disturb Howie, wrapping myself in a thick robe, I tiptoed to the other end of our house to my music studio—a comforting room for me, bathed in bright sunlight, despite the Siberian temperatures outside. My chair encircled by piles of sheet music, is a place where for years clusters of notes have ascended to the spheres or fallen to the floor ignobly discarded. The sounds still resound. Filmy sheers drape the floor-to-ceiling windows and, positioned next to an adjacent wall, rests my cello in its red case. I scanned the room, noting the photographs, signed programs, and posters displayed, including several publicizing my father's performances, which seem to have a deeper significance today. Huddling under a green crocheted afghan, I reached for a pen, and with a deep inhalation turned on the audiotape.

> So... where should I start? Way back? I can start way, way back. I remember my father, Nándor, had bought a summer place in the outskirts of Budapest—30 kilometers [19 miles] away, in Göt and they built it from brick. We called it Katolac, which [*peals of laughter*], means my name Kato, and *lac* means *lacás* or place, ah, but I couldn't call it a cottage. Not as nice. We had 14 fruit trees in long

backyard, and there were local people nearby—country people mostly. Always we went up there in summer. My father he came on Friday. We were waiting anxiously for Daddy, my brother, Tibor, "Tibi" and I, and when we saw him, we rushed like mad, "Daddy!" And we jumped on him. He always brought some ice cream for us, and, uh [my mother takes a breath], my father was very strict man—very, very strict. We were scared of him. But we loved him so much you can't even imagine.

I felt my muscles spasm with emotion. Mama's voice sounded different than I remembered—a singsong tone, higher pitched, and more strongly accented.

When we were older we already went to country before school finished, in May, by train, to school and back, until end September. There was a nice supper place, with a dance band. An older lady, must have been maybe 25 or 30 years old at that time [*giggles*], taught us to dance. We danced grown-up dances really good. Tibi in his white sailor suit—well, he was only about 10, 12 years old, I was about eight—around 1935, 1932? And people sat down to watch how two little ones could dance so well. Oh, we had fantastic memories.

For the first time in years, I pictured my mother and Tibi dominating the dance floor. How they pranced and sashayed cheek to cheek whenever we attended a wedding or bar mitzvah, both of them beaming as if they were kids again, embarrassing Rob and me in front of our friends.

You see, my father stayed in Budapest working hard. He had not a photographic studio—no, it was optometry, and photo-optic store, both—all kinds photo cameras and lenses. He was working already at five in morning printing film. My father's store was on the street level exterior of building. Budapest is built with attached apartment buildings above all the stores, not like here. Yeah, we lived in third floor and our window looked out on so-called *Körut*. A nice curved street, in ninth district of Pest, so we were walking distance to

Danube. We learned to swim there—yes, the Danube river. We went often. And we went to regular elementary school. There was a skating rink on the way. Tibi, he could always dance, even on skates! [*Giggles*].

Tibi was a *nagy vagány*—you know, a type of man who was always doing mischief but got out of trouble? So many times, he wasn' home by 10 p.m. And I was so worried about him, like later I was worried about my own children if they weren' home. When I was teenager, I was allowed out if I went with Tibi. We went to concerts together, we entered and won dance competitions, he took me to school dances. Girls would stand by the wall waiting for somebody to call them, you know? I never had that because my brother always danced first with me, no matter what. I just want to show you what we meant to each other.

I had forgotten. How she chattered! Barely taking a breath. And liberally spiced with laughter. In 1994, the year my uncle died, she was only 69. Well before illness. Her way of speaking diametrically opposed to my father's, whose discourse teemed with reticence, as if he stumbled over his own tongue.

We didn' live in a Jewish area. We were not religious, but my mother kept holidays, and there was not far away a synagogue where we always went. Across the road from where we had our store there was compound for soldiers. Officers came into our store. They liked my father very much. They left films, bought cameras. You know, they didn' even know he was Jewish. The name Horvát—it is not Jewish. Horvát is a Christian name really. Well, look, originally it was Herzka—then it was Hungarianized—I don' even know when it was changed. I don' remember my father's name being different than Horvát—interestingly my husband's family was, I'm not sure the spelling—Herkovitch, Herskovitz, Hershkovitz, they also Hungarianized to Horvát, you say in English, Hor-VA-thhh [*laughter*]. Lots of people did that. My best friend Ada Kuti—she knows they were Klein. It was a very antisemitic country, and you didn' want them know from your name you were Jewish. That's all there is to it.

It's the first time I learn my name is not Horvath, on either side. We'd been amused, Rob and I, that our mother's maiden name was the same as her married name. Surely coincidental. Horvath is such a common Hungarian name—like Smith is in Canada. I scribbled several spellings of the names Herzka and Herskovitz in a notebook. If I traced the names, might there be ancestors in genealogical records, birth or marriage certificates?

In the 1930s, religious education was compulsory. Each week students attended their respective sessions and the Jewish students, in addition to classes, were required to attend Friday Shabbat services or risk a failing grade. Changing surnames didn't help a bit. Everyone knew who was Jewish.

After middle school, most middle-class young people learned a trade. Nándor had worked incessantly to send my mother and Tibi to *Gimnázium*, the high school, but the Jewish kids had a tough time. Harassed by the teachers and bullied by the other students, even when they excelled, their grades rarely reflected their proficiency. Tibi had two strikes against him as a Jew and as one of the shortest teenagers in the school. Because he made the other kids laugh with his rubbery facial expressions and droll sense of humor, his popularity rose, although it sometimes got him into trouble. Whenever Tibor Horvát had to fend off ruffians who pursued Jewish youths, bigger buddies came to Tibi's aid. Not everyone evaded a beating.

My mother's family accepted antisemitism as part of life, as previous generations had—maligned for an eternity. How could they have known that this time incomprehensible brutality would be inflicted upon them?

Tibi did finish *Gimnázium*. By that time, 1940, he turned 18, he couldn' go to university. No Jewish kid could go by that time, because the law, oh there were many laws before I was born, even in 1920s—first *Numerus clausus* [closed number]. It's Latin—six percent of students could be Jews, no more, and then when it got very bad, law became *Numerus nulus*. So, no Jewish students allowed. No, no.

I stopped the tape. Unnerving details. My deficient grasp of the historical facts impeded my understanding. A time line would help, I thought.

World War II Timeline

1918—The Austro-Hungarian Empire is broken up in October 1918. With the signing of the Trianon Peace Treaty after World War I, Hungary loses two-thirds of its territory and more than half of its ethnic population.

1919—Hungarian communist and activist, Béla Kun, seizes power and wages war with Czechoslovakia and Romania.

1920—Authoritarian Adm. Miklós Horthy, an antisemite and rabid anti-communist, becomes regent. He essentially rules until 1944.

1924—*Numerus clausus* is enacted in Hungary. To limit the number of students, and racial in intent, it is one of the first antisemetic laws to be introduced in Europe, well before similar measures in Germany, and restricts the number of Jews to six percent of university students. In Hungary, nearly 300 other anti-Jewish laws are decreed before 1944.

1933—Adolf Hitler is elected chancellor of Germany. Hungary forms an alliance with Germany, signing a trade agreement drawing them out of the Depression.

. . .

1938—Hungary restricts Jewish participation in the economy to 20 percent. Germany annexes Austria. Hitler returns some Czechoslovakian territory to Hungary (and later Transylvania) in return for their alliance.

1938—November 9, *Kristallnacht* (Night of Broken Glass) in Germany and Austria. Nazi violence erupts in a coordinated attack on Jewish homes, businesses, shops, and synagogues. Thousands of Jews are injured and 30,000 are arrested and taken to concentration camps.

1939—Germany invades Poland. World War II begins as Britain and France declare war on Germany. The Hungarian government imposes the *munkaszolgálat*, forced labor "work" units for Jewish men aged 21 to 48. Approximately 100,000 men are conscripted, including my father, uncle, and grandfather. Twenty-five to forty thousand Jewish labor servicemen perish from exposure, starvation, mistreatment, and murder before the German invasion. Antisemitic laws restrict Jews to six percent of the economy.

1941—According to the 1941 census, the Jewish population totaled 825,000, which included 100,000 converts to Christianity. They are barred employment in certain professions as well as citizenship. Twenty thousand immigrant Jews living in Hungary are deported to German-occupied Ukraine and massacred by Nazi *Einsatzgruppen* (special units, mobile "killing squads"). Hungary declares war on the United States, Russia, and the Soviet Union, and enters World War II. Massive killing operations begin. Auschwitz exterminates prisoners. The Hungarian army participates in military actions on the side of the Axis powers and during the invasion of Yugoslavia.

. . .

1942—Wannsee Conference. The "Final Solution" is agreed upon by the Nazi leadership—the decision to begin systematic deportations of Jews from all over Europe to six extermination camps in Poland. More than 3,000 men, women, and children, including almost 1,000 Jews, are murdered by the Hungarian *Nyilas* at *Újvidék* (now Novi Sad, Serbia).

1943—By late in the year, 63,000 Jews in villages and towns throughout Hungary have been murdered. The Hungarian army suffers extraordinary losses. Horthy seeks to negotiate a surrender with the Allies.

1944—March 19, Germany invades Hungary. As a result of Admiral Horthy's duplicity, he is replaced by a pro-Nazi government. Horthy is relegated to the position of a figurehead.

For 1,000 years, relations between the Christian populace and Jews in Hungary ebbed and flowed, from uneasy acceptance to fierce expulsion. As long as there were Jews, antisemitism loomed. Laws in Hungary decreed that Jews wear a compulsory identifying badge as early as 1279. The emblems of shame—a white band; an oval, yellow felt, or taffeta badge; a yellow hat; a cone shaped headdress. Denigrations continued with blood libels in 1349, anti-Jewish riots in 1494, and in the 1700s a "tolerance tax" was imposed on Jews for the privilege of living in Hungarian towns.

These actions were not isolated to Hungary. Pope Innocent III decreed in 1215 that Jews and Muslims wear distinguishing garments to inhibit social contact with Christians. In England, King Edward I specified, "Jews over the age of seven were required to wear a piece of yellow taffeta, six fingers long and three broad, over the left chest of the outer garment" (see USHMM Jewish Badge: Origins).

A movement to grant civil right to Jews gained ground by the

1830s in Hungary. Despite vehement opposition among some parliamentarians, and vicious anti-Jewish disturbances, economic equality was finally approved in 1867; by 1895, the state accorded official status to Judaism on par with the dominant religions: Catholicism and Protestantism. Hungary's population, one of the most diverse on the continent, was 95 percent Christian.

By 1920—with a Roman Catholic majority, and Lutherans, Calvinists, Greek Orthodox, and Unitarians, who didn't get on well either—the country had seen its Jewish population grow to 910,000 —the second largest in Europe.

After World War I, Hungary's citizens fiercely contested Jewish involvement in society. Weren't they responsible for the severe shortages and famine? Waves of violence toward Jews swept the country. Several far-right paramilitary antisemitic organizations agitated for the expulsion of Jews even as early as 1919 (see ushmm.org, The Holocaust in Hungary.) Once a new right-wing regime came to power in 1920, rebellion was temporarily suppressed.

By this time however, more than 25 percent of the university students were Jewish. Not only had they become assimilated, Jews, like my parents, considered themselves proud Magyars and patriots, notwithstanding the prevailing antisemitic ideology.

They wouldn't have wanted to live anywhere else—with its distinguished history, shaped by the grandeur of the Habsburg dynasty, one of the most powerful royal houses of Europe—where culture and scholarship flourished, and gastronomy rose to a dazzling art. Budapest, nicknamed *Pearl of the Danube*, has a rich history of Jewish inventors and scientists, doctors and lawyers, athletes and architects, writers and poets, actors and musicians—such as André Kertész, Edward Teller, Robert Capa, Hedy Lamarr, Harry Houdini, Elie Wiesel, George Szell, Peter Lorre, and Arthur Koestler—Jews you may have heard about.

In 1920, the wildly popular authoritarian Admiral Horthy, "His Serene Highness the Regent of the Kingdom of Hungary," took the helm. An avowed antisemite, he found it intolerable that "everything" had a Jewish presence. They had "too much success." In no time, he imposed the *Numerus clausus* laws, which restricted admission of

Jewish students to universities. Horthy feared the Russians and communism more than Nazi Germany. Besides, Hitler promised to return land that rightfully belonged to Hungary, which had been redistributed by the winning side after World War I. Despite misgivings, Horthy forged close but uneasy economic and political ties with the Third Reich.

During the 1930s, as the Depression tightened its hold, enlightened defenders of the Jewish populace reversed their stance. By 1938, under pressure from both Nazi Germany and the *Nyilas*—the right-wing Arrow Cross Party, which had garnered one-quarter of the vote in Parliament—Hungary enacted the first of three anti-Jewish decrees. The Jewish workforce would be drastically reduced to six percent of the population. Jewish men of military age would be assigned to forced labor units and, more troubling, in 1939, the term Jew would be suffused with racial overtones.

Previously, discrimination had been based on religion. The debate erupted: is Judaism a faith or a culture? The conundrum became an excuse. As in Germany, Jews would no longer be considered citizens of the country with civil protections. One hundred thousand Christians and their children who had converted from Judaism or who had become secular were stigmatized. Sexual relations or marriage between Jews and non-Jews were forbidden.

By mid-1941, the so-called Third Jewish Law further narrowed the definition of a Jew. Anyone with one Jewish grandparent was considered Jewish, thus exposing thousands of Christian citizens of Jewish heritage to persecution—a total of approximately 850,000 people.

The narrowing of the definition is redolent of the derogatory and offensive slave terms in our own US history, which I felt compelled to look up—"mulatto" (a person with one white and one Black parent), "quadroon" (a person having one Black grandparent), and "octoroon" (one-eighth Black)—brought arbitrary racial and social classification to the fore. The prevailing belief of the "one drop of blood rule" as unique to the United States and American Black people had me quaking. I realized the disturbing history is one we have in common.

Many of the Jews of Europe assumed the continuous ostinato of antisemitism was surely another fleeting phenomenon. Painful reflections. I hadn't understood the pervasive history of Hungarian antisemitism (and since I'm Canadian), the horrific persecution of African Americans. With a more comprehensive perspective, I returned to the tape. My mother no longer laughed.

> Tibi he couldn' do nothing. He was only 18 in 1940. So he went to learn optometry. To get a license. That was a trade. A trade you could do. That's why so many people went to be tailors, and all girls, ah, girls you had to learn how to sew. Because. What is going to happen? We heard awful rumors, but didn' believe it. They said it was propaganda. Lies... Yeah... Tibi and Gyuri [George] were exactly same age, born in 1922. You had to go for a soldier at age 21 but Jewish boys were sent to hard-labor camps. So-called *munkaszolgálat*. They took Tibi—where, we didn' know. He had to go with a soldier cap but also yellow star on. Yeah, by this time it was 1943. Gyuri was going to Academy of Music and music school wasn' so strictly controlled. So he got a leave to finish his studies. Of course, he wanted to go too, to university, to be an engineer. He was so good at matematics. We were worried. We heard stories. We thought nothing could happen wrong in Budapest. Because you see Hungary was ally to Germans. Look, until 1944 there were rules and laws but we were still okay in Budapest, but the outskirts—Jews from small towns were taken. Girlfriends who had been taken to Auschwitz already.

One terribly disturbing day, in 1943, refugees from Czechoslovakia pounded on their door. They begged for food, clothing, shelter. Their eyes were empty, their children limp. My grandmother Irma, looking over her shoulder, opened the outside door and urged the outcasts into their apartment. While Irma served bread and her thick bean soup, my mother ransacked cupboards looking for winter clothing and blankets for the haggard family. She listened in horror. "All Jews are being deported. Even nonreligious Jews. We were beaten, raped. Families separated—children from their mothers, young couples from their parents. Our elders, the very young or the sick, and even pregnant women dragged away. Shot or hung in streets like animals. Townspeople, our neighbors jeered. Nowhere to hide, nothing to eat…"

But even the shock of hearing from these refugees didn't convince my mother. This could never happen in Hungary. Extermination camps? It would never come to that, not to them. Certainly Nándor, her father, would be spared. He would protect the family. He'd been a decorated soldier in the Hungarian army during the First World War. A hero would never be mistreated.

She was wrong. A few weeks later the *Nyilas* hoods battered their door. Spewing profanity, they dragged Nándor down the steps, scornful of the repulsive creature, and pushed him into a van—destination, the outskirts of the country for forced labor.

Submerged in disturbing details, I returned to the computer for clarification. It all happened so quickly in Hungary—within weeks. Even prior to the German occupation of 1944, 63,000 Hungarian Jews had been killed. In fact, the first massacre of Jewish foreign nationals occurred in 1941. And of the *munkaszolgálat* laborers, 25,000 to 40,000 perished of exposure, malnutrition, and mistreatment. Another visual representation would perhaps help me absorb the material, but while I read, my ears were clogged from crying, and I had to pause often to wipe hot tears dripping down my face.

1944 Time Line in Hungary

March 19—Germany invades Hungary. Horthy remains regent but a fanatically pro-German prime minister is installed.

March 22—All Jewish shops are required to close.

. . .

April 5—Jews are forced to wear the yellow Star of David. Houses are designated for Jews and labeled with huge stars: "yellow-star houses." Cameras are confiscated. American and British forces begin their bombardment of Hungary.

April 16—Ghettoization begins.

April 28—In the villages and smaller towns, Jews are quickly forced into ghettos.

May 2—Deportation to Auschwitz begins.

May 14—Each day, four trains depart from Hungary transporting as many as 12,000 Jews to Auschwitz.

May 26—George and Katherine (Katóka), my parents, marry.

May 27—My father, George, is deported to slave labor.

May 16–July 6: Eichmann plans to liquidate the entire Jewish population of Budapest. In less than eight weeks, on 147 trains, 437,402 Jews are rounded up and deported to Auschwitz; 10–15 percent are selected for work and the others are gassed upon arrival.

Mid-June—Budapest Jews are ordered into 2,000 designated buildings labeled with the Star of David, "star houses." Bank accounts are confiscated, Jewish businesses are closed. Jews are allowed out in public between 2 p.m. and 5 p.m only.

. . .

July 2—The Allies heavily bomb Budapest.

July 6—Horthy threatens military action if the deportation of Jews is not halted.

July 9—Raoul Wallenberg, a Swedish diplomat, arrives in Budapest. He is credited with saving as many as 100,000 Jews, including my mother.

October 15—Horthy attempts to negotiate peace with the Allies. Hitler orders the kidnapping of Horthy's son, and Horthy is arrested. The Arrow Cross Fascist Party is installed and a reign of terror begins.

October 29—The (Allied) Soviet army backed up by 1,500 tanks begins its assault on Budapest. Hitler orders German troops to hold the city by any means necessary.

November 8—Approximately 70,000 Jews, including my grandfather Nándor, are rounded up at the Újlaki Brickyards and marched to the Austrian border. Thousands are shot; thousands more die of malnourishment and exposure. Those who survive are forced onto cattle cars and transported to concentration camps.

Late November—The Arrow Cross orders the remaining Jews into a closed ghetto. Many perish of exposure and starvation. Through December, several thousand Jews are marched on foot to the Austrian border. Additionally, 70 labor service battalions (*munkaszolgálat* servicemen) and 35,000 civilians, a total of 50,000 to 60,000 Jews, are deported to Germany.

December 26—The Soviet encirclement of Budapest is completed. The 110-day siege of Budapest begins. One million civilians are trapped. Approximately 20,000 Jews, seized from the ghetto, are executed, most of them shot into the Danube river; 120,000 people die due to the fighting, starvation, and illness.

February 13, 1945—The city surrenders. Budapest is in ruins. During the Soviet occupation that follows, some 500,000 Hungarians are deported to Soviet labor camps. Thousands of women and girls are raped.

April 4, 1945—The Soviets drive out the last German troops and Arrow Cross collaborators. The communists dominate postwar. The monarchy is abolished in 1946 and by 1949, the communist takeover is complete. The Soviet occupation lasts until 1991.

Admiral Horthy, admittedly an antisemite, believed that socioeconomic issues could be resolved by simply restricting Jews. He focused on restoring Hungary's stature in Europe, and Jews, he had to admit, occupied prominent positions in the economy, in culture, and in politics. He resisted pressure from the German Reich and from the radical antisemitic *Nyilas* within Hungary. These factions insisted Jews should be prohibited from every activity and expelled. By 1943, Horthy and his prime minister, Miklós Kállay, dismayed by the untold loss of Hungarian soldiers on the eastern front, sought ways to make overtures to the Allied forces and to reject Germany's demand they participate in the deportation of Jews.

Word of Horthy's incessant secret negotiations got out. Hitler summoned him to Germany on March 18, 1944 and Operation Margaret, the invasion and takeover of Hungary, began the following day. Döme Sztójay, a virulently anti-Jewish and pro-German politician, replaced Kállay as head of the government. Sztójay commenced draconian measures, appointing activist László Baky to the position of undersecretary of state to actualize the Final Solution: arrests, ghettoization, exile, and ultimately the annihilation of all Jews, implemented not by Nazis but by the Hungarian gendarmes and police.

Gradually more measures were enacted, but in 1944 restrictions ensued rapidly. Jews were no longer allowed to go to the Danube, to sit on park benches, or to use public transportation. Hateful slurs: *Juden Raus* (Jews not allowed) were painted on storefront windows. Picnics, swimming, and owning pets—forbidden. Cameras, bicycles, and radios—confiscated. Jewish offices and shops—shuttered.

By April, every Jew had to don the yellow Star of David. Forced to use their food rations for the fabric and to make the repugnant identifying label according to strict guidelines, Jews affixed the star onto their outer garments. Only permitted to shop at select stores between 2 p.m. and 5 p.m., pickings were slim. Eventually all Jewish bank accounts would be taken over by the state.

The *Nyilas* militia guarded the streets and needed no excuse to humiliate or beat up any Jew they encountered. My mother, on her way to piano lessons, witnessed doctors, lawyers, professors on their hands and knees, forced to scrub the sidewalks with toothbrushes while boorish thugs pummeled them with clubs—*Serves you right, you stinking Jewish swine*. Hoping not to attract attention, my parents and grandparents rushed through the streets when they had to go out.

My 18-year-old mother refused to acknowledge the dire predictions. Petulantly, she stamped her foot. "I'm strong. I can show those Germans I can work. I'm a proud Hungarian. The Nazis wouldn't deport married women, would they?" Young Jewish women became brides overnight. My mother had to get permission. She was underage. Then my father received his summons. Their hasty wedding ceremony, held in a courthouse, took place on May 26, the night before the Nazis took my father away.

Many years later, my mother told me about her flirtation with my father, a skinny, formal-looking cellist at the Liszt Academy. The prospect of free Budapest Symphony tickets and wearing a pretty frock lured her to date him. *Would she have married him under different circumstances?* It's a question I never asked.

After lumbering to a detention camp outside the city, my father and thousands of other young Hungarian men were deported to the copper mines of Bor, Yugoslavia, for hard labor.

What horrors awaited? Unaware that the Nazis would decimate Budapest's Jews, sending thousands each day to the crematoriums at Auschwitz, he believed there would be no escape from Bor. Surely a death sentence. Three beloved men in my mother's life—her husband, father, and brother—were wrenched from friends and family, to fates too terrible to contemplate.

My own family devoured, annihilated, caught up in the unconceivable carnage. Glancing outside, the activity on the street and grumbles in my stomach interrupted. Time for a dose of reality and some sustenance. I tiptoed downstairs to make myself some extra-strong coffee and peanut butter toast layered with sliced banana. I savored the creamy treat, inhaled the caramel-like aroma of the coffee. After several delicious bites, and thinking about what I'd heard, I felt guilty eating. The tape coaxed me back to the studio.

The streets in their neighborhood had been eerily quiet. Then, on a sunny day in June, my mother heard them, battering the gate next door. Their building was next. Behaving like savages, armed with grenades, the Arrow Cross *Nyilas* hollered, "Every filthy Jew out. If you don't come out, we'll shoot you and blow the place up! You have ten minutes. Pack a small bag. You won't need much where you are going, *féreg* (you maggots)!"

My mother quaked in fear at the sight of the militiamen who forced their way in, large black crosses emblazoned on their green armbands. The men glared as my mother packed in haste, trying to keep her wits about her—a warm coat, sturdy shoes, some piano music. It was impossible to hide keepsakes. My grandmother Irma thrust her wedding ring into a loaf of bread. The louts, after confiscating the jewelry, the silver candelabra, and money, if they found any, smashed crystal and Jewish objects—the menorah, Kiddush cups, Sabbath candles, finally ripping the challah cover to shreds.

> Where we used to live it was really very much Gentile district. Everybody had to move. From our house into so-called *csillágos házak*—yellow star houses—ghetto districts. Buildings where they put yellow star outside the doorway. So we walked with guards, and guns and dogs...Pushed. Even old people. Even babies. An old uncle and aunt of mine was living already in that area, in one of those houses. Small tiny place, and we all moved in. Small rucksacks, belongings piled up in downstairs lobby because there was only room for beds. We had to take turns to sleep.

Uncle? Aunt? I stopped the tape. I knew only of my mother's cousin Trudy and her son Misi. I'd met them on a trip to Hungary when I was in my twenties. Could there be other relatives? What had happened to them, and why had no one ever spoken of them? My father had painstakingly preserved a closet full of old photo albums containing tattered black-and-white photographs. I recall seeing people in bathing suits nestling together, laughing. They stared back at me. Kin? How would I learn whether or not they—whoever they were—survived the conflagration?

And my mother's belongings, the treasured piano, mementos. What happened to them? I reached for my computer to search the term *csillágos házak* and stumbled upon an online site—bright yellow stars and pink teardrop-shaped icons dot the map of the entire city of Budapest like a child's paint-by-number coloring book. The glittering symbols enumerate the detention centers, internment camps, and prisons of Budapest in 1944. The addresses are listed.

I read, "On June 16, 1944 the mayor of Budapest, Ákos Farkas had decreed, 'Every one of these apartment buildings will mark all their street entrances with a yellow star which must be kept permanently intact and clean. The sign shall be a six-pointed canary yellow star measuring 30 centimeters in diameter, on a 51 x 36 cm black background.'"[1] No other city had used this tactic.

A stockpile of Jews. Apartments near the Great Synagogue made it easier to round up the "vermin" for deportation. I tried to envision 200,000 people coerced into 2,000 yellow star houses—one family to a room.

My mother rambled on, now slipping in some Hungarian. The erratic outbursts triggered my imagination, the scene a diorama in my head. Apartments fit for a family of four now held 20 or more people. How could we believe everyone, all citizens, were not complicit? Even more chilling, what had become of Tibi, Nándor, and my father?

Far away, Tibi, the shrewd one, planned his escape from the *munkaszolgálat*. During a morning roll call in late May, the guards announced Tibi's labor battalion would be marched "to the west" for *Umsiedlung*— "resettlement" and toil at a "work farm." After months of hard labor, senseless cruelty, disgusting rations, and brutal conditions, Tibi was filled with foreboding. He had heard rumors. Nazi euphemisms hid their intentions, and he suspected *Sonderaktionen*, special actions, meant certain death. Waiting for a dark night, he and another prisoner attempted to break out. Despite the pursuit of soldiers with their frenzied dogs, and dodging a barrage of gunshots, my uncle evaded capture. After several days of wandering in the remote countryside, Tibi reached Budapest. He found the family, now installed in one of the yellow star houses. Imagine the scene. Tibi emerged from the shadows at their door in the ghetto—skinny, hungry, but alive.

Married or not, the young women and children were targeted next. Signs posted all over the city ordered women between the ages of 12 and 45 to report to the sports arena. Anyone disobeying the order would be severely punished. My mother had no choice but to go.

The cavernous arena was several blocks away. The downpour that day muddied the tangle of streets. From a distance, my mother could already hear and visualize the terrifying scene. Once inside the perimeter, she was thrust into chaos. Shoved, wrenched, menaced—overwhelmed by a confusion of women and children shrieking and wailing, while guards bellowed over the sound of snarling dogs. Gunshots ricocheted all around her and contributed to the crushing hysteria.

Prodded into lines, the dreaded selections began. My mother slipped from the back of one line to the other, keenly observing what was happening. The pregnant and frail women and very small children were sent to one side where they were forced into a truck; the beautiful, lithe young women to another; the able-bodied Jews to another. When nature called, you had to soil yourself. Dusk settled. The SS could not complete the job in one day and the guards were soaked to the skin. *Damn those Jews! Pain in the ass!* An SS officer barked instructions through his megaphone. "You Jew parasites are to come back tomorrow. If you dare stay and hide in the Jewish houses, you will be found and everyone in your family will be shot!"

My mother stumbled back to their house breathless, in terror, trembling uncontrollably. What diabolical subterfuge could be happening here in Budapest, the peerless empire of civility and culture?

She reported the horrific scene to Tibi. He had experienced the senseless brutality himself. Irma, their mother, wrung her hands, helpless, crying softly. They should stick together. These things arose periodically. If they kept quiet and did as they were told everything would work out—no need to overreact. But Tibi was not persuaded. He made the decision on the spot. They must hide. Where and how, he didn't know. He only knew that the alternative was bound to be much worse.

The women over 50 had not yet been called. While Tibi searched for a place to hide, my mother and Tibi's fiancé, Edit, returned to the yellow star house. Concealed in the basement cellar, they burrowed under the lumber and coal stockpiled to heat the building. Whenever anyone came down to replenish their supply, Edit and my mother buried themselves deeper, afraid to breathe. Nightly, Irma crept downstairs with some food if there was any.

Over the next few days, the *Nyilas* came looking for hidden Jews. For hours, the girls didn't dare move. Edit had to pee and my mother's arms grew numb. At one point, they heard the raid directly above. Surely the thumping of their hearts would betray them. Then it was quiet. My mother knew they'd be back, and soon. The girls emerged from the cold, sooty cellar and sprinted away from the ghetto.

Swedish diplomat Raoul Wallenberg came to Budapest in July, determined to save the remaining Jews of Budapest. He bought property, placed Swedish flags on the buildings, and designated them secure embassies; he distributed forged Swedish passports, and certificates of protection, and personally intervened to save arrested Jews. My mother was one of the thousands Wallenberg saved. She spent several nights in one of these Swedish safe houses.

The Allies gained ground over Germany. Admiral Horthy didn't want Hungary to be among the vanquished. Secretly he attempted to broach a deal with the Allies. One hundred fifty thousand Jews were still alive in Hungary including my mother, Tibi, and my grandmothers. Moderates like Horthy couldn't believe the rumors: mass annihilation of Jews? Despite the desperate need for labor? Weren't "death camps" typical Jewish exaggeration and propaganda? Hitler himself had indicated he needed manpower. Even after Pope Pius XII, President Franklin Roosevelt, and King Gustav of Sweden appealed to Horthy to stop deportations, even after a bombing raid on Budapest on July 2, the government—and in particular Lászlo Baky, a leading member of the Hungarian Nazi Party—would not waver.

But what did Horthy know and when did he know it? Hitler had communicated with Horthy in a meeting as far back as April 16–17, 1943, chastising Horthy for his leniency towards his Jews. Horthy had hedged, "What shall I do with them after having almost completely deprived them of their livelihoods—we can't beat them to death, after all." Hitler and German Foreign Affairs Minister Joachim von Ribbentrop retorted, "The Jews must be exterminated or taken to concentration camps".[2]

The watershed moment occurred in April of 1944. Two Slovakian prisoners, Walter Rosenberg and Alfred Wetzler, escaped from Auschwitz.[3] Their eyewitness testimony complete with drawings and hair-raising details were documented in what is now called the Auschwitz Notebook. Although the notebook, hastily translated into German and Hungarian, attempted to save Hungary's Jews, distribution was limited.[4] In late June, a copy of the document was taken to Switzerland, hand copied, and circulated among Jewish groups and the Swiss government. When excerpts of the Vrba-Wetzler manuscript appeared in the Swiss press—and subsequently, the *New York Times* on June 4, and then on the BBC World Service on June 15—Pope Pius sent a telegram to Horthy asking him to save the "unfortunate people."

One excuse after another justified Allied inaction. Bomb Auschwitz? It would divert too much air support from the war effort. Bomb Auschwitz? It would goad the Germans into further retaliation. Bomb Auschwitz? It was inconceivable, preposterous to conceive of 6,000 human beings gassed and disposed of per day.[5]

It isn't known when the irrefutable proof of widespread and systematic butchery first appeared in Hungary—possibly May or June 1944. Had the information in the notebooks been revealed to Hungary's Jews? If they'd known of their fate would they, like my mother, have resisted? Fought back? In her memoirs, Countess Ilona Edlesheim-Gyulai, a known supporter of Budapest's Jewish population and daughter-in-law to Horthy, claims that on July 3 she received the Auschwitz Notebook and passed it on to Horthy himself. He was "deeply shocked" and made another attempt to hold out against Nazi demands to hand over his Jews.

During a radio address to the nation on July 7, Horthy announced he would block further deportations, threatening military action. By then, Eichmann and his Hungarian cohorts had already shipped 437,000 Hungarian Jews to Auschwitz, most to their demise. Not to be outdone, the Nazis devised a scheme to circumvent the order. The *Nyilas* released Nándor from *munkaszolgálat*. They had a better plan for the 58-year-old war veteran, one that would chastise other presumptuous Jews.

Horthy's negotiations with the British and with Stalin seem foolhardy in retrospect. And, indeed, Hitler and the Arrow Cross had had enough. Hitler kidnapped Horthy's youngest son and imprisoned him at Dachau. On October 15, 1944, Germany orchestrated a coup, deposing and arresting Horthy, that sympathizer of Jews, and installed Hitler's puppet to run the country—Szalási, the maniacal *Nyilas* leader. He knew what to do with those remaining Jews. Buttressed by the regime change, the *Nyilas* thugs descended upon the yellow star houses.

Adolf Eichmann, the engineer of the Final Solution, returned to Budapest two days later, confident of the cooperation of the Hungarian fascist police. The evil scheme: extract the Jews from wherever they were hiding. Seize 50,000 of the strongest for forced labor. Prod the rest 220 kilometers [137 miles] to the Austrian border and cram them into cattle cars in a last murderous surge to Dachau, Mauthausen, and Buchenwald in order to annihilate the remaining Jews of Hungary before the arrival of the Russian Army. My grandfather Nándor was among the more than 70,000 men, women, and children forced to trudge to Austria. The *Nyilas* saw them as repugnant creatures. Not content to allow starvation, disease, and frigid temperatures to break them, for amusement, the *Nyilas* escorts beat and shot weaker troublemakers along the way.

Entr'acte 1951

Buchenwald Letter, written to my father, Gyuri [George] from my mother's father, Nándor:

Drága Gyerekeink! (Our dear Children)

1951. November 14.

My kind son Gyuri, in your last letter you asked what happened to me. I don't know what the point is to discuss those terrible times, but now that the war is over and you are safely in Canada, I will try to write my experiences down for you.

From 1944. October 20. to 1945. May 8. I was in the concentration camp of Buchenwald. My registry sheet was 18612 and my internment number was 97867.

These numbers I can never forget. I confirm that the stamped text of the paperwork says: *Concentration Camp Buchenwald—Weimar, signed Bartel. Lagerkomite Kommandant.*

And before heading for home on May 8, 1945, the following text was stamped: *Hungarian Committee, signed Dr. Gyöngyösi and American Colonel Peter Ball.*

Gyuri, you may not know that I was born in Szentes on July 13, 1886. It is a small town in the Hungarian plains on the bank of the river Tisza. So just after the Regent's radio speech the gendarmerie of the Hungarian fascist *Nyilas* took me from our apartment in Budapest. During his speech, Admiral Horthy announced that Hungary was finished with the war. He wanted to make a deal with the Allies. Horthy proclaimed that further deportation of Budapest Jewry would be halted. But immediately after this radio speech Horthy was arrested and taken to Germany as prisoner. One of his sons was killed, the other was kidnapped by the Germans. When Ferenc Szálasi, chief of the Arrow Cross, became the new leader, we knew we were finished. He agreed with Hitler.

Sometime around Oct 11 and 15 in the early morning, the Arrow-Cross gendarmerie raided my apartment. I was taken away. They took us to the trotting racecourse, where we were selected and divided into squadron units. I was taken into the third squadron. Officially there was to be no more deportation but nonetheless we were forced to march that same night until noon of the next day, to a village near the town of Gödöllő, about 31 kilometers [19 miles] northeast of Budapest.

After two days and nights without food, we were ordered into the forests to dig trenches and make weapons. We worked for two weeks, surrounded and strictly guarded by mostly Arrow Cross men.

Then one day we were ordered to march again, this time for two weeks without stopping—169 kilometers [105 miles] to Hegyeshalom at the Austrian border where the German SS were waiting for us. They loaded us into wagons to where we didn't know. Four days in cattle cars before we arrived to Buchenwald near Weimar. Can you believe it? The town of philosophers, writers, composers: Goethe, Schiller, Liszt, and Bach.

Those of us who were not completely debilitated physically were assembled. The Germans wanted people who understood locksmith work. We had to speak up if we knew this work. I was put in the group. The Nazis took us to Niederorschel (Langenwerke AG)—a subcamp of Buchenwald where we made airplane fuselages, run by the Junkers Flugzeug-und Motorenwerke. It was heavy physical work. But this was better than the quarry work others had to do. Some of the prisoners had to build the camp and the road to the entry of the camp. Anyone who couldn't carry the huge boulders was shot. And worse, my children. Lethal injections, medical experiments. I don't want to tell you about these. I was lucky.

Our food was unbearable. For months, we ate nothing but animal fodder and forage, mostly carrots, rotten potatoes and cabbage, which was sometimes boiled, sometimes raw.

Death was a constant, and soon the prisoners were dying of typhus. I was always athletic and fit, so I evaded the epidemic. I was lucky.

Eighty percent of the inmates of the camp lost half of their body weight during this time and this too caused numerous deaths. Many thousands of "unfit" Jews were transported from Buchenwald to Auschwitz. I was not shipped away. I was lucky. By December 1944 transports to the camp increased. There were more than 60,000 of us crowded into already unbearable conditions. Then even more.

We were liberated in 1945, April 11, but many of us had to stay in the camp. There was no way to move us. I was terribly weak and looked like a skeleton. Finally, after three months of medical treatment, I was able to stand on my legs and to make my way home. Open freight wagons just happened to be going our way. I got on. When I reached Vác, I rejoiced at finally being back in Hungary. The Hungarian Committee welcomed us there. We got a few hot meals and bits of pieces of bread. I was lucky to be alive at my age. I send my kisses to you both, good luck, and I hope this information is useful to you.

The letter was signed, "Your *Apu*!" I'd found the letter in a bag of correspondence saved by my father. Singling out the bright blue aerogram with multicolored stamps, I read the letter, then with trembling hands, folded it and put it back in its envelope, bewildered that Nándor, my mother's father, had been writing to my father about these horrific details long after the fact. I felt myself grow cold, contemplating a ghastly version of J.S. Bach's *Well-Tempered Clavier*—a contrapuntal fugue for screeching cattle car wheels with macabre irony from Johann Wolfgang von Goethe: "A man should hear a little music, read a little poetry, and see a fine picture every day of his life, in order that worldly cares may not obliterate the sense of the beautiful, which God has implanted in the human soul."

Blasted by 1,500 tanks and bombarded by the Allies, the Russians closed in encircling Budapest on December 26, 1944. The Führer's edict:

HOLD ON TO BUDAPEST AT ALL COSTS.

The German and Arrow Cross troops obeyed. One of the most

frightful urban battles of World War II—a brutal 110-day siege —ensued.

Tibi and my mother cowered in attics, basements, abandoned factories, and bombed edifices. When Tibi finally located an empty apartment on the outskirts of the city for Edit and my mother, he joined the partisans. Wasn't it better to die in freedom? My mother recalled:

> Me and my girlfriend—we had false papers what actually Zionist underground filled out—false birth certificate. My name Horvát Katalin sounds not Jewish—and, well, I didn' look Jewish. So I went out many times without star on me. Tibi too. But he looked Jewish. And if they stopped him they would tell him to pull down his pants —you know? To see if he was circumcised. Remember how strong he was? Tibi once jumped *off* a rooftop, and once climbed *up* a chimney... to escape.

The inexorable bedlam continued. Bullets flew. Bombs exploded. Buildings collapsed. The stunning bridges linking Buda and Pest were incinerated. Enveloped by smoke, darkness, and uncertainty, Budapest endured the relentless combat.

When the incessant din of explosives, sniper bullets, and salvos of artillery were utterly ferocious, Kato and Edit emerged from their hiding place and went down into the nearby bomb shelter. Most of the people there didn't suspect that the two girls might be Jewish. Each time my mother climbed out of the shelter, she dashed to their building, through the rubble, dodging the curtains of fire, looking every few seconds over her shoulder for militiamen—anyone who might be suspicious of her. Tibi had returned to be with his sister and mother and remained upstairs in a frigid little room. He looked too Jewish. He was more afraid to run to the bomb shelter. Whenever the sirens sounded, my mother shook with fear, wondering if their building had been hit. Was Tibi still alive? And Nándor. Was he? They had no idea Nándor had been marched to Austria and deported to Buchenwald in late October.

Hunger drove them out into the streets. The apricot trees of my mother's childhood, chickens roaming in the streets, and multicolored sweet peppers seemed a vaporous phantasm. Russian guns could be heard. Still, it was absurd to think that the family could survive these final weeks. The Arrow Cross knew the end was near, but despite the shelling, they were still killing Jews.

Once, when Irma ventured out for food, two *Nyilas* militiamen seized and dragged her to the ghetto near the large synagogue, pitching her behind high walls topped with barbed wire. Jews had been held there for deportation but due to the siege, they could no longer be expelled. No matter. The Arrow Cross plotted to liquidate the ghetto.

> That's when I got into trouble. I went out to look for my mother. I needed food, even horsemeat. They caught me in street. I was taken into a place—into headquarters of Hungarian Nazis where they used to torture people. I heard stories. Everybody knows that street, *Number 60*. And when I looked out of window I saw there was a big, long row of Jewish people and they, the *Nyilas*, were forcing Jews to the Danube and they machine-gunned them and their families. Into the Danube.

Gruesome sensations heaved in my abdomen. The number 60 loomed—the address where my mother narrowly averted a horrible fate. I checked my computer to see if I could track down the location, Number 60, the headquarters of the Hungarian Nazis. I stared at the sitemap for several minutes. Then I found it—60 Andrássy Street. On a visit to Budapest in 2000, my husband and I had strolled along the wide tree-lined boulevard bustling with city traffic. We relished the spectacular neo-Renaissance mansions and regal white stone designer shops: Gucci, Ralph Lauren, Armani, and the exquisite fine bone china shop Herend. We explored Franz Liszt Square and the Music Academy—the school my parents attended—an Italian ice cream shop that Howie could not get enough of, and the historic red marble Opera House with wide stone balustrades and sculpted pillars. We must have walked by the address 60 Andrássy Street—

Nazi and *Nyilas* headquarters—several times. In 2002, it became the "House of Terror Museum."

I pictured my mother, a raven-haired beauty, always industrious, always talkative, rammed into a room with a young Hungarian Nazi soldier for "questioning." Whatever she said, or did, worked. He let her go.

> Yeah yeah. It was end of the war, so I tell you actually the Russians liberated the Jews. Tibi used to say, he kissed the Russian tanks. Look, a long story. Why talk about it (*sigh*). We saved some papers. I don' know...locked, ah, in a, how you call it? A trunk. Oh. Oh! Here is my husband.

A clattering sound—a collision with the microphone. My father stood in the doorway to the bedroom, impatient to leave. He'd been looking for her. I could hear Mama standing quickly, sense the blood draining from her face. She didn't want to annoy him. She didn't want him to overhear the conversation. My mother had revealed her story for first time. When the tape ended abruptly, hot tears slithered down my face, the details too painful to fathom.

The grim statistics: 400,000 Hungarian Jews had been deported by July 1944, in an astounding 56 days—on efficient days, 12,000 men, women, and children. Every tenth victim of the Holocaust was Hungarian. Every third Auschwitz victim was Hungarian. The *Nyilas* men behaved with scandalous brutality. Even Adolf Eichmann noticed: "In some cases my men were shocked by the inhumanity of the Hungarian police." He had come to Hungary with only 20 Nazi officers. The *Nyilas*, assisted by enthusiastic citizens, did Eichmann's dirty work. Between early December 1944 and February 13, 1945, they dragged some 20,000 Jewish people from the ghetto—from hiding places, hospitals, and nursing homes—and shot them into the icy waters of the Danube. The Beautiful Blue Danube deranged, red, cluttered with bodies. Budapest was liberated, just in time, before the planned liquidation of the ghetto.

How then did my mother survive? Dumb luck? Destiny? Ingenuity? Chutzpah? Several minutes—or was it hours—passed in a numbed state of suspension. Speculations hovered in my mind. How did she elude the roundups? Endure the siege? Return to life after the inferno?

Despite liberation, the conditions were perilous. My young mother had no food. She had to venture out. Blackening her face with soot, she donned a baggy, worn overcoat and a kerchief over her hair, and tried to make herself look inconspicuous. The city unrecognizable, blowing snow and a frigid covering of frost made it even more difficult to negotiate the tangle of debris. Virtually nothing had withstood the desperate fighting. Jewish and non-Jewish survivors wandered the streets or lay prostrate against remnants of buildings, begging, digging for anything edible.

A skeleton jostled my mother. "Bread! Do you have bread?" My mother hurried on, wary of tripping on chunks of cement, broken glass, charred remains. She dodged the bodies, struggled through the terrifying scene. As she rounded a corner, a Russian soldier accosted her from behind. He grabbed her by the arm. "*Rabota? Munka?* Come to work." She flashed a winning smile, struggled free, and pretended she was expected somewhere. My mother had heard about the Russian soldiers. He might not have good intentions.

Even though Hungary was liberated and the Jews had been freed, disappearances continued. The victors exiled more than 500,000 people—presumably to the Russian gulag—and witnesses reported innumerable attacks on girls and women.

With mud-coated shoes and numb toes, my mother hurried along the banks of the river. What could she do? Her hunger gnawed. Materials were scarce. The city would have to be rebuilt. Surely scavenged hardware could be traded. My mother made her way to what had been a street lined with shops, knelt down, and started pulling nails out of the debris of leveled buildings. Her small hands, which had played the piano so beautifully, bled. But she pressed on —salvaging pieces of wood, wire, and hinges that could be used in exchange for food. I have a vague memory of my mother telling Rob and me about digging in the rubble for nails, perhaps in a moment of frustration with us.

The tape-recording left many questions unanswered. With no infrastructure in place, how did my mother reunite with the remnants of her family? How did my father find her?

Still lost in thought, I hadn't noticed the sun rising. Howie puttered in the kitchen, but I decided to listen to the end of the tape one more time before breakfast. Perhaps I'd missed some clues. What had she said near the end of the tape?

Envision the scene: my father, edgy, impatient with my mother. He had found her in the back bedroom of my uncle's home during Tibi's shiva, and he wanted to leave. I turned the tape on again. Flashing through my mind—the feverish weeks in 1999 when I'd cleaned out my parents' cluttered home in preparation for their move to a condominium; unexplained agitation over a locked rattan trunk, hidden and forgotten for a decade. Within were papers.

My grandfather Nándor. *My grandfather lived in a secular neighborhood, befriended non-Jewish men and fellow army officers, and even changed his surname in his futile quest for anonymity. In the end, none of his actions averted catastrophe.*

Kato—a beauty, at age 17. *My mother had dreams. A talented singer and pianist, why not become an actress? Life was full of possibilities.*

Relatives unknown. *Left side: Top photo my grandmother Irma, my mother's mother; middle left, my grandmother Margaret, my father's mother; bottom left my father playing the cello, a friend in attendance. Center, my father and his twin sister Magda are seated in the front row, in 1928. Who are these scantily clad people?*

Yellow star houses. *How does an army detain 200,000 citizens? The people of Jewish ancestry were forced to relocate into the yellow star houses, widespread throughout the city. The map illustrating very few safe houses and the encircled ghetto (bottom right) graphically signifies the impossibility of escape.* Credit: www.yellowstarhouses.org.

---

1. yellowstarhouses.org
2. ushmm.org
3. Once Rosenberg escaped, he changed his name permanently to Rudolf Vrba.
4. The entire report was not published in English until November 1944.
5. A bitter debate raged regarding not only the purported ignorance of the gravity of the situation, and the issue of bombing precision, but also the ethical dilemma of sacrificing the lives of those enslaved. Besides, bombing in mid-July "would not have saved the approximately 310,000 Hungarian Jews whom the Germans had killed upon arrival between May 15 and July 11, 1944. [ushmm.org; Brittanica.com]

PART III

FROM CHAOS TO CONCERT HALL
GEORGE'S [GYURI'S] STORY

Do not judge, dear reader, do not judge your fellow until you have stood in his shoes. When your identity, your assets, your parenting capabilities, your profession, your capacity to choose, have all been taken away and you have to decide between the survival of your children or your brothers, do you really know what you would have done? And what if you, as a rabbi or layperson, simply couldn't believe—didn't imagine... that all the trains were headed to death?

—Rabbi Joseph A. Polak (1942–), *After the Holocaust, the Bells Still Ring*

9

ENVOI TO ATROCIOUS TIMES

August 2009, my fourth trip to Toronto in as many months. I was determined to raid the trunk at last. After squeezing into the narrow airplane seat, my apprehensions resurfaced. Surely during this visit, my father would be open to questions about the trunk. Probably a hodgepodge of memorabilia, or could there be more? He saved everything. Since the discovery of the documentary and the tape recording, which my father and I listened to together during those bewildering days of my mother's shiva, and his revelations in January of playing with Leonard Bernstein, did I detect just a hint of willingness? My father had alluded to immigrant experiences, perhaps because he was alone, his own health tenuous. With any luck, if I probed carefully enough, I might coax some information out of him. The thought, though, made me feel squeamish.

After the usual sloppy kisses, I entered the apartment. My father rapped his temple with his knuckles and said, "Touch vood Janetkém. Tanks God, you arrived. How you keeping?"

Assailed by the collections that filled every nook and cranny, I wondered, has he acquired more knick-knacks and what-nots? Ten years ago, when my parents moved, I'd pared down precious porcelain figurines large and small, framed photographs, shelves of books, cushion-laden sofas, plants of various shapes and sizes, cabinets full of CDs, VCR tapes and LP-vinyls, and ornately framed oil paintings. The dislocation, followed by my mother's protracted illness, engendered silence—an entire decade whizzing by in a blur.

After hours of small talk, when I had a moment in private with Ian, I connived to meet him early the next morning at the storeroom in the underground parking garage to retrieve the crate. Together we hoisted it into the rental car and I sped away.

Rob and I maneuvered the trunk into the guest bedroom of his Toronto house. Using every tool known to man, we twisted, screwed, and pried. After several minutes of frustration, Rob gave up but I, with one final pull, and bruised fingers, popped the lock open. I lifted the lid. Sticky cobwebs and a haze of dust made me shrink backward. Once the mist subsided, I peered into the trunk stuffed full of mementos, some yellowed and frayed. I spread several handfuls all over the bed: my father's school report cards from the 1930s with a photo of his young face, letters and documents tied together, tiny black-and-white photographs, birthday and anniversary cards, several discolored newspaper clippings, and leather-covered diplomas marvelously preserved. What a find! I'd only just begun assessing the collection when a phone call intruded. "Vat time you are coming already?" Papa would be angry if I dawdled. Not an option. I pulled myself away and decided not to say anything about the trunk, just yet.

Once I ascended the steep hill to the front door and gained entry to my father's condominium, we sat side by side all day. Dialogue with my father had always been strained. I'd become adept at evading subjects of consequence: relations with my brother, my mother's illness, and of course the past.

Later, in the darkness, I drove across town back to Rob's house. He and Sara had retired for the night. The guest room smelled musty from the documents spread out on my bed. Despite the late hour, unable to resist, I rummaged through more high school records, birthday cards, and souvenir programs of concerts my dad had performed. Something old and brittle caught my attention. Gingerly, I unfolded the paper, afraid it might disintegrate in my hands. It crackled in protest. The elegant calligraphy and stylized border-work displayed some Hebrew script. I pulled it closer to my face. (*Why hadn't I studied my Hungarian more carefully*?) Official stamps, signatures, Stars of David, my father's signature, and the date April 27, 1935. I sounded out the large Hebrew letters at the top. *Bar Mitzvah*. Of course. My father would've been 13 years old. He had become bar mitzvah in Budapest's famous Byzantine synagogue, then called the *Dohány Templom*, the largest remaining synagogue in Europe.

Setting the fragile document on a table, I leaned over the side of the trunk to reach down to the bottom. I felt a thick string binding. Heaving everything out of my way to get to it, I pulled the mound of papers to the surface. Positioned on top a solitary photo—my handsome young father, with a mustache and a full head of hair, standing proudly, showing off his gorgeous bride, with his left hand enfolded under my mother's arm, his right hand lovingly holding hers. A spindly group of trees can be seen in the background. He is wearing a nicely cut suit, white shirt, and a swanky plaid bowtie. Mama smiles broadly, her brunette locks fashionably curled and fluffed up. Her chic high-necked dress with tiny buttons all the way down the bodice is cinched at the waist. The soft material drapes gracefully. A coating of perfectly applied lipstick highlights her shapely mouth. The photo, dated July 1950, two years before my unlikely birth, shows no evidence of trauma, displacement, loneliness. A young couple out for a Sunday stroll, one would think. But who dressed like that in Canada?

Under the photo were several documents bound together. The topmost, passport-sized, had a stiff and worn cover. As I opened it, two bright pink cards and a photo fell onto the bed. A memory drifted in—fables about an across-the-sea adventure. Or were they tales, whispered into my young ears? I read:

> (Tourist Third Class) IMMIGRATION IDENTIFICATION CARD, THIS CARD MUST BE SHOWN TO THE EXAMINING OFFICER AT PORT OF ARRIVAL.

Name of passenger: Horvath Georg

Name of ship: Scythia

Civil Examination Stamp: Oct 10, 1948 Canada Immigration Quebec, P.Q.

The second identical card says, "Horvath Katerina."

In the photo, my mother is standing on the steps of the gangplank to a ship, both hands lightly grasping the railing. Her gaze is averted. She looks pale and uncharacteristically shy, with just a hint of a smile. The wind blows her dark hair. It looks chilly. Her duffle coat—the sleeves too long, the bodice too bulky, a scarf tucked into the collar—are clearly secondhand. My parents cannot speak English. On the boat teeming with refugees from diverse nations I imagine communication is problematic. Many of the Jewish refugees from Eastern Europe speak Yiddish, but my parents, assimilated cosmopolitan people, don't.

I picture the journey in steerage—the filth, the nausea, the air rank with anxiety. Men separated from the women. Blustery, gray interminable days. The sea turbulent, the weather cold. Down in the bowels of the ship the stale air compounds the sour, fetid smell, and pails are scarce. My mother is terribly seasick during the voyage, and she isn't the only one. Somehow, they and the cello survive.

Georg and Katerina arrive to a place called Canada. Later, I learned she knew little about the country. They were inexplicably healthy. They proved it by touching their toes, saying *AHHH*. Taking deep breaths. Countless officials grilled them in the strange language.

The Cunard liner *RMS Scythia* docked at Pier 21, at Halifax, on October 10, 1948. My parents disembarked with their few possessions, crossing several parallel railway tracks. They walked en masse to the immigrant sheds to be deloused.

Everyone has to pass a mental health examination upon entry. My mother must've been nervous. Not a good time to let on you're homesick. Stand up straight. Brush your hair and put on a little lipstick. Smile with your teeth. Look directly in the officer's eyes and give the impression that you are strong and healthy—eager to start life anew. Don't cough, for heaven's sake, and don't let on your spirit aches at having left behind parents and siblings, and everything familiar.

I noticed a yellowing bound booklet, uncompromising, authoritative, the letters in bold green ink:

> MILITARY GOVERNMENT FOR GERMANY: Temporary Travel Document In Lieu of Passport for Stateless Persons and Persons of Undetermined Nationality.
>
> Name: Horvath Georg #82793.
>
> Page two:
>
> Occupation: tobacco farmer. Height, weight, eye color, year and month of birth.
>
> Personal details: Immigrant's parents' names, birthdates, and places of birth.
>
> Spouse: Katherina.
>
> Occupation: tailor.
>
> Page three:
>
> Stapled to the page, two passport-sized black-and-white photos.

They look older than their years, grim, and stiff. Both gazing rightward; complying with the requirement their left ear should be visible. (Canadian officials believe other facial features are indistinguishable in foreigners.) They attempted to appear well groomed. In this photo, my father is wearing a shirt, narrow tie, and slightly tattered tweed jacket. His thick hair combed backward reveals unruly eyebrows but his mustache is thin and trimmed. Mama's tresses are curled and draped behind her ears, exposing tiny pearl studs. Her gingham dress seems threadbare.

Above and below their signatures, several official imprints and a dizzying array of permission stamps caught my eye, "Canada Immigration Service, Karlsruhe."

This must have required a great deal of persistence and legwork back in Germany. And money too. Where did they get the money?

After several hours waiting in lines, extremely late at night, they boarded the train to their ultimate destination—Hamilton, Ontario—a small farming community about 60 miles west of Toronto. Why were they headed to a town without much culture, with very little if any classical music?

The 18-hour train ride from the east coast port of Halifax to Hamilton was interrupted for another inspection: immigration. All émigrés had to disembark in Québec before they could transfer to final destinations. My father waited for his turn, anxious. A professional musician, a cellist, how would he reclaim his calling in this foreign place? The inspection officer noted my father's occupation listed on the Travel Document.

"These hands have never worked on a farm."

"But I can learn," my father said.

The official grunted in reply. With a slight hesitation, he stamped page ten of the booklet, the coveted final stamp—the one I had seen on the boat ticket—their visa more precious than gold.

How did they manage it? Every country had Jewish quotas and a reluctance to take in refugees. Especially Hungarians. They could be spies. My parents, learned musicians, might not be admitted to Canada, as in those days, who could make a living that way? Essential professions such as farmers and tailors gained entry—even if they were Jews.

Within a few moments of my parents reboarding, the train personnel passed out slices of something white and soft. "*Mucikám*," my father whispered, "They are giving us cake!" She bit into the flimsy, not very sweet, but agreeable slice. It was their first encounter with Wonder Bread.

A few hours later, somewhere in the backwoods, just as they were lulled to sleep, they heard the squeal of the tires. The locomotive braked. The ragged refugees must have cringed with trepidation when police boarded and rushed through the train compartments looking for saboteurs or infiltrators—their relief at landing in a safe country upended by flashbacks of Nazi arrests.

Carefully rewrapping the document, I returned to the pile in front of me. A large leather-bound, multipage folio, embossed with the indicia of the Ferenc Liszt Music Academy caught my attention. I leafed through the lesson book, reading the professor's glowing comments, reveling in my father's outstanding grades.

Something fell out from the center of the report card. A certificate with a waxy finish, pressed, and hidden from sight. Bold calligraphy, official signatures, and a prominent black thumbprint drew me to the left side of the page:

> Ausweis—Certification. Georg Horvath, 26.2.22 Budapest.
>
> Provisional Identification Card for Civilian Internee of Buchenwald Concentration Camp.
>
> Weimar-Buchenwald May 8, 1945 number 18612, internee number 97587. *Kept in captivity.*
>
> Signed: Lagerkomitee Kommandant Bartel and American Colonel Ball.

I inhaled sharply, disquieted by the sight and feel of the document in my hands. The existence of a Buchenwald pass affixed with my father's photo, official looking signatures, and multiple stamps in

German was mystifying. His enslavement occurred in Bor, not Buchenwald. My father's intimidating demeanor endured even now at age 87, but the time had come to summon the courage to ask questions.

That night I couldn't sleep. The presence of such a tangible document in the bedroom here in Toronto made me nauseous. I dressed hurriedly in the morning and drove, I admit, a bit over the speed limit, to my father's condominium, stopping only for my one indulgence, a triple latte at Starbucks. Still processing what I had found, I considered how to broach the subject of the trunk with my father.

After the usual pleasantries, he shuffled to the living room, dragging his rigid legs, maneuvering his walker along the Persian carpet, which bulged in places. Distance accomplished, he flopped into the wheelchair. His limbs trembled from the effort, and the few wisps of hair on either side of his head came loose. For me to sit down, I had to move an assortment of embroidered, fringed, silk, and velvet decorative cushions, neatly assembled, off the sofa.

I must've appeared ill at ease, which prompted an anxious glance from my father. With a gesture, I reassured him nothing was amiss, at least I hoped not. My throat was dry. Struggling to pluck up the courage, I managed to croak, "Papa, um... can you tell me about your time in Bor? What did you have to do there?"

He frowned, "Vat? Why you want to know that?"

I waited, fiddling with the fringes on a sofa pillow. It seemed he might not answer me.

Several tense moments passed. "Okay, okay. I tell you one story."

I grabbed a pen and notebook. Avoiding eye contact I scribbled feverishly.

"We had to build railway from Bor to Belgrade. Germans needed supplies especially copper. Every morning at 6 a.m. they rang for us to wake up. We had to line up quickly for labor. They watched us all a time, following our every movement. I worked with pickaxe. It was heavy, two sided, and sharp tool. The ground was craggy and full of boulders. I had to break up stones and level ground, then I had to lift enormous rocks and debris into huge wheelbarrows. After I filled wheelbarrow with rocks and stones I had to dump contents into a pit.

Then I had to fill wheelbarrow with sand, go back to spots where were the potholes and dump tons of sand to fill up holes. I had strict quota of number of wheelbarrows I filled. If you cheated, even a bit, and your wheelbarrow wasn't *very* full, you would be shot. Brutal work. Just brutal. I had to push and roll huge cement sphere on tracks too—all alone. It went on tracks. Very difficult to maneuver, so heavy, but I tried to have confidence I could do it. If I broke it, I would be shot.

Once, I remember I was so exhausted, I took chance. I sat down for a couple of seconds. A rotten guard noticed. He rushed towards me. Furious. His vicious dogs waited for his signal. Their long, sharp teeth were bared, and they were ready to tear me to bits. Guard wanted to hang me but Hungarian Commandant that day was a little more sympathetic. Remember how superstitious I am? It was August 20, Hungarian National Holiday, day of celebrations with fireworks. So, commandant decided not to hang me or have dogs rip me apart. Instead my punishment should be to saw wood all day—12 hours, more—I don't remember. Not easy but I could live through that. I thought about Mummy, my wife..."

August 20, Saint Stephen's Day, Hungary's Fourth of July. The merriment typically starts early in the morning with the raising of the Hungarian flag. Parliament opens its doors and Mass is celebrated in the splendid St. Stephen's Basilica, the façade anchored by two massive bell towers. An elaborate Hungarian torte is selected, and the official cake-cutting ceremony precedes the concerts that follow. All the attendees enjoy a slice while listening to the music.

My body throbbed. Howard and I were married on August 20. Rob's first daughter, Ilana, was born on August 20. Certainly, there were other near misses, but this memory—how could it have been so suppressed? My father had never let on the date had such synchronicity. The specter chafed, but I forced myself to proceed.

"Papa. You remember the wicker steamer trunk that was in the crawl space, don't you? I took it to Robert's house and I looked inside it yesterday. I found papers. Letters, report cards, and your boat tickets, and I—"

He muttered something unintelligible. Perturbed by his gaunt and haunted expression, his knuckles prominent as he gripped the armrests of the wheelchair, I probed as gently as I could, "There's a Buchenwald ID card. It has your photo in it. I thought... Wasn't Grandfather Nándor taken there? How did you—?"

"Janetkém. Janet. *Hamis!* But that is *false. FALSE!*"

My father shifted in his chair as if he might bolt, as he so often had in the past. Indignant that he no longer had the strength to get up out of the chair unassisted, he sat motionless. His thoughts seemed to drift away. Finally, he spoke. I grabbed my pen again.

"I was liberated from Bor by Serbian partisans. I hid in forest, walked home to Budapest, to Mummy. I didn't have boots. My clothes were in shreds and stuck to me with lice. Germans mowed the forests so they could find Jews and deserters, and hay felt like needles; my feet were bloody. I begged for bread from some Russian soldiers.

'Please *khleba*,' I said. They wanted to shoot me. They thought I was German spy. I said to them, '*Yid! Yevre!* I am Jew!' and they told rabbi (an army chaplain) to come over. I said Jewish prayer: '*Sh'ma Yisrael! Adonai Eloheinu Adonai Echad! / Barukh shem kavod malchuto l'olam va'ed.*' (Hear, O Israel; Adonai our God, Adonai is One. / Blessed is the name of God's glorious reign for ever and ever.)

I was lucky. It saved me. I had no papers, nothing to say who I was or where I came from. We had to get papers. To get out. Nándor had ID card in Buchenwald. Nazis did that in German camps. Only way to get visa to leave Europe after war was from Germany, from Munich, with ID paper. So we forged it. Put my photo and my birthdate and signature on it."

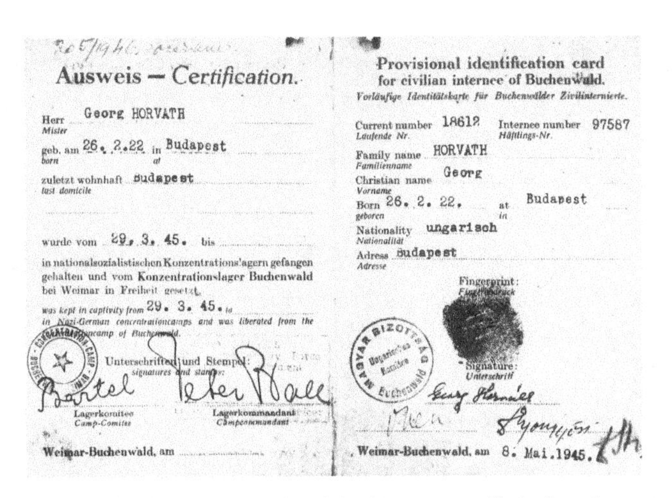

Ausweis — Certification.

Herr / Mister: Georg HORVATH

geb. am / born: 26. 2.22 in / at: Budapest

zuletzt wohnhaft / last domicile: Budapest

wurde vom 29. 3. 45. bis

in nationalsozialistischen Konzentrationslagern gefangen gehalten und vom Konzentrationslager Buchenwald bei Weimar in Freiheit gesetzt.

was kept in captivity from 29. 3. 45. to in Nazi-German concentrationcamps and was liberated from the concentrationcamp of Buchenwald.

Unterschriften und Stempel: / signatures and stamps:

Lagerkomitee / Camp-Comitee — Lagerkommandant / Campcommandant

Weimar-Buchenwald, am

Provisional identification card for civilian internee of Buchenwald.

Vorläufige Identitätskarte für Buchenwälder Zivilinternierte.

Current number / Laufende Nr.: 18612 — Internee number / Häftlings-Nr.: 97587

Family name / Familienname: HORVATH

Christian name / Vorname: Georg

Born / geboren: 26. 2. 22. at / in: Budapest

Nationality / Nationalität: ungarisch

Adress / Adresse: Budapest

Fingerprint: / Fingerabdruck

Signature: / Unterschrift

Weimar-Buchenwald, am 8. Mai.1945.

Buchenwald ID Card. *I peered closely at my grandfather's card, which was forged with my father's birthdate and signature. The middle date, 29.3.45, indicates the date of my grandfather's liberation.*

A dreadful image: my father stealthily hiking in the forest, in the winter, concealed under haystacks during the day, covered in lice, trudging from Yugoslavia to Hungary. This explains why they'd made their way to Germany after the war. Disoriented for a moment, and to divert his attention (and mine), I stopped writing and looked directly at him, every preconception altered. Was he the same father I thought I had—the weakling, the sensitive and volatile one who imploded at the slightest provocation? I fumbled for another question, less loaded. "Where did you get the money for the boat tickets?"

"Everyone who was allowed to live in Germany after war received 250 DM. A lot of money. But mark (the currency at the time) declined. We saved, we worked, our family helped what they could to pay for our passage on ship to Canada. We waited for proper paperwork. I played in popular orchestra in Munich—you know, Strauss waltzes. It didn't pay much. I played some recitals; some programs, and I tried to practice six hours a day. They actually wanted me in Munich Philharmonic, but I still had 'big dreams' to play solo. Your mummy cooked and cleaned for a gentleman."

My father sat limp and exhausted. I closed my notebook. Worried

I had pushed too hard, I convinced him to go to bed, promising we'd watch *Dancing with the Stars* the following evening—a television program he loved. His clutch almost toppled me. With several pecks on my cheek we bid goodnight.

I don't remember driving back to Rob's place, but when I got there, I searched my computer for confirmation of the details my father revealed, staying up well past the middle of the night before I climbed into bed. Then the phone rang. I strained to hear. A knock on my door.

"Dad's having another angina attack," Rob said. "Ian has given him two sprays of nitroglycerin. I told Ian it's okay to administer a third spray if he needs it. Ian will call us back in 20 minutes to let us know if the pain has subsided."

"I'll get dressed. Let's go over."

"No, I think if this doesn't work, I think Ian should call 911, and we can meet the ambulance at the hospital. Maybe it won't come to that, but I'll alert my colleagues in emerg." I wasn't sure I concurred with his plan, but, after all, he was the doctor already in professional mode. After an interminable 20-minute wait, the phone rang again. I knew from Rob's face that we should hurry.

Shocking. My father the survivor, in every sense of the word, failing. No longer the lucid, elegant man I had always known. Confused, angry, weeping—an unrecognizable creature, refusing treatment, and swearing. (Hungarian is liberally spiced with colorful swear words.) The bare hospital cubicle smelled foul. A flimsy curtain draped partially around him offered little privacy.

The ICU nurses apologized. Heart failure, they said. They had to restrain my father when he tried to pull out the IV tubes and remove the oxygen mask. He'd attempted to get out of the hospital cot, unaware he hadn't the strength. When I saw my father, he was combative.

"Janetkém, I want to go home." I cringed and averted my eyes. The drab dingy gown revealed a diaper, spindly legs, and a hairy chest. I turned to the nurse to explain: "You don't know my father. He's not just another wizened, helpless, old man. He has a story, an amazing story of triumph and survival; a life filled with music, art, flowers, and gastronomic pleasures; a life of everlasting love and perseverance."

But it was not the time for stories. "Okay, Papa. I'll take you home."

Surrounded by his art and all the tchotchkes, and my presence around the clock, my father's spirits lifted. Rob arranged for special equipment—an oxygen tank, ample condom catheters for overnight, premeasured morphine syringes, nitroglycerin oral spray to treat his angina attacks, and a visiting nurse in addition to Ian. Two people were needed to shower and shave him. Nonetheless, he recovered remarkably quickly from this bout of heart failure and regained his appetite and impatience. I stayed there all day every day. Ian confided that although my father's Parkinson's symptoms inhibited him, after I left in the evening, he sat for hours at the dining room table. "Lolo scribbles until very late," Ian told me. "But he has been very quiet about it."

Two weeks passed. My father's condition stabilized, so I booked my trip home to St. Paul. Remorseful about the extended period away from my husband, my 15-year-old son, and my job, still, leaving my father pained me. I drove to the apartment for a final day, and more of my father's impulsive smooches, which I hoped might linger on my face. But when I got there, he was not at the elevator.

I entered the stuffy apartment. No effusive greeting. His intent, pensive air and his brusque kiss made me apprehensive.

"Janetkém, we sit down. I want to read to you something."

"Let me set these things down and get a drink of water, Papa. Do you want anything?"

"Have a peach. So juicy. And strudel. Bring me a tea with lemon."

As I boiled the water and washed a peach, Ian assisted my father to the dining room table. He demanded my presence. "Vat taking so long? Terrible long. Come already."

What could be so urgent? I surmised he wanted to show me the endless array of doctor's bills, documents, or tax forms, which I have helped decipher over the years. Even during my years in grade school, I'd been the official letter writer and translator. I glanced across the room. My father's hands shook as he held two or three wrinkled pages covered in dark, cramped handwriting.

"Janetkém. I will read this to you." He cleared his throat several times and took a moment to gulp some tea. With each swallow, one bushy eyebrow, now tinged with gray, bristled up and down. I caught a glimpse of the virtually indecipherable Hungarian script.

"*Itt le fogom irni hitelesen az én szavaimel ahogyan törtent az én déportálásom.*" (I am writing testimony in my words exactly how my deportation happened.)

My breathing became constricted. The late-night writing...

"Papa. Papa. Can you wait a second? Let me get my computer. Then I can type while you read it to me. Would that be all right?"

He responded with a grunt. I stumbled to get my carry-on bag and pull out my computer—my hands trembling as his. He began to read in Hungarian. In the first few moments I interrupted him three times to spell words for me.

"Janetké. *Mucikám. Why* you interrupting me every second?"

Mustn't lose the opportunity. I decided to simultaneously translate into English, typing phonetically, and later I'd look up the unfamiliar words. He took another breath and began again.

> Here I will document in my words exactly how my deportation happened.
>
> I was born February 26, 1922, into a Jewish family. I have no paperwork, documents, or proof of what happened to me. The Germans didn't give any kind of official (*hivatalos*) proof and the Serbian partisans didn't order this kind of record. This type of evidence, which you are inquiring about, is not among my belongings. Allow me to write how my deportation occurred.
>
> My family was a Jewish family and we lived in Budapest. We were a very assimilated family and proud Hungarians. I had always wanted to be an engineer but by the time I was of age for university, Jews were prohibited from studying at universities. I was a talented

cellist so I pursued that avocation. By the 1940s I already had played with the Budapest Philharmonic.

"Janetkém, was March 19, 1944. During Sunday afternoon concert. The Germans marched into Hungary. Never forget that day. We were playing Berlioz, *Symphonie Fantastique*. Nazis stopped concert and told us to go home. Public gatherings were illegal. Can you imagine? All Jewish members—who were left, some already rounded up—fired on the spot."

Berlioz. A piece I've played so often. The glorious music, about love and despair, the life of an artist and his self-destructive passions, accompanied by air raids and Sutka dive-bombers whistling and booming as they fell. The artist depicted in the music has poisoned himself—the hallucinatory themes and the *March to the Scaffold* movement forever transformed to a sardonic metaphor.

Restrictions for Jews escalated. They could only shop in certain stores at specified times—when there was little food left. Jews had to wear the Jewish star on outer garments. Radios and bicycles confiscated. Pets disallowed. Parks off-limits.

"You know, anyone who had money got out in early 1930s. In 1933, I must been 11 or 12 years old, we had chance. One of my mother's sisters Janka *néni* (aunt) lived already in Chicago. She left long time ago, and she sent us tickets. But we decided not to leave. We knew no English and really nothing was wrong yet then. Everything mainly normal. We were Hungarians. Deportations, persecutions could never happen in Hungary!"

A shockwave charged through me. They had the opportunity to leave and didn't? The suffering could have been avoided. After all the rumors from elsewhere in Europe, they still had faith they would be spared. And what had happened to the relatives in Chicago? No one ever mentioned them.

I continued typing, sounding out the Hungarian words to translate them later.

In the middle of May 1944, I received a letter from the Hungarian government (*Hatoság*) that I should report immediately and turn myself in for deportation to Vác. I was a student at Hungary's Liszt Music Academy, as a cellist, and this would have been my final year that I would receive my diploma as an artist.

Events started escalating for Jews during the war. Even though we Hungarians were certain that deportations and persecutions could never happen in Hungary. I had acquired as insurance, a document from the government that I would be allowed to complete my cello studies for my diploma as an artist graduate of the Budapest Music Academy. I took this letter to Hungarian military headquarters (*katonai parancsnokság*). A captain snatched it from my hands. He tore it to shreds in front of me while shouting, "You will not get any kind of postponement! You have to report without delay."

Rumor had it that if Jewish women were married they would not be deported. So Kato and I were hastily married by a judge on May 26, 1944. Maybe I could save her.

"Janetkém, it was evening before they took me away... We had to get my father's permission because Mummy was not 18 years old yet. I was so happy to marry Katóka, your Mummy."

My father squinted at the page. Placing it down onto the table, he reached for a fragile document. I heard delicate crinkling sounds as he flattened the page—his marriage certificate. 1944. They'd proclaimed their religion as Roman Catholic. Sitting stock-still saying nothing, I waited for him to fold the document, his fingers, which once scurried up the cello, now fumbling with the simple task.

My mother Margit at this time was considered an essential worker and allowed to continue her work in a leather store, *Vigodni*, which was turned into a factory by the Germans to make boots for the German soldiers. She was able to make a wonderful, strong pair for me. I wasn't allowed to take much beyond those boots. These turned out to be invaluable in the coming months. I hid one small photo of my new bride in an inside pocket of my jacket.

On May 27, carrying a small rucksack, I was ordered to go alone to the train station and I took a train to Vác. As soon as I arrived, I

> could see the Hungarian soldiers (*Nyilás*) waiting to order me where I should go. There were hundreds of Jewish men, all of us believing and hoping that we were going for work.
>
> We had to line up in groups. Almost immediately they made the selection to send me to the group, who could work, that would be deported to the Bor company or division (*Boriszázad*). By 1944 we knew that virtually no one returns from that place, the mine (*Banya*). That is what I thought. I was 22 years old.

During the previous year, many hundreds of Hungarian Jewish men had been rounded up from the countryside. At that time, the men had no idea where they were going. They were transported to Bor, coerced into working in the mines under brutal conditions. By 1944 everyone assumed no one would return. The remaining Jews of Budapest—women, children, the elderly, the ailing—were forced into ghettos and then deported. Hungarian Jews, hundreds of thousands of them, immediately shipped "to the west," and gassed upon arrival. All of the trains that departed after my father's train went to Auschwitz.

> We were loaded into cattle wagon like animals, standing, cramped, rammed together in complete darkness. The car doors nailed shut. We had to take turns sitting down. Men and women were separated but we all had to do our business together in pail that soon overflowed. The stench just unbearable. We traveled for days without food or water.

Papa's hand shook as he took a sip of tea. I skimmed through what I had just written. Unimaginable. Neighbors and friends stood by as the Nazis rounded up all the Jews of all ages, from whatever station in life, shipping them to destinations unknown. Never to return. Did the bystanders know by this time in the war? Of 825,000 Jews who lived in Hungary in 1941, almost 600,000 perished. I railed against the majority of perpetrators who evaded punishment; several lifetimes would not be sufficient to expiate for these offenses. I closed my eyes and conjured eternal damnation—a Prometheusean punishment.

"On the way, train stopped. Allies were bombing. The Hungarian *Nyilas* cowards jumped off trains and cowered in fields but left us on sealed trains. Luckily, we weren't blown up. Our transport arrived June 1 at night. Guards had grenades (*gránát*). We were pushed into warehouse and left overnight, no beds, no straw even. In morning, we couldn't believe our eyes. We could see long line of lynching poles (*akasztás*) to hang prisoners."

Gruesome punishment. Men would be tied to the pole with their toes just touching the ground. They would be left for hours. Often the victims were hung by their wrists tied behind them, their shoulders soon wrenched from their sockets. My father learned Hungarian sadist guards had contrived this brutal abuse. The new arrivals stood in the blazing sun while the guards assigned each prisoner to one of about 30 camps between Bor and Belgrade, a distance of 222 kilometers [138 miles]. The prisoners consigned to work in the mine shafts were shrouded in darkness for days at a time. Half of German copper came from Bor, an indispensable material for the war effort.

> When we arrived in Bor, 4,000 men were separated into groups of three to 400 men. Half of all the men went to the mine. Others were assigned to build a railway. Each group was identified and named after small German villages. Mine was named *Röhme Tábor*. Each "village" consisted of six to eight groups of men who were housed around 500 meters away from each other. My group's assignment was to build the railroad tracks. We built in both directions to "tie together" tracks from Bor to Belgrade. The tracks had to be built in sections and eventually were supposed to meet in the middle.
>
> Each laborer was assigned a number. My number was 1, 1, 8, 5, 6.
>
> I am very superstitious and I added up the numbers. They totaled 21. I thought that was a good omen. I was a good card player and 21 had always been a number that meant good luck for me.
>
> The Bor Század were all Hungarians so the commandant was a Hungarian as well. His name was Lieutenant Colonel (*Maranyi Alezredes*).

> When we came back to the camp for dinner hour, we had black water that was supposed to be coffee, watery boiled cabbage, and a piece of bread—one loaf of moldy (*penészes*) bread for every five men. If you didn't force yourself to eat it you would starve. After these pitiful offerings, most nights we performed for the Hungarians. They wanted us to work until nightfall so they forced us to wrestle in the mud (*birkózás*), kick dance, exercise. These were humiliating (*megalázó*), and demeaning "torture". Useless activities.

"Until nightfall, Janetkém. Entertainment for Goddamn antisemitic bastard guards. We worked 12-hour days but we couldn't sleep. Our shacks had many small friends—mice, rats, bedbugs, lice, fleas. On Sundays, they would select people with dreamed-up charges for special punishments. All commanders were Nazis. He was sonofabitch bastard."

The commander of the entire camp system, Ede Marányi, a virulent antisemite, condoned beatings and ruthless punishments. My father had already described the work he had to do—breaking up boulders with a pickaxe, loading wheelbarrows with stones and dirt, and shoving cement spheres, all under constant threat of violence.

By late fall, the Germans were losing the war. Nonetheless, my father explained, the Nazis had every intention of completing their de-Jewification agenda. On September 16, 1944, they divided the camp into two groups of about 4,000 men each. One group would march "home"; the other 4,000 would remain behind in the camp. My father, desperate, convinced those left behind would be shot, did everything he could to try to move into the group making the trek home. As it turned out, he was wrong. The roads became littered with beaten, emaciated bodies of the 4,000 men who marched away. Shot on the spot if they stumbled, if they stopped to urinate, if they fell from the cold or from exhaustion. They went without food and water for days. The prisoners who evaded a bullet, who didn't starve or freeze to death en route, were sent to other concentration camps.

My father angled his eyes over his reading glasses to peer at me. "You know famous, just fan-tas-tic poet Miklós Radnóti? He was in Bor too. He was in first group, marching, and still writing protest poems. He was carrying his messages, and a friend too, who was very weak. Radnóti made guards angry. He kept 'scribbling,' so they beat him and then shot him." Papa shuddered, "My lucky number 21 saved me."

Radnóti, I later learn, had actually been assigned to the second group, and like my father he'd tried to switch to the first contingent of prisoners "going home." Tragically, Radnóti's entreaties were successful. Almost two years later, on August 1, 1946, a mass grave, discovered and excavated, exposed corpses; among them, Radnóti's body. A small notebook was found in the pocket of his overcoat with his last five poems. Today the poems in Radnóti's Bor Notebook have been translated and internationally recognized—a moving testament to the brutality that prevailed.

Papa continued reading.

> In November, the Serbian partisans liberated us from the Germans. By this time my coat, my shirt, and my pants were in shreds and falling off. I would have perished over the winter without proper clothing. I weighed 115 pounds. The *Nyilás* fled. As soon as the Serbs entered the area, we dispersed in every direction, wherever we could, into the forest.
>
> By then the Russians had also arrived in the area. All this time I kept hidden the precious photo of my wife Kato in my old worn leather wallet (*briftascni*), in an inside pocket. As I stealthily made my way on foot northward, I saw a Russian soldier cutting bread. I begged for a piece but this fellow denounced me. He told the Russian commander that I had a gun and that I had tried to shoot him. The Cossack captain thought I must be a German defector, but all I had were rags on me! "*Yevre*," I said, "I am Jew." He asked me to prove it.

"This is when I said the Sh'ma prayer, Janetkém."

> The Russian found my photo of Kato and he took it from me, probably to show it off and brag that this beautiful woman was *his* girlfriend. He then noticed the wonderful and still sturdy boots my

mother had made for me. He stole them right off of my feet, leaving me barefoot.

I wandered in the country, hiding under viaducts in the woods for weeks with very little food, walking at night, toward Szeged, Hungary. I hiked barefoot until my feet bled. The Serbs had mowed the straw (*szálma*) in the countryside so they could search for German defectors, and it was as sharp as needles.

I trudged all the way from Bor to Szeged on this ground. I remember that one night it started to pour and I tried to take cover under a haystack (*szénaboglya*). In the morning, I was drenched and the rags of my jacket had dried frozen and were stuck on me.

Reaching for my phone, I Googled the distance my father had lumbered through Yugoslavia. From Bor (now Serbia) to Szeged, the border of Hungary, is 459.8 kilometers (almost 286 miles). A healthy person can walk 20 miles in eight hours. So, 286 miles could take 114 hours on foot, that is, if you could walk in a straight line.

Szeged, the town known for exquisite, sweet Hungarian paprika. The red metal container imprinted "Pride of Szeged" was filled with the pungent delicacy, and permanently ensconced on our kitchen counter. Thinking back to my childhood, I recall we rarely took walks when we were growing up in Toronto, except for our visits to Edwards Gardens, the lovely public park on the east side of the city. Our family never took road trips, or hiked, or camped. What pleasure could there be in sleeping outside? My father didn't even own a pair of tennis shoes. I attempted to visualize the trek my father made, but it's unfathomable.

Life was full of inconsistencies (*következetlenségek*). At one point, I hooked up with an Italian who also had been wandering in the countryside. Soon we ran into more Russian soldiers. One of the Russians wanted to shoot us. He had a grudge. An Italian had injured him at the front and the Russian wanted revenge. I happened to be standing right there with the Italian. Fortunately, just as he took his aim, another Russian soldier there pushed his hand away just in time.

The next morning this same soldier, our savior, cut a small piece of bread for himself and gave me the rest, the larger portion. So you see there were always some decent human beings.

"Remember I told you once there was guard who pitied me? I think he loved cello. He gave me gloves to protect my hands from hard labor in Bor. I was lucky. One guard broke all fingers of another musician prisoner."

Another narrow escape. I marveled at my father's magnanimity. What had happened to turn him into the negative, disheartened man I knew, who used to say he was cursed? Often enough, Rob and I, and our mother, were pummeled by his fury at the world.

When I finally got to Szeged (a city at the southern border of Hungary, which was already liberated and dealing with millions of refugees) after weeks of wandering, I was covered in lice. This could spread the dreaded disease, typhus. Contracting typhus, in these filthy circumstances, with no hospitals and medication, meant certain death. I had to go to an assigned place where the rags I was wearing were boiled in hot water to get rid of the lice. And there I was also fumigated. I spent several days in Szeged wandering, sleeping on the ground, cold and miserable, begging for food.

Covered in lice? Sleeping on the ground? Stifling my queasiness, it dawned on me why he'd been so fanatic about fastidiousness, cleanliness, order. When the Nazis coralled my father, if he'd known, if anyone had known, would he have smuggled a piece of soap into his boots or rucksack? Or would he have been shot for the infraction? No one could fathom such heinous conditions. Each morning when I take a shower and moisten my bar of soap, I breathe in the sweet-smelling lavender, and think about it—the luxury of hygiene.

One day I noticed a Russian cargo train (*szálito teher*). It was unguarded. At night when the streets were deserted, I decided to hop on the train headed to Temesvár (now Timisoara, Romania), 117 kilometers [73 miles] west, which I heard had already been liberated

> and was in Russian hands. [Author's note: they joined the Allies in late 1941.] Budapest was still not liberated (*hartzok fojtak*) I could not go there. My hometown surrounded *(körülvett)* and barricaded. The rumors of brutal street fighting (*utcai harcok*) were terrifying. I could hardly imagine what conditions might be like. I dared not think about my beautiful wife and my mother. I had no idea if they were still alive.

For a moment, my father stared at the floor, mute. In the silence, confounded and distressed, I became aware of my own sensations—seared innards, swooshing sounds, an irregular heartbeat. Each interchange raised more questions. How did he survive the winter? How did he maintain hope? My father was a cellist, a classical musician, not an athlete. I tried to imagine enduring such a trek.

"Papa. How did you find your way?"

"Hmm? I don't know. I stumbled at night along bombed roads. Janetkém, I don't know. I don't remember. Had to get home... to find Mummy."

My father tapped his fingers and gaped at me, as if he didn't recognize the present or trust his memories of the past. Then he continued.

> I made it to Temesvár on the cargo train. A Jewish relief organization had been set up there. They were attempting to help. They gave me some clothing and the addresses of Jewish families who might take me in. I was lucky again. I happened upon a Hungarian Jewish couple. I told them what had happened to me. The woman played the violin and her best friend, a Romanian Jewish woman, often invited me to join her family for dinner. We became very friendly
>
> Lucia, the Romanian, had a beautiful daughter who was a fantastic violinist. The daughter fell in love with me. Yes, she was a beautiful talented girl. They also had a son, about my age and size, and he played the cello! So this family generously took me in, gave me some of their son's clothing, and decent shoes. I actually looked like a gentleman. Their son was a student in Bucharest, away at the

time, so I was able to play their son's cello. I started the arduous task of moving my worn fingers. I was so lucky.

I'd often heard this phrase from other survivors. Lucky they weren't shot on the spot; lucky they weren't sent directly to the gas; lucky they defied the odds. Can any of us imagine what enduring the brutality could have entailed? They had to have had, in addition to something or someone to live for, unwavering perseverance and hope, chutzpah, good fortune, psychic insight. What about faith? Did my father have faith?

My muscles and fingers feel tight and weak even after a few days of not playing the cello. Following harsh manual labor, my father must've been so grateful he could play again, relieved there was no permanent physical damage. I thought about the survival skills he'd had to cultivate, which likely included learning how not to feel, in the face of such cruelty. My father performed chamber music in Temesvár with Lucia and a neighbor of theirs, a pianist. Beethoven piano trios, full of musical vision, the slow movements deep and profound, the quick ones dramatic and aggressive. I imagine the most difficult task: how to revive smothered emotions in order to make music again.

He turned to me and reminisced about a pleasant memory, "I remember we played Schubert *Quintet* for two cellos with Gábor Magyar. One of our favorite pieces of chamber music. Isn't it? Just gorgeous. Just fan-tas-tic."

Allowing our minds to drift, we heard the beautiful strains of the music. Papa's fingers started their tapping dance on the arm of the chair, as he imagined playing the soaring opening of the piece, the cello duet. I also recalled the sublime melodies of the quintet, the second cello adding a chocolaty richness to the dark sound. The slow movement—a prayer, hummed in the violins without vibrato, creates a silken sheen of sound, while underneath, pizzicato bell-like thrums from the cello resonate. The depths of color, the vivid changes of light. Revelatory sounds. After this conversation, I would never play the piece the same way again. Many years later, when I performed during a festival to honor my father, the Schubert *Quintet* evoked precious memories.

The Russians prevailed and liberated Budapest on February 13, 1945. An orgy of violence followed surrender. The numbers of casualties cited varies. With few photographs taken, and the political upheaval and state takeover that followed, the statistics were manipulated. Today right-wing interpretations further muddy the truth. Estimates indicate that 40,000 civilians perished during the last days of the siege, 20,000 of them Jews. Of 30,000 soldiers who made a last-ditch attempt to break out rather than capitulate, only 785 escaped hot pursuit. Two thousand wounded men suffocated in fires. Russian casualties are estimated at from 100,000 to 160,000 men, and hundreds of thousands of Hungarian and German civilians succumbed. The "Paris of the East"—leveled. Historic buildings—Ottoman, Moorish, and Art Deco—reduced to rubble. Bridges linking Buda and Pest demolished. The uncommonly cold winter contributed to the agony, and there was not much more than horsemeat to eat.

Like other desperate refugees, my father hovered around lists of names—of the victims, of the survivors as they discovered them, of the occupants of DP camps, once they were displayed by the Red Cross, United Nations Relief and Rehabilitation Administration (UNNRA), and refugee service organizations. Often the lists were stuck haphazardly on walls, not alphabetized, and replete with misspelled names. Families searching for missing loved ones posted desperate notes on message boards. My father, after days of searching through countless slips of paper, caught sight of his name—*Horvát György, we are alive at the Swedish safe house in Pest.*

"I lived and waited in Temesvár when, finally, Budapest was freed and I could go home—straight to Vigodni leather store, remember? Turned into boot-making factory? I ran upstairs so fast. I looked on message board. That's how I found out my mother was with friend in ghetto. I was so weak but I ran to ghetto. There stood my mother! I couldn't believe my eyes. We cried. She told me my wife Kato was alive! Katóka was in Swedish safe house. I sent message to her. When Kato got the news I was alive too, she hurried through bombed-out streets, and rubble to my mother's place. What a reunion! We didn't have bed, so we slept on dining room table. We couldn't believe it when Kato's father, Nándor, came home a couple of months later from Buchenwald concentration camp."

Seriously ill, and with an injured leg, Nándor could barely walk. A friend from the camp helped him make his way home. Although not a young man, Nándor defiantly stayed alive. The story I remember hearing as a little girl: he'd smuggled a small square of sugar into the camp. Each day, despite being ravenous, he ate a tiny square of the sugar. It saved him from starvation.

Sifting through the detritus of the city, while my mother dredged for hardware to trade for food, my father attempted to earn a little money playing the cello. The populace yearned for entertainment, for music, for an escape from horrifying memories. My father auditioned for the Opera House and he performed in small cabarets, but his meagre salary had to be spent the same day. It was worth less than half by the next morning.

> Budapest was divided into zones at that time—Russian, American, British, and French—and it was necessary to have permission to travel from one to another. Life was still precarious for Jews. As I walked the few blocks on my way to a concert, a Russian soldier accosted me (*megszólított*). He was standing under an awning by an apartment. "Come over here," he said. "I want you to come to do a little work (*robitni*)." Do a little work, we heard these words hundreds of times a day. I suspected that he wanted to send me to Siberia! Several people had disappeared that way and never came back. I had my cello with me. I said, "Look! I have my instrument and I am on my way to play a concert!" I also had a paper in Russian that gave me permission to travel to the concert. With a furrowed brow, he scrutinized (*megvizgált*) the paper. The Russian held the paper upside down so I knew he was illiterate (*írástudatlan*). He pretended to weigh the implications of the letter. I pointed to my

name on program. Finally, he let me walk away.

My father slowly raised his head, straining to return to the present. He glanced at his watch. It was after six o'clock. We had sat motionless all day.

"Okay, Janetkém. We stop now. Time to eat. Terrible tired. You must be tired."

"Papa. Let me heat up the chicken paprikás I made for you yesterday."

"Iy-awn, please heat up Janet's chicken. Make a toast and soup please."

Ian busied himself assembling the various courses for dinner. "Janetkém, lie down. Go lie down on the couch. Move pillows."

I felt stiff from sitting all day. Wasn't he? But I listened to my father and limped to the sofa. At least 20 decorative pillows perfectly aligned had to be shunted over once again to make room for me on the seafoam-green sofa. Ian warmed up the meal and within a few minutes, we silently ate our supper.

My father insisted. He would finish the story with some last details. I continued with my transcript.

Discussions over the next months were intense, he told me. They felt unable to continue life in a Europe drenched with Jewish blood, among them Hungarians who were vicious antisemites. My parents made the gut-wrenching decision to escape from their native country. The family planned how the young people could find a way out.

My father and mother, and Tibor and his wife, Edit, knew they had to get to Munich, where they could obtain the necessary exit visas to leave Europe. They pawned a Leica camera from Nándor's "photo-optic" store. The elders chipped in whatever money and scraps of food that could be had to bribe a Russian truck driver. He agreed to smuggle the young members of the family in the back of his truck under heaps of hay during one of his regular trips from Hungary to Germany. My parents packed a few small bags, some jewelry, and the cello, and left behind precious family members.

Had they known their next embraces would not be for a decade, I doubt they would have left. The Soviets took over, a reality I contemplate now: I could have been born in Budapest, barely subsisting during the Soviet occupation, or not born at all.

I visualized the scene described to me as if I had been there. My parents planned to leave in the middle of the night sometime in 1946. With as much confidence as they could muster, with the promise to bring their parents out of Hungary as soon as possible, and after tearful goodbyes, they climbed into the cargo bed. It was difficult to breathe under all that straw, vital no one sneeze or cough as they crossed various checkpoints at each zone and finally the border into Austria.

They came to a sudden stop. What happened? Was there some obstruction or had the driver lost his nerve? Tibi, always the perceptive one, hissed, "Quickly, quickly. Throw everything off the truck and jump!"

"Rubbish," my father told him.

"Let's go!"

My father looked up at me to explain, "You know, driver, maybe he was afraid? Maybe he wanted to steal everything we had. He just left us in countryside somewhere on outskirts of Vienna. In Russian sector. Just as we catched our breath, Tibi—who was such a good swimmer—jumped into Danube! He wanted to get to Vienna and get help. We—Mummy and me, with the cello and Edit—hiked in Austria at night.

My dear sister Magda, already in Vienna, to meet us, was dressed like queen. Magda worked for American army—General Clark's office in Munich, as translator. You remember she spoke five languages? So she knew what to do. She took us to consulate. "Just come with me," she said. Magda looked so beautiful, guard almost fell on his face! She arranged permission for us to stay in Vienna, and then after while she got Jewish pass from Vienna to Salzburg, which was in American zone, and then at night, we traveled across Austrian border in truck to Munich. We stayed in Windsheim lager (DP camp). I think in Bavaria. Janetkém. I don't remember... Maybe before we could go to Munich? I don't remember."

Hiking farther at night, in fear. Moving from one place to another. It must've been arduous. Would I have been as brave under those circumstances? This was the first time I'd heard my parents had been in a DP camp.

"Iy-awn," my father shouted as he tried to get up from his seat. Ian hurried over to help. He angled the walker and grasped my father under his arms to give him a boost. I thought my father needed to go to the bathroom, but he gestured for me to follow. We got up slowly and shuffled to the walk-in closet in his bedroom. The photo albums, at least 50 of them, stacked high in the closet, four deep on top of an upper shelf, were thick with history. I had thrust them in there in a heap when my parents moved, happy to stash the collection, giving not a thought to the memories held within.

Papa peered into the closet. Then he recognized the album he was looking for. It took all three of us to dislodge the brittle and yellowing scrapbook from the others. We went back to the table, then my father lovingly leafed through several discolored pages, each crackling a protest. On the front of several of the photos—tiny black-and-white snapshots neatly lined up, dated, and shrink-wrapped—my father wrote in his indecipherable cursive: *Windsheim*.

"There. There is Mummy in 1946. Windsheim."

I stared at the photo. My mother is leaning over and stirring the contents of a two-handled pot, which has been placed on a broken-down stone—what is it? A primitive cooktop? She's cooking outside amid dirt and debris. Swaths of decaying weeds surround my mother's feet. Even so, she's wearing open-toed shoes with little bows at her ankles. The turf is enclosed by an uneven fence of mismatched slats and branches. I crouched for a better look at the next photo. The area is crumbling, shabby, littered with pebbles, shattered pipes, and bordered by dirt roads and ramshackle buildings. She is smiling as she snuggles a small child. Splintered wood roped together fashions a makeshift table. I notice another woman in the background. She and my mother are wearing twin gingham dresses—the tattered one I saw in the photo of my mother on the boat. They must have been donated dresses.

My father turned to another page. Sixteen one-inch photos from Munich, of Tibi and Edit, of my mother posing flirtatiously in 1946, seemingly unscathed, several shots of my father playing the cello, an upright piano in the background, and faded photos of breathtaking views of mountains and ski lifts, identified in block letters: Garmisch-Partenkirchen, May 1947. I had so many questions, but didn't want to disturb my father's reveries. While he gazed at his younger self, I searched online for information about these places and read: "Windsheim – Jüdisches DP-Lager / Jewish DP Camp *Bewohner* / Population: 2,800 *Juli*/July 1946. US zone." Puzzling information to piece together. I needed to look at a map, to get more background and a better understanding of where these places were to trace my parents' journey.

1945 Refugee Repatriation

Between 1945 and 1950, immediately following the war, the Allies had to assume a formidable task—some ten million people to repatriate, tens of thousands of them barely alive. Jewish prisoners from crematoriums and slave labor who had fled from the Nazis to Russia, who'd hidden in the forests of Europe, fought as partisans, survived concealed in caves, sewers, root cellars, or pigpens had no homes to go to and no surviving family members. The Allies initially assumed uprooted Jews would return to their native countries. Those who tried found an unwelcome if not hostile reception. Citizens who'd seized property and possessions were reluctant to give them back.

The Allies organized displaced persons camps to house the refugees. DP camps hastily set up in Austria, Italy, and Germany were woefully inadequate to feed, clothe, house, and treat this mass of humanity, thrown together with previous animosities still intact. Antisemitism raged. The Allies needed help. They enlisted the support of the Jewish Joint Distribution Committee, JDC, formed in 1914 by three influential philanthropists: Jacob Schiff, Louis Marshall, and Felix M. Warburg, a respected banker. The organization had been active in war relief efforts since World War I, providing millions of dollars in Jewish and nonsectarian aid.

During the 1930s, the JDC provided relief to Jews suddenly without resources. They provided medical care, food, and shelter, and they allocated funds to support emigration. By the end of 1939, the JDC organizations had enabled approximately 110,000 Jews to flee Nazi-occupied Europe. By the following year they were active in more than 40 countries.

With support from the JDC, the International Red Cross, and UNNRA (which had been created in 1943 by 44 nations), the Allies provided DPs with economic assistance and repatriation services.

But the Jewish refugees needed special attention. They couldn't be housed in the same camps and hospitals as their tormentors. Germany had become their unwanted refuge. Survivors detained in DP camps throughout Bavaria endured miserable, overcrowded conditions—in military barracks, abandoned hotels, airports, hospitals, former concentration camps, and even, in Feldafing, a training center for Hitler *Jugend* (youth).

Jewish refugees were finally relocated to separate camps through the efforts of Joseph Schwartz, JDC's European director. He called for a "partnership between the army, UNNRA, UNNRA's successor agency—the International Refugee Organization—and the JDC," and together they allocated aid. "The JDC distributed supplies that nourished both body and soul: funds that supported medical facilities schools, synagogues, and cultural activities..." Their work continues today (see www.jdc.org).

The US camps had more to offer than those administered by the British, French, and Russians, but the shortage of food, supplies, and medical care persisted throughout Europe. Landsberg, the largest DP camp in the US zone, located about 60 kilometers [37 miles] from Munich (and the location of the concert with Leonard Bernstein), housed over 4,000 refugees.

During the spring of 1946 my parents arrived to Windsheim—a small DP camp in the American zone, by then well over capacity at 2,500 people. The camp's population soon swelled to 3,200 with teeming cellars and jammed garrets. As in other DP camps, the detainees struggled to return to normalcy in squalid and dispiriting conditions. They organized schools, synagogues, and sports teams. They established theaters, performed concerts, and wrote and distributed newspapers—the specter of lost or missing family members never far from their thoughts.

Even as early as 1943, the enormous issue of displaced persons became apparent. It had to be addressed. How would families dispersed all over Europe find each other? The British Red Cross initiated the International Tracing Service (ITS), and they began to collect whatever written documentation they could find—birth or death records, Gestapo lists, concentration camp and forced labor registrations, and notes from prisoners scratched on bits of paper in quivering handwriting. The Germans kept thorough records.

To date, the ITS has processed nearly 12 million requests. Their unique historical archive includes 30 million documents. One thousand queries are received each month, even today—from people wrested from their parents' arms as infants in the 1940s, and from children of survivors searching for ancestors—people like me. Many of these records, now digitized, make it easier to connect people. Thirty to 50 families continue to be reunited each year.

Holocaust victims held in DP camps prayed for a better life, for visas, for a country to call home, for freedom. They were stunned by the callousness of bystanders and the cruelty of local perpetrators who willingly, if not eagerly, participated in the mass murders. No one spoke for them; no one opened their doors for them. Most countries, including the US, refused to accept Jewish refugees, despite learning of the horrific details well before the end of the war, of gas chambers and mass murders.

US Congress, entrenched in their viewpoint that aliens were likely spies and saboteurs, adhered to restrictive refugee policies and immigration processes. In 1945, President Truman stepped in, loosening quota restrictions. The Truman Directive gave preference to displaced persons. Of the 35,000 to 40,000 DP visas issued between 1945 and 1948, with hundreds of thousands of debilitated survivors sequestered in camps in Germany, fewer than half went to Jewish refugees.

The overwhelming majority of Jewish survivors firmly believed their future could only be relied upon in a country of their own—to absorb and heal them, to help them regain their humanity, and to establish a national identity: *Eretz Israel*. But the State of Israel wouldn't be established until late 1948 and the British strictly controlled immigration to Palestine.

Disturbing clashes occurred. In 1942, the *Struma*—a ship carrying 800 Jews fleeing Romania who'd been extorted 1,000 dollars for the passage to Palestine—floated unmoored outside Istanbul. Turkey wouldn't allow the passengers to disembark, and the British wouldn't extend visas to enter Palestine. After 70 days of wrangling, the ship was towed to the Balkan Sea without a working engine and abandoned. The following morning, a Russian submarine torpedoed the *Struma*. All but one passenger perished.

Another incident captivated world attention. In 1947, the ill-fated ship, *Exodus*—with 4,500 Holocaust survivors aboard including orphaned children—embarked for Palestine. After a 24-day hunger strike and a three-week standoff, the boatload of pariahs was intercepted and turned back to Europe to a DP camp in Germany.

Lest you think the Americans eschewed such behavior, in 1939, after two weeks of sailing, another vessel, the *St. Louis,* loaded with 937 Jewish people attempting to escape Nazi Germany, reached the shores of Miami. The passengers who had purchased expensive Cuban visas could see the lights on the mainland while immigration authorities quarreled about their fate. Cuba revoked the visas and refused the passengers. America and Canada also prohibited entry, sending the *St. Louis* back to Germany —a death sentence for nearly a third of the refugees on board.

In 1948, Congress finally passed additional legislation to expand the number of DPs allowed, accepting 202,000 DPs into the United States. But only 80,000 of them were Jewish.

Where did these inflexible isolationist viewpoints originate? I took some time to explore the history, and learned that after the First World War and the Bolshevik takeover in Russia, anti-immigrant fervor rose to a fever pitch. Weren't the newcomers arriving to US shores by 1900 predominately from "lower classes?"—people from Poland, Hungary, southern Italy, Russia, and Eastern European countries, many of whom practiced odious religions. According to several members of Congress, Eastern European Jews were particularly undesirable. Anyone behaving in an "un-American" way was suspect. Aliens, agitators, dissidents, and "Reds" subsisted everywhere and, allegedly, organized rebellion.

The government employed strong tactics, including surveillance, surprise raids, and arrests. Anti-immigrant rhetoric spearheaded by Rep. Albert Johnson, the chair of the House Committee on Immigration and Naturalization, and a young J. Edgar Hoover led to the first mass deportation in the 20th century. Two hundred and forty-nine people, among them the American feminist and rebel Emma Goldman, were expelled from Ellis Island in 1919, across the Atlantic, away from this country, for their political views or backgrounds. By the 1920s, thousands of people were incarcerated in unheated cells, given little food or water, in cities such as New York, Detroit, and Boston. Some of them were roughed up; some died of pneumonia.

Louis F. Post, the acting secretary of labor, stepped in to prevent more deportations much to the chagrin of those in power. Post defended the prisoners who were detained without evidence.

With the election of Warren Harding in 1921, the anti-Bolshevik frenzy diminished. To mollify isolationists, Congress enacted the Johnson–Reed Act in 1924, limiting immigration through a strictly controlled quota system. Capped in 1927 to allow no more than 150,000 émigrés per year and still in effect 40 years later, the law prevented those fleeing the Holocaust from finding refuge in the US.

Hungarian Jewish immigration had been curtailed and my parents were rejected. Hungarians could be infiltrators. After all, the country had allied with Germany. Willing to go anywhere, my parents considered themselves lucky to receive visas to Canada—their third choice I later learned, after Argentina.

Setting the photo albums aside, my father continued his tale. They reached Munich safely sometime in 1946. Magda had made connections. No crowded, unsanitary DP camp would do for her twin brother. Windsheim was temporary, a way station.

"These photos... I didn't know you were in a DP camp, Papa. How long did you have to stay there?"

"Janetkém. Doesn't matter anymore."

"Yes, it matters—I mean, to me," I said in quick diminuendo. "I'd like to know."

"Miserable times. Just miserable," Papa said. "I don't know. Weeks? I don't remember."

Magda, ever industrious, arranged permission to transfer them to Munich. Then she heard about an orchestra, a Jewish orchestra, of Holocaust survivors. She made contact with the musicians and took my father to meet them. Of course they needed a cellist! My father became one of the members of the St. Ottilien Orchestra, the group comprising of just a handful of musicians, sometimes 15, sometimes more—the musicians who'd managed to stay alive, those who were anxiously awaiting exit visas, and those who'd received their papers and expected to sail away at any moment. The group bussed twice a week throughout Bavaria in the American zone, performing in cities such as Frankfurt and Stuttgart and Dachau. A mere few weeks earlier, it had seemed improbable my father would ever belong to any orchestra or make music in a concert hall again.

Entr'acte 2009

As we often do, Howie and I curl up at home and listen to *Rhapsody in Blue*—a work I have played many times in the Minnesota Orchestra —a lone clarinet trills and ascends in a long jazzy wail; a muted, guttural trumpet introduces the piano, which enters with swagger, sizzling and sultry; and melodies swirl long after the piece ends. I think back to what it must've been like in 1948. Did the musicians know the piece, composed just over 20 years earlier? Did my father know of George Gershwin? Papa was only 15 years old when Gershwin died of a brain tumor in 1937, age 38. Although originally composed for jazz band, we typically play *Rhapsody in Blue* with large forces—a hodgepodge of percussion, a bevy of brass instruments, a lush string section. The St. Ottilien orchestra had only 17 members. In my imagination, I see Bernstein tossing off the solo piano part, lifting his hands to conduct whenever he could, and—like a juggler—filling in any and all missing instrumental parts, willing everything to come together in that memorable concert.

Howie and I watch inspirational documentaries about Leonard Bernstein, the maestro, a master in every sense of the word. Charismatic, flamboyant, earnest, he is idolized for his generosity of spirit, his deep understanding of music, his celestial vision, and his devotion to the education of his audience, whatever their background, age, or musical taste. Seated with the ever-present cigarette, in a powder blue ascot and denim shirt, his luxuriant white hair spilling over his forehead, he seems immortal as he urges us to be better human beings. If only his presence would leap into the future; if only post-Bernstein humanity would act upon his words and deeds. Committed to creating beauty, he believed music could one day bring people together in harmony.

For me, his appearance in Landsberg and Feldafing overshadows his other activities in 1948, but there were other memorable successes. Bernstein recorded Gershwin's *An American in Paris* in the US and he spent two months in Palestine conducting the Israel Philharmonic through December as their music director, the musicians never missing a concert, despite the fact that everyone—men and women—had been drafted.

The fledgling state was established on May 14, 1948, just four days after the concerts in Landsberg and Feldafing. War broke out immediately. Five Arab nations including Lebanon, Syria, Iraq, and Egypt formed an alliance and launched an air attack on Tel Aviv that very night. By September, Bernstein was on a plane to Israel. In an amphitheater-like archeological dig, through constant air raids, Bernstein sat out in the open at the piano, impervious, propped up on cement blocks, in the center and between the musicians, and surrounded by thousands of admirers—the dawn of a lifelong love affair with the Israel Philharmonic.

None of us had ever been to Israel. Well aware that my parents would not be comfortable visiting on their own, in 1989, I booked an all-inclusive tour—hotels, meals, and the important sights included—my treat. To explore the country and our cultural heritage together would be a gift. It didn't occur to me that my father would allude to wearing a yellow star for the first time.

Our guide, a swarthy, broad-shouldered veteran of the 1948 War of Independence, the Six-Day War in 1967, and the Yom Kippur War of 1973—so-named when Egypt attacked Israel on the Holy Day—was a scholar of both Jewish history and Jewish faith traditions.

Imagine: all the marquees and street signs printed in Hebrew. Almost everyone is effusive and unrestrained. Almost everyone is Jewish. My parents and I had never experienced being in the majority. I'd seldom traipsed around with them, certainly not scaling cliffs, exploring Bedouin markets, and surveying ancient archeological sites. To see them in wide-brimmed straw hats, white shorts, dusty tennis shoes, and holding hands, was unusual to say the least.

One day, we made a stop and encountered a peddler at the side of the road. He claimed to be smitten with me and offered my father seven camels as a dowry for my hand. *What? Only seven?* To prove their excellence, the peddler coaxed my father onto one of the enormous camels sitting at the edge of the road. When Papa unwittingly placed his rump between the two humps, the beast rose to its feet with a spit and a bellow. My mother and I shrieked, "Oh my God! *Yay Istenem! Yay Gyurikám!*" My father grinned with hysteria or hilarity, I'm not sure which. He towered several feet above ground, holding on with a vice grip. While I snapped several photos, the peddler eased my father safely back down to earth, who, once his feet returned to terra firma, winked, "My daughter, I am not giving away for all camels in the world!"

The only friction: dinnertime. My parents insisted on trekking all over the city to find Hungarian restaurants. Israel is considered a culinary superpower, and I hoped to try popular Israeli foods: shakshuka, a baked dish of eggs in a spicy sauce of onions, garlic, peppers, and tomatoes; bourekas a puff pastry filled with cheese and potatoes, or mushrooms and spinach; and of course the quintessential street food, falafel, hummus and salad stuffed into a pita pocket. But only Hungarian would do. When at last we found one, my father drained an entire glass of Tokaji—a sweet Hungarian white wine—and said, "*Egészségedre!*"

During our explorations of the awe-inspiring sites, breathtaking panoramas blazed: Caesarea, the ancient Roman port now undersea; Masada, the stone fortress on a massive plateau above the Dead Sea; Temple Mount, an elevated walled-in area in the Old City of Jerusalem; the Dead Sea Scrolls, displayed in the Shrine of the Book section in the Israel Museum; the Church of the Holy Sepulchre, built on the site of Jesus' Crucifixion and subsequent burial; and Al-Aqsa Mosque, the third holiest site in Islam with its golden dome dominating the landscape. The ravishing ochre stone of Jerusalem, glorious art, aqua seas, hot breezes, desert sands, harsh sunlight, vibrant blooms, I witnessed the beauty of Judaism and the religious curiosity with awe and a sense of wonder. Until this trip my perspective had been limited. My cultural heritage began and ended with the Holocaust. When the Nazis invaded Hungary, my parents were young adults. They had a patchwork of fond prewar memories. But for Rob and me, and other children of Holocaust survivors, the encumbrance began in the womb, oozing into our genes.

"Goddamn antisemitic bastards," my father had spewed as if Jew-hatred triggered every insult or provocation. We did celebrate the Jewish holidays, but in retrospect, I see my father participated halfheartedly. It took me many years to feel a sense of pride in my heritage.

Our tour schedule included a visit to Yad Vashem—the World Holocaust Remembrance Center. I didn't know what to expect. I didn't think my parents would come. We toured the exhibits grief-stricken, especially at the Children's Memorial. There, descending stone steps into a hollowed-out underground cavern, we found a depiction of the 1.5 million murdered children—representing approximately 95 percent of all Jewish children ages 0–18 who perished in occupied Europe (www.yadvashem.org). The towering inner room, dark and narrow, is lined in mirrors and reflects candles, multiplied a thousandfold, shimmering around us and above us—a luminescent sky in a distant hemisphere. We stood in homage as a relentless drone named each child who perished, their age, and where they were from—in Hebrew, English, and Yiddish.

Perhaps he was overcome. Perhaps something released in him, but when we entered the next room with a display of artifacts and the chronology of the war, my father pointed to one of the glass cases and said, "I had to wear star like this. My number was 1, 1, 8, 5, 6." Then he turned to stare at nothing. Although by then in my thirties, I'd never heard him speak of his own experiences during the Holocaust.

With another labored exhale, my father continued his testimony. "Music saved us. We had decent life in Munich. We could recover a little." He remembered the concerts, the passionate outpouring of human expression, which after years of suffering, stirred hearts. During my parents' two-year wait for necessary exit papers, they were well fed by UNNRA and the American Joint Jewish Distribution Committee, enough to sustain the entire family: American packaged goods like macaroni, cereal, and peanut butter—foods my parents had never tasted.

My father continued cello lessons in Germany, with Anton Walter, a prominent teacher. Another paradox—Papa hid the fact that he was a Jew from Walter, an ardent antisemite, and Walter, who yearned for good students to bolster his own failing career, ignored the possibility. "I took private cello lessons three hours a week and I tried to squeeze in six hours a day of practice too. That's what an *artist* has to do."

He performed several solo concerts during that period. To show the program to his teacher and boast a little, proud of one of his recitals, my father tore off the letterhead, which indicated the program was sponsored by a Jewish organization. I found a few of them. November 1947: *Jüdisches Komitee Fürstenfeldbruck* (a town 32 kilometers [20 miles] west of Munich) included Mendelssohn *Trio*, Op. 49, No. 1 and several solos. Anton Walter, I discovered, fraternized with *some* Jews. Walter performed for years as the cellist of the internationally famous Rosé String Quartet, led by Arnold Rosé, the concertmaster of the Vienna Philharmonic for more than half a century until the 1938 Nazi Anschluss (annexation of Austria). Rosé escaped with his life but his daughter, Alma, died in Auschwitz.

While my father continued his cello-playing career, my mother answered an ad in the local paper from a Mr. Goldberg, who wanted a Jewish woman to cook and keep house for him. Goldberg had been a wealthy and well-known businessman. During the war, the Nazis confiscated his apartment as well as his successful fabric and textile factory and deported him to a concentration camp. My father didn't remember which one. Goldberg survived. The Allies returned the apartment to him, but the plant, on the outskirts of town, lay in ruins. They compensated Goldberg by giving him a fabric factory in Bad-Reichenhall near Salzburg, hence he was out of town for weeks at a time. My parents, and my mother's brother, Tibi, and his wife, Edit, moved into Goldberg's spacious third-floor Munich apartment at 48 Jahnstrasse. From 1946 to 1948, my mother shopped for necessities, prepared Hungarian delicacies from whatever provisions she could find, and scoured the apartment for the gentleman.

Saving money for the cost of tickets to Canada and the immense amount of paperwork necessary to emigrate remained a bewildering task. Goldberg wanted to help. He entrusted my mother with belongings from the apartment. Clutching porcelain, fabric, coats, comforters, and goods my father received in payment for his concerts from the Americans—coffee, American cigarettes (these were like gold), sugar, and chocolate—my mother dealt on the black market, selling the items to desperate people foraging the streets, openly engaging in the risky business.

> So we lived in Munich at 48 Jahnstrasse freely for two years. It was a gorgeous apartment. He left money for us too. Hundreds of German marks were left in a jar. Katoka was the only one who had a key and she shopped and paid his bills. He trusted her to handle everything. He of course loved the food Katoka cooked... We were able to save a lot of money.

My father laughed. "I remember funny story. Gasoline was very rare. Even more rare, Goldberg had small car. We collected gas for him whenever we could find some, and we kept it on balcony. Mummy had to cook in fireplace. One day, a stupid cleaning woman of building came and she put some hot pieces of coal from fireplace next to gas tank on the balcony. It exploded. It burned like the devil! A Nazi who lived under us in apartment below wanted to arrest Mummy, Goddamn antisemitic bastard. But debris just landed on courtyard below and burned out. No damage was done! Goldberg had to bribe Nazi tenant to keep him from pressing charges."

Baffling times. Living side by side, victims and persecutors, neighbors and friends who had turned against them, now neighbors again. Moving forward as if the atrocities hadn't occurred. In retrospect, the expediency of silence, the self-aggrandizing deeds, the ease of evil, is not lost on me. It smacks of behavior we know all too well. Is the world any less absurd today?

My father didn't pause. He shuffled his pages and continued his recitation and I kept writing.

> Goldberg was very good to us. In fact, Goldberg loaned me money to buy the *Panormo* cello on the black market. It cost 100 dollars, a lot of money at that time. We promised to repay Goldberg when we were in Hamilton. It was the cello I performed on in the Jewish Orchestra.

The *Panormo* cello powerfully raising spirits. The sounds of the music flowing from soul to soul. I'd wondered how the St. Ottilien orchestra members procured instruments. The exquisite, handmade 18th-century Italian instrument, which traveled with my father for two years, to 100 DP camps, and weathered the harsh conditions of the boat trip to Canada, was the cello I played as a teenager for my first recital in the Art Gallery of Ontario. With light fluting, the extra turn into the eye of the scroll, the textured varnish, and the exotic flame of the wood. *How could I have known?* My entire being seemed to pulsate with this revelation.

By late 1947, my aunt Magda, my father's twin sister, the quick-witted one, had already made her way to the US by marrying a Chicago relative. I subsequently learned Milton Jack Friedman was their cousin, their aunt Janka's daughter Ilona's son. Without even setting eyes on her new husband, Magda settled in New York where she started to work. As always, protective of her twin brother, she made the final arrangements for my parents' immigration to Canada. She'd located a guarantor and met the train when my parents arrived in Toronto.

"So Papa, you finally got all the papers together and money for the boat tickets in 1948?" I asked.

"Janetkém. It was Magda. She found Hungarians in Canada who wanted to help Hungarian refugees. Ben, a farmer in Hamilton, said he would sign for us. We would do *anything*. If they needed farmers, what you think? My papers said I was farmer! The inspector said to me, 'These hands have never worked on a farm.' And I said to him, 'But I can learn.' They gave us white bread on train. I thought it was cake!"

At this my father laughed. He'd told me this story before. "Ben offered us work. We scraped and painted, and washed wood floors, sometimes for no payment. Amazing Mummy didn't get splinters."

Letters from Budapest, 1949

Longing. The letters are full of longing. My father had saved a large bag of neatly folded letters, bound together and placed in the trunk. The correspondence, although one-way, allowed me to creep into the fissure of time before my birth in Canada. The letters from my grandparents took time to decipher not only because they were in Hungarian. The ink had bled from one side onto the other and to save paper and postage, the cursive handwriting was miniscule.

With insatiable curiosity, I squinted at the letters, a hint of my parents' life during those initial two years. Immigration had been virtually impossible for Jews. Once they arrived in Hamilton how did they adapt? Two skilled artists who craved to play music consigned to washing cars, cleaning office buildings overnight, dishwashing, scraping paint, scrubbing floors. How else could they make a living? Plagued by anxiety, homesickness, and a terrible sense of impotence, my father had lost weight. He yearned to go home. They lived in a furnished flat with no heat and a small hot plate; rent: $4 a week. What did they eat, I wonder? Hot dogs and white bread aren't exactly Hungarian fare.

My mother, determined to tough it out, supported my disheartened father. Their English was poor. Prospects undetermined. They explored the possibility of moving to the US. Perhaps life would be easier there? But the US still considered them a "bad risk."

With clumsy hands, I unfolded the first letter.

My dear Little Katóka!

From Grandfather Nándor

May 9, 1949

I fear I will have to cover your pictures, because they break my heart. Unfortunately, this wicked, evil world creates such sad and painful situations for us and millions of other people. I'm inconsolable and I will be until we can find a solution. Dear Gyuri! I'm so glad you have finally managed to have a solo concert. Any news on the move to Montreal? Vancouver? We are unhappy about your job Katóka, and hope Gyuri you can finally play in an orchestra. Gyuri, your mom found a tuning fork and a big piece of rosin, should she send it to you?

Apu (father)

A move to Montreal or Vancouver? Searching through my notes of conversations with my father, I didn't see any references to relocating to another city.

A career in music in Canada seemed hopeless, especially in

Hamilton, truly just a small farming community. Evidently, even common music supplies had to be sent from Budapest.

Citizens justified employing foreigners for menial labor with extremely low pay. Weren't they taking jobs away from real Canadians? Probably infiltrators or communists who couldn't be trusted, who couldn't even speak English.

After several months of despair my father managed an introduction to the president of the musicians' union in Hamilton, a man named Anderson, who told him, "A musician like you should be in Toronto." Anderson allowed my father to join the musicians' union there, but the president of the much larger and established chapter in Toronto found out. Incensed and in a fit of pique, he tore my father's union card shouting, "You have to be a resident of Canada for two years to apply. A musician may not perform until he joins the musicians' union."

My Dear Beloved Children

From Grandmother Margaret

September 7, 1949

Your letter didn't exactly put my mind at ease. What are you thinking, son? First things first, I must tell you not to have any illusions. To just come back with no consequences? There are strict laws in effect here. You know I'll be fined for holding a room in my apartment...

Gyuri dear, it looks like you'll have to put your music aside completely; because it seems to me you won't be able to get into the Union. And if you're not allowed to visit Magda in New York for 5 years that would be terrible, and I blame myself for letting you leave. Take care of yourselves and try to get jobs in your own professions. My God, back here you wouldn't have needed to do things like that. It drives me crazy. Not because of the work, but you are a musician, and so is Katóka, and you could have been respected professionals back home, back here...

My father's breakthrough occurred when he took a four-hour bus ride to the town of Lindsay to meet the director of their choral society. After obtaining the union's permission, the society engaged my father not only to play during the church service but also to play a recital, for the grand fee of 100 dollars. No longer a mere laborer, his beautiful playing and musical talent identified him as an artist.

My Dearly Beloved Children

From Grandmother Margaret

November 22, 1949

My mother bawled her eyes out in happiness over your successful concert, son. I told her not to cry but be happy and laugh. The concert must have been beautiful! Our only regret is that we could not hear it. Son, what do you get for playing on the radio and in the orchestra? Do you have any prospects for a good contract? Did you wear a tux while playing? Or don't they do that over there?

Katóka, I can't come to terms with sewing. All that sitting hunched doesn't do you any good, it would be better if you opened a shop and employed some girls. I really want you, my dear daughter, to keep practicing, and to continue your musical career with Gyuri. Remember, dear son that I am listening to you from afar, and if you think of us, you will always play well.

Goodbye, God bless you until we see each other again,

Your loving mother (Margit mama)

My mother, an expert seamstress, bluffed her way into a higher-paying job as a fur finisher in the sweatshops of Toronto. She hand-sewed silk linings into fur coats, with the heavy garments draped over her lap even during the summer months when the temperatures hovered over 90 degrees. Few windows could be cracked open. An excellent worker, my mother charmed Sam Pollack, one of the foremen. He generously offered to rent a room to my parents in his family home for $18 a week. I remember meeting the Pollack family as a little girl and the story my father told me about him.

"At first, he complained I was always 'fiddling' and Mummy, such a beauty, worked so hard. Then a friend from Hamilton sent message to me late at night. I should not tell who called me. There would be auditions for a cello position in Toronto Symphony, the next morning. TSO was against foreigners, afraid of refugees, so nobody told me about audition. I had no time to prepare but I did go to conductor's room and he asked me to play everything—all sight-reading. He liked my playing and offered contract for 1950–51 season. Oh, we were so happy! When Pollack heard our news, he was finally impressed with my 'fiddling'. He was fan-tas-tic person. He even took me to tailor to make me a very elegant black suit. It was $100. Very expensive. A loaf of bread was five cents just so you can imagine."

The Toronto Symphony. Employment playing the cello in an orchestra even if only for the 24-week season. My father still had to hustle. He accepted every engagement, especially during summer months—radio and television commercials, weddings, picnics, funerals, solo recitals. Once his reputation grew, a synagogue invited him to play *Kol Nidrei* on Yom Kippur.

My mother, the major wage earner, endured the factory work although she was desperate to have a child. By 1952 my parents had saved enough money to purchase a tiny bungalow in Toronto—958 Castlefield Avenue—and, eight arduous years after their marriage, when I was born, Mama left the fur-finishing business. My arrival made the struggle for existence and all the fear and hardships worthwhile.

With a grand exhale my father concluded. The piercing declaration, fragments of scribbled notes, and piles of carefully preserved but tattered letters in the rattan trunk would take time to absorb. The mail from Budapest, dated 1949 through 1956, became glimmers of light, which illuminated my parents' refugee life. I never dreamed there might be information about missing relatives. The letters disclosed in-depth information—whispers I wasn't privy to as a child. Puzzling over the complexities, I began to unravel the enigma and ambiguities of my existence.

But before I could sift through more material, my investigations had to be suspended. Shortness of breath, exhaustion, and confusion intruded. My father's Parkinson's symptoms dramatically escalated, and the alarming indications of congestive heart failure filled us with dread.

***The young couple, Toronto, 1950.** They couldn't have been more delighted. Gyuri, with abundant tenderness, clasps Kato's hand as they lean into one another. There is ease and harmony, and not a hint of the demons that haunt them.*

Kato onboard the **Scythia*****, October 1948.*** *Later, I learned Canada had been my parents' third choice.*

Prison camp escape and despair. *When my father trudged barefoot through the forests of Yugoslavia to Romania, he encountered fellow cellist and Hungarian, Gabriel Magyar. Magyar's drawing conveys the bleak countryside, and the desolation."* Credit: Marianna Markus (married name Tiborné Tóth), niece of G. Magyar, from Budapest, Hungary. Gabriel Magyar was the cellist of the Hungarian String Quartet 1956–1972 and cello professor at the University of Illinois in Urbana.

Open-toed shoes, and a donated dress—Windsheim DP camp, 1946. *She's preparing a meal on a makeshift stove out in the open. Next photo: Kato is happily nuzzling one of the many children born in the DP camps. This child could very well have been me.*

Papa inadvertently rides a camel. *The unlikeliest scenario: Papa riding an animal, any animal. Papa chortling. Papa in a straw hat, tennis shoes, and a polo shirt. Papa in the desert.*

10

PAPA'S DEATH AND NOTES OF TRANSCENDENCE

My father died in his own bed on Thanksgiving night. Our family encircled him, agonizing over the futility, as if we could keep him within our embrace. Only a few weeks earlier, he had disclosed deeply hidden secrets submerged for all five decades of my life. Buoyed with hope for more details, I had asked Papa to consider a filmed interview. He acquiesced. I made the arrangements with a crew sensitive to recording a Holocaust survivor. No bright lights, no visible recording device or microphone, just a small camera with a soft-spoken interviewer. But it was not to be. At his bedside that November night, amid hushed caresses, I hummed a cherished cello melody and prepared to let him go.

"Janetkém. Long time not seen. How you keeping?" I busied myself shuffling papers in my parents' airless condominium, shouting to be heard over the sound of the television. Day after day, he watched the same inane programs instead of listening to one of hundreds of cello recordings that lined the living room walls. The jarring noise made my headache. Later, with a vague sense of foreboding, I understood how he missed the music. Each disc triggered yearning and a painful reminder of a lifetime of offering and receiving solace, which was no longer possible.

Despite the deafening laugh track, my father nodded off. Rising from my perch next to his wheelchair, my legs numb, my stomach grumbling, I slipped over to the TV to kill the volume and take a lungful of silence.

November 16. My last visit with my father, although I didn't know that yet. Rob hurried to North York General Hospital for his shift and Ian had gone out for a rare breath of air. We were alone together, my father and me. The previous night, I'd landed at the Toronto airport after hearing the news that my father's time might be at hand. He seemed to be asleep. I tiptoed to the kitchen to crack open a window, but a profusion of flowers impeded my access to the blinds. The orchid, its lavish blooms of iridescent purples, occupied most of the table.

As I gulped some icy mango juice (relished by my father), I fondled one of the petals and couldn't resist leaning down for a whiff of the earthy, moist loam. A mirage made an appearance, of Papa's magnificent garden behind my childhood home. Usually we weren't allowed to play in the backyard, just in case we might trample the grass or handle the murderous, hooked thorns of the rose garden. But one year, inexplicably, Papa sanctioned an ice rink. Rob and I ran back and forth from the house with our electric tea kettle, pouring boiling water onto the snow-covered grass. It took forever, but eventually we were able to skate on the bumpy surface. Photos of us both on our butts show no sign of either parent hovering uneasily to restrict us from this dangerous activity. My reveries returned to the abundant flowers, which surrounded the table.

Perhaps my playing would soothe my father. I unpacked the cello he bought for me with his life's savings, the cello I played when he tried to influence me as an uncooperative 20-year-old to audition and go to study with Starker, the instrument's appearance as familiar to me as my own skin—the deep golden luster of aged wood on the belly, each tree-ring growth visible, the heart-shaped ebony pegs, the flamed maple back. Papa's torso listed leftward over the armrest and his head lolled back. I pulled the cello toward me, sat very close, and played the opening of the Bach *Cello Suite No. 1*, the *Prelude*. With a steady oscillation of my bow, organ-like tones bloomed, the harmonies G and D echoing through the room. The triumphant climax imminent, I glanced at my father. His stooped and salivating figure urged my fingers to sprint faster across the strings, the arpeggiated figures vibrant. As the last chord dissipated, my father's sudden movement startled me. Sitting erect, eyes blazing, he said,

"Janetkém. What fingering you used in bar 9? And *why* you slowed down so much in the middle? At the long D? Play more in time! Play it again."

So I did, careful to keep the tempo steady in the middle of the piece.

Papa's mind had remained sharp, but by the third week of November, his thoughts seemed to hover and swoop gracefully. Mellow and charming asides revealed a refreshing sense of humor. We hired a palliative nurse to supplement the compassionate care of Ian and Cristy.

The nurse asked, "Is there anything I can do for you, George?"

"Make me rich," he replied.

My father turned to me, "What you think, a woman undoing my pants?"

He insisted that he had to go. He was late for work; he had to be somewhere. "I need a taxi."

The nurse asked, "To go where?"

"Getting ready to get young! But we have to go. Where do you want to go, Janetkém? Hungarian restaurants are all very bad."

My brother and the hospice nurse, Carla, a kindhearted, middle-aged woman with slender fingers, agreed our father could continue on like this for days or weeks. I dithered. Harris wanted me home for Thanksgiving. With barely a goodbye, I decided to leave rashly, thinking... I don't know what I was thinking. That in my dad's dream state he wouldn't miss me? Wouldn't notice? My stop home was short-lived. Rob called two days after my arrival in St. Paul.

"You'd better get here..." he said, "soon."

By the time I landed in Toronto, the situation was critical. Rob's wife, Sara, waited for me in her car, and when I sprinted out of the terminal, we drove as fast as we dared on the black, ice-covered roads down Yonge Street to my father's high-rise. Once there, the security guard opened the double doors with his ready smile, perhaps surprised I'd returned, again. But he must have noticed my heavy breathing, my face wet and pale.

Sara and I ran to the elevator and punched the up button—hard. As if that would make the elevator appear more quickly. The pings at each floor made 14 seem so distant. My heart thrashed erratically. *Please go faster. Please, please don't let me be too late.* I had not been there for my mother's death. The thought of losing my father without a final goodbye was too much to bear.

We burst into the apartment and hurried to the back bedroom. Propped up on several pillows, he lay in his hospital bed, an oxygen mask on his face. Looking terrified, he struggled to breathe.

My father had held on for a last glimpse of me. So relieved to see him, and to see that he could see me, I collapsed into sobs. Grasping his cold frail hand, I murmured into his ear. We held him: Rob and Sara; one of my nieces, Danielle; the caregivers, Ian, Cristy, and Juliana.

"I've never seen anyone in this state hang on so long," Rob whispered. This, from a doctor, gripped my heart.

Sara crawled into the bed and lay by my father's side. Leaning over the edge of the bed, I wrapped my arms around his shoulders purring I loved him. Thirty minutes later, on Thanksgiving evening, he passed away. My throat felt suctioned when, with a great whoosh, the door opened and the funeral home employees slid into the bedroom and out into the hallway with a stretcher, my father zipped up in a black rubber-boot-like body bag. Within a year, Rob and I had lost both parents, two more souls, among the last witnesses to an atrocious time in history.

I'm often asked to play at funerals. The melancholy, lustrous cello sound is a mystical intermediary and the regal tones imbued with the deceased's spirit offers a special succor. Performing at any funeral requires composure. Until that moment, I couldn't fathom summoning the requisite self-possession to perform at the funeral of my own parent. Nevertheless, I did. The Bach *Suite* I played for my father the previous week echoed with fleeting beauty in the funeral home.

The deceased must be buried as soon as possible—if feasible, the next day. It's Jewish law. Howie and Harris arrived the following morning. On that bitterly cold November afternoon, we drove to the cemetery where the frozen earth had allowed a fissure. It's a double plot, the headstone carved in the shape of a book open in the middle. Mama's side is not only topped with stones but strangely festooned. My father had continued to write voluminous love letters and to inscribe fancy cards for every occasion after my mother's death—Mother's Day, their anniversary, her birthday—sealed in gallon-sized Ziploc baggies and left leaning against the tombstone, buffeted in the wind, rain, and snow—a symbol of his undying love.

Somehow the coffin got stuck. The plot seemed too tight and narrow, but I knew it was an indication of Papa's reluctance to go. The rabbi said a brief prayer then handed Rob a trowel to drop the newly dug earth onto the coffin. The hollow thud pierced with finality.

According to Jewish custom, this last mitzvah is an act of respect for the dead and closure for the family. While the leaves blew in a frenzied dance, we took turns shoveling the earth into the recently dug gravesite, shivering in silence, using the back of the spade to symbolize our misgivings. My heels sank into the wet mud, and the air smelled of sorrow, damp with all the tears shed here and mixed with mine. I wrenched myself away from the mound of earth desolate, inconsolable, but at last with some understanding.

My parents were now eternally conjoined. They had always been enmeshed: my father easily unhinged, my mother, uncompromising, resilient, but mollifying. Because they were fiercely protective of each other, and of my brother and me, I perceived their behavior as weak, even reprehensible. Now their fortitude stuns me. They began anew, in a strange country, knowing no one, and through their musical talent, they were able to bring beauty and meaning to their lives and the lives of others. I didn't know then how my parents' story—a story of perseverance and fortitude, of love and hope, and of the transformative power of music would continue to shape my life. I promised my father I would persevere. I pledged to stand in his place, to commit myself to convey their story despite a deep-seated, lifelong disquiet about revealing myself as a Jew.

Entr'acte 2005

The cry of the shofar. To hear it is to draw me close. Generations of Jewish people are linked by the shofar blasts, which herald Rosh Hashana, the New Year. Three brilliant blasts of the ram's horn—*Te-ki-ah—She-va-rim—Teru-ah*, a long note, a series of short staccato notes, then a prolonged note—signify we can heal from brokenness to wholeness; we can be among those who will be tranquil and not tormented. God encourages us to see that a profound and lasting peace is possible if we remember, if we express regret, if we wrap ourselves in light and turn our faces to the future. In synagogues everywhere, we commemorate Rosh Hashana followed by the Days of Awe—ten days of spiritual yearning and reflection, which crescendo to the holiest day of the year for Jewish people—Yom Kippur.

In my family, the observance of Yom Kippur has an added dimension. My father would prepare for months practicing *Kol Nidrei*, his left hand fingering furiously on my mother's back, even in his sleep. On the eve of the Holy Day, he would ascend the bimah with his cello, his complexion strangely pallid. Once he set bow to string, the eloquent sounds enthralled, entreating us to open our hearts, to calm our uncertainties, to inhale serenity.

The lament mirrors the anguish of covenants breached because of religious persecution, those who had to say yes when they meant no. But even more important, we are duty-bound to ask for forgiveness from parents and children, friends and coworkers, acquaintances and neighbors, for wrongs committed here on earth, intentionally or not. On Yom Kippur our sincerity is tested.

For over three decades, I have had the awesome privilege of performing the ancient chant on the evening preceding the Day of Atonement—three times, opening three services at our Temple, to accommodate all the congregants. No one misses Yom Kippur.

As I concentrate on the gripping emotions of the piece, my heart swells and I'm mindful that the service begins with the *Kol Nidrei* prayer all over the globe. My father and his playing are with me. I hear the creamy tones of his cello, coaxing spaciousness, his voice soothing. My bow mournfully glides across the strings, and the rhapsodic cello sound resonates, then drifts into the spheres. "You made me weep" is my precious reward. Sitting directly in front of the ark containing the sacred hand-scribed Torah scrolls, my father and I have set the tone for this day of reflection for more than 60 years.

The following morning, on Yom Kippur day at Temple Israel between the morning service and the closing healing prayers at sundown, there is a study session for the congregation. This year, in 2003, Fr. Michael O'Connell, of the Basilica of St. Mary in Minneapolis, is the guest speaker. A familiar presence at our synagogue, he's a diminutive man with a sweet face, drooping jowls, and bushy eyebrows, prone to wearing slippers and wool vests. Our Rabbi, an attractive brunette, dons short-tailored skirts, shoes with impossibly high, spiked heels, and no stockings. They couldn't be more different. But the religious leaders share a common zeal for inclusion and cross-cultural conversation.

Two other guests join us, creative artists Stephen Paulus, composer of liturgical, choral, and orchestral works, and the distinguished poet and librettist Michael Dennis Browne. We jam the auditorium after the morning service. Once the chatter subsides, Father O'Connell recounts a story:

The basilica provides quarters, which are comfortable enough. His wood-paneled room has a fireplace, mismatched furniture, and plush if slightly worn carpeting. His closet, though, is a disaster. Piqued the door never quite closes, and its contents frequently spill onto the floor, he resolves one day to clean it out. The sorting takes several hours, until finally he reaches the deep recesses of the closet. There he finds a small, worn, leather-covered box. *What might this be, hidden for only the Lord knows how long?* Father O'Connell opens the unassuming box. A glimpse of the contents triggers a quick reflex. Snapping the container shut, he prepares to throw it away, certainly before anyone else catches sight of it. But he hesitates and pockets the noxious artifact into the folds of his cassock. Later, after many days of reflection and prayer, he knows what the Lord is calling him to do.

I am intrigued. What significance could this discovery have for us on Yom Kippur? Father O'Connell stands. He's brought the curio with him. Extending his arm, slowly turning so we all could see, he proffers the miniature, which is nestled in the furrows of his palm. The specter taunts. Within the box are a pair of fiendishly blue lapis lazuli cufflinks in the shape of swastikas.

We all need several moments to recover. "My first impulse," Father O'Connell says, "as you can well understand, was to throw this ghastly trinket away. But a Voice called me. This is not just some relic, with sentiments from somewhere across the ocean and decades ago. This is right here in your own space, in your own church."

The timing couldn't be more opportune. The sixtieth anniversary of the end of World War II and the liberation of the death camp Auschwitz in 2005 coincide with the fortieth anniversary of *Nostra aetate*, the Vatican's historical document of 1965, which represents a major shift in Roman Catholic teaching about Judaism and Christianity's relationship to it. The document decries contempt for the Jewish People and denounces perpetuation of the myth that the Jewish People are responsible for the death of Christ.

"Our two peoples are spiritually conjoined," he says, "as our elder brothers and sisters in faith." That's a foreign concept, I can't help thinking. Despite this decree, antisemitism is alive and well.

Father O'Connell's life's work has been to dispel

misunderstanding and mistrust between Jews and Christians. Galvanized by the swastika cuff links, he decided to approach the Basilica leadership with a proposal.

Believing art is a powerful messenger, which penetrates deeply and endures far beyond the spoken word, the church, *their* church, should commission two noted Minnesota artists to create a musical work—an oratorio for choir, vocal soloists, and full symphony orchestra as a memorial to the past and a legacy for future children. The composition, he hopes, will act as a conduit to transport audience members and participants toward understanding, foster a vision of peace, and perhaps redress wrongs against the Jewish People. He foresees young musicians performing the oratorio in the future to promulgate words of reconciliation.

The funds have been raised, he says. Paulus and Browne have accepted the commission, and the work will be a gift from the Basilica of St. Mary to Temple Israel and the Jewish community.

As the shock of the jeweled swastikas fades, I envision the groundbreaking project and imagine performing the oratorio as a member of the Minnesota Orchestra—unaware I'll have a prominent and much more challenging role in the program.

Stephen and Michael travel to the United States Holocaust Memorial Museum in Washington, DC, where they delve into the chasm of the Holocaust. Haunted by the photographs of murdered children, of towers of shoes, toys, and precious teddy bears left behind, and suitcases emptied of family mementos, Stephen chooses a title that reflects hope—*To Be Certain of the Dawn*—from the writings of the scholar and theologian Abraham Joshua Heschel. To anchor the work aurally to the Jewish People, Stephen imagines weaving the thrilling summons of the shofar and ancestral chants into the music. Father O'Connell's only request of the artists: the basilica's youth choir should be included in the work to musically depict the one million voiceless victims—the children who perished in the Holocaust.

A full year before the concert, Osmo Vänskä, our maestro, invites me to his studio at Orchestra Hall. Vänskä, a native of Finland, is a deeply religious man. He sits comfortably with his arms crossed, his expression intent. Multiple crinkles extend from his eyes, indicative of years of intense music making—his pale complexion and thinning blond hair in stark contrast to his dark framed glasses. Observing a collection of framed photos of barren hilltops, multiple snapshots of his three children, distinguished artists, and the maestro himself sitting helmetless on a motorcycle in skin-tight black leather, I sense a paradox. Not the straitlaced classical music conductor we've come to expect. Uncertain why I've been summoned, I ease myself into the plush white sofa opposite him.

He wastes no time. "Janet, the program in 2005, featuring Stephen's oratorio, will be called *Reflection and Liberation* and have a meditative theme. I would like you to perform Max Bruch's *Kol Nidrei* as the cello soloist on the first half of the program, immediately prior to the oratorio." I'm unnerved. An invitation to perform as soloist with a major orchestra is a rare honor, but instead of enthusiasm Osmo perceives my reticence. To fill the silence, he reaches for two bottles of water from the minibar. When I take the bottle and glass from him I spill all over myself and the white carpet. Stammering apologies, struggling to subdue the painful misgivings whirling through my mind, I can't help thinking: Osmo certainly has no clue about my background. How much involvement has he had with Jews? He's aware I perform the piece often, but does he understand the profound meaning of the work and its hallowed place in the synagogue? It's difficult to imagine playing *Kol Nidrei* in a church. Could I do it?

Osmo listens attentively as I attempt to convey my deep connection to the piece and the emotional undertones of the interpretation—the lamentation, which delineates the centuries of persecution of the Jewish People; the possibility of repentance; and the promise of redemption. After several moments of discourse and indecision I agree to perform.

The specter of the basilica haunts me for months, the hollow in the pit of my stomach far deeper than my normal pre-performance jitters. The orchestra has often performed Handel's *Messiah* there, but this is different. When I envision playing the revered piece so central to the Jewish faith in a Catholic church, I doubt I'm up to the task. *Had the piece ever been done in this setting? Would I be able to bare my soul and communicate the depth of feeling and ancient meaning of this work to people who have no prior history with it? Would the audience be hostile?* These are minor considerations compared with the larger issue of my fraught history as the heir of the Holocaust.

The fear of entering a church overwhelmed me as a child. Perhaps I thought I'd be struck down. Perhaps I thought we would always be universally vilified. Despite the enormous weight to live for those who perished, I understood my role—to exceed my parents' expectations and succeed in ways they were unable to. But even now, as an adult, I shrivel at the label—Jew. It's ingrained. I hear my mother saying, "We are Jews; we are always afraid. Never tell *anyvone* you are Jewish," as if even to us it's an expletive. Is this how other minorities feel? After years, I'm only beginning to decipher the incoherence of my upbringing, attributing my parents' behavior to experiences of persecution, restriction, humiliation, deprivation, and loss.

One night, after particularly troubled dreams, my churning wakes me. Google beckons. I type "*Kol Nidrei* in a church" into the search bar and a photograph appears—Pope John Paul II and Rav Elio Toaff, the chief rabbi of Italy, together, at the Vatican. In 1994, they presided over a special event—*Papal Concert to Commemorate the Shoah* to honor the six million Jews who were systematically annihilated by the Nazis. An audience of 7,500 guests, Holocaust survivors among them, attended the program conducted and conceived by Gilbert Levine with London's Royal Philharmonic Orchestra and cellist Lynn Harrell, one of my idols, who played the luminous solo. The program included the Jewish prayer for the dead, *Kaddish*, from Leonard

Bernstein *Symphony No. 3*. Heartened and with a plan, I sink back into bed.

Father O'Connell and I have a good relationship. He attends Yom Kippur services at Temple Israel every year, and he's heard me play *Kol Nidrei* many times. I make an appointment to see him. On the appointed day, a frosty January afternoon, I drive on snow-covered roads to the church. A receptionist leads me to Father O'Connell's quarters. He's sitting near the fireplace in deep contemplation but as soon as he sees me he smiles and with a gesture invites me to make myself comfortable. The embers from the hearth cast yellow hues and an ambiance of warmth. I feel enveloped by radiance. Still I hesitate: *What do I want to say? That I fear exposing myself as a Jew; fear playing in a church, especially this piece; that I'm uneasy about the reception?*

Father O'Connell senses my agitation. Without a word, he rises from his chair and reaches into his now nicely organized closet. Removing the little leather-covered box, he sits down very close to me and opens the box. There, gleaming in the reflection of the hearth, are the bright blue swastika cuff links. They're engraved, and the insignia of the manufacturer is prominently, proudly, imprinted in silver letters on the ivory silk lining of the box, evidently custom made in this country, and commissioned by Nazi devotees.

The malevolent symbol has caused so much pain, so much loss. The swastikas, especially so decoratively carved, strike like a dagger at my very core. I rage for my helpless parents—dispersed and separated from friends and family forever, the ashes of victims scattered in the wind.

"The opportunity is a blessing, Janet." Father O'Connell says, "You need not bear the burden of victimization you have inherited. Trust the voice of the cello to guide you."

Elie Wiesel's words echo in my heart:

> I swore never to be silent whenever and wherever human beings endure suffering and humiliation. We must always take sides. Neutrality helps the oppressor, never the victim. Silence encourages the tormentor, never the tormented. Sometimes we must interfere.

> When human lives are endangered, when human dignity is in jeopardy, national borders and sensitivities become irrelevant.
>
> —from Wiesel's Nobel Prize Acceptance Speech, 1986

My doubts begin to dissolve. Heady from the encounter, I resolve to perform for my parents, and for those who perished during those brutal years—for the righteous Gentiles who put themselves in harm's way to do the right thing, and for the larger goal of reconciliation. With this intention, I hope I will overcome the fear of being condemned for who I am.

The basilica is packed that November evening. As I walk out with the conductor and take my seat prominently in the center, in front of the orchestra, my breath falters, and for a moment my heart flutters like a trapped bird. Bowing my head, I feel embraced by the spirits of the victims. Motionless, transported by the ambience in the basilica, whispering strings quiver around me. As the introductory notes dissipate, a hush descends upon the audience. I inhale deeply, close my eyes, and begin to play *Kol Nidrei*. Sublime golden tones resound in the sacred space, which ascend effortlessly imparting a profound level of spiritual consciousness. The lament resolves, ending in utter serenity, and my cello breathes stillness. I am certain my father is with me.

After a pause, the stage is set for the oratorio. Three hundred participants, the orchestra, chorus, soloists, and the basilica youth choir take their places. Massive images of the children who vanished from the *shtetls* (villages) of Europe, photographs by Roman Vishniac, are projected onto scrims suspended from the ceiling. The photos and the text of the oratorio, in English, Hebrew, and German, call attention to the Holocaust's victimization of children. Vänskä enters while the basilica lights dim. He raises his arms, and as the audience quiets three brilliant sounds interject. The spine-shivering shofar blasts:

Te-ki-ah—She-va-rim—Teru-ah—
Sh'ma Yisrael! Adonai Eloheinu Adonai Echad!
Baruch shem kavod malchuto l'olam va'ed.

Hearing these words intoned takes me to another plane. The *Sh'ma* saved my father's life when he fled from the slave labor camp in Bor, Yugoslavia.

Vocal solos of transcendent beauty magically enthrall—soaring, tingling high notes, luxurious tenor notes, buttercream low notes. The violin bows tremble so fast the air turns to crystal, and the uplifting text is etched with divinity.

Create a great emptiness in me.
Send a wind.
Lay bare the branches.
Strip me of usual song.

Drop me like a stone,
send me down unknown paths,
send me into pathlessness,
into the lost places,
down into echoes
to where I hear
voices, but no words:
a place of weeping
below any of earth's waters.

Teshuvah, Teshuvah, Teshuvah.

The text praises:

We thank You for our hope.
We thank You for our dreams.
We thank You for sunlight.

And admonishes:

Jews may not be citizens.
Jews may not meet in public places.
Jews may not attend school.
Jews may not marry outside their race.
Jews may not imagine; may not dream.

Hundreds of tapers, which have been distributed to audience members, are lit during the *Veil of Tears*. The moment is reminiscent of the children's memorial at Yad Vashem, in Israel. And the children sing: "Where was the light we should have been?" Testimony of local Holocaust survivors, woven into the text of the libretto, exclaim,

"Why did I survive?
The Rabbi said: 'God kept you on earth to write the story.'" (*Henry Oertelt, survivor*)

"I dream of a sculpture of a
bird—I try to touch it. I wake
up touching the bird. I think
it is a miracle." (*Robert Fisch, survivor*)
A final prayer brings the oratorio to a close.

V'a havta le reacha kamocha.
(You should love your neighbor as yourself.)

Haunted and yet healed, the audience members hold their applause. Differences are extinguished by the mystical blessing of the music. For me, experiencing the sanctuary as a sacred, holy place, is transformative, and during the performance the attendees and I share unforgettable spiritual moments together. With reluctance, I leave the basilica, musing upon newfound sensibilities. I couldn't have known then, this sanctification, and life-changing departure from past perceptions, would become the impetus for metamorphosis.

Years later I receive a message from a woman whose name I don't recognize—Mairi Dorman Phaneuf, a cellist, who has been trying to track me down to learn the history of her instrument. When she purchased the cello from a prominent firm in New York, the dealer told her the cello had belonged to a Holocaust survivor. Months of research led Mairi to my father's name and then to mine.

> Janet, I'm so glad to find you on Facebook. I'm writing to you because I performed *Kol Nidrei* today at the Museum of Jewish Heritage—A Living Memorial to the Holocaust, in NYC. I was struck as I entered the building.
>
> What an honor to play this piece on your father's cello, and to explain the instrument's history to the audience—that the cello once belonged to a Holocaust survivor! I know I'll think of him again Friday on Yom Kippur.

When my father passed away in 2009, I lost track of the instrument after it was sold. Mairi performed in the museum where upstairs cherished artifacts are held: the photos with Leonard Bernstein, and the program to the 1948 concert my father played in Landsberg. With trembling fingers, I call her. During our conversation, Mairi mentions she plays *Kol Nidrei* every year at a prominent synagogue in New York on Yom Kippur. I'm astonished. After seven decades, the cello still sings.

My father's cello: the Panormo. *From the late 1700s, the flawless, textured varnish in golden hues gives no hint of its fraught history and the journey with my father to Canada.*

Father O'Connell's discovery of the swastika cufflinks, the symbol that brought and still brings so much heartache, became a divine catalyst.

To Be Certain of the Dawn ***performance Basilica of St. Mary, Minneapolis, 2005, by Stephen Paulus.*** *Since then, the piece has been recorded and performed more than two dozen times by college and professional orchestras across the country, and in Europe at the gates of concentration camps.* Credit: Photo by Michael Jensen; courtesy of the Minnesota Orchestra.

Basilica of St. Mary exterior. *Janet with the other soloist, clarinetist Burt Hara.*

PART IV

MY STORY

The sweetest music is not in the oratorio, but in the human voice when it speaks from its instant life tones of tenderness, truth, or courage.

What lies behind us and what lies before us are tiny matters, compared to what lies within us.

—Ralph Waldo Emerson (1803–1882)

11

A MUSICIAN AFRAID OF SOUND

Musicians often share this favorite anecdote. A violinist strolls down the streets of New York, carrying his instrument. Someone asks, "How do you get to Carnegie Hall? His answer: "Practice, practice, practice!" Even after numerous concerts there, we relish the opportunity to travel to New York, to perform on the venerable stage and savor the vapors of artists past. The 125-year-old ochre and terra cotta brick building, at 57th Street and Seventh Avenue, with its Italian renaissance façade, has attracted luminaries in every genre onstage and in the audience.

That year our schedule book announced: February 2010, Carnegie Hall presents the Minnesota Orchestra with conductor Osmo Vänskä. The program included a clamorous work. The elation I felt as a young cellist when I first performed in the famous auditorium rapidly changed to dread.

I'd hurtled through 2009. Looking after my father and learning my parents' story took precedence over everything. When he ceased to breathe, I began to. Submerged for a year, wallowing in avoidance, I surfaced. The grief engendered a newfound sense of awareness, and induced me to take on the mantle of living witness—to impart wisdom, and to speak truth through music as my parents did. But I could no longer deny the affliction that had assailed me for months.

Flying back and forth between St. Paul and Toronto, caretaking and doing research, I'd managed to practice, teach, perform countless concerts, and take care of my own family, with no time to look after myself. By the end of the year, after my father's death, music hurt. Sound hurt. Even my own voice hurt.

That February night at Carnegie Hall, we performed the epic choral piece *Kullervo* by Finnish composer Jean Sibelius—73 minutes of visceral and savage music for chorus, vocal soloists, and orchestra. An unforgettable evening. My ears throbbed—the pain like a knife pirouetting in my ear.

By spring my husband couldn't kiss me, even on the cheek, because the slightest touch set off ripples of pain in my head, my face, and my jaw. Every noise felt like an assault—a car alarm going off, a baby squealing, a group of giggling teens racing into the elevator. The ping of an ATM machine. Cicadas chirping. And especially the roar of a leaf blower. In sympathy, my husband and son tiptoed around me and recoiled with each ding. When I had to go out, I stuffed my ears with custom earplugs and wore noise-cancelling headphones, but they didn't help much. At any time, noise could bring me to my knees. How had I become a musician afraid of sound?

I should have realized my career ended that night—August 2006—an evening of Broadway favorites. I sat dead center in my spot as principal cello with the drum set, piano, electric guitars, keyboard, and conductor directly in front of me. During classical music performances, we rarely use microphones, but for our "pops" programs we present vocalists who do use them. This program featured three Broadway singers wearing brilliantly colored sequined outfits who pranced across the stage clutching their handheld microphones. Speakers blasted the music back onto the stage toward us, so the singers could hear themselves. The stage would hold three of these monitors for a typical non-classical concert, but this time there were eight black beasts, all the way across the stage—one of them no more than two feet from my left ear.

The speaker seemed perilously close. The stage manager said that with only one rehearsal immediately prior to the concert, they couldn't take time to make adjustments, so I stuffed my ears with musician's earplugs and swallowed my objections. I'd be a bit shell-shocked, I assumed, but nothing more than a temporary annoyance.

After an encore from *Phantom of the Opera* the program came to a close with thunderous applause. As I exited the stage, I experienced an excruciating sensation in my ears, which radiated down my neck and into my face, neck, tongue, teeth, and jaw. Pain hardly describes it. A fluttering sensation in my head made me feel faint.

I hurried out of the building to escape the backstage commotion —every noise, I quickly discovered, made it worse, including the sound of my own voice—and I drove home, barely able to see through my tears. That night I lay in bed praying the pain would simply subside overnight. But it didn't. The next morning, the schedule called for a three-hour dress rehearsal of the opera *Carmen*. I had spent hours perfecting my solos and preparing the cello parts for the entire section. During the rehearsal the voices of the singers, usually thrilling, triggered agony. I had to wear earplugs for a classical program for the first time in my long career.

Over the next few weeks, I saw otolaryngologists and neurologists, audiologists and neurotologists, heading from one appointment to another in a flurry of anxiety. I didn't tell my father, of course. The ENT exams, neurological assessments, and MRIs revealed no abnormalities—in fact, my hearing tests came back better than normal. I could actually be a spy, I heard so acutely. It seemed like the world's volume was stuck on high. The specialists recommended psychiatric tests. Perhaps meditation, relaxation exercises, or therapy would help, they told me.

Finally, one of the many doctors offered me a diagnosis: I had sustained an acoustic-shock injury to my left ear. Ear trauma is permanent, with no real treatment. He suggested I try to load up on vitamins, abstain from caffeine and alcohol, and keep my life as silent as possible to see if the pain would subside.

For three months, I withdrew to near-solitary confinement, and hoped healing might occur. I lived in silence. I avoided social situations. I restricted all communication to emails and texts. No TV, no radio, no grocery stores with their infernal scanners, no telephone (except to call home pretending all was well)—and, worst of all, no music.

The silent exile seemed to help. I returned to my position, with a major compromise: I would always have to wear a left earplug, and, for the time being, I'd be excused from performing in amplified programs. Soon, my brain adjusted to hearing with the earplug, and I adapted to this new normal. I believed my playing hadn't deteriorated, but as a precaution I kept all noisy activities at bay, even avoiding the car radio. At home, my husband did the vacuuming and the dishes as quietly as possible; my son kept his friends out of the house when I was home, and he listened to his music and the TV with headphones. My personality quelled. I became reclusive. Even walking my dog seemed risky. If I encountered a leaf blower, saw, or lawn mower, or children cackling with glee, I'd run in the opposite direction in a panic.

When I visited Toronto that year I alluded to headaches. My father agreed to turn the television off. Beneath it all ran an undercurrent of worry: would I be able to maintain the highest level of playing? Would the condition get worse? And most distressing of all, how could I admit to my father that I was losing the music?

Terrified to admit the health crisis ahead, I continued to play the full symphonic schedule with earplugs, flinching with every forte. But despite precautions my condition deteriorated, and in 2009 my right ear started to hurt too. After a second months-long round of doctor-hopping, I finally met an ENT who seemed to understand the disorder.

When the doctor sprinted through his explanation my first reaction was one of relief. *So,* I thought, *I'm not going crazy after all.* The severe pain, the dizziness, the fear of sound, and the strange fluttering sensation were caused by my brain processing noise much louder than it actually is.

Although hearing tests came back normal, I had developed the noise-induced ailment hyperacusis, an injury within the auditory system caused by intense and repeated exposure to high decibels. My brain perceived sound disproportionately. The result—an abnormal sensitivity, in other words the total breakdown of tolerance to all sound.

Hyperacusis may ensue after one ear-splitting sensorineural auditory event—an acoustic shock, as in my case, when the particularly loud concert torpedoed my ear—or the injury can occur from cumulative exposure to noise.

Onstage, during a classical or rock concert decibel levels often climb precipitously. And musicians do like to make a lot of noise. In fact, we would say only half in jest: fast is good, loud is better, fast and loud is best. Imagine being surrounded by 100 musicians wailing—the piccolo trilling, the brass blasting, the cymbals crashing.

The doctor told me prolonged exposure would only make things worse. With decades of hearing ahead of me, it would be best if I left my job and did something else, something quiet.

Do something else? Unthinkable. Playing the cello and making music *was* my life, the core of my identity. How could something I loved so much bring me such pain?

Entr'acte 1979

The Indianapolis Symphony season had ended in late May. Earlier in the year, I auditioned to participate in the famous several-week chamber music festival in Vermont during the summer, Marlboro Music Festival, and I was accepted. I couldn't wait. It would be a thrill to play with the elite artists and faculty who gather there to make music.

My first performance featured the lovely Dvořák *Serenade for Wind Instruments, cello, and double bass* in D Minor, Op. 44, which has a wonderful but tricky cello part. The next morning, the director of Marlboro, Frank Solomon, asked to see me. Not wasting a moment, he said, "I'd like to invite you to be the cellist for the "Music from Marlboro" concert tour in the fall." What an honor! The five-member ensemble would perform in some of the most important chamber music venues in the country. Would I be available?

Beyond excited, even before calling my parents, I telephoned the music director of the Indianapolis Symphony. Would he excuse me from the first 10 days of the season in September to perform in the Music from Marlboro tour? I was certain my appearances would reflect well on the orchestra as well as give me an opportunity for musical growth. He said no. He wouldn't release me.

Heartbroken, I considered my options. That year, a contract negotiating year for the orchestra, meant theoretically, I had no binding agreement. Thinking the Marlboro tour would be the experience of a lifetime, I submitted my resignation.

"Whaaatt? *Jaaannaaattte!* Don' quit your job!!"

"Mama." I assured her in a slightly cocky tone of voice, "I can *always* get another job." But in reality, orchestral openings do not occur all that often, especially leadership positions, and I knew the Minnesota Orchestra had already held auditions for associate principal cello without choosing anyone.

After three sets of tryouts without an outcome, the personnel manager of the Minnesota Orchestra had extended invitations to several assistant and associate principal cellists from around the country for an "invitation only" audition. Ron Balasz had called me. "Can you fly to Minneapolis next week?"

"What's the list?" I asked.

When he rattled off 10 or 12 excerpts from the standard orchestral repertoire, pieces that the audition committee might choose to hear, I thought, why not? Despite not having time to prepare as I normally would for an audition like this, I decided to try my luck.

Sitting on the stage of Orchestra Hall in Minneapolis behind a bulky, blue velvet screen on wheels, I played for the committee. They barked their requests—Strauss *Ein Heldenleben*, Mendelssohn *Scherzo* from *Midsummer Night's Dream*, Beethoven *Symphony* No. 5 slow movement section cello solos, Brahms *Piano Concerto* No. 2, the famous cello solo from the slow movement... So far so good. Then they asked for Tchaikovsky *Symphony* No. 4 slow movement—the cello melody in 5 flats—and they asked me to play it all on one string, which meant a leap into no-man's land. I missed it—the long shift. Then I missed it again. "Thank you," someone said and I was dismissed.

Afterwards, as we walked backstage my head hanging, Ron Balasz said, "Janet. I don't think you're ready for this orchestra."

"Oh yes, I am!" I countered, immediately regretting my loose tongue. I knew I'd try to return to audition truly primed. Hadn't I just blown it with my impudent remark?

Months later in addition to packing up my apartment in Indianapolis, I squeezed in every moment I could to practice for the Marlboro tour, as well as the cello audition that was bound to be announced soon. One of the chamber music pieces we'd be performing, the gorgeous Dvořák *Piano Quintet* No. 2, with the divine opening cello melody, is a lengthy work requiring lots of rehearsal.

When I arrived in New York for two weeks of intensive rehearsals, I learned that the Minnesota Orchestra would be again holding cello auditions, scheduled on the day before our first performance in New York City. There was no way around it. I had to make an appointment to see Frank Solomon.

During the elevator ride to his office on an upper floor of a towering high rise, my stomach sank. Solomon invited me into his musty office. I broached the subject in an unsteady voice, "Would you excuse me from a day of rehearsals in New York to fly to Minneapolis for the orchestra audition?"

With an expressionless face, without so much as a response, he motioned for me to take a seat in the anteroom.

Later I learned that as soon the office door closed behind me, Frank had called the Minnesota Orchestra.

"Hello. Personnel manager's office, Ron Balasz speaking."

"Ron. May I call you Ron? Does Janet have a prayer of winning the position during the upcoming cello auditions?"

Ron's response came back to bite me, "Neville Marriner is very particular… We've had several auditions, and you know she auditioned once and didn't even get past the *preliminary round*!"

Solomon summoned me. He said no. He wouldn't release me.

But I went anyway. The day of the audition I rehearsed for three hours in the morning in New York with the chamber ensemble, then I hurried to the airport, and flew with my cello to Minneapolis. I auditioned late afternoon once again behind the unwieldly, blue velvet screen. After I played, I waited in the cold, windowless dressing room, tired, thirsty, and hungry. Ron returned with a smile inviting me to play for the semi-finals. I clutched my cello, set up behind the screen, and this time I didn't miss any of the long leaps in the repertoire.

While I nervously waited, the committee deliberated. After perhaps 30 minutes, Ron appeared. Would I follow him to the stage to play for the finals, this time without a screen?

Somehow, despite exhaustion setting in, I mustered the strength and determination to play yet again. It helped to know that the committee liked my playing. Momentarily daunted by the group of distinguished looking graying gentlemen, I braved the grueling final round, one excerpt following another. All the solos and difficult passages in the repertoire went quite well, I thought, and I left the stage. Retiring to the tiny dressing room, I stared at the white, concrete walls, and the grey carpet, praying it was good enough.

By this time, it was well into the evening and I was starving. Ron reappeared. The competition was down to two candidates. Would I return to the stage to play some chamber music with the concertmaster and other principal string players? By luck the committee had chosen the Beethoven's *String Quartet* Op. 59 No. 1 to play with me, a piece I had performed many times.

When we took our seats, the violist turned to his colleagues and asked, "What's the tempo of this movement?"

Before the concertmaster could answer, my sassy tongue responded. "Oh! It goes like this," and I sang the opening melody. This time my retort didn't seem cocky. Neville's barely discernable smile reassured me as I led the ensemble with self-assurance.

After my final effort, time seemed to stand still. When Ron finally peeked inside the door of the warm-up room he had a big grin on his face. "Janet. You won the job. The committee would like to congratulate you."

A member of the orchestra invited me to his home to stay the night, and to enjoy the delicious Japanese dinner his wife had prepared. There was little time for sleep, though. Back on a plane by 7:00 am, once settled, with the cello in the seat beside me, I pulled my coat over my head, and wept with relief and elation the entire way back to New York.

The thrill sustained me through the evening performance. It was a coup for a very young woman to win a titled position in an elite orchestra. I would be the only woman sitting in the "inner circle" closest to the maestro. After years of practice, I had won the associate principal cello position of the Minnesota Orchestra. When I called my parents with the news, elated squeals could be heard all the way from Toronto to Minneapolis.

The ear has 20,000 to 30,000 hair cells, the nerve endings responsible for carrying the electrical impulses through the auditory nerve to the brain. These delicate receptors bend or flatten as sounds enter the ear, typically springing back to normal in a few hours or overnight. But over time, loud sounds can cause more permanent damage as hair cells lose their resilience. Frequent and intense exposure to noise will cause these receptors to flatten down, stiffen, and eventually break. The damage can interfere with the ability to determine the location of a sound, cause extreme sensitivity and pain, and make it impossible to discern language with background noise. One in 20 Americans, or 48 million people, report some degree of hearing impairment.

An alarming statistic—but hearing protection isn't a health habit that's often discussed. The National Institute for Occupational Safety and Health (NIOSH) and the Centers for Disease Control cap the continuous exposure to decibel levels at 85 decibels (dB) for an eight-hour day. Decibels work logarithmically: permissible exposure times must be halved for each increase of three decibels. Any exposure above 115 decibels, even for a few seconds, is unsafe. But life has become toxically noisy. City traffic can reach 85 dB. Restaurant racket exceeds 100 dB. At its peak, a full orchestra measures 120 decibels, the volume of a rock concert or jackhammer—and the exposure time and the proximity to the sound exponentially compound the risk of damage. In crowded spaces, such as a stadium, the sound can be debilitating—a Kansas City game in 2013 made the Guinness Book of World Records with "record-breaking" noise clocked at an astonishing 137.5 dB. It's important to know the highest frequencies are the most injurious.

Still, people willfully jeopardize their hearing every day. Sound exposure is cumulative, creeping up on those who listen to music with ear buds for hours at a time or multiple times a day. According to the American Medical Association, one in five teens now suffers from hearing damage and cannot hear whispers, raindrops, or consonants. Tinnitus or the constant "ringing" or roaring in your ears affects millions of young people. Noise, not ageing, is the leading cause of permanent hearing injury—and even a small amount of hearing loss can have a profound, negative effect on comprehension and social development. Untreated, hearing impairment can affect brain function and is associated with early-onset dementia.

In hindsight, continuing my full schedule had been reckless. I continued to play solos, to teach, and to play. The orchestra's schedule in 2010 included several cacophonous and massive works and soon entering Orchestra Hall for rehearsals without earplugs became intolerable. Cowering in a corner of the building to avoid sound, I wondered if my colleagues thought I was being antisocial. Ignoring the doctor's advice, and the pain, I persevered. Although I yearned for silence, I could not imagine being away from people, away from the cello, away from life as I knew it. My inviolable promise to my father spurred and sustained me.

Who was I without the cello?

Playing on the stage of Carnegie Hall. Credit: Photo by Stephanie Berger; courtesy of the Minnesota Orchestra.

Janet's last concert. *This appearance in Amsterdam's Concertgebouw, with violin soloist Gil Shaham, would be my last with the Minnesota Orchestra—or any orchestra.* Credit: Photo by Greg Hegleson; courtesy of the Minnesota Orchestra.

On tour with the Minnesota Orchestra. *Osmo Vänskä, our music director, gestures for the orchestra to stand.* Credit: Photo by Greg Hegleson; courtesy of the Minnesota Orchestra.

12

PILGRIMAGE

Our orchestra prepared for a three-week tour of Europe's most prestigious concert halls in August 2010—Philharmonie in Berlin, the Concertgebouw in Amsterdam, Musikverein in Vienna, and Royal Albert Hall in London, the pinnacle of any musician's career. A few weeks of vacation followed the tour, an opportunity to make a pilgrimage to the places my father performed. I couldn't miss that! Surely, I would be able to hang on at least a few more months.

The programs on tour included Beethoven's *Symphony No. 9*, with its famous *Ode to Joy*, which calls for massive forces onstage: a 250-voice chorus, vocal soloists, and more than 100 orchestra members.

Traveling from country to country, always hectic even when you're not on tour with an orchestra, became complicated by my affliction. Flight attendants reprimanded me for wearing enormous noise-cancelling headphones. I cowered in city traffic, hid in hotel rooms, writhed through concerts. Anxiously penciling little marks onto the sheet music, I noted where there might be enough time to put in earplugs and, if there was a solo, when to remove them, often glancing into the audience, paranoid that all the thousands of people in the hall noticed. I had to resort to heavy-duty earplugs, all the time. Deeply disturbing thoughts plagued me. *What kind of a musician am I now? The conductor and my colleagues must be able to hear a difference in my playing.*

The worst pain struck during one of the last performances, which took place in London's most iconic venue Royal Albert Hall, at the preeminent festival The Proms. The elliptical, red granite building holds more than 5,000 audience members and the triumph, tumult, and jubilation was paralyzing. Weeping afterward in the recesses of the dressing room backstage, I knew I was done. The final concert, in Amsterdam, would be my last as an orchestral musician.

My upcoming pilgrimage to find the places my father had performed would now serve two purposes—to dig much deeper into my parents' past and to ask: What future did I have without music?

In preparation for Europe, I reviewed what I had learned from my parents and made note of the unanswered questions. Although I had the address of the apartment where my parents lived in Munich on Jahnstrasse, information about the places my father performed in Bavaria was negligible. Nonetheless, I would definitely visit at least the St. Ottilien Monastery, which became the survivors' hospital, located 45 minutes by car west of Munich, between Munich and Landsberg.

The two displaced persons' camps where my father performed as a member of the Jewish Orchestra with Leonard Bernstein, Landsberg and Feldafing, had been dismantled, but I'd heard of several memorials in both towns. And just 30 kilometers [19 miles] northeast, Dachau, a small suburb of Munich, would be my first tour of a concentration camp. After viewing scores of films and documentaries, and reading innumerable stories, I felt compelled to experience a camp in person, especially Dachau, where the seeds were planted to address the "Jewish Question" and the annihilation of an entire people.

My parents, ironically enough after liberation, had to make their way to Germany, the country of the perpetrators, to wait for appropriate papers to leave Europe. Still, my own nerves almost overwhelmed me. How would I handle being alone in Munich, with virtually no knowledge of the language, no idea how I would get around the city, and with apprehension about being a Jew in Germany? Howie and Harris joined me for the tour performances, sightseeing in London and Amsterdam, and the first leg of my odyssey to Budapest. They then had to leave Europe to return home in time for Labor Day and the start of the school year.

With the physical agony of performing behind me, wearing earplugs at all times, we proceeded on the journey. In truth, I didn't know what I was seeking; I didn't know if I was running from or toward a new path.

Budapest

My roots beckoned. I looked forward to the first part of the trip: a reunion with my cousin Mihály (Misi), the son of my mother's first cousin Trudy, and his daughters, Andrea and Monika; introducing my 16-year-old son to them for the first time; and exploring Budapest. In the midst of laughter, gastronomic indulgences, and sightseeing, there would be poignant discoveries. On September 6, 2010, just after the tour ended, Misi picked us up in his tiny vehicle to take us to his home, the same home his family had owned and lived in since before the war. He fumbled with a tarnished key. The one modest room houses a tiny kitchen and a cubicle of a bathroom. A curtain is drawn in the evening to create a bedroom.

Hungarians love to eat. As soon as we entered, we inhaled delicious aromas—garlic, paprika, onions, the smell of freshly baked bread. Misi served a cold supper of Hungarian salami, *körözött*, a savory cheese spread, pâté, cucumber salad, thick rye bread, and an assortment of favorite desserts—*beigli*, a sweet dough filled with ground walnut or poppy seed, and chestnut purée, overflowing with whipped cream. (My mother often reminisced about the vendors who sold sweet earthy-tasting roasted chestnuts on the streets of Budapest when she was growing up.)

Misi is as short as I am, a nonstop smoker, and has the beginnings of a paunch. Although he speaks no English, the luster in eyes and his impish expression convey a droll sense of humor. Somehow, he has maintained a positive attitude to life despite hardships during the communist regime. He makes a living weaving sweaters, though trained as an airplane mechanic.

We hadn't seen Andrea in more than a decade—a captivating young woman, with a radiant smile, endearing attempts to speak English, and striking looks. Her thick hair draped over her neck in riotous waves. Andrea moved in with her sister so we could stay in her apartment and really, Howie didn't mind the six-floor climb with our suitcases. The next day, we were ready to explore. Andrea took a half day from her job to help me find my father's family apartment. No small feat! We drove back and forth, up and down the ancient and narrow one-way streets, until we finally found Lónyay Utca. Howie's parking karma, which always works in the US, was in fine form in Budapest. A tiny opening appeared. We got out of the car and started to walk the several blocks toward my father's address, number 42.

Many of the buildings pockmarked by bullets unsettled me—evidence of the siege 65 years before—and restoration is still incomplete. I noticed a gaping hole ahead. *Would his building be there?* My pace increased. Then I saw my father's apartment building, which just skirts the edge of the excavation project. I took several photos of the street signs, IX. Ker. Ferencváros, Lónyay Utca 34 46, indicating the district as well as the avenue—Ninth District, City of Francis, Lónyay Street. I took a snapshot of the hall and interior courtyard of the apartment building and the sign over the doorway: "*Respectable tenants. Clean house.*" In 1944, were my father's family considered "decent, honest, or respectable" residents?

Afterward, on our own for a few hours, we hurried over to Gerbeaud, one of the most legendary pastry cafés in Budapest. With more than 150 years of history, the elegant, gilded tables, surrounded by glass cases of confections, amazed my son—*dobos, krémes* oozing with vanilla cream custard, sandwiched between a flaky pastry, the famous *Eszterházy* torte, several flavors of strudel, layer cakes, and truffles, the mouth-watering smell of chocolate, with tinges of vanilla saturating the air. He didn't ogle the sparking chandeliers, velvet drapery, and silk-carpeted walls as Howie and I did. After the war, the state took the establishment over; not until 1984 could the family purchase the café and restore their name.

I ordered several luscious brunch specialties for us—dumplings stuffed with meat and sauerkraut and doused with a mushroom sauce, chunks of goulash on thick toasted and buttered rolls, an oblong platter of pastries with dollops of apricot and vanilla sauce, and for me, Gerbeaud's extraordinarily pungent coffee. My fluent Hungarian amused them. Howie and Harris had never heard me speak the language—not an easy one to learn if you're not a native speaker. Belonging to the Finno-Ugric branch of Uralic languages, it is unrelated to virtually every other language except Finnish (very distantly). Unlike most alphabets, which contain five to seven vowels, Hungarian uses 14 vowels and the alphabet contains 44 letters. Howie often says the language sounds as if the speaker is always complaining. Perhaps they are, I think.

Both my parents studied at the famed Liszt Academy. In the heart of the city, the striking neo-Renaissance edifice eclipses everything nearby. Between massive columns, a bust of Liszt presides over the porte cochere. Inside, my every sense was aroused by the aura of splendid sonorities, the aroma of emerald and gold, mahogany and velvet, the riot of emerald variegated marble walls. And the gold medallions embedded in each jade tile, aquamarine tiled floors, and an embrace of gold and amber cornices.

I heard mellifluous tones, fingers scurrying along a violin fingerboard. I heard a coloratura soprano straining to master a high C, her vocal timbre thinning with each attempt. I heard the hostile beat of a metronome driving a pianist through thunderous arpeggios. I heard the breakneck tempos and pulsating polyrhythms of cool jazz 5/4, 9/8, 6/4, the sounds that emanate from every surface even today.

To walk onto the stage in the main concert hall with its inlaid balconies, decorative ebony walls, and a massive organ, is to encounter the phantoms of notable alumni and teachers: composers Béla Bartók, Zoltán Kodály, and György Ligeti; maestros George

(György) Szell, Eugene Ormandy, George Solti, Fritz Reiner, István Kertész, and Antal Doráti; pianists András Schiff, Franz Liszt, Lili Kraus; soprano Éva Marton (I am leaving out so many others), my mentor, pianist György Sebök, and my cello teacher János Starker, as well as famous Hungarian gypsy, folk, and jazz bands. Why so many? My teacher had a theory. The Hungarian language has a unique feature. Each first syllable of every word is accented. Ingrained at infancy, Starker believed this incessant cadence instills a sense of musicality and rhythm in Hungarians.

I wandered the halls and imagined my young parents, here. When my father first spied the beautiful young singer and pianist and fell in love. Where they encountered strict teachers; where they practiced hours every day to perfect their fingerings, sound quality, ease of expression, and depth of emotion. They didn't know then how well their dedication would serve them in the years ahead.

Later that day, Misi drove us to the Jewish cemetery to visit Trudy's gravesite, the first of many somber moments. Located a fair distance outside of the city in an industrial area, the *Kozma Utcai Izraelita Temető* (Kozma Street Jewish Cemetery), one of the largest Jewish cemeteries in Europe, dated from the early 1890s, is now more than two thirds overgrown by vegetation, vines, and bushes, and crowded with crumbling and shattered headstones. The burial grounds are usually unattended and closed for visitors. An unexpectedly poignant Holocaust Memorial dominates with several white marble columns arranged alphabetically. Each column represents a concentration camp and is inscribed with names carved in neat rows on the marble of individuals who are known to have perished in those camps. There is a separate monument in tribute to victims who were murdered without a trace:

"IN MEMORY OF HUNDREDS OF THOUSANDS OF OUR NAMELESS MARTYRS."

I inched closer to one of the monoliths, dodging rocks, trying not to step on any fragments of headstones and looked up. Hand-scrawled and barely legible, between the engraved names, in pen, pencil, razor-sharp knives, anything (*fingernails,* I wondered?), more names had been scratched onto the pillars. Dozens of names—of vanished loved ones, disclosed sometime after the installation of the marble columns. Overcome, I had to turn away.

We walked through dense growth to get to Trudy's grave. Her mother, Misi's grandmother, perished in Auschwitz.

Years before, when I'd already left home, my parents had saved enough money to bring Trudy to Toronto for a visit. It had been decades since my mother had seen her cousin. They were so alike—ample flesh on their small frames, their hand gestures barely keeping up with their tongues, and facial expressions revealing every emotion. But after the elation of the first few days, Trudy's mood plummeted. Perhaps she couldn't reconcile the struggles of her life in Hungary with the freedoms of our Canada.

I'd heard about life behind the Iron Curtain. My uncle Tibi often would say, only half in jest, that the Soviets behaved worse than the Nazis. The government requisitioned larger properties. They ordered Trudy to divide her house in two and accept another family into the other half. A tiny refrigerator amounted to an entire year's pay. Tremendous shortages of food and housing necessitated constant hustling to make ends meet, and travel restrictions, secrecy and censorship, and the constant specter of deportation to the Russian gulag, never strayed from her thoughts. Expressing one's opinion freely is a luxury we rarely contemplate in this country. But for my parents' courageous decision to emigrate this could have been their life and mine.

The *Dohány Templom,* now named "the Great Synagogue," the largest synagogue in Europe and one of the most impressive sights in Budapest, also houses the Hungarian Jewish Museum. The spectacular Moorish building of pink, turquoise, and gold Byzantine decor, and an exterior of alternating rows of red and ochre brick in Picassoesque stripes, is always crowded with visitors. Gilded onion-shaped twin towers dominate. The exquisite details sparkle in the sunshine—eight-pointed stars, rose windows, stained glass, and gold and red filigree that looks like mosaic.

After the *Nyilas* party bombed the synagogue in 1939, it was used as a stable. What we see today is the result of a massive reconstruction begun in the 1990s, funded in part by Estée Lauder, co-founder of the international cosmetics company and influential business expert (her parents were Hungarian Jewish immigrants). In 1944, one of the Jewish ghettos was located right here, in the synagogue, where the *Nyilas* trapped Irma, my mother's mother.

The interior glows pink. Massive chandeliers hang from the inlaid ceiling. I walked along the mosaic floor to the front, as my relatives had in the past, toward the ark to get a better look. The gold and cerulean blues shimmered. An imposing 5,000 pipe organ from 1859, on which composers Camille Saint-Saëns and Franz Liszt performed, is still played today. I placed my hands on the wrought iron gate. No doubt my father took hesitant steps as he ascended the bimah to say the blessings during his bar mitzvah in 1935 when he was 13, the ceremony that formally welcomes a Jewish boy into the faith as a man. The entire community's respirations slithered into my soul.

One of the most heroic figures of the Holocaust, a man who saved many thousands of lives, is honored in the back courtyard of the synagogue. Raoul Wallenberg, a Swedish diplomat, traveled to Budapest in July 1944 determined to save the last major Jewish population of Europe. He enlisted a team who forged and issued Swedish documents to imperiled Hungarian Jews. Wallenberg rescued thousands with his fearlessness, even going so far as to leap into the frigid waters of the Danube himself to save 80 drowning Jews. Feverishly he purchased abandoned property, slapped a Swedish flag on the exterior and pronounced them protected Swedish embassies—a safe haven for beleaguered Jews at least for a night or two. During the last days of the siege he personally intervened to prevent the planned destruction of the ghetto. My mother and grandmother took refuge in Swedish safe houses with false identity papers.

In Raoul Wallenberg Park, in the courtyard behind the synagogue, a large memorial surrounded by stones is dedicated to his valiant efforts. Emblematic of the ancient Jewish custom, we place a pebble on the headstone to indicate we've visited the grave to pay our respects. There is further symbolism. Unlike flowers, stones represent permanence. The soul of the departed is, at least for a time, weighed down on earth, ensuring a lasting presence in our memory. In the biblical era, rocks were often the only marker to indicate the final resting place of the deceased. A disturbing thought—the countless mass graves, remains in cinders, and bones crushed into pits during the Holocaust forever denies the solace of visiting any sacred spot to pray for and remember our loved ones.

Four red marble plates commemorate 240 non-Jewish Hungarians who also saved Jewish people during the Holocaust.

The centerpiece of the park, the Tree of Life Holocaust Memorial, designed by Imre Varga in 1991, sponsored by the Emanuel Foundation of New York, was founded by the actor Tony Curtis to honor his Hungarian-born father, Emanuel Schwartz. A towering stainless-steel willow represents an overturned menorah, a striking symbol of mourning—each leaf of the weeping tree inscribed with the name of a victim. Shielded by the canopy of silver is a mass tomb. Synagogues typically do not house graveyards, but since 2,000 people perished here in the ghetto from 1944 to 1945, it has been preserved as hallowed ground.

We explored the edifice for many hours. The sacred space, not so long ago soiled by horse manure, throbs with a palpable descant.

Today Budapest boasts a community of approximately 100,000 Jewish citizens with some 20 synagogues, although many Hungarian Jews are unaffiliated, and intermarriage is widespread. The pretense of acceptance has been short-lived. The fledgling community lives in fear after a spate of antisemitic incidents from Neo-Nazi extremists and adherents to the right-wing *Jobbik* party. Do they wonder if it's time to flee again? Budapest's hypnotic effect has its hold on me, too —a peculiar brew—equally beguiling and repugnant.

We strolled along the Danube for the spectacular scenery and views of the eight ornamental bridges, all of which were blown up by retreating German troops and rebuilt years later, but our purpose was to see the "Shoes on the Danube Promenade." Behind us stood the magnificent parliament building, which from a distance looked like lace. On a buoyant summer day with a luminous sky, how can one make sense of the unimaginable? On these very shores, forced to strip naked, forced to face the river, the captive Jews were shot, the discharge propelling them into the water, which swiftly sucked the bodies into the depths.

Sixty pairs of bronze shoes are rooted to the ledge to memorialize the spot. Some are stylish. Some are threadbare. Some are tiny. There is no handrail. They rest at the very edge, facing the swirling river. I noticed a pair of stylish open-toed sandals, the back strap hastily flung off, fashionable pumps, men's boots ripped open, tongues pulled forward, and a solitary red rose laid next to a child's high-topped laced shoes, worn at the toes. Do musicians who, like me, annually perform the famous waltz by Johann Strauss II—*The Beautiful Blue Danube*—and tourists who sail on cruise boats know this despicable history? I gazed into the depths of the watery tomb mumbling a mournful prayer to the bones beneath.

Behind the sculpture created by Gyula Pauer and conceptualized by the filmmaker Can Togay lies a stone bench with cast iron signs in Hungarian, English, and Hebrew: "To the memory of the victims shot into the Danube by Arrow Cross militiamen in 1944–45. Erected 16 April 2005."

|

That night my dreams are disturbed: A man races to the shores of the Danube. In the piercing December wind, a group of naked Jews huddles, mostly women and children, wrenched from their beds in the middle of the night. Shoes and nightclothes thrust in a pile. The *Nyilas* henchmen brandish their rifles. The Jews are chained together in threes. No sense wasting bullets. Shoot the middle Jew and the impact will pull the others down into the blue-black icy waters. The hoodlums scream, "Dirty Jews, filthy pigs, you are coming with us!"

The victims trudge down the street to the shores of the river. Resistance is futile. Stragglers are shot.

A voice sounds. "Halt! I am Raoul Wallenberg from the Swedish Embassy. These people are Swedish citizens. You cannot touch them." A wiry, tenacious man hurries down the hill to the hellish scene. His sheer bravado causes the brutes to hesitate. Grabbing a pair of frail icy hands, he leads them away from the death ledge.

The river plunge averted, my eyes open. Next to me is my snoring husband swaddled in thick quilts and soft sheets. I remember listening to the audiotape—my mother's voice, telling her story. Chilling. One of the Jews on the shores of the Danube could have been my mother.

We spent our last day wandering along the elegant boulevard Andrássy Avenue. Howie and I had strolled the wide tree-lined boulevards bustling with city traffic a number of years ago. We will again relish the grandeur of the neo-Renaissance mansions and stone façades, the chic boutiques and mouth-watering pastry shops, the fine china shop Herend, and the richly decorated Opera House. Statues of celebrated composers adorn the façade. But this time, for me, the address loomed—60 Andrássy Street, Nazi and *Nyilas* headquarters. The brochures boast: A Wonderful Museum of Terror. Huge letters on the outside of the building—TERROR MUSEUM—leave no doubt as to what went on in this building. We hastened away. Hounded by morbid fascination, in the comfort of the apartment, I steeled myself to learn more.

Budapest has the highest number of museums per capita in Europe. The Terror Museum is the most visited. Portraits of the victims in black oval frames hang outside, affixed to the stone facade. Inside, the exhibits related to both the fascist and communist regimes memorialize the victims—those detained, interrogated, tortured, or killed in the building, a towering wall insufficient to display all the victims' photographs. The three-minute plunge in the elevator sinks into the bowels of the edifice. Slamming the computer lid down, I tried not to imagine my mother on the descent to the chambers below, where wails went unanswered, where voices were silenced.

She was taken here, to Number 60. Did she evade the elevator? Perhaps my mother encountered a handsome young guard who let her go. Perhaps she used her good looks and bartered for her freedom.

Some historians believe the museum portrays Hungary as the victim of foreign occupiers, rather than the perpetrators they were. And it appears, at least to me, more space is dedicated to the communist terror than the fascist one. The argument that a Holocaust museum has been built in the city doesn't convince me. Consideration of atrocities toward the Jewish People are given short shrift.

Despite the traumas my parents suffered, Budapest, the bedrock of my heritage, feels like home to me. And I believe they, who were staunchly Hungarian, who had been culturally adrift as Canadian newcomers, would have relished the visit. My father returned to Budapest only once, on tour with the Toronto Symphony. I know he visited Misi and Trudy and went to his old apartment on Lónyay Utca, but he never shared his feelings about being there.

The following day, Misi drove Howie and Harris to the airport, while Andrea took me to the train station for my trek to Germany. A porter indicated I could wait in a private business-class lounge with free coffee and just the treat I needed, a chocolate croissant. When the train pulled in, he let me know and even helped me find the right car and my assigned seat. Quite civilized, I thought, unlike previous experiences in Hungary during the Soviet-imposed People's Republic, when everyone endured scrutiny, when every corner was examined, and everything was suspect. An inspection came to mind during a previous trip—a flashlight wielded like a weapon directly and deliberately in my face and down my chest, the contents of my purse dumped beside me, despite a Canadian passport. Did my Hungarian name cause extra scrutiny? Or that I'm a Jew? I shook myself out of sinister reveries and took my seat on the train. Communist rule finally ended in 1989, followed by full Soviet withdrawal in 1990.

Emotional as always, I shed some tears when the train left the station. Goodbyes are difficult, or had I qualms about arriving alone in Germany? My father eschewed separation. To be alone the worst possible fate. I realize with a jolt the anxiety is entrenched in me.

A somber visit to the Kozma Street Jewish Cemetery. *I could not hold back to tears at the sight of this heartbreaking memorial to the hundreds of thousands who perished in the Shoah.*

One of the pillars dedicated to Holocaust victims. *Opened in 1891, the Kozma Street Cemetery is the oldest in Budapest and one of the largest in Europe with over 300,000 graves, many submerged under dense foliage after decades of neglect.*

The Dohány Street Great Synagogue. *Opened in 1859, the Moorish building, with rare rose shaped and stained-glass windows.*

Tree of Life monument to the victims of the Holocaust in Raoul Wallenberg Holocaust Memorial Park. Credit: Budapest, Hungary - 19.10.2019: "Tree of Life" monument to the victims of the Holocaust in Raoul Wallenberg Holocaust Memorial Park —The Dohány Street Synagogue, Great (Tabakgasse) Synagogue; Jordan Joy from Shutterstock ID: 1635413551.

Standing near the bimah. *Built in 1859 to seat 3,000 worshippers, the robust community now gone, a babble of languages can be heard as the tour guides lead visitors through the ornate compound. I sense my father's presence as I approach the bimah to see the arc holding the Torah Scrolls, where 75 years before my father had his Bar Mitzvah.*

Entr'acte 1957

The photograph has yellowed. Risking more fissures, handling it gingerly, I gaze at the fragile document—a glimpse conjures my younger self and my elegant mom. The scene is tranquil. My face inclined lightly grazes Mama's right arm as she lights the candles—not your typical American frosted cake. This torte is home baked, ornately decorated, and Hungarian of course—with a creamy chocolate buttercream, sandwiched between layers of sponge cake, glazed with apricot jam (my father's favorite) and garnished with melted chocolate. There are pretty little puffs of whipped cream encircling each of the five birthday candles. It floats on the exquisite white lace tablecloth.

I remember the navy-blue dress my mother is wearing, the one with tiny white polka dots, a crisscross bodice and deep V neckline, which accentuates her curvaceous figure. Mama's raven hair is swept up so we can see her pearlescent skin, the white-beaded choker and matching earrings. This, for a fifth birthday gathering at home.

My dress is all satin and tulle. A too wide collar drifts off my shoulders. My hair is cut short, haphazardly, with home scissors, and my arms awkwardly hang by my sides.

We gaze intently at the candles, seemingly unaware of anything but each other. The delicate beauty of the photo belies my mother's resilience and the deeper meaning, which I am aware of now from my present-day perspective.

What must it have meant to her to be able to celebrate with an Eszterházy Torte—named after a 19th-century prince of the Austro-Hungarian Empire—in Canada, her new home, with her daughter—the daughter she might never have had, the daughter she hadn't dared envision just a few years ago, 17 and alone, desperate to survive, starving, emaciated, cowering in deserted tunnels and bombed buildings barely daring to breathe lest she be discovered by the Nazis.

I scrutinize the photo, searching for clues. With pursed lips and suddenly clammy hands, I undress, slip on the navy-blue polka dot dress, which still hangs in my closet, and wonder: how can she look so unscathed? How did she start anew, never looking back, never remembering, never alluding to those harrowing years?

My mother's overprotectiveness makes sense now. I perceived a deep wound only my impeccable behavior could salve. As the living, breathing embodiment of survival, I tried not to cause them further pain, resolved to become what they couldn't be, attempted to make up for their losses and fulfill their dreams.

As the years passed, it became more and more difficult to live up to expectations. It was never enough. I had become an accomplished professional musician, married well, had a beautiful son. But I had left them by moving away. Life had become a perpetual farewell.

Eszterházy Torte. Mama used to say that the greatest pastries originate from Hungary.

Munich

Once over the border, lush golden pastures brim with windmills; on the hills perch neat elfin houses; cows curl their tongues around the grass among rows of groomed fields. Modern highways and developed towns line the autobahn. I imagine my parents traveling on this route from Budapest to Vienna beneath the hay under which they were hidden in the back of a Russian truck, probably overcome with anxiety. When they left home for a new life, they would have seen quite a different landscape than I, if they could have peeked. No doubt their fear of being stopped at the border, not the scenery, occupied their thoughts. The journey, in 1946, would have been dreadful enough, even though by that time locked cattle cars no longer transported people to unknown destinations. But the streets teemed with refugees.

The train reached the Vienna South Station. I glimpsed stately historic buildings as well as trim balconies, contemporary high-rises, and eclectic graffiti on tunnel walls. A mélange of people boarded—multicultural, young and old, every shade of skin color, and conversations in various languages except for Hungarian. I quickly felt unmoored.

We pulled into the station in Munich on time. Several weeks prior, I had booked a favorite American hotel in Munich, thinking the familiarity of a Marriott in a quiet residential area would ease some of my discomfort at being in Germany, and I needed a quiet haven from noise. It turned out to be a fortuitous choice.

I struggled with my suitcase in the massive train station while zillions of people rushed by. Suddenly uncertain of myself, I had difficulty figuring out where to find the taxi queue. The cabdriver didn't speak English. Did he understand I would need to pay by credit card?

The gloomy, drizzly weather descended upon me. The Munich Marriott seemed to be remote from the center—isolated from what I would later discover is an energetic and bustling city that pulsates with people barreling down the streets, driving cars, and riding bicycles. Too tired to explore, I eased myself into bed under the plush comforter and ordered room service.

In the morning, feeling a bit more confident, I decided to attempt the underground to find the Jewish Museum and new Orthodox synagogue I'd read about. I thought it would be the best place to inquire about a private guide to take me to Landsberg am Lech and St. Ottilien. Descending into the bowels of the subway station, I encountered my first challenge. How would I figure out which metro ticket to buy with only an automated machine and instructions in German? Determined not to let my nerves get the better of me, I fumbled with my Euros and managed to get the machine to spit out a ticket. When I exited the subway, the sights overwhelmed me—tiny boutiques and elegant department stores, modern and historic edifices, cafés and bistros, and the streets crowded with people. The old town square houses the Neue Rathaus. Directly in front of me: a magnificent festooned neo-Gothic building from the turn of the century with its famous glockenspiel. The figurines twirl every few hours in the tower. And resembling spokes on a bicycle wheel, a multitude of streets project in every direction. I wandered. It was thrilling when I found Maximiliansplatz—the street address of the Regina-Palast-Hotel where my father performed his ambitious recital program on January 18, 1948—the memory transporting me to St. Paul and my music studio. The area has been renovated, the hotel supplanted with brightly adorned designer shops, ultramodern skyscrapers, and flagstone walkways. Nevertheless, I summoned my father's presence, imagining his alluring cello sound.

Eventually I stumbled upon the synagogue museum and community center. The main exhibit features personal accounts of Munich's Jews, recorded and broadcast from small screens suspended from the ceiling. A huge carpet maps the city and indicates where those who perished had lived and worked. The Jewish population of Munich today is a mere sprinkling of the numbers who lived here before the war.

The gray concrete of the museum and the metallic paint colors, reminiscent of the Daniel Libeskind Jewish Museum in Berlin, felt cold, unfriendly, claustrophobic, and probably intentionally unsettling. Hurrying through the exhibits, I resisted the urge to flee.

Engulfed by long gray corridors, square blocks of stone, masses of cement, and stark architecture, I bolted to the sanctuary. Although a bit more uplifting, with transparent skylights allowing filtered light to shine onto the rows of seats, overall, the atmosphere seemed unwelcoming.

When I had entered the museum, an English-speaking ticket seller had greeted me. I returned to her desk to ask about a guide. She suggested I call a friend of hers, an Israeli who lived in town and who would be a knowledgeable and trustworthy escort. With the cell number placed securely in my purse, I walked over to see the community center building. Security was tight. The young Israeli security guards examined me head to toe. I asked how they came to live in Munich. A groundswell of mostly young, educated, cosmopolitan Israelis, descendants of German citizens, who've been offered dual citizenship, have flooded modern German cities—especially Berlin, a city with a great deal to offer. My queries about World War II elicited puzzled expressions, although they tried to be helpful. Was the history forgotten or unknown to them? Or were they eager to create new identities unencumbered by the devastating past?

Upon my return to the hotel, I called the Israeli guide. My mood plummeted even further at his officious tone and exorbitant price. A personable guide I realized, might be a challenge to find.

Gray weather contributed to the oppressive atmosphere I'd experienced the previous day. I wallowed in the comfy bed in the morning and then treated myself to a late breakfast of tasty soup and a panini German style, hoping it would lighten my mood. Just as I finished the meal, the sun broke through and as it turned out the perfect day to take the walking tour I'd heard about.

Brochures emphasize a trip to Munich, Germany, is positively incomplete without their most popular outing—a three-hour "Third Reich Walking Tour" and, for a few dollars more, a "bonus visit to Dachau." For many tourists, this is their first to a concentration camp. Like me, people feel compelled to experience the concentration camp in person. I signed up for both tours.

Our group of 20 consisted almost totally of non-Jewish people, and they no doubt looked forward to the three-hour tourist's adventure. For me the day would expose harsh and horrifying truths. Our guide, a young British man, began the tour by saying, "We will start at the beginning." While we stood under a tree he traced German history and attempted to put Hitler's improbable rise to power in perspective. The shade did little to mitigate the burning sensation in my throat.

Germany's surrender after World War I caused widespread humiliation. Stripped of their territories, required to pay tremendous reparations, the country began to go bankrupt. Discontent festered. Blaming a "foreign group" for the ills of society conveniently targeted the Jewish population.

At the time, Hitler seemed an unlikely hero—brash, coarse, unqualified, seemingly someone government officials could manipulate. But Hitler's hypnotic allure and grandiloquence whipped people into a frenzy. The population, soon trained to hate, summarily accepted that Jews ought to be at the base of society; once there, they were only steps away from dehumanization. The words of Ben Ferencz, a Nazi prosecutor at the Nuremberg trials, pulsed through my mind, "War makes murderers of otherwise decent people."

The 20 of us strolled to the huge beer hall Hofbräuhaus, one of Munich's most famous tourist attractions, where Hitler founded the Nazi party. I steered my attention to the beer steins consumed by famous visitors, and to Wolfgang Amadeus Mozart who'd lived nearby. Still, stepping inside unnerved me. Within the massive space, rows of enormous wooden tables were arranged from one end of the room to the other. Lights hung from the curved, ornately painted ceiling that had been festooned by swastikas during the Nazi era. The cavern reminded me of a cross between the Gryffindor cafeteria at the "Hogwarts School of Witchcraft and Wizardry" and an airplane hangar.

Fewer than 100 people came to hear Hitler in 1920, but soon his harangues drew crowds. The beer hall couldn't accommodate the 7,000 to 8,000 people who flocked to town to attend weekly meetings and catch the shrieking rhetoric.

Nearby the *Schutzstaffel* held their meetings. The fierce elite guard, the SS, controlled the German police and eventually the concentration camp system. Strolling a little further along the neighborhood streets, we came upon the art gallery. The architecture of the Haus der Deutschen Kunst building was designed to propagate German ideals with its square, solid shape and wide columns—ostensibly to represent German vigor. Inside, the art is massive and imposing, showing authority and manliness and power, acclaiming the purity of race, and epitomized by the slogan "blood and soil." In this context, the word blood specified that cultural identity could only be defined by purity of blood; the word soil promoted the ideology that those who tended the land should be celebrated.

Abstract and unrealistic art, and modernism, such as Dadaism, expressionism, and surrealism, were eschewed. These styles were considered a dangerous influence on the German people, Jewish or not. Artists Marc Chagall, Paul Klee, Wassily Kandinsky, Max Ernst, Pablo Picasso, Vincent Van Gogh, and Henri Matisse challenged authoritarianism and had to be suppressed. I wondered how many geniuses fled? How many could no longer produce art? How many works were destroyed or never came to be?

Joseph Goebbels, Hitler's Minister for Public Enlightenment and Propaganda, an infamous Nazi, controlled not only the arts but also the radio, the press, the theater, and publishing. He'd staged a colossal book burning in 1933 and had already begun ousting Jews from their positions. In 1937 Goebbels staged an exhibit in an adjacent building near the Haus der Deutschen Kunst to display the derided and ridiculed "degenerate" German art—Jewish, communist, abstract, and expressionist artists—the pieces considered poisonous, un-German, unacceptable. The shunned and subversive paintings, hung haphazardly with derisive placards next to them, provoked the attendees. Goebbels didn't anticipate the hordes of people who would gather to see this immoral art.

The paradox: Goebbels, a gifted orator who inspired terror, who promulgated the ideology of Nazi supremacy, and helped implement the Final Solution, was a passionate art collector. After forming the Commission for the Exploitation of Degenerate Art, Goebbels masterminded the plunder of thousands of artworks—priceless pieces seized from galleries as well as from Jewish homes and stored in various locations or sold. In fact, a huge cache of stolen art was found as recently as 2013 in a Munich flat. Restitution continues today.

The Nazis enacted fierce tactics—the confiscation of valuable musical instruments, and the suppression of theatrical performances, literary works, and musical compositions. "Degenerate" music comprised not only the masterpieces of Jewish composers Gustav Mahler, Felix Mendelssohn, Arnold Schoenberg, and others. Specific musical styles were considered odious and perilous, such as the music of George Gershwin, Paul Hindemith, Igor Stravinsky, and jazz and atonal music. The Reich Music Examination Office, a bureau within the Reich Ministry for Popular Enlightenment and Propaganda, controlled "undesirable" and "dangerous" music, reminiscent of Russian and Chinese suppression of Western art, music, literature, as well as book banning over the ages. It made me think of our own society—the proposed defunding of the National Endowment for the Arts [NEA] attempts to ban books, even this last decade, documented by the American Library Association. Does this signify that we, too, may be heading in the direction of devaluing the arts, culture, and free thinking?

The Haus der Kunst gallery now shows anything but German art. Although it has no permanent collection, it features a wide variety of contemporary art, including creations of Chinese human rights activist and artist Ai Weiwei, who due to stiff censorship in China is unable to live and work in his native land.

A massive long-term public monument stands at the Haus der Kunst entitled *The Joys of Yiddish*, designed by American sculptor Mel Bochner. Ten sarcastic Yiddish words spoken in the ghettos to improve morale are emblazoned across the facade in huge yellow block letters—the color a visual reminder of the stars and armbands Jews had to display:

PISHER, NEBBISH, KIBBITZER, KVETCHER, NUDNICK, MESHUGENER (Loosely translated as brat, nerd, joker, complainer, nuisance, crazy person).

I couldn't help wondering what Hitler and his cronies would think now.

Our group continued to the next site at the Hofgarten in front of the Staatskanzlie, the Bavarian War Memorial. There a tall, black stone memorial is dedicated to the handful of students: The White Rose—a nonviolent resistance group—founded by Hans Scholl, a medical student, and his sister Sophie, who dared defy the Nazi regime in 1942 and 1943.

Hans was outraged by the apathy of German people. He'd witnessed mistreatment of Jews and heard rumors of mass murders and deportations; he urged resistance. Other students from cities as far as Vienna joined their ranks. Their goal: to be as disruptive as possible, to sabotage, and to distribute anti-Nazi leaflets calling for opposition to the Nazi regime and the rejection of fascism. It was dangerous work. Trains were well guarded. Young men were confronted. The scarcity of stamps and paper necessitated duplication of leaflets on hand-operated machines before stuffing them into envelopes. One evening, Hans and two cohorts went so far as to paint "Down with Hitler" and to X out swastikas on houses in Munich. They managed to distribute six resistance leaflets before a custodian at the university betrayed them to the Gestapo. The five student leaders and their philosophy professor were executed in 1943—Sophie and Hans, by guillotine.

Today there are 30 sites in Munich that honor Hans and Sophie Scholl, the most renowned members of the resistance. The monument we saw looked to me like an oversized headstone topped with hundreds of stones. The guide referred to the puzzling stones. Periodically, the groundskeepers remove the stones and place them on the pathway, yet they mysteriously reappear. Our escort and other tourists in the group seemed unaware of the ancient Jewish symbolism of placing stones on a headstone. In addition to embodying permanence, the word for pebble in Hebrew means bond—the deceased is connected to the bond of life through the visitor. I explained to the group that to me, the stones indicate deeply honoring the heroic efforts of Sophie and Hans and others, who tried to speak out against the regime.

Making our way down a narrow street, northwest at Odeonsplatz, we came upon one of Munich's most beautiful squares, Feldherrnhalle, "Hall of Bavarian Generals"—an ornate, eggnog-colored wall of three arches adorned by statues, the spiritual center of the Nazi movement. The street took on an eerie glow. In 1923, during the so-called "beer hall putsch," Hitler made an attempt to overthrow the Weimar government. Two thousand men had marched from here to the center of Munich, to Marienplatz, where just yesterday I had strolled and admired the fashionable shops. Several of Hitler's followers were killed and Hitler's bodyguard took several bullets to save Hitler. The publicity thrust him center stage. The putsch, an act of treason, curiously resulted in a sentence of just four years, and Hitler served only nine months at the Landsberg am Lech prison. There, in cell 7, he wrote *Mein Kampf*. During Hitler's ascendance, more than 4,000 young people belonging to the *Hitlerjugend* (Hitler youth) organization made their pilgrimage to cell 7, perhaps hoping it still oozed with his repellant decrees.

The history and events that shaped Landsberg, a town 97 kilometers [60 miles] from Munich and approximately 55 kilometers [34 miles] from Dachau, began to coalesce. During the war, Landsberg housed the prison, a German military compound, and Kaufering—a network of subsidiary forced labor camps associated with Dachau.

I'd recently learned that Sonia Beker's mother, Fania, and her aunt, Henia, toiled at Kaufering, where they were forced to dig a network of tunnels within the hills, undetectable by the Allies, to house subterranean munitions factories. The prisoners lived like rats in partially entombed huts where thousands died of exposure and malnutrition. Their skeletons litter the hills.

After the war, the Allies converted the German compound into the Landsberg DP camp, one of the largest in Bavaria, and the location of the transformative concert with Leonard Bernstein and the St. Ottilien Orchestra. The symbolism of the music *Rhapsody in*

Blue couldn't be denied—American jazz, triumphant, performed by Bernstein, an American Jewish icon, and composed by George Gershwin, an American Jewish composer. My father learned to love the infectious swing of Gershwin's music and so did I. (In 1948 at only two decades old, there was no hint of *Rhapsody in Blue*'s future popularity.)

Further down, we sauntered beside the state university for music and theater, which survived wartime bombing. Students ran in and out carrying musical instruments, and lilting melodies drifted to where we stood. In 1936, the edifice had a more nefarious role as the "Fuhrer building," Nazi Gestapo headquarters. The Munich Agreement of 1938, signed by British Prime Minister Chamberlain, Hitler, and representatives of Italy and France, occurred here. The document was intended to appease Hitler by allowing Germany to annex the Sudetenland territories of Czechoslovakia. In retrospect, Chamberlain's myopic eyes failed to assess not only Hitler's arrogance, but also his agenda. Soon after, Germany invaded Poland. And here I stood at this very building. I could visualize swastika flags suspended from the balconies and florid red carpets adorning the grand entryway. And now the structure houses the music school. What a conundrum. I believe art creates wonder, is a vehicle for creating community, an expression of what it is to be human. To imagine making music in this building seems repugnant, the melodic phrases imbued with fumes of the horrific past.

Flanked on either side by gorgeous parks, busy traffic, and extravagant shops, the area bustled with activity. People dawdled in cafés with glasses of champagne or cups of coffee. I noticed women in vibrantly embroidered dirndl dresses, townsfolk mainly my age and older animated and relaxed. I observed average people like me. Some kind, some not; some friendly and educated, some not; some rude and unrefined, some not. What did they know? What did they remember? And the question my generation asks: are we different?

As our group disbanded, my meditations faded. The five-hour Dachau walking tour would give me plenty to cogitate upon the following day and I had barely sufficient time to get ready for *Erev* (evening of) Rosh Hashanah, the Jewish New Year, which would begin that evening; I'd arranged to attend services at a local Reform temple prior to my trip.

Carefully scrutinizing the city map, I spotted Beth Shalom. It was quite a distance away from the hotel. But Jahnstrasse, where my parents' 1940s Munich apartment is located, appeared to be very near the temple. I decided not to risk the subway. Perhaps with a cab driving me, I'd have time to make a stop there.

It was impossible not to engage the doorman of the Marriott Hotel in conversation. After the usual pleasantries, he regaled me with his adventures on the Continent. A chatty man, he was accustomed to lodgers who thought it odd to see an African American at the Munich Marriott. He mentioned he'd been in the US army, stationed in Afghanistan; afterward, he'd decided to stay overseas, in Europe. I loved the stories but itched to begin my adventure.

The hotel has a code of honor regarding the queue of cab drivers lined up in front, and the doorman strictly controls the protocol. I hadn't as yet divulged my ulterior motive—that I was looking for a guide who might know the outlying areas of Bavaria.

When he finally took a breath, I gingerly approached the subject. I explained why I needed a cabdriver who could speak English. The beaming doorman strode confidently to the entryway of the hotel and proceeded to march past the long line of taxis. He proclaimed for all to hear that no other driver could fill the weighty role but Alexander, his buddy. The doorman greeted each driver by name and explained the need for a fluent English-speaking driver for "*die Dame*" waiting by the door, who was about to embark on a special odyssey.

Well down the line of cabs, Alexander waited. Charming, tall, good-looking, with a curly head of dark hair and a winning smile, he was enthusiastic when he heard what I hoped to find.

I showed Alexander a copy of one of my father's Munich radio recital invitations, with the address, Jahnstrasse 48. Alexander found the distinguished multifloored gray apartment building easily. It's without a doubt the original structure. We got out of the car so I could take a few photos. Alexander had to stretch to his full height to photograph the address for me, which was buried under an overgrowth of bushes and revealed flower boxes in each window. When it started to rain, Alexander seemed in no hurry.

He turned off his taxi meter while he carefully read the directions to the temple. We discovered the address hidden behind a tall white gate. A high-rise in a relatively deserted area couldn't be further from my idea of a gathering place, let alone a temple. Alexander worried that we were too early and there wasn't a soul to indicate where we should enter. He jumped out to find the doorway—perhaps in the back? By then a police car arrived, evidently scheduled to monitor the gate all evening. It occurred to me that tight security is necessary here, and, I realized with a shudder, all Jewish structures need protection once again.

Certain no other cabs would be driving around this area late in the evening, Alexander insisted on waiting for me until the end of the service. I ventured up a long staircase in the back of the ordinary-looking apartment building.

At the top of the stairs sat a man with a checklist. When he found my name, he invited me in with a friendly gesture. Women bustled with preparations. A spectacular spread of cooked foods and desserts assailed me with divine smells—a mélange of cinnamon, cloves, tart lemon, pungent mustard, and roasted meats beautifully arranged on several long tables. After the prayer services the Kiddush or blessings would be recited over wine and challah, and would be followed by the more substantial fare.

Everyone greeted me exceptionally warmly, "*L'Shana Tova*" (Happy New Year.) Someone led me to the synagogue downstairs where all the seats were occupied by about 75 congregants, mainly younger people, several Americans among them. I observed a hodgepodge of men with ponytails wearing jeans, ladies in sparkly blouses, and gentlemen in suits, but all the men wore the traditional head covering, a *kippah*.

Instead of a *bimah*—an altar or podium in front of the ark (the recessed sacred container in which the Torah scrolls are kept)—the room held a simple lectern draped by a white cloth. Silver embroidery outlined a Star of David, a few Hebrew letters, and two large red pomegranates. The only other adornment in the room were two matching silver candlesticks. The young rabbi and cantor conducted the service informally and entirely in German, but I sang along, the prayers familiar, with all the melodies I'm accustomed to.

It had been so many years since I was able to spend Rosh Hashanah with my parents in Toronto. Rosh Hashanah is celebrated with a festive meal and I remember dipping apples in honey for a sweet New Year; I remember Mama's honey cake, the delicious round challah with raisins; her aromatic brisket, the rich gravy teeming with tender carrots and potatoes; I remember a side dish of pomegranates. Closing my eyes, I fantasize about the succulent, crimson seeds—the redolent, tart juice staining my lips.

Every year at Rosh Hashanah, I look forward to the challenge of digging deeply into the pomegranate rind and fishing out the sweet seeds, which offers delicious rewards and symbolizes the renewal of hope for good fortune in the New Year. Now, many years later, as a parent, I replicate the customs for my own family and explain the deeper significance of the pomegranate.

The round shape, topped with a calyx, or crown, is one of the most ancient and perennial symbols of Judaism. Some Jewish scholars are convinced that the pomegranate, not the apple, was the forbidden fruit of the Garden of Eden.

The Bible describes images of the pomegranate adorning the garb of religious leaders. The fruit, it is said, was depicted on the pillars in front of King Solomon's Temple in Jerusalem, and his coronet emulated the design of the crown of the fruit.

By the Middle Ages, the symbol of the pomegranate embellished the Torah, the sacred Jewish texts that consist of the five books of Moses. The tops or staves of the Torah rollers, the metal ornaments crowning the Torah Scroll, became known by the Hebrew word for pomegranate: *rimmonim.*

The fruit laden with spiritual significance symbolizes fertility and renewal, and is emblematic of the parameters of good and righteous behavior. According to traditional beliefs, there are 613 seeds in the pomegranate, each signifying one of 613 commandments, or *mizvot* (good deeds). The Torah requires the Jewish People to abide by these commandments, in order to live a righteous life. Even dreaming about pomegranates is considered an omen of wisdom.

Meditating upon these images, I realize this perennial metaphor maintains its vitality in the 21st century. The Jewish People, in spite of centuries of persecution, have achieved the fertility and renewal promised by the pomegranate. From its seeds have grown a generation—my generation—raised by Holocaust survivors, who aspire to pursue good and righteous behavior.

I peered around the room observing the small Jewish congregation with... I'm not sure—curiosity, admiration, apprehension? Why attempt to establish life and religion here in Munich where the Jewish community was so pitilessly decimated? The 250-member assembly is dedicated to renewal, even going so far as to commission architect Daniel Libeskind to design a permanent home.

The congregation laughed often. Despite my own qualms, it felt comfortable and like any Jewish congregation—people chatted, sauntered in and out, stared at everyone, then again sauntered in and out. After the traditional blessings on the wine, bread, and apples and honey, people rushed to get to the food—again typical. If you're petite, you understand the disadvantage in situations like this. I managed to snatch a piece of cake before Alexander appeared. The police were not pleased with his loitering. We hurried out, a baggie of goodies pressed into my hands as I exited.

On the ride back to the hotel, amiable chatter bolstered my confidence, so I revealed the full scope of my mission—to track down the places where my father performed with the St. Ottilien Orchestra. Despite the limited information I had, I was determined to retrace my father's footsteps.

Alexander offered his services for a day of sleuthing. Coincidentally, he'd lived in Landsberg for seven years. Unlike the cocky Israeli guide who insisted he needed an address, as there wasn't a DP camp at Landsberg, and maintained Bernstein didn't conduct in Munich until the 1960s, Alexander, who was exactly my age, had served in the German army in the 1970s in Landsberg and had knowledge of the town and its history. The Israeli wanted to charge by the hour for a minimum of four hours, which would've added up. Alexander agreed to do all three sites—Landsberg, Feldafing, and St. Ottilien for a flat rate with no time limitations. My quest had become his quest.

He suggested we first stop at the Rathaus, the government offices, for historical records and to be sure we knew where we might find old monuments and plaques. He also proposed going on a weekday, that is, Friday, as the offices would be open. (The Israeli had recommended a Sunday excursion.) Meeting Alexander was *bashert* as we say—a Yiddish word that means "meant to be," providential. We agreed to rendezvous at 8:30 a.m. In the meantime, I braced myself for the visit to Dachau concentration camp—beyond what I've experienced in my imagination.

Entr'acte 2010

I don't sleep much that night. In the morning, the tube takes me to the main station, the Hauptbahnhof. More train tracks than gates at an airport crisscross in front of me. Trains whistle, babies cry, travelers stumble, and the overpowering stench of diesel fuel wafting through the air makes the abundant varieties of pastries and sandwiches on display somehow unappealing. Every direction seems to lurch upstream as I try to find track 32, the tour company booth, where my group and I are to gather for our three-hour tour.

After several moments, the guide appears. Carelessly tossing his worn backpack onto his shoulders, he leads us toward the underground, we tourists scurrying like so many mice after him, hoping not to get lost. I keep my eye on the impossibly young guide—lanky, with long unkempt hair, torn jeans, and a couple of black tattoos on his spindly arms. What could he possibly know of the clamorous emotions that prickle through my bones?

Twelve of us manage to board the train. An older couple sweetly holding hands speak French in hushed tones. Near them a pretty young blonde on leave from the Peace Corps adjusts her hiking gear. Two big women with enormous dark sunglasses, straw hats, tote bags, and sensible shoes sit erect to avoid leaning on anyone next to them. A group of boisterous teenagers just released from their semester of study abroad elbow each other, and a young Japanese couple with several expensive cameras dangling from their necks heave a baby carriage. Last, the most petite woman of the bunch, smartly dressed, hair coiffed just so (as my mother would have expected), slouches with trepidation.

What a lovely day—the countryside green and lush and quite beautiful in the sunshine. Dachau is a 1,200-year-old picturesque and affluent town close to Munich. Through the train windows, I can see flower boxes, which adorn charming little homes, cobblestone streets, and breathtaking views of the Alps. The townsfolk ride bicycles past the city bus station marked Dachau and cross Dachau Street—older Frauen laugh, taking bites out of perfectly formed crimson apples (paying no mind to the cores) and young people lick melting ice cream cones. A sign blares:

TOUR DACHAU GERMANY. IT IS A BEAUTIFUL CITY LOCATED JUST NORTHWEST OF MUNICH, WITH MUCH MORE TO SEE THAN JUST THE CONCENTRATION CAMP!

We disembark and gather in an expansive area covered in gray stones for a few introductory remarks from the guide. Even for those who know some of this history, the details give perspective—how the general public, many with moral rectitude, were inexorably caught up in the maelstrom of fascism. For me, it clarifies the relentless descent into anarchy.

"Let's go back in history for a moment," he says, "to the 1920s. The United States stock market crash in 1929 led to worldwide financial collapse." He went on to say that the mood in Germany was particularly bleak. Disgraced by their defeat after World War I, Germans suffered 30 percent unemployment by the 1930s. The agitated nation, frustrated by inept government, began to support the Nazi party—a previously unknown political group—to free them from the dismal depths. Despite winning only one-third of the vote in the 1932 elections, the party formed a coalition after full-scale backroom machinations. Paul von Hindenburg, president of Germany, reluctantly appointed Adolf Hitler chancellor. The party advocated extreme nationalism, totalitarian rule, and views that bordered on the fanatic, including virulent antisemitism. Democratic ideals ended. So often, I think, partisan gerrymandering to solidify political advantage has ebbed and flowed.

Dachau opened as a concentration camp for political prisoners just a few weeks after Hitler was appointed chancellor of the Reich, on March 22, 1933. The National Socialist German Workers' Party adopted emergency measures, seized political power, and subdued all opponents of the regime. Stripped of their rights, political adversaries and protesters, clergy and communists, foreigners, artists and the intelligentsia were incarcerated in Dachau. No trials. No recourse. "Protective custody," they called it. The goal: to subvert all norms by intimidation, sedition, and complete suppression of civil liberties. Many of the prisoners were systematically murdered—some worked to death, others executed. Initially, regular prison guards ran the camp. Heinrich Himmler soon saw to it that SS men replaced them.

I can't help silently posing the question: What might have halted the trajectory? How many citizens resisted Hitler in the early years? Over and over, we have seen tyrants hoodwink the populace. Even today, we are duped or disbelieving when the truth is apparent.

Moderates first dismissed Hitler's incendiary remarks—*Must be all bluster. Couldn't he be tamed?*—a dictatorship could never occur in a country where laws protecting freedom of speech and thought had always been inviolable. But within months, Hitler introduced the Enabling Act of 1933, which allowed him to impose edicts without a vote in the Reichstag. I shudder to think of our own complacency. Self-serving politicians and partisan politics is not new.

A murderous rampage by 80 members of the Nazi Storm Troopers leadership [SA] consolidated Hitler's power. Suppression of any organization deemed a threat followed. When Hindenburg died in 1934, Hitler assumed the roles of chancellor and president, naming himself führer, the supreme ruler; before everyone's eyes, he made the transformation from a failed artist from Austria to a demagogue. Freedom of speech and the press were suppressed, alternative political parties outlawed, civil liberties suspended. Books, music, and art deemed "degenerate" were banned. Nonetheless, the populace, seduced by Hitler's mesmerizing oratory skills, failed to halt his inexorable ascent.

Even as early as 1920, Nazi party members had the goal to separate Jews from "Aryan society." They eschewed anyone who didn't meet the ideal of blond hair and blue eyes, white unblemished skin, a perfect body, or "pure blood." Between 1933 and 1939 when the war broke out, more than 400 laws restricted Jews. The regime confiscated cameras, radios, and bicycles. Forbade sitting in public parks, and limited shopping to between 2:00 p.m. and 5:00 p.m. at designated stores only (enter by the back door). They prohibited school attendance, and padlocked businesses. Roving gangs of hoodlums claiming to be militia assistants needed no excuse to harass, to humiliate, to plunder—which is exactly what my parents had told me happened in Hungary with the *Nyilas*. The parallels to today are startling. It occurs to me that here in the US we have several unmonitored paramilitary groups. By the 1990s, all 50 states had active groups; 334 armed militia factions were documented in 2011 at their peak by the Southern Poverty Law Center.

The SS had complete control of Dachau by 1935, with the ability to extinguish all adversaries. Eventually those who passed through the one-way gates *Arbeit Macht Frei* (Work sets you free) represented people from 34 countries and included German dissidents, "antisocials" (which could conveniently include anyone, I think), Jehovah's Witnesses, Romani people, homosexuals, Black people, anyone with physical or cognitive disabilities, and Jews. I'm surprised to hear that two-thirds of all Dachau inmates were non-Jewish political prisoners. Communists, trade unionists, Social Democrats. The priest barracks of Dachau alone held several thousand clergy members restrained to "de-Christianize" Germany. Exact numbers incarcerated vary widely. It is believed that the estimates—200,000 imprisoned and 40,000 murdered—may be vastly underestimated.

But Dachau turned out to be good for Germany's economic development. Germany needed a workforce for their war machine, and the munitions industry benefitted from the prison workforce. Huge amounts of money could be made using abundant slave labor. Townspeople justified, rationalized, or feigned ignorance of what was going on, not suspecting, at least then, that the operations would lay the groundwork for the infrastructure employed to address the "Jewish Question."

I didn't know that Dachau, the longest-functioning concentration camp, came to be the "parent" camp, the first of thousands built all over Europe. For 12 years, the Nazis solidified their ideology and refined their strategies for the brutality that ensued all across the Continent—a school for violence, you might say. Everything that occurred in subsequent concentration camps was initially tried at Dachau.

I look around. The entry to Dachau now has a large grassy area and a modern building with a bookstore, snack bar, and restroom facilities like any other tourist attraction. There's a big crowd—older and younger tourists, from many countries, and the majority do not seem Jewish. It's difficult, at least for me, to dissociate these contemporary additions from the actualities of this place.

The guide points out the original guard towers. A large stone platform had been unearthed, the spot where prisoners first encountered the SS officers; where fates were sealed. The chief guard barked to each prisoner in line *Rechts*, you to the right (young men and women, those deemed old enough and strong enough to work, and the attractive, shapely young women for a more ominous purpose). *Links,* you to the left (the dispensable prisoners, who were immediately murdered: those who were pregnant, elderly, disabled, injured, or anyone who had annoyed the guards for whatever reason). A triple layer of barbed wire encases the enormously high walls. Adjacent to the fortifications—a deep, wide trench, which surrounds the complex so any escape attempt resulted in suicide, oftentimes intentionally so.

The two large women in the group lead the way and enter through the wrought iron gates, walking under the sign with the facetious slogan *Arbeit Macht Frei*. Hanging at the entrance of several concentration camps, the mantra "work sets you free" taunted the slave laborers who marched daily to and from their forced labors. Ghastly sensations prickle up my spine when I notice teenagers mugging next to the infamous sign, taking selfies.

We walk beyond the gate to a huge open area covered in stones where daily roll calls took place before dawn—*Rechts*, you to the right. *Links,* you to the left—and each evening after 12 hours of labor in the muck, the piercing wind, torrential rain, blistering heat. The specter real to me, I envision attention drawn to an unfortunate prisoner, however incidental, any misstep, which causes a provocation for a merciless rampage upon the entire group, the inmates in constant terror of thrashing, whipping, and lynching. One horrendous tactic: shooting every tenth prisoner while they were in standing formation.

The tour guide leads the group into the barracks. The bunks are new and the earthy, warm smell of freshly hewn wood, and clean floors, is disconcerting and deceptive.

The first barracks, for political prisoners in the years before the war, assigned one person to a bunk. As groups move through each room intended to represent the "progress" as the war continued, we come to the last room—the barracks that held Jews. It's a squeeze to get the 12-member troop and a baby stroller inside.

Initially, in the early 1940s, these barracks housed 60 Jewish men, but, later in the war, the cells held hundreds. Prisoners slept on their sides contorting like embracing sardines jammed four to six in a bunk. The only consolation—they were warmer that way. To see the space makes me despondent. One medieval toilet hardly sufficed. Dysentery hit. Too weak to rise, wedged in their bunks, prisoners soiled themselves. Often, overnight, of the four or six men on the bare wooden slat, half died. Ironically, typhoid makes the skin smell fragrant, like freshly baked bread. Even so, the effluvium of rotting flesh, unwashed bodies, diarrhea, and decomposing carcasses pervaded.

Food consisted of a moldy piece of black bread and a little watery soup. Unable to wash, captives wore the same threadbare prison garb for months. A typhoid epidemic ensued as lice crawled from one body to another. But no matter how sick you were, you tried to show up for roll call—*Rechts*, you to the right. *Links,* you to the left—to avoid the fancy modern medical facility set up in the square, ostensibly to offer treatment, where instead, appalling medical experiments were carried out.

Our guide continues. Dachau had been a camp exclusively for men. Bewildered for a moment, I decide to speak up. "I know of at least two women who were prisoners in Dachau," I say. Everyone in the group peers at me as if they hadn't noticed me before. The guide asks me to elaborate. "My friend's mother and aunt—two sisters, Fania and Henia, toiled as slave laborers at the Kaufering concentration camp. Near the end of the war, corralled and paraded through the main streets of the nearby town of Landsberg, they marched to Dachau on the way to their deaths."

He stammers and checks his notes, then he clarifies. Dachau had been used as a transit camp to many other locations. Thousands of prisoners passed through Dachau. As each transport arrived selections were made. The guards dispatched able-bodied men and women to slave-labor camps wherever workers were needed to build roads, railways, or mining the quarries; they conveyed the very young, very old, and disabled people to their deaths at Auschwitz or other extermination camps. *Rechts*, you to the right. *Links,* you to the left. Several tour members seem astonished. An older lady with no inkling there may be living offspring, asks, "You know some people who survived this place?" Her incredulity makes me squirm.

A museum has been built at the campgrounds. On display: photographs and belongings of those who perished; videotaped interviews of those who survived; and posters scorning the pernicious Jew.

The liberating army, totally unprepared for what they found, unwittingly encountered the macabre site. The general had followed a putrid odor for 48 kilometers [30 miles] until they stumbled upon the carnival of horror, Dachau. They found 39 railway boxcars teeming with more than 2,000 corpses just outside the gates, and emaciated skeletons impersonating humans within.

The bestiality was documented in graphic and intensely revolting photos. American soldiers required the citizens of Dachau to tour the camp, to see firsthand what they had refused to acknowledge. The citizens were mortified, stupefied. Tourists can never experience, of course, the putrescence of the camp—the reeking feces, decaying cadavers, festering wounds. In a contemporaneous film on display you can see many of the townsfolk who covered their noses, who turned away to vomit while they carried shovelfuls of carcasses to a crude final resting place. At this point, overcome, the sweet older couple and I leave the room.

The buildings that remain are the crematoriums and gas chamber. The crematoriums incinerated executed prisoners, but it is not known if the gas chamber was used except for "training." A posted sign says, "This is the center of potential mass murder. The room, disguised as 'showers' and equipped with fake shower spouts, misled the victims to prevent them from refusing to enter the room. During a period of 15 to 20 minutes, up to 150 at a time could be suffocated to death using prussic acid poison gas (Zyklon B)." Tourists are welcome to go in. The Japanese couple refuses. But I, taking a moment to shutter my mind, with a gasp, barrel through.

In a fever dream, I observe a square, dirty, dank room, with walls and a floor of tarnished but smooth brick cobblestones, without any cracks or spaces between them—hermetically sealed. The shower heads, which released the lethal gas, were clearly visible before they were stolen by tourists as souvenirs. Some light seeps in through a small window from where the Nazis viewed their victims; I imagine naked victims, who expect their first real shower in months, crammed into the vault, who slowly asphyxiate; their shrieks resonate in my ears. Barely able to see through my tears, I sprint out to the bright, sunny day. Our guide notices and walks over to put a protective arm around me at the exit. At least there is one now.

Around the corner, suddenly there is some color, which offers a break from all the bleak grayness. Bright pink and red begonias surround a beautiful stone memorial adorned with a Star of David—

one of three memorials at Dachau, which represent three of the world's religious groups: Jewish, Christian, and Russian Orthodox.

A bright sculpture catches my eye, but the cheer is deceiving. Look closely at the sculpture. You'll notice that within three immense circles, which depict a super-sized chain-link fence, the artist incorporates superimposing triangles. They form multiple Stars of David. I and the other tourists learn about the sinister imagery. The Nazis kept track of their captives meticulously. Prisoners didn't have names. Colored cloth badges classified them. Communists and enemies of the state had to wear the red triangle; foreign forced laborers, mainly Poles, wore blue; the German "criminals" wore green triangles; Roma sported brown triangles; the pink triangle represented the homosexual group; and, of course, the Jews wore yellow. Black people living in Germany, especially African Americans, endured extremely harsh treatment.

Most prisoners were classified into two offensive groups (almost everyone could be classified as an enemy of the state)—a Jewish communist, a gay criminal—two triangles superimposed formed a Star of David. And the other malevolent classifications? Some prisoners wore the colored insignia with a black bar across the badge, which marked these men for vile mistreatment; the circle shaped emblem arbitrarily singled out inmates for the most dreadful work: the penal colony, rock quarries, and almost certain death. Even anonymity, the only protection available to the prisoners was virtually impossible—*Rechts*, you to the right. *Links,* you to the left.

Silently we lumber to the final shrine: a black marble headstone-like monument dedicated to all who perished. The group peers into the sun to read the inscription:

May the example of those who were exterminated here between 1933–1945 because they resisted Nazism help unite the living for the defense of peace and freedom and respect for their fellow man.

While thinking about my parents I propel these sentiments into orbit with a silent prayer.

It's approaching closing time. I hear multiple languages—Italian, Spanish, English, and German (no doubt like the internees)—as we move toward the exit to board one city bus that will stop for a last pickup. On the way out, there's a final signpost:

Dachau—the significance of this name will never be erased from German history. It stands for all concentration camps which the Nazis established in their territory.

The crowd of sightseers somehow crams onto the bus. It's an uncomfortable closeness if only for the ride to the train—nothing like a cattle car to an unknown destination, I remind myself. We are silent. There is nothing that can be said.

I extricate myself at the Hauptbahnhof station and board the subway to head for my plush hotel room. Once I unlock and relock the door and strip off my clothes, I step into a hot shower, as hot as I can stand, but scrubbing doesn't wash away my turmoil. Once again, I ponder life as a free person, and the years when my family had no such escape. Despite reading everything I could about the Holocaust at a certain point in my life—about being swept into the madness, the suffering, the dread, the anxiety and death—nothing prepared me for the experience on this sunny day. At Dachau, I explored the question, how did this happen? But the answer to my plea, *how could this have happened?* remains unanswered.

Entr'acte 2013

I shudder awake from a horrifying stupor. Rousing myself, stumbling to our bathroom mirror, I see puffy eyelids and a deep crease down the left side of my face resembling a knife wound, like I used to see on my mother's morning face. I'd thought it odd then. Now I wonder, did she wake terrified? Their revelations still churn.

"Darling, I don't know how you do it," says my 82-year-old aunt Eva. "Why are you bringing back the dead? I can't talk about it. I have nightmares every night."

Gently probing, I ask, "How did you avoid being rounded up?"

Eva resists speaking about it. Once, years ago, she told me about crawling across the Danube on her belly. In the dark; in the cold. Bullets whirred. She witnessed the *Nyilas* shooting several of their group, vicious dogs ravaged some others, but she scrambled to safety.

"They hid me in a vegetable bunker. I had a bench to lie on. The bunker, it wasn't high enough for me to even stand up. Afraid of the dark, and always cold, I could hardly stand the musty smell. I couldn't get out. There were mice."

"Who's they?" I asked.

"My [Christian] stepmother's parents. They had a little home outside of Budapest. You know, it was at the end of their garden, a hole really, in the mud where they dried vegetables for the winter. That's where they kept me. They brought me food if they could late at night. I heard the screeching bombs."

"How old were you then?"

"I was a little girl. I must've been maybe 13? I can't talk about it. I have nightmares every night."

When I was growing up, Eva was my confidante, a gorgeous Hungarian woman—think Eva Longoria with raven hair, flirtatious eyes, and sensuous lips; think Zsa Zsa Gabor glamorous with her splendid accent, every sentence prefaced with *anyukám* and *Daaahlink*; think Samantha Bee irreverent and outspoken, with cheeky asides dripping with sarcasm. Eva and Tibi sparkled with wit. They'd travelled to exotic places, were always the life of the party, and so unlike my conservative parents. One of very few people my father might listen to, Eva was the only person who could mollify me after conflicts with them. But she never alluded to her distressing past.

Now I am having her nightmares: I stare at the ceiling in the middle of the night, debilitated, with terror in my heart. I'm plagued by my father's insomnia. Sleepless at night and headaches all day, I didn't associate his ills with memory, with separation, with trauma. I feel anxious and alone as he did, despite my sweet, understanding spouse lying beside me.

I thought I'd stay in the Twin Cities a few months, maybe a year or two. Instead, I stayed, leaving my life behind. How did a nice Jewish girl from Toronto end up in Minnesota? A place I'd never heard of. Even now I wonder—especially since Harris has moved out, especially since my only close relatives are Rob and Sara, their children, and Eva, in Toronto. Perhaps I came to Minneapolis because—you know—it was utterly different from home, away from people who'd known me, a city with wide-open spaces, rivers and lakes, its few Jews hidden underground. But my life here, I admit, was isolated, still protected, still shielded from the world. Onstage every day of my life for more than 34 years—I'd drive straight to Orchestra Hall and back after concerts, never spotting a pile of trash, some graffiti, a tenement, or people scurrying to work. When I wasn't performing, I stayed home to practice, seldom seeing a person of color or hearing an accent. I rarely encountered vagrants or anyone inebriated, and never hung out at bars or clubs. I didn't drink or smoke. My parents hadn't either. I suppose our Muse, music, served as the bubble in which we floated, hiding from the pain of the world.

St. Ottilien

Once a miserable haven for Holocaust survivors, Germany's St. Ottilien Archabbey had no resemblance to the grainy 60-year-old photos in my possession. Like a film noir suddenly colorized, the verdant pastures, lush farmland, and neo-Gothic monastery with its octagonal spire emerged before me. On a glorious day of azure skies, warbling birds, and spectacular vistas surrounding the grounds, the Alps hazy in the distance, it seemed absurd to visualize what my father must have experienced here.

Alexander parked, and we walked along a stone, tree-lined path on the grounds toward the church, encountering a cafe, shops, and sculptures. The expanded site, like a small village, now comprises a school and library, a spiritual retreat center, private dwellings for guests of the Benedictines, a printing facility that publishes spiritual texts, and an agricultural wing.

We stopped at the office. While Alexander explained our fact-finding mission to the monk behind the reception desk, I read placards describing the good works and contemplative life of the Benedictines who serve 55 monasteries in 20 countries.

The abbot explained that no one remembers the 1945 concert for the DPs that took place here, but the Benedictine missionaries were mindful of those challenging times. The Gestapo appropriated the entire monastery in 1941, driving the monks out. Those who'd opposed Hitler were incarcerated; others joined the battle to fight against the Nazis. What a contrast to the reflective, prayerful life of service the Benedictines are known for.

After the war, the monks made their way back to St. Ottilien, and committed to the renewal of their country, the restoration of their abbey. They established a Jewish hospital for survivors. Only one of the buildings remains today. Although many survivors still perished, 427 babies were born at St. Ottilien between 1946 and 1948, among them a friend of mine, and friends of Sonia. New life amidst the chaos.

I would return to St. Ottilien a few years later with these very friends, but in 2010 I had no forewarning of what was to come.

The cleric proffered a map of the St. Ottilien grounds and drew a circle to indicate a place we shouldn't miss—the Jewish cemetery. Alexander and I meandered along a dirt path flanked by clay walls. I posed for a photo at the magnificent church—the Gothic door adorned with grape-like shapes in turquoise and black iron, a breathtaking interior in all-white stone, ribbed-vault ceilings, crisscrossing floor tiles, and a colossal organ.

Farther down the path, we came to a wrought iron gate gilded with a Star of David. Within the pristine Jewish cemetery, a tall hedge stands guard over the headstones. Topped with hundreds of pebbles, the largest monument is carved with 16 names of those who died all within one week, in May 1945, and so many more after liberation, too sick to be saved. I laid some of my own stones in honor of the deceased, while the somber peal of bells rang in the distance.

Just 19 kilometers [12 miles] away, about an hour due west from Munich by car, the medieval town Landsberg am Lech nestles in a vale on the river. Neither the DP camp nor the barracks where Alexander served are there today but I knew of monuments and memorials in the town, somewhere. I'd brought the address of the city's archive offices with me, but despite traveling here on a Friday, we found the doors locked. In the adjacent square stood a distinguished gentleman wearing a terra-cotta camel hair blazer and a white striped shirt, his briefcase brimming with papers. Although he was talking to someone, Alexander interrupted, "Might the gentleman be aware of monuments to World War II?"

Franz Xavier Rößle, the former mayor of Landsberg, had been personally responsible for seeing to the installation of these memorials. *Once again bashert*, I thought. He told us about several tributes in the city and its environs, none of which we would have known about. Viktor Frankl, their most famous native son, the author of *Man's Search for Meaning*, received the city's cultural award and the avenue named him was just down the way. Unaware of aspects of my story, the mayor anticipated learning more about Leonard Bernstein's Landsberg concert for their city archives. I promised to send him a copy of the program. Waving *Auf Wiedersehen*, he assured me we would meet again.

Alexander and I headed well up into the hills, on zigzagging roads flanked by tiny houses, to Kaufering VII, which belonged to the network of Dachau subsidiary concentration camps. Prominently displayed—a headstone engraved in English, with a heartbreaking dedication from a son to his mother who perished here.

Jewish slaves slept in the frigid air, barely covered by skimpy huts after long days of labor building bunkers and trenches for German soldiers. No matter how famished, withered, or battered, 3,555 Jews between the ages of 11 and 70 were marched back and forth each day. The vast majority didn't survive the brutal conditions in Kaufering, the camp where Sonia's mother and aunt, Fania and Henia, were enslaved.

Imagine: in Kaufering I, seven Hungarian women gave birth to seven babies in the ice-covered huts. Someone took pity, found a tiny stove, and smuggled it into the hut for the shivering infants, but a Nazi guard found out. He beat the offender mercilessly. Inexplicably the babies weren't put to death as so many were, by a lethal injection into their hearts.

American soldiers liberated the seven women and their babies in 1945 and wept at the sight. After the war, one of the women moved to Toronto with her husband and baby. Eventually she established a business: Miriam's Fine Judaica Gift Shop on Bathurst Street, one of the main north-south routes in Toronto. It's still there. I've driven passed Miriam's hundreds of times. If my mother knew the family, she never spoke about it.

Difficult to fathom how such bestiality could occur in this charming, archaic town, deep in the countryside.

Farther up, we encountered a particularly disturbing relic sheltered by a pergola-like wood structure and surrounded in stones —an original cattle car, used to transport unknown numbers of prisoners to their deaths. Wide metal bars thrust through metal loops firmly sealed and locked the doors from the outside. Mounted on the wood slats, next to the cattle car, sagged a lone memorial from a son to his father. I needed to remind myself why I was here. I dug my fingernails into my thighs to transport my consciousness back to the present, while Alexander read the inscription: The Nazis' endless supply of free labor consisted of Jews considered fit enough to be shipped from Auschwitz to Kaufering to work. Once the slaves had been physically ravaged and on death's door, they mounted the trains for their final trip—back to Auschwitz and the gas.

Slowly we retraced our steps to find the site of the concert with Bernstein, now the town's kindergarten. Prior to the war, Landsberg had been a German army base, the Saarburg Kaserne. By May 9, 1945, there were 6,870 people housed at the Landsberg DP camp—and not all of them Jewish.

Like in other DP camps before the JDC stepped in, they lived in anguish with their oppressors, encircled by a double barbed wire fence. According to the US Holocaust Memorial Museum, "Major Irving Heymont, an officer of the 5th Infantry Regiment of the US Army that liberated the Gunskirchen concentration camp, a subcamp of Mauthausen, was awarded the Silver Star for gallantry in action. When the war ended, he was tasked to run the displaced persons camp in Landsberg Germany." In September 1945, with a keen sense of the plight of the DPs, Major Heymont moved all non-Jews out of the camp. Later, I read that Heymont hadn't divulged that he too was Jewish. His father had fled Russia to escape persecution.

There's a memorial on the walls of the kindergarten marking the site of the former DP camp. The playground, renamed Anne Frank Platz, is full of life and, I hope, a brighter future.

On the way to our next stop while we drove along the main thoroughfare, a large stone and iron sculpture caught my eye. Adjacent to the old city fortress walls chiseled in bas-relief, the monument depicts a death march. Prisoners stumbled the almost 80 kilometers [50 miles] from Kaufering to Dachau right through the town, on these very streets. Commissioned by a German businessman, the memorial is inscribed, "How was it possible that the townspeople did not know or did not see?" The benefits of free labor, burgeoning factories and industry, and, to be fair, following orders to save their own skin, must have taken precedence. I often ask myself the question: *What would I or any of us have done in similar circumstances? What could we—should we—do today as we witness atrocity?*

I was ready for a break. We ambled around the cobblestone streets of the town, noting the pinks, blues, and yellow pastel shades of the ancient buildings, until we found a place with a splendid antipasto spread. My first bites were tinged with sorrow. Over lunch, Alexander regaled me with colorful anecdotes, and, hard to believe in retrospect, we laughed a great deal. Picture the scene: a petite, blonde, hazel-eyed, second-generation American Jew, with a tall, dark-haired and dark-eyed, second-generation German. The levity was primarily due to our successes so far. Alexander's patience, perseverance, and eloquence had made the difference. He stopped people on the street for directions and information—which I could not have done, and almost everyone we encountered was helpful.

As we gobbled garlic calamari, artichokes stuffed with feta cheese, and angel hair pasta with white cream sauce, the fragrances such a contrast to what I'd imagined at Dachau, he told me his life story. Born several years after the conclusion of the war, Alexander had a tough childhood. His mother had signed him up for the army as a young teenager—to cast Alexander aside. With little or no education about World War II, silence surrounded the years between 1938 and 1945. In fact, the films and photos had been unavailable—neither released nor shown on television—until after the reunification of Germany in 1990. Generation three, my son's generation, receives little education about the Holocaust and other watershed moments in history. Are we humans forever destined to repeat our mistakes?

Distress and disbelief transformed Alexander when he finally saw the Holocaust footage. Today he often takes people to Dachau. The tourists, he says, for the most part are unprepared for what they encounter. Dumbstruck English, German, Italian, and Spanish visitors wonder if their grandparents might have been involved. Some of them delve into their own histories as a result, to learn how their predecessors behaved, sometimes uncovering painful truths.

At Feldafing, our last stop, we encountered resistance. The proprietor of the main hotel, the person who could have helped, was dismissive and brusque. He wanted nothing to do with us, and would not be swayed even after hearing that Leonard Bernstein had appeared at Feldafing and performed for thousands of DPs.

Originally a *Hitlerjugend* summer camp about 32 kilometers [20 miles] from Munich, Feldafing DP camp, established in May 1945, housed 3,000 Hungarian survivors. It had stone and wood barracks and little else. As in Landsberg, it took some convincing to replace the non-Jewish Polish and Hungarian DPs with Jewish survivors from Dachau. The Americans still firmly believed in repatriation, but the news spread. Jews who returned to their villages in the countries of origin faced further persecution, even death.

Feldafing DP camp was the first of its kind to regain normalcy despite the lack of sanitation and the poverty. Residents organized secular and religious schools, established an extensive library, the first all-Jewish hospital, and a rabbinical council. Several newspapers were published, and two theatrical troupes and an orchestra entertained. Feldafing became another example of cooperative living, similar to the *kibbutz system*.

The DPs' priority to create community and educate their children was evident in the photos I saw of my mother at Windsheim lager—she cuddled someone's child, cooked on whatever makeshift stove she could find, pitched in with farm work. My parents, like others, continued their education—learning trades like dressmaking, carpentry, tailoring, welding, or, as in my father's case, practicing music.

Alexander and I didn't find the original location of Feldafing but we ventured up into the hills on winding roads and stumbled upon yet another cemetery. This one has two sides. The Christian side bloomed with flowers and trees and stately monuments, but in the back, behind and over a thick hedge, an obscure side, a Jewish side, lay emblems dilapidated, neglected, and crumbling. Of the graves that had a headstone, most indicated 1945 as the year of death. Several square stones in the ground had no names or identifying features.

Calmed by silent spirits, the skin in my throat loosened. It was nearly 6:00 p.m. Time to return to the Marriott to unwind, and to toast our success. The African American doorman joined us for dinner. After a cathartic day, the conversation turned to justice and tolerance—our insights heightened by the doorman's experiences of racial inequality. I wasn't aware that during World War II, platoons were segregated. A Black and Asian troop, the 183rd Combat Engineers, participated in the liberation of Dachau, and the all-Black 761st Tank Battalion liberated Gunskirchen, a subcamp of Mauthausen, as well as Buchenwald. (*Perhaps they freed my aunt Magda and my own grandfather?*) One of the soldiers, E.G. McConnell, PFC, a recipient of the Purple Heart for bravery, was born in Jamaica, New York, where racial strife was a daily misery. When he trod into the abyss of the camp, McConnell had an epiphany. "This," he said, "is what hatred can do."

The seeds of our world's near apocalypse germinated in Munich, but after encounters with so many helpful and sympathetic German people, my preconceptions altered. A serendipitous day, one that only the word *bashert* sufficed, through remarkable coincidences, I found what I had hoped to find. Even more telling, I no longer had the urge to flee.

After dinner, back in my room, I reached for the snapshot I'd brought with me of my father in 2009—when he first glimpsed the grainy photograph of the St. Ottilien Orchestra in Landsberg. In that photo he's handsome and young, standing with the other musicians and Leonard Bernstein. My elderly father's eyebrows are contorted in surprise at the sight. Faltering for a moment, I pulled the photo to my face. "*Papa, I did it!*" I said. Overcome by the highly charged day, tears trickled down my face for the rest of the night.

So much has changed 65 years later. The Shoah seems distant here, even more than in Budapest. I feel the absence of the lost Jewish community, a population now of fewer than 10,000 Jews. Nonetheless life has gone on. With the implicit understanding Hitler was a madman, the events and locations of those times described factually, unapologetically in Munich guidebooks, do not mention that the nation had followed him—some enthusiastically, some willingly, some as bystanders, and a few as rescuers. In Munich, heartened by the remorse, atonement, and acts of clemency I encountered, I feel able to move forward in my own spiritual journey.

At 5:00 a.m. the next morning Alexander picked me up to drive me to the airport. I bid Alexander farewell, knowing the fond embrace could never convey my gratitude. Although I left Europe with reluctance, the unforgettable pilgrimage gave me closure and perspective at a fortuitous time in my life. Ironically, upon my return home, my orchestral career would officially be cut short—another parallel to my father's life. Over time, I would navigate the murky passage, I would absorb all I had learned, and I would acquire the courage to break free from the past.

The pristine Jewish Cemetery at the St. Ottilien Monastery.
The stones represent permanence and indicate our presence as I silently recite the blessing over the dead

The bronze sculpture on the streets of Landsberg. *The monument dominates the main street in Landsberg, the very location of the forced march from Kaufering to Dachau in 1945, and is inscribed: "How was it possible that the townspeople did not know or did not see?"*

Munich memorial stone. *The sculpture has been erected where the main synagogue once stood. The inscription refers to the persecution of the Jews and the razing of the synagogue, demolished Kristallnacht, November 9-10, 1938.*

Entr'acte 2009

What was I thinking? A few dollars for one of Mama's handbags? Now, they signify my connection to her. I retrieve the package from My Sister's Closet, a local vintage consignment store, throw off my coat, and unwrap the exquisite suede handbag, clipping off the offensive tag. The delicately scored sides and the filigree of pliable silver suggest lace. Two shimmering buttons affix the handle. I peek inside: "*Le Goût du Jour, Paris 12. Rue Cambon*."

During a trip to Toronto to take care of details after my mother's death (almost a year ago), I rashly attacked her closets and emptied them of shoes, hats, and clothing so as not to prolong the pain. My father, silent, watched from his wheelchair. The drawers brimmed with scarves of silk, wool, and velvet—azure, amber, scarlet, and jade—and the vintage leather gloves, dresses, and shoes barely fit into three or four hefty lawn and leaf bags. I resisted tackling her collection of purses that had signified a taste of luxury. With a sigh, and a glance at my father, I remember kneeling to clasp them in my arms, when he wasn't looking.

The close encounter at My Sister's Closet spurs me now to scrutinize my highboy. I spread them on my bed—satins, brocades, silks and velvets, rhinestones, sequins, and needlework. An elaborately embroidered, gold-framed clutch creates the impression of tapestry. Its tiny white beads shape a cascade of florets, and petals, and blossoms.

Mama cherished her sequined reticule—a geometric gray and black appliqué with interlocking faux pearls that form a kissing-lock closure. Hesitating a moment, longing for her scent—Chanel No. 5—I draw the purse to my face. But the odor is dank and stale.

As a youngster, handbags seemed to contain the mysteries of womanhood. Decades later, the mystic provisions revealed bobby pins, toothpicks, and face powder; a hand mirror concealed in black suede, an ornate little fan for incessant hot flashes, and a hair-teasing comb for emergency makeovers. But most important, and ever-present, there was a photo of my brother and me.

And there were other accessories to consider. Mama found the prodigious snowfalls of Toronto winters challenging. No clunky mukluks for her. High-heeled upscale boots—even if they were second-hand—a black pair and a brown pair sufficed until we arrived at our destination. My mother always carried her shoes in a felt bag. To enter a person's home with soiled boots was unthinkable, but it was even more offensive to barge inside wearing stocking feet. I assumed it violated her sense of fashion. Subsequently I learn the deeper significance. Only during shiva, the eight-day mourning period after the loss of a loved one, do we walk barefoot. Adornments such as mirrors and makeup are not allowed as mourners mustn't focus on their appearance. While grieving, we sit on low stools to symbolize "being brought low" by the loss. Friends and acquaintances are honor-bound to bring meals, to visit, to comfort, and to enfold the bereaved in their communal embrace.

I see her face when I look at a mirror—the same hazel-colored eyes, pristine complexion, prominent forehead. People say we're alike—feisty, prudent, and opinionated, but surely, I'm not as critical.

The deeply embedded behaviors make sense now. Hunted for being Jewish as a teenager, my mother craved refinement and decorum, grasped for beauty and harmony, and endeavored to extirpate the past.

My mind is drenched with images of my mother as a young girl—barefoot, in a threadbare and patched cloak, fearing for her life. I try to grapple with the phantasm. Hiding in basements, empty warehouses, and rubble, in distress. Despite deprivation, fear, and loss, she never complained. As far as Rob and I were concerned, the past had been excised from her consciousness. Only now do I appreciate her determination—to build a life in Canada, to fashion a proper family, and to ensure my father, and Rob and I, thrived. She forged ahead with gumption, resilience, and a generous dose of chutzpah.

Children of Holocaust survivors have needed a lifetime to process the genetic trauma passed down to us. Quite aware we're alive today by virtue of our parents' survival, our internal gauge makes it visceral, as if we'd been there ourselves experiencing the horrors. To our parents, we came to signify the inexplicable paradox—why they lived when so many died. Our generation, the implausible progeny, represent them. The standards demanded of us are especially high—to excel, to behave irreproachably, to be impeccable inside and out, to impart and proffer beauty, and to never be complacent. But I'm cognizant that the role of chronic worrier has been passed down to me. Have I unwittingly conveyed my fixations onto Harris? I hope not.

Both of my parents are gone now. I've learned enough of their story to fulfill a destiny I never thought possible. But uncertainty assails me: Am I prepared to take on the mantle of survivor-at-large? My character quirks still stand in the way. I've embodied determination, perseverance, and discipline, but it's challenging to let my guard down, to stop driving myself, to squelch anxiety and guilt, to experience pleasure or frivolity or peace. And, everything smacks of privilege compared to what my parents faced, compared to what people of color experience every day. Even though my skin is white and my hair now blonde, I'm acutely aware of the maligned minority I belong to. Going forward, how will I fashion some kind of truce with the turmoil that resides within?

13

LIVING IN ISOLATION

"My ears can no longer bear performing," I murmured, sotto voce. After several seconds of dead air and a somber nod from the maestro, I stumbled out of the room.

Once I returned to the States, I'd made an appointment with the management of the Minnesota Orchestra, resigning my position as associate-principal cello. Seated in Osmo Vänskä's Orchestra Hall studio, sparsely decorated, Finnish-style, the concert grand piano positioned beside a black lacquered desk strewn with musical scores —where we'd rehearsed, where we'd greeted artists, where we'd explored countless pieces of music—I snuffed out a 31-year career in a few-minute meeting.

Unable to face my colleagues, I left them each a note with my goodbyes and departed the hall for the last time. Bitter tears flowed as I drove home to a cloistered existence, a musician afraid of sound. Accustomed to being among thousands of people, an unrelentingly scheduled existence, and my position as an artist, performer, and advocate for the arts, I sank into a deep depression. Many months would pass in mourning, my father's death now compounded by the end of my career.

Of all the things that swirl in my soul sound predominates viscerally, emotionally, psychically. My earliest memories are infused with exotic, quivering, hushed diaphanous layers of infernal choruses, late-night chamber music. Fantastic, floating hums lapped and lulled me to sleep. Melodies echoed constantly in the recesses of my marrow. It called and I had listened.

Thousands of symphonies later, notes and notes upon notes, sounds that had stirred now disturbed. Emotionally charred, relegated to silence as it self-emptied, I couldn't bear to enter my studio—a still life of sheet music in piles on the floor and heaped on the music stand. Musical phrases practiced for decades swirled in the spheres unhinged. My cello, my constant companion since childhood, lay dormant in its case. Taunted by a closet full of long black clothes—our required uniform—of smooth silks, creamy taffeta, gossamer velvet, and lissome lace, I wrenched each dress off its hanger, tossed them onto the floor, and thrust them into bags: destination, Goodwill. Awakening each morning in a fog of loss, with pangs of anxiety, only my puppy roused me from under the covers. My sense of identity crumbled. Who was I in the wake of this terrible new ache?

Once animated and outgoing, I became subdued, soft spoken. Released from the incessant clatter of life, isolated from human contact, stripped of music, the perpetual blackout amplified my hunger to create.

Entr'acte 2011

One of the first things I learn as a young cellist is that a page of music waits, quietly. A musical score, says pianist Jeremy Denk, is "at once a book and a book waiting to be written." The act of playing music is an act of re-creation—which brings to life the intentions of the composer. To hone our skills, we still the mind and the body, to think through a masterwork, to fashion the space for the soul to create and to dream. In the silence of our studios, after we've mastered the notes on the page technically, we improvise, invent, and conceive of an interpretation, which is an amalgamation of the composer's intentions with our personalities.

Art cannot thrive in isolation. A writer needs to be read; an actor needs to be seen; a musician needs to be heard. Beyond our ateliers our conception blossoms in the domain of relationships and connections. During the rehearsal process and performance, our music is shaped by those with whom we are playing, those who performed these works before us, and by the ambience of the hall and the reaction of the audience.

A concert engenders a sense of collective concentration, an atmosphere, which allows each listener to dwell for a moment in deeper realms, to surrender to the emotions of the music. As in theater, the ebb and flow of the drama is shaped by an inhalation, an exhalation—each pause allowing the music to breathe, each phrase like a caress, each section a moment of repose. A concert presents the impossibility of recurrence; hence an artist gives their all to create something singular, perhaps unexpected, and larger than ourselves. Deprived of silence, music flounders in a nebulous mass; without time to decipher or comprehend the sounds before us.

Soundlessness, a foreign notion in our noisy world, can be a powerful force. Moments of silence express mourning, elicit reflection, inspire meditation or prayer, offers us opportunities to explore vital truths. But silence is not the complete absence of sound, for the winds blow, the waves crash, the birds sing, and our hearts still beat.

We musicians who've had the discipline to spend hours upon hours of time alone with the music know that time spent in stillness can be rejuvenating. No worthy invention, thought, or masterpiece was ever conceived otherwise. But for me, the silence is my undoing.

Doctors confessed: my rare condition had not been thoroughly researched. There really was nothing more I could do. Howie, undeterred, probed tenaciously for months, until finally, he stumbled upon a clinic that specializes in hyperacusis and tinnitus, at the Oregon Health and Sciences University in Portland. It would be three months before they could see me.

When the time came to make the trip, I boarded the airplane with the heaviest-duty earplugs I could find and with apprehension about the upcoming appointments with a team of otolaryngologists and audiologists.

We squeezed into a tiny examination room. Multiple specialist tested my hearing, my ears convulsing each time they were touched. After 12 hours over two days the doctors fit me with specially programmed devices. These attenuators, they said, could be controlled with a remote, and would reduce the world's volume without altering its clarity.

The final step: to test them. I recoiled with anticipation before the doctor even made a sound. He brandished a spoon then emphatically clanged a dish. But it didn't hurt. We went out into the common areas of the hospital, even passing by the noisy café. But it didn't hurt. A woman wearing high-heeled shoes clattered by. But it didn't hurt. That I experienced no pain felt miraculous.

With the protection of my new hearing devices, they told me, I could embark on the next phase of treatment—a desensitization strategy to teach my brain to accept sound again. I would need to tune out the noise around me. In other words, I'd need to unlearn my musician's finely-honed ability to pay close attention to sound. The specialists provided an armload of CDs of pleasing sounds—rainfall, blowing wind, ocean waves. I was to play them for a few minutes, gradually increasing to several hours a day for the next few months as low-volume background noise to my normal daily activities. I should take it slow, they warned me, perhaps a year or more, *adagio*, boosting the volume by degrees. Eventually my tolerance might start to improve. Then a dreaded caveat: with my endurance so compromised, my hearing likely would never return to normal levels.

I asked the question I'd been steeling myself to ask: what about music? Their answer was noncommittal. I would never again be an orchestral musician, might never tolerate noisy venues—but, although the retraining program couldn't guarantee success—improvement could occur...perhaps enough to play the cello?

Averse to being whittled by despair, I became a zealous patient; within months, my sound sensitivity decreased. With my hearing devices in, my husband and I could venture out to see a quiet film, invite a small group of friends over, and dine in quaint restaurants if we avoided the weekend crowds. But my fingers itched to play. Two years after my trip to the Oregon clinic, and two years of desensitization, I entered my studio, took the cello out of its red case, and delivered us both from hibernation. Gingerly at first and with the left earplug in, I moved my rusty fingers. My muscles ached, and my fingers chafed against the slender metal strings. To my ears I sounded like a complete beginner. But I was persistent. Somehow, albeit away from the massive sound of an orchestra, I would play *Kol Nidrei* again, and integrate music to tell my parents' story.

Moving to Minneapolis in 1980 necessitated summoning courage. I felt trepidation not because the orchestra had high standards, and not because of the heaps of snow and frigid temperatures. Minneapolis, I learned, had the distinction of being one of the most antisemitic cities in the United States. In the 1930s elite Protestant families dominated politics and business, and there was a commonly held prejudice that Jews did not deserve equal standing in society. "Restricted" or "exclusive clientele" became the pervading euphemism for Gentiles only.

Minneapolis made no such pretense. Prominent companies such as Dayton's, 3M, General Mills, and Pillsbury did not hire Jews. Sports and service clubs (Kiwanis, the Lions Clubs, AAA) refused membership to Jews. Signs appeared, even at the trendy Calhoun Beach Club, "No Jews, peddlers, and dogs allowed," "NJA," "Christian preferred, Gentiles only," malevolently aligned with hateful "whites only" policies. Areas of the city refused to sell homes to people who were "not full bloods of the so-called Caucasian or white race."

Even in Howie's day, in the 1960s, secretive Nazi-like groups had 800 members. Jewish medical students and doctors were barred from residency and hospital jobs, and lawyers from certain firms. "*Pssst! Don't make trouble! Keep a low profile,*" people hissed—precisely what my parents felt.

In the 1930s and '40s, the unusual number of blondes living here induced many of my coreligionists to Scandinavianize their Jewish sounding names, fearing persecution, just as my family Hungarianized theirs—yet another generation of Jews who changed their names and dyed their hair. I admit my dark tresses became lighter too. Unwilling to admit being a blonde made me more comfortable in my skin, I colored my hair as my mother had, convinced my intentions were simply to cover the gray.

I'd grown up in a city with a large and visible Jewish community. Jewish homes beckoned with their mezuzahs, and restaurants flaunted bagels, matzo ball soup, pastrami sandwiches on rye, and famous pastries such as chocolate *babka*, nut-filled *rugelach* and *hamantaschen* stuffed with apricots. Disconcerted, I circumvented having to adapt to an invisible and vilified community. The music world is insular. Being onstage most hours of the day meant little contact with "civilians." Intense performance schedules disconnected me from real-world concerns.

My resignation from the orchestra was the opportunity to confront these issues and prompted me to examine my values. Too often, dehumanization of and prejudice toward other human beings who may appear different or believe differently has led to violence and atrocity—a perspective my very existence underscores. Had the Holocaust taught us anything? Active genocides continue, of the Rohingya in Myanmar, the Nuer in South Sudan, Christians and Yazidis in Iraq and Syria, and others, let alone the ongoing racial strife here in this country between White People and People of Color. Despite discomfort about "coming out" and speaking more openly as a Jew, I've lived long enough in isolation. To educate people about the Holocaust, to do my part against the recurrence of bigotry, and to pursue *Tikkun Olam*, the Jewish precept to heal the world, is the obligation of my generation.

The names of individual heroes hummed in my ears—Raoul Wallenberg, Chiune Sugihara, Oskar Schindler, Carl Lutz, Varien Fry, Sir Nicholas Winton, Hanna Szenes, Ho Feng-Shan, Irena Sendler, Jan Karski, and more than 25,000 others who risked their lives to save Jews. And in our time the people who've spoken out for the powerless have been shining examples: Rosa Parks, Nelson Mandela, John

Lewis, Martin Luther King Jr., Nobel Prize laureate Malala Yousafzai, climate activist Greta Thunberg, and, of course, Ruth Bader Ginsburg, notorious RBG. Still, the path ahead unnerved me. Blinded by the ear injury, I had plunged through the looking glass adrift, paddling feverishly to keep myself from sinking into a whirlpool.

To boost my confidence and to find my way forward I needed guidance. A friend suggested The James P. Shannon Leadership Institute—a yearlong program through the Amherst Wilder Foundation in St. Paul that offers the opportunity for community leaders to renew, recharge, and reflect. I would learn how to redefine my purpose, gain clarity, and increase my effectiveness, she told me. Just what I needed.

My partners from all over the country comprised the most diverse group I had ever associated with—individuals from different cultures, nationalities, and faith traditions, with varying skin colors and backgrounds—and who were, for a change, not musicians. During the Shannon program's weekend retreats, Steve, our facilitator—a Tom Hanks type, with a goatee, a compact physique, and mischievous facial expressions—prodded, cheered, and challenged us; we discussed how to integrate personal changes to improve our direction and focus. We developed strategies, we role-played, and we tackled issues of social justice and community service. The writings of Parker Palmer, Paul Hawken, and the wise words of Bertrand Russell resonated with me, "Man is a credulous animal and must believe in something. In the absence of good grounds for belief, he will be satisfied with bad ones." At each session, I felt my energy and optimism evolve through even the outlandish assignments, endeavors I'd never dared to try before.

Our year-end goal was to formulate a five-year plan to present to the group. Five years? I had no idea what the next few months would look like.

The deadline approached. I sat at my desk in front of a blank computer screen, impotent, the muses: Calliope, Euterpe, and Clio—poetry, music, and history—were nowhere to be found. My parents' story whirled, free-wheeling nearby, but a vision of my future, and how to convey all I had learned, eluded me. After several days of writer's block and frustration, I reread some of my father's testimony. Then the tale alighted, gently, into a rhythmic poem (although I have never written poetry). Perhaps a multimedia theater piece—a presentation with narration, a slide show, and cello-playing, to chronicle my parents' experiences during the Holocaust—would fulfill the aim of initiating conversations about racism. The thought of playing for people again galvanized me to start the cello anew.

I compiled 180 archival and personal images—photos of my family from the 1940s, from the US Holocaust Memorial Museum, of individuals from several different cultures, and of recent genocides. Integrating the old with the contemporary, I arranged them to coincide exactly with my recitation. Beginning with the statement "we are much more similar than we are different," I put the images together: A buck-toothed boy; a Navajo shaman in full-feathered headdress, a Somali woman wrapped in a shawl, an infant swaddled in her arms; giggling Palestinian youngsters; a Peruvian boy tending his sheep; a kimono-clad Japanese geisha, cherry blossom petals in her hair; an Amish farmer; a Hindu woman in a turquoise sari, hiding behind her scarf; an African American man snuggling with his daughter; blonde, redheaded, and brunette children singing joyful songs.

Humans hope. We all relish family. We pursue food and shelter, yearn for freedom and love. Nonetheless the inexorable descent to hell and madness did occur. I placed those photos next: of homosexual prisoners wearing the pink triangle, and of ghettos, roundups, cattle cars, barbed wire, skeletons, and slaves; images of the swastika, and the Star of David in multiple languages: *Juif, Jood, Jude*; a sign "Help wanted: whites only," and the bronzed *Shoes on the Danube* monument at the edge of the shore. I inserted snapshots of my mother, her ID card pronouncing her STATELESS, and concluded with a shot of Papa playing again, of hands enfolding the globe; of heroes, and the memorable words of Elie Wiesel: "Being silent is the greatest sin of all."

At five key moments, I planned to play cello works, evocative music my father performed, from five different countries, ending the presentation with the piece I played at my father's side during his final days, the *Prelude* from Johann Sebastian Bach's *Solo Suite No. 1*. For the first time the technology, though complicated, proved to be the easy part. The cello seemed totally alien in my hands. But if my father could restore his playing after slave labor, I could heal too.

My Shannon cohorts were bemused when I dragged a PowerPoint projector, my computer, a little straw suitcase, a music stand, and my cello into the lecture hall on presentation day. I took my cello out of its case, then set up the computer and screen, and opened the small straw valise. Garish carpeting offset my display items: a baguette, a menorah, several ancient snapshots, and plastic shackles that looked real. When I donned a yellow star imprinted with the word *JUDE*, a hush descended over the group. I tuned, turned the slide show on, and opened with Ravel's sultry *Pièce en forme de Habanera* using my father's sheet music, copied in his own hand. Gradually taut muscles in my neck released. I stood for my rhythmic oration, the images timed to coincide with the recitation. But most important, even if my hands and arms strained with the effort, the cello tones echoed, the Bach flowing as it once had, an eon ago.

When the concluding chord dissolved, I noticed Steve's lower lip quivering and several people dabbing their eyes. I thought I heard Mama's *Bravo-oh-OH*. The classroom, awash with emotion was tangible evidence of the transformative power of music. I knew I had been shown the way forward.

Surveying the room, grateful for the guidance of my partners, I pledged to foster dialogue. It would take another two years of healing, but I had faith that the simple act of sharing our stories with one another would lead to understanding and to what connects and elevates us as human beings. Through my words and my cello playing I'd venture forward to impart *Tikkun Olam*, assured my parents' story might impart lessons to future generations.

Raoul Wallenberg, Swedish hero. *Budapest, Hungary, May 12, 2012: A stamp printed in Hungary shows Raoul Gustaf Wallenberg (1912–1945?).* Credit: Olga Popova, Shutterstock Royalty-free stock photo ID: 559569658.

Raoul Wallenberg Holocaust Memorial Park

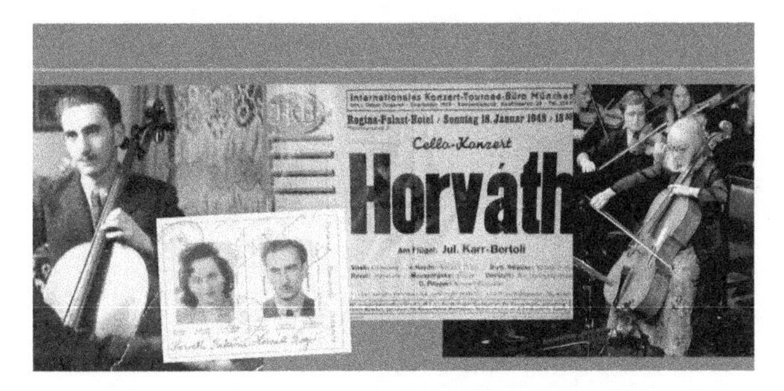

The newly created social justice presentation. Credit: Photo illustration courtesy of Bettina Dehnhard, Communications Coordinator, the Germanic-American Institute, Saint Paul, Minnesota.

A class shares their thoughts *I was invited to perform my social justice presentation for a class at St. Cloud State University, and to lead a discussion for Create Comm*UNITY*, an annual event to foster dialogue about race. First row L to R: a student from Sierra Leon, my piano accompanist Heather MacLaughlin, me with a Jewish star donned; behind me and to the right Hedy Tripp, Professor, Department of Ethnic and Women's Studies for the Asian American studies program, St. Cloud State University, Saint Cloud, MN.*

14

WHEN HISTORY IS REVISED AND DENIED

> "A-S-S-H-O-L-S: I've formed an Association of Auschwitz Survivors, Survivors of the Holocaust and Other Liars... Oh, you think that's tasteless? I don't see any reason to be tasteful about Auschwitz. It's baloney. It's a legend. I'm going to sink the battleship Auschwitz."

That evening in the movie theater, Howie sensed my shivers. I gripped the armrests to steady myself through the slander and lies. A wheezing sound emanating from my chest disturbed the silence.

When the movie *Denial* was released in September 2015, based on the acclaimed book *Holocaust History on Trial* by American historian Deborah Lipstadt, Howie and I intended to see it. Holocaust denial is a hot topic for Jews. The transcripts of the infamous lawsuit and trial brought against Lipstadt by Holocaust denier David Irving in 1999 was carefully reenacted in the film. Oscar-winning actress Rachel Weisz played the protagonist Lipstadt: a much-admired scholar, author, and Dorot Professor of Modern Jewish History and Holocaust Studies at Emory University in Atlanta, a professor with a feisty demeanor, flaming red hair, and an unwavering belief in truth and justice.

Lipstadt repudiates the growing assault on truth and memory. In the late 1990s, she denounced the movement of writers and speakers who falsify the very existence of the Holocaust, and targeted the infamous Holocaust denier at the forefront of the crusade, right-wing extremist David Irving. Irving retaliated. Accusing Lipstadt and Penguin, her publisher, of libel, he sued.

European Jews who'd survived the inferno expected Lipstadt to represent them; to speak for them, to attest to the suffering and slaughter inflicted upon them. But no survivors were called to testify. Even Lipstadt did not testify. It would dignify the deniers. The legal team implemented a shrewd strategy: not to prove the most documented genocide in history did indeed happen, but to confirm Irving deliberately lied, fabricated, and distorted the facts based on his antisemitic views. International press packed the courtroom.

Irving proclaimed Lipstadt had spearheaded a worldwide conspiracy in an effort to discredit him. Well regarded in some circles, having written some 30 books as a World War II chronicler, wasn't he a reputable academic? Lipstadt's barristers solicited opinions from several expert historians who assessed Irving's vast output and scrutinized his writing for accuracy.

The movie reenacts Irving's outrageous assertions. As we watched the macabre testimony I wriggled lower and lower in my seat. He discounted architectural drawings of Auschwitz and the eyewitness accounts. He claimed the Holocaust was a myth invented by Jews, justifying the deaths as "everyday casualties of war." He attributed the photos of thousands of corpses to propaganda perpetuated by the Allies. *The Diary of Anne Frank*, according to Irving, was "a romantic novel, rather like *Gone with the Wind*." Discussion about "alleged gas chambers" resulted in abhorrent calculations. "How many cadavers could realistically be piled into elevators?" goaded Irving, oozing sarcasm. "You say there were no doors?"

Emotionally beaten black and blue by the footage, barely stifling the urge to scream, I descended into a flashback: my mother's friends and family annihilated at Auschwitz, the largest cemetery in the world. I remembered Ada, my mother's close friend, sterilized without anesthesia, her parents and siblings murdered; I remembered my 90-year-old acquaintance Mary Neumann orphaned at age 16; I remembered the mother of my Mama's first cousin Trudy murdered at age 39. No remains to trace, no dates to commemorate, no headstones to visit. Can anyone discount the Block 5 display cases, which hold enormous piles of shoes, suitcases, eyeglasses, and crutches? And Block 4, Room 5, which hoards hair shorn from the heads of 140,000 victims? One-third of those murdered at Auschwitz were Hungarian. Neither the victims nor the bystanders or the perpetrators deny what happened there.

Initially skeptical about the accusations against Irving, Richard Evans, a graduate of Oxford, author of *In Defense of History*, and an expert on 19th- and 20th-century German history, conceded, after tracing Irving's footnotes and sources, that Irving deliberately falsified the past.

"I was not prepared for the sheer depths of duplicity... His numerous mistakes... calculated and deliberate... A knotted web of distortions, suppressions and manipulations."

When Lipstadt prevailed, the euphoria surrounding the international headlines led Jews to hope other Holocaust deniers would be delegitimized. But that was not to be. As we recede from the horrors of the Shoah more people are ignorant of the past and this history in particular.

On the drive home from the movie theater we were deathly silent. As soon as we arrived, with ghastly curiosity, I searched for Irving's website to see for myself. A photograph reeked of self-aggrandizement. His posts made me recoil in disgust—vituperative slander so utterly repulsive I felt slimy like a voyeur. I whacked the computer lid down.

Entr'acte 2015

That night, my dreams are a chorus of lamentation. My parents weep, and my son calls out. David Irving towers menacingly over me. *I don't even look Jewish*, I think. My hazel eyes widened in panic, stare up at him:

I hear the vicious dogs barking.

I suffer the backbreaking toil.

I taste the animal fodder masquerading as food.

I feel the overpowering fear, humiliation, and degradation.

I hear the silence of death.

I smell the constant stench of unwashed bodies, feces, and the black fires of burning corpses in Auschwitz: 1,000 every 15 minutes.

I shiver through the exhaustion of frigid marches, and days without food or water.

I witness the merciless bestiality.

I struggle for air in a cattle car, with men, women, and children crammed in like so many sardines.

I shrivel in the complete darkness.

Still not fully conscious, my curly blond hair in disarray, I realize this dream is reality—a nightmare that engulfs me. Holocaust deniers like Irving strike at my very core.

The anguish and ire, the shame and secrecy. To protect their offspring and to try to move beyond the contagion, survivors remained silent about their experiences. No one really wanted to hear the details of their suffering anyhow, not Americans, not in the 1950s. The Holocaust was too recent, too raw, too deplorable. Besides, Communism was the real threat; Germany the new ally. Families barraged by the specter of nuclear war hastened to build bomb shelters. As a child, I saw posters:

SURVIVAL UNDER ATOMIC ATTACK—HOW TO PROTECT YOURSELF, YOUR FAMILY, YOUR COMMUNITY IN THE EVENT OF AN ATTACK—This book may save your *life*!

My parents yearned to fit in as Canadians, to be inconspicuous, to live in peace. They didn't talk about it. Even so, all their friends belonged to the clandestine club. Holocaust survivors had a grisly commonality.

Despite my parents' efforts to shield us, their pain was bestowed upon my generation. We gleaned the terror, humiliation, and loss, which oozed through our skin, our psyches stamped with anxiety. One thing I learned early on. You could be killed just for being a Jew.

Throughout their lives my father and mother remained suspicious of authority, fearful of anyone in uniform, secretive about their faith. They endured lifelong scars, both physical and emotional, and, I admit, so do I. Their efforts to inculcate the fear of admitting my Jewishness is difficult to shake.

After a concerted effort to speak about being Jewish without fear of repercussions, I thought I'd come out of my shell; I believed I'd processed life-changing losses and the challenges of my upbringing, convinced of the direction my life should take. That is, until the political events of 2015, when my qualms pulled me back into a dark cubbyhole.

The crusade underfoot triggers insurmountable fury and helplessness—Holocaust denial, a scourge, an affliction, arresting my nascent plans. My background persuades me to see it as an abominable omen of more to come. Sure enough, it has resurfaced. Muslim, Black, and Asian people, other ethnic and religious minorities, and Jews are once again denigrated. Vile chants from the "alt-right" and white supremacists echo in my ears, "Your race needs to be collectively ovened"; "White lives matter." "Hitler should have finished the job." Today's "fake news" ricocheted and fused with propaganda of the 1940s.

You may think I'm overreacting. These are just isolated extremists and crackpots. Although Holocaust deniers may seem irrational, theirs is a virulent form of antisemitism that perpetrates stereotypes and lies in a world of fake news and alternative facts. Their words encourage others, especially the younger generation, to cause more harm; to feed antisemitic and Neo-Nazi sympathies; to deliberately obscure truth, and to provoke, cause outrage, and incite violence.

Scholars claim Holocaust denial, the "new antisemitism," recycles many of the elements of pre-1945 antisemitism in a post–World War

II context. Deniers discredit reports of the Holocaust as a vast shadowy plot to shame and disgrace the white, Western world. Even during the 1940s, people in the United States vacillated between belief and disbelief. German massacres of Jewish civilians must surely be propaganda designed to force the government to grant Jews special treatment and consideration.

Some argue that, above all, the supposed hoax serves the interests of the State of Israel. Denying the Holocaust attacks the legitimacy of the country. Others contend Nazism is a laudable political philosophy. They make their case by claiming to be legitimate scholars: their goal—to reestablish fascist laws and Nazi ideology put in place in the 1940s, to convince the world the "myths" of the Holocaust were created by Jews to serve their own purposes. These groups freely recruit and promulgate their inflammatory right-wing ideologies, made easy on the internet, and they extend beyond Neo-Nazi groups to include terrorist groups bent on destroying Israel.

To protect my parents and other Holocaust victims, and their offspring from this further assault, I cannot skirt the issue.

The Holocaust represents a schism, a horror on a scale never before disseminated so widely. Such atrocity was largely unknowable to the world at large before the internet. The government mandated the destruction of an entire people—state-sponsored and condoned —to systematically annihilate all Jews regardless of age, sex, gender, or station in society, in whatever country they resided, to make their race extinct.

Tragically, other mass killings have occurred all too often, before and since—Armenia, Rwanda, Cambodia, Darfur, Bosnia, and notorious mass murders committed by Mao Tse-tung in China and Stalin in Russia.

The term *genocide* didn't even exist before it was coined by Raphael Lemkin in 1944. The United Nations established the Convention on the Prevention and Punishment of the Crime of Genocide in 1948. (The term currently does not include the murder of social classes and political groups.)

Here in our own country, 80 percent of our Indigenous American population was murdered between 1492 and 1900. Enslavement endured by African American people persisted as government dogma and racism continues. I ask: were these acts of barbarism by uncivilized people?

The near consummation of the extermination of an entire people, the Nazis' "Final Solution" and the subsequent murder of six million Jews in what we deem an enlightened world, a world that has learned lessons from history, seems untenable, inconceivable.

Although antisemitism is nothing new, the racial classification of the Jew beginning in the late 1800s changed everything. A Jew was a Jew, wherever they lived—outcasts, not citizens, not merely a group who practiced a non-Christian religion. Is this still the case? Am I an American who happens to be Jewish, or am I looked upon and set apart as a Jew? Am I to be assessed as non-white? Shouldn't classification be arbitrary, and race, ethnicity, or religion irrelevant when it comes to our path and obligation to one another?

Cloaked in unassuming clothing, the deniers claim to be merely revisionists—correcting "errors" in history. The Holocaust is not the only history deemed inconvenient and worth refuting. The continuous denial by the Turks of the genocide of Armenians comes to mind. We know it happened. As with the Holocaust, it's well documented. Certainly, there are many occasions when politicians have distorted the truth to suit their own agenda.

Inundated with hot-off-the-press news, our lives are too hectic to thoughtfully delve into anything but a sound bite. It becomes easy to promulgate biased views and ignore other perspectives. It seems our weak-kneed and indecisive behavior impedes our road to civility, to diplomacy, to listening to each other even if we differ. But today, heightened tensions with nefarious or totalitarian governments has the potential not only to be catastrophic but apocalyptic.

Despite the organizations that promote peace and understanding, demonstrate higher forms of ethics, and establish a culture of conscience and integrity, moral backbone eludes us. Is imbuing the world with justice and peace beyond our grasp? Is the lengthy history of racism and bigotry, fueled by fear of people who are different, getting worse? We have access to global news coverage through the internet, and we see the suffering around us. Refugees who need our help. Aren't we all witnesses and bystanders? Aren't we the people who observed Jews being marched to the camps at Dachau? Today it's preposterous to say, "we didn't know."

Reflecting on the movie, repulsed and riveted, I try to suppress my trepidation, compelling myself to admit at least inwardly, if I don't tell the story, who will? The year 2016 reeks of denigrating, abhorrent, bigoted sentiments. It's the most contentious and offensive political mêlée in my lifetime.

Until November, I'm convinced the racist rhetoric cannot possibly represent the attitude of the American people. Then, Donald Trump wins the election.

Jews rounded up in 1943 and sent to Treblinka. *This occurred after the Warsaw Ghetto Uprising—a four-week-long rebellion by Jewish resistance fighters. The terrified little boy has never been identified but the German officer brandishing his rifle, Josef Blösche, has been immortalized in photos taken by Major General Jürgen Stroop as proof of his 'skill' in taking care of Jews fighting back with little more than stones.* Credit: Courtesy of the United States Holocaust Memorial Museum, Washington, DC.

Original cattle car, 1940s, near Landsberg. *Three cattle cars are preserved in the hills above Landsberg. The exterior locks tight.*

Broken headstones in Budapest. *Now becoming a common sight: crumbling headstones and monuments in Jewish cemeteries, which have been defaced, or vandalized.*

The stereotype of the menacing Jew. The caricature from the 1940s makes its way back into present-day. Credit: United States Holocaust Memorial Museum —An antisemitic poster entitled: "Behind the enemy powers: the Jew.

15

THE FEAR OF RISING ANTISEMITISM

I didn't suspect the mail that day would be loaded. A thick envelope said, "Map Enclosed." When I tore it open, I saw an accordion-pleated booklet. The red and black letters seemed to shriek: "917 ACTIVE HATE GROUPS IN US IN 2016."

Suddenly clumsy, my hands clammy, I flattened the pamphlet and beheld a map of the US dotted with crayon-colored icons representing extremist groups. My eyes are drawn to the vivid blue and red graph at the bottom of the page that says: Anti-Muslim groups up 197%. The number of anti-government organizations exploded from 200 groups during the George W. Bush years to 998 during the Obama administration. In early 2016, it had settled a bit down to 917, at least for now.[1] Except for a handful of states, every state in the nation has a Neo-Nazi presence.[2] We Minnesotans brag about our quality of life, but in 2016 the chart indicates we have ten active hate groups here, while Alaska and Hawaii are the only states without racist organizations. The Southern Poverty Law Center is tracking more than 1,600 extremist groups operating across the country.

The fraught and dreadful year of political campaigning brought out the worst in this country. Donald Trump lashed out. His diatribes

—misogynist, xenophobic, isolationist, and racist—had all but become normalized. Extremist groups and individuals came out from under the rocks, voicing similarly offensive views.

Convinced the opinions expressed were isolated (weren't they from fringe groups?), for the first time I participated in phone banks, signed petitions, and vocally expressed my political ideology: Stronger Together. On November 8, election night, Howie and I chilled champagne ready to celebrate. But red clumps leeched over the map, eclipsing blue, frothing towards the inevitable 270 electoral votes needed. We sat on our sofa, champagne untouched. Howie retired at 2 a.m., but I remained motionless, unable to process the outcome, unable to utter a sound.

With the inevitable weeks away, a prodigious pressure formed inside me. Despite repugnant declarations against women, people with disabilities, and Muslim, Black, and Latino people, as well as reckless quips about the environment, the press, foreign governments (both allies and foes), and derogatory remarks regarding international agreements, Trump was elected—without any political background, with a history of malfeasance and nepotism, and with limited support outside the white male population. To me, the similarities to the unexpected ascent of Hitler punched me in the gut. Violent clashes at political events and the sudden rise of hate incidents after the election—1,094 in the first 34 days—engendered an absence of moral boundaries. Religious and ethnic groups have been subject to harangues; confrontations between right and left and the rise of antisemitic rhetoric have occurred daily, and not just in the US. The rightward tilt has spread around the globe. Hate is once again dividing us.

Entr'acte 2016

"Emergency Survival for All Situations"—*Get yours on Amazon, at REI, My Patriot Supply*. I'm reading up on the latest 'Top Best-Rated Survival Kits' with the sound of Mama's voice echoing, "Don' tell anyone you are *Jewish*. Be nice!" Contradictory thoughts whiz by: outspoken behavior would reflect badly on the entire community, in fact all the Jewish People. Keep a low profile; we must stand up for what is right. Speak out; we should have a packed bag ready with essential supplies—especially soap—just in case we have to flee.

Racist incidents have targeted the Muslim community and immigrants, but once again even more vindictive harangues are aimed at my race and me. I'm concerned about the views of people who live in my neighborhood—in the stately turn-of-the-century homes of stone and brick, with turrets and pillars and wrap-around verandas, and those who rent the modest stucco duplexes and studio apartments around the corner—where American flags proudly hover.

That November day ironically, the skies shimmer a brilliant aqua blue and golden leaves flutter in the light breeze. But, when I walk my dog, my bowels congeal. A five-month-old Dalmatian, a golden retriever, and an affectionate shih tzu nuzzle each other. They all seem to get along. When the young owner of the Dalmatian ambles by me, she wishes me a happy Sunday. *Would she say that if she knew I was Jewish*? When I pass a parked police car. I wonder, *is he watching me? Have I done anything wrong?*

Attempting to keep my equilibrium, and to stay hopeful and positive, I'm wrenched in the opposite direction. Potential disasters clutter my mind: banning immigrants, climate change, nuclear war, violence in the streets. Consumed by the paranoia my father exemplified, I feel too near the precipice. Me, a human rights advocate? I don't think so. I pour over the Hate Map.

"Aren't there any *love* groups?" Howie asks.

The recent election has spurred urgent conversations among Jews. Those of us who are children of the Holocaust vacillate between the impulse to hide, and the pledge to resist. Of two conflicting views, to which group do I belong?—the Jews who were convinced if they kept their heads down, stayed calm and quiet, it would all pass? Or those who predicted a terrifying outcome and took action?

What would my parents have wanted me to do? They brought me

up to exemplify the tenets of ethical behavior; to seek solutions to human conflicts; to respect the freedom, the dignity, and the rights of every human being. Yet every part of my being squirms when I think about interceding—like Perseus confronting Medusa's destructive eyes, terrified of snakes and caves, and of being turned to stone.

When Harris was a little boy, I cast aside my qualms and endeavored to instill Jewish values—sharing with those less fortunate; modelling altruism, compassion, and patience; and, through piano lessons, imparting creativity and perseverance. We enrolled Harris in Sunday school and in 2007, he became bar mitzvah. That year, after Harris begged for a puppy, we relented like so many families do, and we brought Oreo home, for the companionship Harris would experience, and the responsibility he'd learn. But I confess, since Rob and I were never allowed a pet, acquiring a dog was as much for me as for him.

I tried to teach Harris about his grandparents' history without instilling in him some of the trauma I'd lived with. During a Minnesota Orchestra tour, we played in Amsterdam. Howie, Harris, and I visited the Anne Frank House. Like any child, he enjoyed exploring all the nooks and crannies at the Secret Annex, where the Frank family lived hidden for two years until they were betrayed. I took Harris' little hand in mine, pointed to a display, and said, "Honey, Grandma had to wear a star like this." I think he understood.

But the photos provoke me and for a moment my mind drifts. September 1944: a phantasm all too real—while my father labors in Bor, everyone in the Secret Annex arrives at Auschwitz following a three-day train ride. The train doors are flung open. Get out. *Get out. Schnell.* The floodlights blind the prisoners, but the sound of snarling dogs and cracking whips leaves no doubt as to their fate. The men and women are separated. Some are immediately sent to the gas. It's the last time Anne sees her father. Two months later, the sisters, mere skeletons, are transported to northern Germany, to Bergen-Belsen, where typhus rages. Anne and Margot die within days of each other —two of the 1,000 people per day who succumb to the infectious disease at Bergen-Belsen—just weeks before liberation in April 1945.

With a jolt, I find myself back in 2016, disoriented, with a nagging urge to make sense of the past. Our family lives a secular and assimilated life. Although we never miss going to temple on the High Holy Days, Howie and I have a culturally mixed group of friends with whom we share Christmas and Easter dinners, Chanukah and Passover Seders.

We come together as people, and only rarely do we struggle for understanding. Now it's an effort to recover the sense of reconciliation I experienced after performing at the basilica years ago. How have I been caught in my mother's shackles again, the screw pin prickling, turning tighter? Revealing my background and religion is a struggle. My voice drifts in a rapid diminuendo, "Sorry, that date won't work to meet you/teach/perform/attend. You see. It's a ... *Jewish holiday*." *Pfff.* The bitter residue slides down my thighs and settles in my feet.

The following year, in 2017, our fear and disbelief intensifies. The number of hate groups rise to 954 and antisemitic incidents surge. Bomb threats, toppled headstones, vandalizations, graffiti. All over the country. The largest synagogue in Washington State is plastered with the sign,

"Holocau$t i$ fake hi$tory!"

Outrage intensifies when the Idaho Anne Frank Human Rights Memorial in Boise is defaced. One of the marble tablets surrounding the life-sized bronze, the only US memorial in her memory, etched with the Universal Declaration of Human Rights, "contained a racial slur and a message declaring black people aren't human."[3] The country erupts when the Unite the Right rally in Charlottesville, Virginia occurs in August, with Neo-Nazis gathering from across the country, marching and screaming "Jews will not replace us!"

How could this be happening here? Do we even recognize our country anymore? Although these hate groups despise minorities, immigrants, women, and homosexuals, the principal ideology of Neo-Nazi and alt-right groups is their animosity towards Jews. They insist we are the primary enemy, responsible for all the ills of the world. If promulgating these falsehoods weren't so chilling, it would surely be preposterous. Jewish people represent only 2 percent of the US population and merely 0.2 percent of the world's population.

Our temple now has a constant police presence. I worry our house is the only one on the street without Christmas lights, without an exquisitely decorated tree visible from the boulevard. When I perform my multimedia social justice piece, my anxiety multiplies.

The nationalist, isolationist, white supremacist propensities predicted by my parents can no longer be denied. Neo-Nazi, anti-Muslim, anti-gay, anti-immigrant, anti-government, racist, and radical right groups are in our midst. The outward veneer has crumbled to reveal the putrefaction beneath.

I want to throw up my hands (and throw up) at the unique challenge of "fake news," that contagion, *Truthiness*, originally coined by Stephen Colbert, of people who loudly and belligerently make pronouncements, leaving little room for debate or reasonable fact-checking. The age of the conspiracy theorist who deliberately plants fables at a time when a large percentage of people get their news from social media is particularly troubling to me. How can anyone separate the legitimate from fabrications?

Although propaganda is not new, still, I'm discouraged, deflated, crestfallen. With my energy waning I'm tempted to cut off the computer, the internet, my phone, the television, the radio. But I can't assume the head-in-the-sand approach. It's not a viable solution. Not for anyone whose family suffered through the Holocaust.

***Recent antisemitic graffiti in France.** Vandalism occurs here in this country too. In addition to destruction of property and bomb threats, attacks on Jewish people are on the rise.* Credit: Quatzenheim, France - Feb 20, 2019— Sunset over Jewish cemetery in Quatzenheim near Strasbourg with vandalized graves with Nazi symbols blue spray-painted on the damaged graves. Royalty-free stock photo ID: 1319923592.

***Harris and Oreo,** our newest and sweetest member of the family injected light and levity into our lives.*

Entr'acte 2011

Rob's dog is terrified of the scowling Beethoven bust that has sat on our family grand piano for as long as I can remember. She's shivering and shaking, and her antics lighten the mood. It's nice Rob and I can share a moment of levity as we've gathered at my parents' condominium for the last time. My parents' paintings, and prints, which we'll distribute, lean against the walls. My 25-year-old nephew, Aaron, Rob's eldest son, dons one of my father's dapper hats and sashays to the floor-to-ceiling mirror in the hallway. Although Aaron has dark eyes, his resemblance to my father at that age is uncanny. I have to hold my breath and wait for my pulse to return to normal.

When my father passed away, Ian and Cristy continued to live in the apartment rent-free until everything could be finalized, but now the condo has been sold. Rob has taken care of the real-estate paperwork and the tasks as executor of the will.

Since Ian and Cristy don't own much beyond their bed and clothing, we give them the furnishings, the kitchen gadgets and utensils, and the extra sets of fine bone china. Each grandchild chooses from among the paintings, the knick-knacks and whatnots, and small pieces of jewelry, and, as my father wished, they'll all receive a stipend for their education. I give some of my mother's gorgeous shawls to my parents' former music students, but not before I take a whiff of each one. Some still have a lingering odor of Chanel No. 5 Paris, the smell that made me gag as a child. Even most of the embroidered, tasseled, decorative pillows have been dispersed.

The overwhelming finality hits me once everyone leaves, the apartment empty except for the decades-old seafoam-green sofa, with wood trim. When I was growing up the ever-present plastic covering stuck to the backs of my legs. Uncovered only when guests came over, the sofa shows very little wear, but no one wants to take it.

I lay back against the velvety cushions, and whispered, "Oh, Mama." Memories, so unbearable she could never speak of them, especially not to Rob or me—her own children. It's painful to revisit my father's often-misconstrued rages. In truth, they never overshadowed his generosity and love, never outshone the learning he instilled—a tremendous work ethic, the love of literature and art, and his passion for music and beauty. This is where we learned about the value of speaking truth, pursuing altruism, and seeking justice—yes, even though the Holocaust hammered incessantly.

I wondered: hadn't my father, just 22 when he was rounded up, formed traits—paranoia, suspicion, distrust, anger—which perhaps saved him? There had to be more. Shrewdness. Recklessness. Vigilance. Courage. Hope. Without weaponry, and stripped of all property, what remains? Only the strength of will and spirit—the soul's resistance. In his transformative work, *Man's Search for Meaning*, Viktor Frankl asserts that even during the worst horrors he did not have "nothing." He had his mind. He had purpose. He had freedom to choose how he responded to vicissitudes however terrible. Is this not resistance?

Would resistance have taken on other forms had the Jews of Europe and the Diaspora known with certainty what would become of them? That we cannot know. Enemies of the Reich and 20,000 to 30,000 Jewish partisans did not go like sheep to their slaughter. In great peril, they took to the forests and used sticks and stones, and subterfuge and sabotage, to disrupt the Nazi war effort. They forged documents, distributed leaflets, joined guerilla fighting groups, carried messages, and damaged munitions they were forced to make. They assisted Allied air force soldiers and smuggled children to safety. Some led refugees on foot through mountain passes. Others tried to preserve recipes and songs, held covert prayer services, gave Hebrew lessons. They furtively pursued activities, which instilled hope, with the will to resist and with culture food—writing poetry, playing music, staging dramas, singing, and composing, as a last testament. Is this not resistance?

These musings saturate the atmosphere in the apartment. I hear a melody tapping and feel my parents' presence. They claimed luck was on their side, but I know better now. No need to speak or to make a sign.

I glance around the room one last time, grab Beethoven, and decide to take the sofa.

---

1. In 2018, the numbers rose to 1,020.
2. California has 79 groups.
3. Southern Poverty Law Center Hatewatch, May 2017.

PART V

COMING FULL CIRCLE COMMEMORATION AND RECONCILIATION

This is the task: in the darkest night to be certain of the dawn, certain of the power to turn a curse into a blessing, agony into a song...
to go through Hell and to continue to trust in the goodness of God—
this is the challenge and the way.

—Rabbi Abraham Joshua Heschel (1907–1972)

16

PLAYING FOR MY PEOPLE IN GERMANY (LANDSBERG, 2018)

The faint ring could barely be heard in the din of the restaurant. Digging into my purse for my cell phone, I see a several-digit number beginning with +49 on the screen. *An international call? From Europe*? A dusky voice trembling with emotion whispers, "Is this Janet? Oh, Janet. It is wonderful to speak with you. I am calling from Landsberg. You see, there are so many things to speak about." Years have passed since I'd been in Landsberg, but this call thrusts me back. In music we say, *D.C.*, *Da Capo*, repeat once again from the beginning. I have no inkling the coda, the ultimate conclusion, is yet to come.

Exactly eight years after that slushy day in January 2009, the day my father revealed he'd played with Leonard Bernstein, Howie and I made a spur-of-the-moment decision to fly to Miami. Still reeling from the 2016 election results, we thought if we were to head for warm weather, stress would simply melt away. Why not escape the frigid temperatures of Minnesota and the chill of apprehension washing over us? We happened to choose a hotel on the ocean but close to the Jewish Community Center. They had just suffered a bomb threat. Orthodox Jews sauntered along the boardwalk openly, unafraid—the women covered head to toe in long black garb, even for a dip in the water, with a scarf or a wig to cover their hair as required by Jewish law. The lulling swells of the ocean soothed as we walked along the pristine, white sand beach.

By chance, Sonia Beker and her husband were vacationing in Miami. We hadn't seen each other in years. Sonia suggested meeting at Hakkasan, the Chinese restaurant at the Fountainebleau Hotel. Festooned in red to celebrate the 2017 Year of the Rooster, it's a maze of dark wood paneling encircling a luminous blue bar. The equally colorful food—delicately scored meats topped with greens, pomegranate seeds, and purple flowers; bright orange stuffed dumplings served in individual bamboo steamers—was a perfect spot for a reunion, a scrumptious meal, and nonstop conversation.

During our week in Miami, Sonia received an email from Landsberg, from two people neither of us knew. The letter outlined a grassroots effort by the German townspeople to organize a concert, to be held in May 2018, to commemorate the seventieth anniversary of the program with Leonard Bernstein and the St. Ottilien Orchestra. They hoped to establish the first Wolf Durmashkin Composition Award, an international award for composers, in honor of Sonia's uncle—a gifted musician, conductor, and composer who perished during the Holocaust. The concert and accompanying exhibit would be supported in part by the Bavarian Ministry of Cultural Affairs. *Might we be able to attend?*

Surprised they conceived of the program with no prompting from us, we replied immediately. *Of course, we'll come!* A woman named Karla Schönebeck, one of the directors, followed up:

Jan 26, 2017

Dear Sonia,

I've just met the son of one of the former German doctors who was at St. Ottilien. At that time, he was only 15 years old. The piano your mother, Fania, played, belonged to him. It still exists, had been restored some years ago and is now in Munich. I asked him to take a picture of the piano, which he promised to do. He will come to the concert I Landsberg too, to meet you.

Best regards, Karla

A trip to Germany next May? Why not. It could be lovely in the spring. My ambivalence about going to Germany had largely been dispelled during my 2010 pilgrimage. Sonia and I discussed how to make the trip truly meaningful. Perhaps we could erect a small plaque at St. Ottilien in honor of our parents? I remembered the ancient little town Landsberg am Lech—picturesque, perched upon a lake, with a 15th-century basilica, a turreted gateway, a fairytale-like stone castle, and a Baroque town hall. Pastel façades in mint green, coral, lavender, and yellow overlook the cobblestone streets.

Sonia and I imagined—I don't know what we imagined—their community orchestra would play a few tunes? A certificate would be awarded to a deserving young German composer, presumably presented by Sonia? A handful of people would come together to remember the program 70 years ago?

Karla, we later learned, would work tenaciously and with vision. The event unfolded over the following months and captured the imagination of the entire region. Eight founding partners offered their support, including Kulturefonds Bayern Kunst, the city of Landsberg am Lech, the Bavarian Philharmonic, and the association die Kunst BauStelle.

The 2018 event would coincide with worldwide celebrations of Leonard Bernstein's 100th birthday. Global media coverage and thousands of concerts would feature performances of Bernstein's compositions, *Mass*, *Age of Anxiety*, *Jeremiah*, and *Kaddish*; new stagings of his Broadway hits, *Candide*, *On the Town*, and *West Side Story*; and rebroadcasts of his Harvard Lectures, Young People's Concerts, documentaries, and filmed performances.

In August, I received the first draft of the program, its scope much broader than either Sonia or I expected. The *International Jewish-German Week May 2018* would not only include a concert and the

Wolf Durmashkin Composition Award, but also a gala dinner, sightseeing tours, a press conference, and an official ceremony to mark the anniversary of the founding, in 1948, of the State of Israel. The documentary produced by John Michalczyk—the film I viewed with my father in August 2009, which spurred his testimony ("Unbelievable Janetkém. It's me! There. There I am! I had so much hair"): *Creating Harmony: The Displaced Persons' Orchestra of St. Ottilien* —would receive its German premier, the producer in attendance.

After receipt of the program, I received a note from Karla.

August 2017

Dear Janet,

Although I didn't wrote (sic) to you within the last month, I havn't (sic) forgotten you, of course not. We have changed bit the program. I would prefer to have a call with you as it makes the things from my kind of view more simple. Be so kind to give me your telephone and I call you. Is this ok? The orchestra will be the Bayerische Philharmonie (Bavarian Philharmonic) who's chief conductor is Mark Mast, a former scholar of Leonard Bernstein. You see, there are many things to speak about.

Warm wishes, Karla

When my cell phone rang with the prefix +49 at lunch time, I had to hurry out of a noisy café to hear. Not a great connection. While Karla spoke, I paced in the parking lot, the gravel crunching under my feet, "Janet. It is my honor to speak to you. We are so pleased you and your family are coming to Landsberg."

I struggled to express how meaningful this trip would be. Karla asked if my father ever spoke about playing at St. Ottilien. No, I explained, he never spoke about those times, or about the orchestra, not until my inadvertent question about Bernstein. But I did remember hearing the name repeatedly St. Ottilien, St. Ottilien, St. Ottilien as a child, without knowing what that meant.

Strangely silent for a moment, she murmured, "I am again and again touched what the Nazis had done with wonderful people as your parents. We cannot bring the people back, but we have to do everything we can to educate the next generations. It must come from people like me, ordinary German people." I stopped moving to savor every word. "With the rise of antisemitism now again," she says, "we must ensure it can *never* happen again."

For a moment, both of us were overcome. After regaining her composure, Karla filled in more details. "On May 10, 2018, we will have two concerts as Bernstein did 70 years ago, on that day in Landsberg. We plan to imitate the program as closely as possible, *Rhapsody in Blue* of course, etc. But what could be more meaningful to all of us, to your family, and all the Jewish People, if you will play *Kol Nidrei*? Will you play? It would be our honor."

More than a decade had passed since I'd played *Kol Nidrei* in the basilica in Minneapolis. To play in Germany, where so many perished, in the town where my own father performed after his harrowing escape from slave labor, would be a privilege and, at the same time, an even more daunting responsibility.

I conveyed the association my father and I, and the Jewish

People have had with this piece through sound waves wriggling into a handheld device—implausibly enough—the signals floating across the ocean. I knew we understood one another. The original program of 1948 would be reenacted, the synergy between Landsbergers and descendants sending an extraordinary message to my father.

Returning to my seat in the restaurant, I couldn't eat a thing.

The directors, Karla Schönebeck and Wolfgang Hauk, announced a global call for musical scores for the competition: sponsored by The Wolf Durmashkin Concert Association, WDCA.

The association die Kunst BauStelle promotes art and culture, cultural education, and cultural youth projects.

May 10th 2018 marks the 70th anniversary of the concert of the DP-Orchestra along with establishment of the State of Israel (14th of May 1948). It is with this historical background we call upon young people to consider the circumstances, moods, feelings, defeats, fightings, and also the rebellion as a framework in their compositions for submission to the contest.

For months emails flew back and forth from Germany. Plans changed daily—or so it seemed to me. Karla and Wolfgang had a superabundance of ideas, ambitious undertakings for even professional music ensembles. I must admit some skepticism.

But my own issues consumed me: practicing and playing *Kol Nidrei* and, the thorniest concern, flying overseas with my 18th-century handmade and irreplaceable cello. Cellists purchase an extra seat on an airplane for their instrument, or risk irrevocable damage in the unheated baggage compartment or through clumsy handling. The cost of an additional ticket would be prohibitive. Shuddering at the thought of someone tossing my instrument onto a luggage turnstile, I decided to borrow a cello. When inquiries in and around Munich yielded nothing, Sebastian Toettcher, a former classmate, who'd moved to Berlin, offered to lend me his valuable Italian instrument. It would mean a stop there, a train to Munich, and another to Landsberg. Wielding a cello and several pieces of luggage, especially with multiple stops, is never without complications, but a reunion with Sebastian and a chance to see some of Berlin would more than compensate.

We planned to arrive a few days early to recover from jet lag, and to familiarize myself with the cello, which would likely be larger and more resistant than mine.

The program began to take shape. Guy Mintus, a young Israeli jazz pianist and composer, would play *Rhapsody in Blue*, and tenor Yoel Sorek would sing some of the Hebrew and Yiddish songs that had been on the original program. The tentative schedule called for numerous rehearsals in both Munich and Landsberg with two different orchestras. *Kol Nidrei* is only a 12-minute work. Why so many rehearsals? Back-to-back practices would require a great deal of stamina, especially on a strange cello, let alone the ever-present concern, my ears withstanding the onslaught.

I wrote for clarification. (*Was I being a nuisance?*) Transporting a cello from Landsberg to Munich and back would require a large car or a van. Cello soloists, I also pointed out, usually perform on a hollow wooden podium similar to what a conductor stands on—a rectangular box long enough to accommodate the metal endpin or spike holding the cello. Raising the cellist off the stage floor helps project the sound. Might the Bayerische Philharmonie (Bavarian Philharmonic) have one?

The finalized program triggered consternation. Jam-packed with pieces and songs, speeches and tributes, my eyes were drawn to my name in bold:

The Cast of the Bavarian Philharmonic Orchestra

(to replicate the historical one from 1948)

9 Strings: 4 Violins, 2 Violas, 1 Bass, and 2 Cellos (one Janet Horvath) 9 Woodwind/Brass/Percussion: (1 Bassoon, 1 Oboe, 1 Clarinet, 1 Trumpet, 1 Horn, 1 Flute, 1 Trombone (only Gershwin), 1 Percussion, 1 Accordion

My tightly packed schedule, with two different orchestras, two different locations, daily travel from Landsberg to Munich, and a ridiculous number of rehearsals suddenly made sense. Karla and Wolfgang had assumed one of the 17 musicians in the orchestra would be me. The anguish of the last few years resurfaced. How would I explain that performing in the orchestra would be impossible? *(I* was *being a nuisance.)* As gently as I could, I described hyperacusis and how it had affected me. Within the orchestra, the volume is all-encompassing but when a soloist sits in front of an orchestra the sound level is very different. A somber, poignant work like *Kol Nidrei* is rarely strident but the instrumentation for *Rhapsody in Blue,* even in the small version, comprises a flamboyant pianist, cymbal crashes, and a shrill high-pitched clarinet. Rehearsing and performing my solo, other orchestral works, and three contemporary pieces would be untenable. Regretfully I had to withdraw. I hoped Karla and Wolfgang would understand.

My apprehensions intensified as the embarkation date approached. Would I get the cello on the airplane unimpeded? When were the rehearsals with the school orchestra? Would someone pick us up at the Landsberg train station? Was there a dressing room at the theater for me to warm up before the performance? I struggled to focus more intensely on what I could control and my important mission—to bring peace to my forebears, to build understanding with subsequent generations, and to stir the audience through the evocative meaning of *Kol Nidrei.*

The Chamber Orchestra of the Bayerische Philharmonie had already begun rehearsing for the Bernstein program and the competition pieces. Karla busied herself designing exhibits for the community, illuminating the tragedies of what had occurred in Landsberg and environs during the Holocaust.

With juggling-like expertise, several volunteers made arrangements for the 40 of us—performers, children of survivors, and distinguished guests—who would be coming to Landsberg. They'd arranged meetings, airport pickups, lodging, exhibit viewings, guest speakers, dinners, and film screenings. They moved the piano, created elaborate brochures and concert programs, and organized tours of Holocaust commemorative sites. And there would be many more surprises.

|

Howie decided to travel to Europe with only a backpack. Considering the load we'd have to carry—my suitcase, which would be laden with dress shoes, a performance gown, other stylish clothing for receptions and dinners, my carry-on with my wedge-shaped cello cushion, the music, and extra strings, our computers, and of course the cello—I asked, "Wouldn't it be better if you checked a bag?" He disagreed. It wasn't worth arguing about. I still had to find an appropriate outfit for *Kol Nidrei* in keeping with the mood of the piece. My dress shouldn't be too formal or too flamboyant, and long enough to sit with my legs spread to hold the instrument comfortably. (I've often offended shopkeepers when I slash between my legs to see if the material will stretch to accommodate the cello.) And forget the stilettos. Toppling over while making one's way onstage is a musician's nightmare. My doubts about Howie's decision fizzled into the background.

I'd practiced my fingers to the bone, repeating passages as familiar to me as my own skin. I'd gathered all the documents, the music, the addresses, the tickets, and the passports, and I'd fussed over every aspect of the trip. On the day of the flight, I woke strangely relaxed. Howie, who rarely gives a thought to planning in advance, was not.

The backpack idea seemed foolhardy to me, but Howie was resolute. He grunted and grumbled and squeezed and pressed, until finally he managed to zip the bag, barely. His tennis shoes, loafers, and dress shoes had to be squeezed into an outside pocket. Loaded down, we made our way to the airport. Once we checked in and entered the terminal, my husband hoisted the backpack onto his shoulders, almost. I recoiled at the sight. Bent backward by the weight, like the arc of a bow without the arrow, he could barely put one foot in front of the other. With miles of walking ahead, just to get to our gate, I insisted, "Howie. Sit here. I'm going to find wheels for this thing. You can't carry that all over Europe!"

Sprinting through the corridors, I hunted for what might be a hopelessly archaic item: a luggage cart. Several salespeople in various luggage stores did raise their eyebrows. Perhaps I wanted to trade up to a rose-gold American Tourister Hardside Spinner? After checking numerous stores, feeling defeated, I retraced my steps, stopping to grab a bottle of water at a variety store. And there I found it, among the magazines and souvenirs—a luggage cart, a bargain at $29.99. Howie perked up when I returned triumphant. Together we strained to stretch the bungee cords around the rotund bag. No sooner had we hooked the plastic clasps around the backpack, we heard a sharp twang. One of them snapped. For several minutes Howie grappled with the cords, trying to tie them so the bag wouldn't slip off the wheels. He resorted to affixing the bungee cords to clips on the outside pockets of the backpack.

The airplane was cramped. Despite Howie's talent for sleeping, he didn't. By the time we arrived at our first stop, London's Heathrow airport in the wee hours of the morning, his footsteps slowed to a crawl. Still, we managed to find our luggage, hail a taxi, instruct the driver where to take us, and at the hotel, unload and check in. Neither of us paid much attention to our belongings. I longed for a meal and a hot shower and Howie desperately needed a bed. The concierge, with a contrite expression, informed us our room would certainly be ready in a couple of hours.

The hospitality floor welcomed us with delicious smells of a splendid English breakfast—freshly baked crumpets, eggs Benedict, back bacon, British sausage with fried bread, black pudding, grilled tomatoes, house-made baked beans on toast, an assortment of marmalades and Nutella, and tea (or if you must, coffee). We indulged. Hours passed before the staff, apologizing profusely, offered us a "lesser" room where we could at least shower and change. They promised to move our bags to the temporary room and then to our final destination for us when it was ready.

Howie had scheduled a lunch meeting in the main restaurant of the hotel. The luggage didn't arrive, and with barely time for one of us to shower, Howie met his client unshaven and disheveled. I followed after I'd luxuriated in the hot spray, keeping my left-hand fingers as dry as possible. (A cellist cannot afford softened fingertips.)

After consuming a three-course lunch, and straining to appear coherent until late afternoon, at long last hotel staff presented a key to our proper room. My husband collapsed into bed, instantly comatose. I puttered with the luggage, removed a few toiletries, rearranged some items that might crease, then noticed Howie's backpack—the bungee cords slack, the outside pockets empty of their contents. I shook Howie awake,

"Howie!! Your shoes are gone! They spilled out somewhere."

"That's nice, dear," he mumbled.

I called security, the front desk, the lost and found. They combed the place without any luck. The British pound signs swelled in my mind. Due to a leg injury, Howard wears only "the world's finest footwear"—Mephistos. Quickly Googling Mephisto, I found a store very near the hotel. After a fitful sleep, worrying not about my upcoming endeavor but footwear, we made our way to the shop in the morning. Thankfully, their prices were much less than they are here in the US, and the store actually had stylish options. A blessing in disguise. Fashion still not his forte, Howie's 15-year-old scuffed, worn tennis shoes could be replaced, and I wouldn't be embarrassed to be seen with him!

After the temporary distraction of the shoe adventure, my qualms came roaring back. What would the cello be like? Would the student orchestra be any good? Would Harris and my brother and sister-in-law arrive safely? Would we? I grappled with the formidable task ahead—to keep my emotions in check while I played in the place my father performed just months after he was liberated from slave labor. And perhaps the ultimate test—did I have the courage to appear onstage openly as a Jew?

The next day, shoes secured, Howie and I flew from London to Berlin, and once we arrived, we took a train to Sebastian's home. He and I had been Starker students at Indiana University. We'd met periodically while he was in the US, but now that Sebastian lived in Berlin it'd been many years since we'd seen each other. Our friendship hadn't suffered from the years apart, but our waistlines had. He and his wife warmly greeted us. During a splendid meal, we reminisced. We both tried to imitate Starker's manner of speaking—his thick Hungarian accent, his brisk speech, his habit of spitting out every consonant. "You play at a very high level." "With instrumental playing, efficiency is motivated by musical and artistic goals."

As dessert warmed in the oven, my fingers itched to try the cello. I wondered if Sebastian would trust me to take the instrument to our hotel room, or would he expect me to practice at his home? With details as yet unresolved, Sebastian led me upstairs to his studio. There, in a position of honor the cello waited. Lovingly, he undid the latches, loosened the straps securely holding the instrument, and he released the cello from its case.

A soft suede wrap encircled its shoulders, like a bib—to protect the varnish on the back and sides of the cello from any nicks from buttons, cufflinks, necklaces, or belts. The deep chestnut wood had not a blemish. Sebastian recommended his preferred bow, suggested I try the other (each bow handles differently and affects the sound), then he handed the instrument to me and left the room. I held my breath and drew a downbow. The sound emanated: smooth, sonorous, deep. Swaddling the instrument in my arms, my left-hand fingers pressed the strings, and within a couple of hours of persuasive seduction, the cello began to unearth its secrets. The instrument, larger than mine, did feel more resistant with its higher bridge; the strings were more taut and further from the fingerboard than I was accustomed to. I'd have to use more power to coax the sound and be very careful not to strain myself.

When I stopped working, Sebastian returned to pack up his baby. I broached the subject of practicing and the travel to Landsberg. Sebastian couldn't have been more gracious. He not only felt comfortable letting me take the instrument to the hotel and on the train, but he also intended to drive to Landsberg, hear me perform, and then take the instrument back to Berlin.

The following morning, after practice, Sebastian came to our hotel for a day of sightseeing. We visited the Neue Synagogue, built in 1859 with its striking eastern Moorish architecture; Checkpoint Charlie, where many East Germans made attempts to gain their freedom from the yoke of Communism; the Brandenburg Gate, a landmark that became a symbol of Nazi power; and some of the hip modern areas of Berlin before we settled into a neighborhood café to sample the spring delicacy—*Spargel*—thick, white asparagus drowned in garlic butter and served with potatoes. After lunch, Sebastian surprised us with tickets to an evening performance of chamber music at the Berlin Philharmonic's home, the Philharmonie, where a decade ago I had played programs with the Minnesota Orchestra. The first glimpse of the structure triggered pangs of distress. How I missed performing in these stellar halls. The program that night included Schubert's *Piano Trio No. 1* in B-flat major, a piece I'd loved to play, but within moments I forgot about everything but the beautiful music.

That night my anxieties roused me. It would be a challenge to convey my polka-dot carry-on bag, enormous suitcase, Howie's offending backpack and cart, and the cello in its white fiberglass case to the Berlin Hauptbahnhof—the largest train station in Europe: a multilevel, all steel and glass edifice with impressive, curved ceilings and vast escalators. Very high tech. We learned that once you've determined where your train will pull in, screens along the track guide you to where you should stand. It's important to wait close to where your seat is located, as the train stops only momentarily. Relieved we figured that out, Howie sat on the benches at our preassigned spot and dozed while I ran to get coffee and snacks.

The train arrived precisely on time. We and hundreds of passengers boarded without noticing that moments before the train arrived, station employees reversed the direction of the train. Car 20 was now in position 1, and car 1 was now in position 20. As the train gained speed, we tried in vain to locate our seats—realizing they were at the opposite end of the train.

"*Entschuldigung. Entschuldigen Sie mich. Vorsicht.*" I tried to force through the narrow aisle stuffed with suitcases and other passengers who likewise shoved the opposite way. Muscling upstream, I lifted the cello up and in front of me so no one would crush the instrument. It would have been easier to walk to Landsberg. By the time we managed to get to our seats, sweat poured down my back, my arms felt like limp noodles, and my torso trembled from the effort.

After a more than five-hour trip, our train pulled into the Landsberg station. I noticed a pink-jacketed, charming-looking blonde woman holding a canary-yellow purse and a matching yellow sign, imprinted: Janet Horvath. What a welcome sight! The staff of the WDCA, as promised, had arranged for a large vehicle and Conny Kurtz, ignoring parking regulations, had pulled up close by. No cello-schlepping required.

On the way to town, Conny's chatter offset my sense of déjà vu. I craned my neck to see places I'd visited during my pilgrimage in 2010.

The pastel and frescoed façades—light-rose, celadon-green, powder-blue—the timeworn gray cobblestone, the medieval church tower, the smell of *Kaffee mit Schlag*, *Knockwurst* and beer. Hard to imagine chaos and cruelty here.

She turned into the narrow driveway of an ancient building mere steps from the town square. Our hotel proprietor, Michael, skittered toward us. We couldn't help noting his shaved head and trim physique; his denim shirt and Bavarian lederhosen—a combination of up-to-date stylishness and German tradition. Michael steered us into the unadorned breakfast room. Leaning on a tiny reception desk, he signed us in, gave us the keys to our room, then grabbed several pieces of our luggage. The exterior spiral staircase was narrow and entirely made of cement—treacherous, especially with a cello.

Michael bounded up, and deposited our belongings into a bare, square room with uncarpeted dark wood floors. Perfectly adequate, I thought, with its billowy jade-green curtains, an unpainted wooden bed and matching wardrobe, a miniature private bathroom, and tucked in the corner, a desk and an armless chair, just right for practicing. Howie and I were the first guests to arrive. I decided to practice a few hours, eager to loosen muscles still sore form carrying the cello through the entire length of the train—meanwhile, Howie napped.

Conny picked us up for dinner. As we ascended the steep road through town and veered left, Howie chimed in, "Landsberg looks just like a ski village." I caught sight of the towering monument I'd seen before. Engraved in bronze, it depicts a distressing scene—skeletal bodies marching to their deaths down this very street, to Dachau. My innards turned queasy thinking the sight for locals is part of the landscape now. Conny whizzed by, turned onto a side road, and parked facing a familiar-looking entrance. She had chosen the restaurant where I'd had lunch with Alexander during my pilgrimage in 2010. The din of animated conversation and the delicious aroma of sizzling meats took me back to eight years before.

Conny led the way to a table. Felicidas, another volunteer, was already seated. After an effusive welcome, we indulged in a scrumptious meal of antipasto, calamari, pasta, and more than a couple of glasses of Lambrusco. Felicidas looked quintessentially German, her blonde tresses carelessly pulled back, and cat-eye glasses perched on her upturned nose. She regaled us with details about the upcoming events, and added, "I'm the helper to take the guests wherever they need, whenever they need." With just a trace of an accent, she told me she speaks fluent Yiddish and sings Yiddish songs although she isn't Jewish. I sensed pride and more than a little determination.

Felicidas poked Conny, "Don't be so modest! Tell them. You are a wonderful photographer and will take wonderful photos this week!"

Conny blushed, "Not really. Not so." She spoke barely audibly in the boisterous café. Hesitating, then taking a mouthful of air she confessed, "I need to tell you something." Then even more quietly, "I've never met any Jews and no Holocaust survivors' children of course. I was so nervous about meeting you, so uncomfortable about being involved and hearing the stories. How would you react to us? To Germans? But you are so very, very dear." She reached to grasp my hand and with each bite of pasta, uncertainty on both sides of the table began to dissolve.

In the morning, the scent of freshly baked rolls, butter and jams, cheeses and coffee, steered us to the bright little breakfast room. Each booth, separated by beechwood latticework, had already been set with silverware, a seasonal centerpiece, and the mouthwatering repast.

A young woman hurried in holding a basket of hand-painted hard-boiled eggs in glimmering hues—green, pink, blue, yellow. They looked too beautiful to eat. She warbled a friendly greeting. "Hallo! Gut morning. I am Michael's sister. I take care of you during the day. I can help with laundry, directions, and snacks anytime, anything you need. Wolfgang Hauck will pick you up, Janet, in the afternoon, to take you to the music school for a meeting with Birgit Abe, the orchestra conductor." The first rehearsal with the students would follow immediately. With plenty of time to warm up, I retired to our room while Howie roamed the town to enjoy the picturesque views of the lake from the boardwalk.

Wolfgang pulled up and with a quiet nod, he hopped out of the white SUV, reached for the cello, and hoisted it into the hatchback. He seemed younger than I'd imagined—his rugged complexion, muscular physique, and rawboned features a contrast to his thinning hair. Wolfgang's emails implied a brusque demeanor, but he seemed relaxed as we drove in silence to the music school.

We parked in front of a stately stone building. The exterior features an ornately carved bas-relief, in the shape of a horseshoe, of cupids playing musical instruments sculpted over black double doors, and a curved portico engraved with the name *Stadt. Sing-u. Musikschule.* The massive building has no elevator, of course. Pausing often to catch my breath, I struggled with the cello up four flights of stairs. Sounds emanated from several classrooms—trombones blaring, horns buzzing, cellos tuning; the sight of piles of music stands, a table covered in violin cases, and along the lengthy hallway, blue, red, and black cello cases took me back to my conservatory days. Ms. Abe, the violin teacher doubling as the conductor, was also younger than I expected—petite and slender with a close-cropped hairstyle and a soft voice. I hoped she commanded the respect of the students. Once introductions were made I unpacked the cello and discussed the piece: I indicated where I played extra softly, where the rubatos, or freedoms, occur, where I liked to move the tempo forward.

The fluttery feeling found its way into my chest as the students sauntered in. They were young. *Really* young. The trombone player couldn't have been more than 12!

Each young musician unpacked and began to warm up, the room echoing with a cacophony of sounds. Just when I fumbled for my earplugs, Wolfgang raised his arms. The pupils listened raptly to his explanation of my role in the events of the week, and the importance of their participation as the accompanists of *Kol Nidrei.* Once he concluded, the students readied their instruments and Birgit gave the downbeat. The tempo moved much too fast, much too matter-of-fact. I stopped the orchestra and asked the conductor if I might say a few words about the piece. Turning my chair around to face the group so they could see and hear me better, I gesticulated passionately, even though I wasn't sure how much English the students understood.

"The piece is a solemn plea for forgiveness opening the holiest day of the Jewish calendar. It opens with grief-stricken yearning." I turned to Birgit. "How do you say this in German? Yes. *Das Verlangen* and it becomes more anxious, even melancholy. Use your deepest sound with lots of warm vibrato. At letter B, the orchestra and cello solo alternate. The cello line is *dolce*—sweet, tender, loving. Please accompany lightly here, but when the orchestra responds, imagine you might be disagreeing with me! This should be forte and articulated with a firm, declamatory rhythm."

I stopped speaking to allow the students to mark their parts. As I tried to illuminate the piece for the students, Birgit waited patiently, throwing in a German word here and there.

"The next phrase I'd like to move forward in tempo, *vorwärts*. It's breathless and full of despair. Perhaps use a grittier, more coarse timbre of sound," I suggested. "Then at letter E, everything changes. A lovely harp solo enters. The transcendent melody in the major key is as if the sunshine comes out—offering hope, *hoffen* and optimism, becoming more and more confident. Use lots of bow and air in your sound here. The music suggests a positive resolution. *Perhaps we humans* are *worthy after all.* The ending quietens. Filled with serenity, we ascend to the heavens, assured of His forgiveness."

Fifty pairs of eyes gawked at me. I paused a moment, hoping they understood, then made one more request.

"It's easy to overpower the cello because of its mellow, baritone voice. Accompanying a cello requires careful listening and a lithesome approach."

We began again this time much slower, *Adagio ma non troppo*. The intonation was spotty at best and there were places I thrashed like a duckling in a bog. We stopped again. "Sorry. *Bitte*. We mustn't linger here. Not slower. Winds. Would you please try this spot alone, for tuning?"

Student and amateur groups tend to ignore the conductor, losing themselves in their own parts, faltering whenever accompaniments become more difficult. We repeated the passage three or four more times. The room, although windowless and warm, happened to be large enough so the overall sound didn't feel too overpowering.

We focused for more than an hour, on each measure of music, and soon they began to understand. I swayed, I sang along, I nodded my head—the room suffused with my melancholy cello sound.

"That's great! *Gut! Danke!*" When we reached the midpoint of the piece, the conductor stopped the orchestra to say our time was up. Just as well. Sweat oozed down my back and my arms and shoulders were beginning to ache. To my ears this cello didn't project. Several people assured me I could be heard, but I felt drowned out by the kids. We'd have to address that next time.

Several students ambled down the stairs with me chatting enthusiastically. They waited until Wolfgang picked me up. Once back at the hotel, before I did anything else, I sent Birgit a link of *Kol Nidrei* from the last Yom Kippur service at our synagogue. She'd have a better understanding of the context of the piece, which would help her convey the intense mood to the youngsters. The next rehearsal wouldn't be for a couple of days. I hoped the students would retain what we'd worked on.

During the rehearsal, Howie had strolled on the boardwalk along the lake, taking in the scenic views of the medieval towers, the charming dwellings, the outdoor cafés, and colorful birds spiraling in the wind.

Just in time for dinner that evening our friends from Washington, DC, Anat and Avi Bar-Cohen, arrived from the airport. Also a child of Holocaust survivors, Anat heads the Children of Survivors (Generation After) group in Washington. Just a few weeks prior to the trip, Anat had at last procured a copy of a fraying and stained document confirming her birth—May 9, 1947, Türkheim, Germany. Anat had known she was born in a DP camp near Munich, but she'd never seen a birth certificate and had no knowledge of the location of the town. I glanced at Anat's photocopied birth certificate again and noticed the date. May 9. I'd be playing *Kol Nidrei* on her birthday.

Michael, our proprietor, recommended a restaurant just steps from our hotel in the main square. The tantalizing aroma of schnitzel pulled us into an enchanting historic restaurant. During the delicious repast, Anat showed me photos and the memorabilia she'd brought with her—even an address, Barhofstrasse 235, and a photograph of the front of the building where she was born. Nonetheless Anat would need help to find the location of the DP camp in Türkheim. The staff I'd encountered so far had been marvelous. They'd be able to assist during the week.

The following morning, the four of us hiked along the river into the woods, breathing the peaceful air. We caught sight of three deer munching on blackberries and saplings in the forest. We wandered into the town and chose a bistro to sample more white asparagus dishes—the long thick spears smothered in sauces and surrounded with meats—a startling discord between our experience and that of our parents 70 years ago.

Later in the evening and Monday morning, the other visitors and participants arrived—an impressive roster of people from all over the globe, including our friend Deb Filler—actor, comedian, and producer of the film *Mr. Bernstein*. Deb's father, Sol Filler, an Auschwitz survivor and a witness to the concert of 1948, was persuaded to go on living after hearing Bernstein's inspired playing of *Rhapsody in Blue*.

German–Jewish week
The Cast of Characters

Durmashkin Family:

Sonia Beker, daughter of survivor Fania Durmashkin, and Sonia's husband, Steve

Rita Gurko Lerner, Vivian (Gurko) Reisman, and Abe Gurko, the three children of survivor Henia Durmashkin

Horvath/Kleyman family:

Janet and Robert Horvath, daughter and son of survivor George Horvath

Howard and Harris Kleyman, my husband and son

Sara Shiewitz, Robert's wife, whose parents were also survivors

Performers and presenters:

Birgit Abe, conductor of the Landsberg School Orchestra

Deb Filler, actor, comedian, writer, daughter of survivor, and the spearhead behind the film *Mr. Bernstein*

Mark Mast, conductor, Bayerische Philharmonie

John Michalczyk, filmmaker of *Creating Harmony: The Displaced Persons Orchestra at St. Ottilien*

Guy Mintus, pianist and composer

Yoed Sorek, tenor

Students of the Landsberg School Orchestra

Honored Guests:

Anat and Avi* Bar-Cohen, (*z"l since then deceased) from Washington, DC

Michael Bernstein, nephew of Leonard Bernstein

Max Lewkowicz, New York film producer

Abba Naor, vice-president of the International Dachau Committee, survivor of the KZ subcamp Kaufering, and patron of the WDCA

Hannah Rosenbaum-Erlichman and her husband, Irving, from Israel. Hannah's parents were survivors

Franz Rößle, former mayor of Landsberg

Emanuel Rotstein, Munich film director

Professor Alexander Tamir, a survivor, originally from Lithuania, who lived in Israel (z"l since then deceased)

Sebastian Toettcher, cellist and friend

Hosts:

Karla Schönebeck and Wolfgang Hauck

Volunteers:

Patricia, Andrea, Conny, Felicidas

Wolf Durmashkin Composition Award Winners:

Brach Bdil, first prize
Rose Miranda Hall, second prize
Otto Wanke, third prize

Karla worked tirelessly on the exhibit "From Lithuania to Landsberg," which opened Monday afternoon, May 7. After several speakers welcomed us, we perused the historical photographs and the posters illuminating the sobering history—one side written in German, the other in English. No detail was left out. Located here—the 11 Landsberg and Kaufering slave-labor concentration camps, subcamps of Dachau—where Henia and Fania Durmashkin toiled. By a hairsbreadth they survived the inhuman conditions.

In June 1944, they and other Lithuanian and Hungarian Jews were coerced into building three massive underground bunkers and, while hidden underground, produce fighter jets. After our idyllic morning, an unfathomable juxtaposition: the subjugation and mistreatment of more than 30,000 prisoners in Landsberg alone, in plain sight. Once liberated on April 27, 1945 by the 12th Armored Division of the US army, the townspeople—perhaps relatives of the attendees with us that day—were forced to tour the carnage and bury corpses with their bare hands. When Landsberg became a DP camp, it remained a miserable sanctuary until 1950. Still in dispute: the number of victims who perished here. Estimates range from 14,500 to 44,000 Jewish inmates murdered.

A few hours later we viewed another display, this time in the town hall foyer. Suspended on the yellow brick walls hung sizable photos and posters of the orchestra members who played here with Leonard Bernstein. The piano upon which Fanny Durmashkin had performed looked impressive, prominently exhibited on the upstairs landing, and next to it stood Franz Rößle, the former mayor, who had steered me to the memorials during my previous visit.

Once we had greeted one another, the entire group gathered for a feast in a Greek restaurant. Several long tables pushed close together, topped with small bouquets of flowers and white tablecloths, just contained our boisterous group. English, German, Yiddish, and Hebrew mixed with the tantalizing smells of dolma, souvlaki, moussaka, and baklava. But we didn't linger. At 8:00 p.m., the documentary, *Creating Harmony: The Displaced Persons Orchestra at St. Ottilien*, would be screened with German subtitles followed by a conversation with the filmmaker John Michalczyk.

As the images whirled by, my mind drifted to 2009, when my father and I viewed the film for the first time. I could hear his voice, his presence palpable: "Janetkém, it's me! How did you find this?" Many of the guests, and Landsberg residents, had never seen the movie before. Especially on the heels of the exhibits, it had a profound impact.

The next event: a visit to St. Ottilien Benedictine Archabbey. Early Tuesday morning, Howie and I, the Durmashkin family, the rabbi from Munich, and 45 guests boarded busses. We were met by several brothers of the abbey, who led us to a clearing for an official ceremony. A wooden music stand had been placed there on the grass, covered by a simple white cloth. Akin to unveiling a Jewish headstone, Sonia and the rabbi lifted the fabric together revealing a bronze commemorative plaque. Before Sonia read the inscription aloud, the archabbot proclaimed our presence an act of "extraordinary remembrance." We remembered Dr. Grinzburg who established the hospital here; we remembered Robert Hilliard and Edward Herman, the two soldiers who through a tireless letter-writing campaign brought the heinous conditions of the DP camp to the attention of the American government; we remembered the musicians of the DP camp orchestra who in 1945 first performed at St. Ottilien. The plaque will be permanently installed where we stood, adjacent to the maternity hospital, where between 1945 and 1949 more than 400 babies were born.

Every few moments while we toured the grounds, we heard recollections from our cohort—the parents who'd started a school for the children; a father and his brother who'd spent four years as policemen within the camp; a mother who'd worked sewing buttons;

the couple who met and married here—each reminiscence revealing an irrevocable bond to St. Ottilien.

We wandered further along the dirt paths. Eight years earlier with my guide, Alexander, I'd visited the pristine Jewish cemetery. We made a final stop there. The graves, still immaculate, with names of so many who despite liberation died in May 1945, who lie alone with no families to visit them, prompted us spontaneously to chant the Kaddish—the Jewish Prayer of Mourning. As we wiped tears from our eyes, the abbey church bells chimed.

After a simple lunch for staff and guests, most of the group embarked on a tour to Dachau from here. I returned to Landsberg, to the music school for my second rehearsal. Although I'd been to Dachau in 2010, I missed sharing the experience with the others. Dachau continued to operate as a refugee camp into the early 1960s and has since been rebuilt. The existing gas chambers, shower rooms, crematorium—the indelible images of ghastly human experiments—no dirge of mourning mitigates our profound horror.

The Landsberg Music School students were on their toes this time. They'd had a day to practice their own parts and to assimilate what I'd taught them about the piece. Birgit, grateful to have heard *Kol Nidrei* in context, rolled up her sleeves to whip the group into shape.

We started where we left off, at the radiant second theme, from the musical setting of a poem by Byron, "Those that Wept on Babel's Stream." The harp solo creates an atmosphere to arouse us—to light, to faith, and to resolution, stirring us with expectation. Birgit wisely put the young harpist front and center so her sound wouldn't be swallowed by surrounding sonorities. During our sublime duet, the ambiance in the room transformed. Our musical concept began to coalesce. The next two hours seemed to go by quickly as we worked perfecting passagework, intonation, rhythm, and, most important, the softest, most tender sound quality.

That evening we spent eating—what else? Enormous, juicy Wiener Schnitzels, with roasted new potatoes, red cabbage, and thick dark bread, in the company of people who, although we hadn't met until this week, felt like newly found relatives. I didn't stay too late for the revelry, or for the wine consumption. Early in the morning, Harris, Rob, and Sara would be arriving for the gala and my performance.

The rest of the group geared up for another tour by bus at daybreak, this time of one of the slave-labor camps—Camp Kaufering VII. Franz Roßle offered to pick me up to join the group later if I had time before the dress rehearsal.

Two thousand three hundred inmates worked there in squalid conditions. Only the remnants of the camp remain now, but our imaginations, unfettered, could sense the overcrowding, disease, cruelty, and utter malevolence of it all. It's wedged in our hearts. Sonia and Deb glimpsed a planter with profuse flowers placed for the annual Day of Remembrance, Yom HaShoah, overturned, kicked apart, vandalized. They and an unknown German woman gently set the planter upright, restoring the flowers and the strewn earth.

Climbing farther, on an overgrown path, I wondered what or whom I tread upon. There was a railcar, which locked from the outside, and a crumbling plaque with a dedication: *Unbekannter*: "Grave of thousands unknown." How powerful and poignant it was to be together here, arm in arm, thinking of the many survivors who lost loved ones, who have no gravesites to visit.

I hurried back to the town hall for the last touch-ups. Like many dress rehearsals, it didn't go very well. A medley of accompanying sounds didn't help. The staff vacuumed the hall carpet, volunteers ripped pieces of colored tape, sticking them onto the reserved seats—the swish, not a sound one associates with the mood of my piece—audio and video engineers fiddled with microphones, and the kids quietly tittered. To add to the mayhem, since the school orchestra would begin the program with a Mendelssohn *Overture*, the hosts quarreled about how long it would take the students to take their places onstage, while dodging chairs, vertical microphones, music stands, and the conductor and cello podiums. Should the youngsters enter, then leave the stage, and enter with me? Or sit through the 11 people slated to speak, prior to *Kol Nidrei?*

We finished abruptly. The piano tuner had just arrived, and the other performers, waiting for their turn to try the acoustics in the hall, patrolled the tight quarters around the perimeter of the stage.

With no backstage to speak of, I escaped to the hotel to change into my gown and to compose myself. A few minutes before concert time, I walked over to the hall. Not an easy task to maneuver the cello around the garbage bins, wood pallets, and motor vehicles, and to locate the well-hidden stage door, as usual in the back alley. An all-cement gray passageway leads backstage. I wheezed up three flights of stairs, my heels clicking on the tiled floors, until finally I reached the bare-bones cubicle assigned to me for the evening. The chilly room had no chair, no room to even draw a bow. Joining the 50 kids tooting and bleeping their instruments in the hallway, I tried to concentrate on setting the tone for the evening—confident music might clear the haze of distrust, might spark compassion, might unite us as humans.

The space was tight. We lined up three deep on the staircase. Once we were given the signal, the little trombonist played a lick from *Star Wars* and the students filed onstage. I waited for them to get settled, then, clutching the cello, carefully maneuvering down the narrow dimly lit stairway, I emerged from behind the sapphire velvet curtain and took the stage. Uplifted by the full house, the presence of family and friends both old and new, I steadied myself, secured the cello, and reached for the microphone.

My words of introduction, translated into German by Karla, described the importance of this piece to the Jewish People, and particularly to my family. I told them my father played *Kol Nidrei* every year in our synagogue for 30 years, and I've continued that tradition another 30 years and to this day. *Kol Nidrei* represents our obligation to ask for forgiveness and inspires our resolve to lead better lives of *teshuva*, *tefillah*, and *tzedakah*, empathy, compassion, and justice.

Fingering my mother's cherished pearls, I took my seat center stage while the lights lowered. The audience was pitched into darkness. Adjusting the tautness of my bow one last time, I sensed my father's strong embrace and the spirit of ancestors beside me. The mournful opening motif—D' D-D-#C' C#-C#-A'— shimmered in the half-darkness of the hall. My bow skimmed along the strings, the somber hues of the cello unfolding in an exquisite tapestry, guiding the audience inward to deeper realms; imbuing reverence, contemplation, exultation. We soared into a mystical dimension, channeling the spirits of those who had perished here, and those who sought reconciliation.

Fading away in tranquility, the concluding high A drifted upward, *morendo*. A mist of tears onstage and a lingering sigh from the audience restored us to this earthly plane. My entire body quivered as I slowly rose to my feet. I acknowledged the extraordinary playing of the young musicians and the enthusiastic applause, a testament to the unifying sentiments we experienced. Together we had ascended through the tenth dimension of infinite possibilities.

Several Yiddish and Hebrew songs from the ghettos, songs of hope, performed by Yoed Sorek and accompanied by Guy Mintus, followed. A beautiful aria by Wolf Durmashkin, which likely had not been sung for 50 years, perhaps the only remaining work of the composer, received its premier. The sheet music, it was discovered, resides in the US Holocaust Memorial Museum.

Proud family members beamed as the three prize-winning composers came onstage to receive their awards. Closing the program —*Yerushalayim*, Jerusalem, an optimistic ballad about the precariousness of freedom, the prospect of a reprieve, and the notion of a better life.

We didn't want the evening to end. During the reception in the lobby, family and friends and the students and presenters clasped me in emotional embraces. The parents of the Landsberg School Orchestra musicians, thrilled their children had the opportunity to play *Kol Nidrei*, believed the performance would have a lifelong impact. Audience members of varied backgrounds, religions, and nationalities drank toasts to us, to each other, and to the transformative spirit in the town hall. For me it was even more extraordinary that Harris, Howie, Rob, and Sara could be part of the experience.

The next day people from all over the region packed the house for the Bernstein Jubilee Concert program. A black car pulled up to the door, where inside sat the head of the Jewish community surrounded by his bodyguards; an elderly Jewish woman who'd been hidden during the war by a priest's housekeeper appeared; the mayor Franz, a brother from St. Ottilien, and a rabbi from Munich entered; Michael Bernstein, Leonard Bernstein's nephew, who represented the Bernstein family, arrived with an escort; and Alexander Tamir, a survivor and music professor from Israel, settled in his wheelchair near the front to celebrate Bracha Bdil, his student, who garnered first prize in the competition. Tamir had studied with Wolf Durmashkin; as an 11-year-old, he won a competition organized by Wolf in the Vilna Ghetto in 1942. Surely *bashert*—meant to be, or could it have been a mere coincidence?

We eagerly took our seats—the righteous Gentiles, the supporters of the festival, the young German musicians, the award winners and their families, and of course our new kinfolk with whom we'd shared this extraordinary adventure.

The three competition pieces, and Deb's award-winning film *Mr. Bernstein*, preceded George Gershwin's *Rhapsody in Blue* featuring piano soloist, Guy Mintus. Accompanying him—17 members of the Bayerische Philharmonie with conductor Mark Mast. Guy's electrifying playing, and the breathtaking atmosphere, captivated and thrilled us. After the final flourish, the audience went crazy. Between euphoria and giddiness, I couldn't help speculating: if we could go back in time, what would our parents have thought of this gathering?

Our hosts had one last surprise for us on our final evening in Landsberg—a Shabbat service and dinner. According to the Torah, Shabbat commemorates the day God rested after creating the world. At the end of six days of work, He indicates we too should observe a day of peace.

Wolfgang and his team converted their offices into a sanctuary flanked by a dining room. The Munich rabbi brought a makeshift bimah and prayer books from the 1940s, and he conducted this first Shabbat service ever held in Landsberg. Afterward we adjourned to the adjacent room. A long table had been set with flowers, white tablecloths, challah, tall white candles to light and bless, and a kiddush cup for prayers over the wine. When the festive meal concluded, we sang songs, Deb told jokes, we toasted our new German friends. I glanced across the table and gazed at Rob, Sara, Howie, and Harris as they marveled at the scene before us.

Our group reflected upon the events of the week, experiences we could only describe as out-of-body moments: Anat found the house where she'd been born in 1947. When the current occupants let her inside, she saw a poster hanging on the wall promoting a performance of *Rhapsody in Blue*. A German couple whose life's work has been to create a Holocaust Memorial presented Hannah Rosenbaum-Erlichman with a never-before-seen photo of her parents. We installed a plaque at St. Ottilien, as Sonia and I had envisioned. We came together as people, during just a week of sharing experiences. And with reverence for my parents, and for all who lost their lives in the conflagration, I played *Kol Nidrei* in Germany.

Music opened our hearts and fed our spiritual hunger. The undulating harmonies wrapped us, enveloped us, and transported us in ways we could never have imagined. Then, with fervent embraces and promises to meet again, we bid each other shalom—peace, contentment, freedom, and the blessing of wholeness.

***Our group.** L to R: John Michalczyk, Vivian Reisman, Guy Mintus, Sonia Beker (next to Guy, partially hidden in the second row); Bracha Bdil, winner of the competition, seventh from the left, and next to her survivor Professor Alexander Tamir of blessed memory (who had been a student of Wolf Durmashkin); Hannah Rosenbaum-Erlichman, nineth from the left. R to L: Howie, Anat Bar-Cohen, third from the right, and I'm standing next to her in the light shirt fourth from the right. Behind me is Avi Bar-Cohen; Rita Lerner, seventh from the right and Abe Gurko, ninth from the right, Deb Filler, tenth from the right.*

***Rob, Sara, Harris, and I pose next to the display photos.** We stood in front of the poster of my father. (Howie, not pictured, was taking the photo.)*

***Janet introduces* Kol Nidrei.** *I conveyed not only the deep significance of the piece but also how momentous the occasion felt, to play in the very place my father had performed 70 years ago.*

***Janet performing* Kol Nidrei.** *I pray the ripples of reconciliation will flow through the atmosphere for a long time to come.*

POSTSCRIPT

One of the most important tenets of Judaism is to honor one's parents. Perhaps this is why so many children of Holocaust survivors, like me, obsess about learning their histories, especially while our parents are still with us. We strive to mold these stories into something that lives on in tribute.

My parents loved and lived the only way they knew how. Their lives capsized without warning. Perhaps to prove to themselves that not all life is chaos, they yearned for order. Music provided order and a much-needed emotional outlet for our family. Through music, my parents interacted with other human beings and reached beyond this world, enjoying the intangibles of life. Today I have a different understanding of why they behaved in such demanding, preoccupied, paranoid ways.

Resilience can be defined by how quickly the symptoms of trauma fade. My mother personified resilience. The worst had happened. No longer afraid, she lived with audacious optimism. Outspoken, and an advocate for the oppressed, she was intent on our moral education. My father embodied the symptoms of his experiences. Now that I've learned a little about epigenetics—that trauma can be passed on genetically to future generations—I'm able to see I have carried his fear and anxiety into my adult life.

Haunted virtually every day, the painful flashbacks of childhood imaginings often interrupted daily activities. To finally know my parents' story—after living life with the enigma, the panic, the mistrust, the rage, and the obsessive love—is a blessing. It's no wonder I've inherited the traits that make me a chronic worrier, a compulsively hard worker, a defender of the downtrodden. I feel responsible for those who were murdered, and guilty for every indulgence—plentiful food, hot showers, sweet-smelling soaps, soft beds, a roof over my head, freedom. It's the very essence of my being.

I couldn't know that the innocent question I asked my father in 2009 would yield such richness. Once I'd pierced the silence, I began to feel more content in my own skin. I've ruminated about how to use all I've learned. How to focus my skills to educate the next generation about discrimination and injustice beyond or in addition to this memoir. I feel fortunate to have had the opportunity for closure for myself, and for my family, and for everyone who was present in person or in spirit in Landsberg. And I feel blessed to have learned I can hold onto the past and move into the future committed to making a positive impact on the world through the transformative power of music, as my parents did before me.

We children of Holocaust survivors continue to struggle with our histories and the resurgence of antisemitism. Our rabbi likened it metaphorically to a virus fomenting in an immune-suppressed body. When dangerous microbes attack, we are more vulnerable to life-threatening contamination. Similarly, the vilification of the Jewish People may be the first sign of a civilization in decline. Other bigotries inevitably follow. The strength of our society depends upon the well-being of every person, no matter their faith, gender, or color. As the world tilts toward authoritarianism, the instinct to forget and deny will be enormous. As our way of life is endangered, rather than allow fear to resurge, we have the opportunity to act. This feels urgent now.

A GENOCIDE DICTIONARY

LANGUAGE OF DECEPTION

"Nazi-Speak Then and Now"

Research indicates that there were more than 35,000 terms (many abbreviated), phrases, and euphemisms that were used in official Nazi correspondence to conceal or otherwise mold traditional language, to disguise intentions.

Code—noun

1. A system for communication for brevity or secrecy. A systematic attempt to avoid direct language. To disguise or camouflage acts of terror.

2. A set of standard laws, rules, or regulations set forth as standards by a government for the protection of public safety.

Below, a listing of some genocides and terrorist groups who have perpetrated genocides or mass murder before and since the Holocaust, and the words or code language that exists then and now.

A

Afghanistan Crisis: Considered a genocide emergency, the Taliban have waged a violent insurgency against the Afghan government since 2001, resulting in 100,000 civilian casualties, mostly young girls, women, and non-Muslim minorities, with hundreds of thousands of people displaced. (See genocidewatch.com)

Aktion 1005: Also known as *Sonderaktion* (Special Action), the secret Nazi internal operation for concealing evidence of mass-killing operations begun in 1942. *Sonderkommandos*, or the forced laborers and prisoners, had to exhume bodies, often from mass graves, and burn the remains, then crush or grind the leftover larger human bones.

Aktion T4: The mass murder or forced euthanasia of intellectually, physically, or mentally disabled individuals (Jewish and non-Jewish) and the elderly.

Aktionen: Other missions to find Jews and murder them.

Al-Assad Regime: Refers to the president of Syria from 1971 to 2000, Hafez al-Assad, who participated in the 1963 Syrian coup d'état. The conflicts during his regime caused the displacement of half of Syria's population, with over 500,000 deaths.

Al-Qaeda: A network of Islamic extremists and Salafist jihadists. A terrorist group, as designated by the United Nations, the North Atlantic Treaty Organization (NATO), the United States, and several other countries.

Al-Shabaab: Militant group linked to al-Qaeda; imposed a ban on the UN World Food Program to prevent aid to famine-stricken areas of Somalia, where it is estimated that 258,000 people died of starvation between 2010 and 2012. Somalia is also the target of US air strikes. Militants from areas under al-Shabaab control are responsible for terrorist attacks with car bombs resulting in civilian deaths.

Armenian Genocide: The 1915 mass murder of 1.5 million ethnic Armenians by the Turkish government (then, the Ottoman Empire).

Anschluss: The Nazi propaganda term for the annexation of Austria in 1938 by Germany.

Antifa: Originating in Italy from the word *fascio* or *fascisti*, and its opposite *anti-Facisti*, these words were anglicized as well as used in Germany in opposition to Hitler's fascism i.e. *antifaschistisch* or

Antifaschist. By 1930 abbreviated to *Antifa*. A left-wing anti-fascist and anti-racist political movement; it is largely decentralized and emphasizes direct action against far-right groups. While much of their political activism is nonviolent, there is a prevailing attitude to directly confront the issues of white supremacy, Neo-Nazism, and fascism, sometimes through violent means.

Antifaschistische Aktion: Anti-Fascist Action or Antifa, a militant political group formed during the Weimar Republic by the Communist Party of Germany and in existence from 1932 to 1933. Later inspired extreme left-wing political movements with anti-capitalist, anti-fascist, anti-imperialist, and anti-Zionist sentiments.

Arbeit: Work.

Arbeit Macht Frei: "Work sets you free." The slogan which appeared on the gates of several concentration camps. Sarcastic and cynical, as the hard work did set them free: to death.

Arbeitslager: "Work Instruction Camps," i.e. forced labor camps. Used throughout the war but even as early as the 1930s.

Aryan: Racial designation of a "master race," a noble or superior race. The pure white race: blonde, blue-eyed, and Nordic or Germanic. People considered to be superior to Semites and people of color. The promotion of a racial hierarchy.

Ausgemertz: The term used to exterminate insects, i.e. murder. Used euphemistically to mean murder of Jews.

Ausschaltung: Elimination, used euphemistically to mean murder of Jews.

Aussiedlung: Evacuation, used euphemistically to mean murder of Jews.

CAMPS:

- Auschwitz, also Auschwitz-Birkenau, Poland—extermination camp.

B

Babi Yar: A ravine located in Ukraine, the site of several massacres of Jews carried out by German forces, the first occurring in 1941—a two-day mass murder of 33,771 Jews. Several thousand more Jews as well as non-Jews including Roma People, communists, Soviet prisoners, and Soviet civilians were subsequently massacred.

Badeanstalten: Bathhouses, i.e., gas chambers.

Blitzkrieg: Lightning war, quick army invasion aided by tanks and airplanes. A form of attack used by terrorist groups and generally associated with the German armed forces during the Second World War. *Blitzkrieg* tactics were particularly effective in the early Nazi conflict.

Blood and Soil: White nationalist and right-wing chant evoking Nazi ideology (see below).

Blut und Boden: "Blood and Soil." Nazi slogan and official policy that ethnicity and identity should be based only on the purity of blood and epitomize the national sense of pride of farmers who tended German land.

Boer War: Also known as the Second Boer War, Anglo-Boer War, and the South African War; fought between the British Empire and the joint forces of two independent Boer states, the South African Republic and the Orange Free State, lasting from 1899–1900. The British deployed "scorched earth" tactics to gain the upper hand by burning thousands of towns and farms. Civilians were rounded up into concentration camps.

Boko Haram: Jihadist terrorist group based in northeast Nigeria.

Bosnian Genocide: The ethnic cleansing of the Bosniak (Bosnian Muslim) population, occurring during the Bosnian War (1992–1995).

CAMPS:

- Bergen-Belsen, Germany (where Anne Frank died).
- Belzec, Poland—extermination camp.
- Birkenau (Auschwitz-Birkenau), Poland—extermination camp.
- Buchenwald, Germany (where my grandfather was incarcerated).

C

Cambodian Genocide: The systematic persecution and killing of Cambodians by the Khmer Rouge under the regime of Pol Pot in 1975. Between 1.7 and 2.2 million Cambodians were killed.

Christians Preferred: Euphemism for restricting Jews.

Codex Judaicus: Laws to deny rights to Slovakian Jews. Included 270 articles.

Colored: Derogatory term for races other than white.

Concentration Camp: Where large numbers of people are forcibly incarcerated, forced to labor, mistreated, and/or executed.

Congo War: Also known as the Great War of Africa; began in Democratic Republic of the Congo in 1998, and involved nine African Countries. The Second Congo War and the aftermath lead to 5.4 million deaths. The *Effacer le tableau* refers to the genocide of Mbuti and other Pygmy tribes occurring from 2002 to 2003, during the Ituri conflict. The cycle of violence and turmoil continues. More than 13 million Congolese need humanitarian aid.

Conspiracy/Collusion: Secret plots to deceive, often on a grand scale and with a political motivation.

Crematoriums: Specially built furnaces in several concentration camps to incinerate the bodies of people murdered by gas.

CAMPS:

- Chełmno, 50 kilometers (31 miles) from Lodz, Poland.

D

Darfur Genocide: The systematic killing of Darfuri ethnic groups, including the Fur, Masalit, and Zaghawa tribes, by Western Sudan. In 2013, the UN estimated a death toll of 300,000 people. The conflicts, although decreased, are still ongoing.

Deep State: A conspiracy theory suggesting a clandestine network within the US government and/or in cooperation with foreign governments.

Der Angriff: "The Attack." German newspaper founded by Joseph Goebbels that encouraged support for Nazi ideals and was full of propaganda and motifs.

Der Ewige Jude: Antisemitic propaganda film, *The Eternal Jew*, 1940. A pseudo-documentary depicting crude, vile, and gruesome stereotypes in which Jews are represented as rats carrying contagion.

Durchgangslager: Transit Camp. Holding facility until prisoners were transported to Auschwitz and other death camps.

CAMPS:

- Dachau, Germany.
- Drancy, Paris—detention/transit camp holding Jews later deported to killing centers.
- Demblin, Poland.

E

East: As in "resettlement to the east"; deportation often to Poland and Auschwitz.

Ein Reich, Ein Volk, Ein Führer: Nazi propaganda slogan that appeared on countless posters, in publications, and heard as a chant on radio and in speeches. One Reich, One People, One Führer.

Einsatzgruppen: German paramilitary death squads, task forces, or security forces that conducted mass shooting operations.

Einsatzkommando: Subgroup of the *Einsatzgruppen*: mobile killing squads.

Endlösung: The Final Solution, annihilation; the term referred to the plan to systematically exterminate and murder the Jewish People from every country, whatever their origin, even those who had converted to other religions, and even those who had intermarried in previous generations and had Jewish descendants.

Entartete Kunst: Forbidden or degenerate art that didn't adhere to Nazi ideology; included authors Thomas Mann and Bertolt Brecht, Jewish musicians Felix Mendelssohn and Gustav Mahler, and painters Marc Chagall, Max Ernst, and Paul Klee.

Ethiopian/Eritrean Civil War: Civil war between Ethiopian military junta communist governments and Ethio-Eritrean anti-government rebels (the Derg) from 1974–1991. The Anuak have been targets of restriction of basic needs, resettlement, murder, and more sinister decimation attempts since the 1980s and continuing today by the Derg and later Ethiopian governments. The repressive Eritrean government continues to subject the population to forced labor, and restricts civil liberties.

Eugenics: Beliefs and practices to improve the human population through genetics. United States; those deemed unfit for society, or inferior, became victims of federally-funded forced sterilization initiatives. African American women, Hispanic and Native American women, the poor, and people with developmental or physical disabilities were targeted. Forced sterilizations continued for decades and occur even today in women's prisons.

Evacuation: Before 1942, the Germans planned to expel or force Jews from Europe. At the Wannsee conference of 1942, evacuation became the Nazi euphemism for annihilation.

Exclusive Clientele: Code for no Jews allowed.

F

Fake News: A current term for propaganda.

Final Solution: *See* Endlösung.

Forced Labor/Slave Labor: Many camps utilized young, fit people to make munitions, dig ditches and mass graves, and to work in mines, factories, quarries, etc.

Führer: Leader or guide with absolute authority; supreme ruler.

Fremdblütig: Alien-blooded.

CAMPS:

- Flossenbürg, Bavaria.

G

Gas Chamber: Efficient system for mass murder. Prisoners were duped, thinking they were to have a shower. They disrobed, then were forced into chambers, locked in, and gassed with Zyklon B.

Gentiles Only: No Jews allowed.

Ghetto: Jews were forced and crowded into specific sectors of the city, with little or no resources, often surrounded by very high walls with barbed wire. They were not allowed to leave.

Gleichschaltung: Coordination, or the process of Nazification. Music, along with other aspects of culture, was subject to Nazification from 1933. The policy of coordination meant that music had to conform to the Nazi ideal.

CAMPS:

- Grini, Norway.
- Gross-Rosen, Germany—a network of up to 100 camps spanning Germany, Czechoslovakia, and occupied Poland.

H

Hamas: A Palestinian nationalist, Sunni-Islamic fundamentalist organization with a powerful military wing; they are considered a terrorist organization along with the Shiite group Hezbollah. Both groups battle Israel and arose as a result of the Arab-Israeli conflict. Hamas formed in 1988 during the first Palestinian intifada against Israel, while Hezbollah formed around 1982 during the Lebanese civil war. Hamas is based in Gaza, whereas Hezbollah is based in Lebanon, but both have had backing from Iran. With grievances against their Arab rulers, they also fight Sunnis, other Shias, and Christians, and call for the destruction of Israel.

Hate Groups: The number of hate groups in the US rose to 1,020 in 2018, according to the Southern Poverty Law Center. White nationalist groups espouse white supremacist or white separatist ideologies, often focusing on the alleged inferiority of nonwhites, promulgating eugenics and antisemitic, anti-Muslim, and anti-Black views.

Hezbollah: *see* Hamas. A Shia Islamist Lebanese political party and militant group.

Hilfsmittel: Auxiliary Equipment, i.e., gas vans used for murder.

High Yellow: Derogatory term used to refer to a light-skinned Black person.

Hitlerjugend: Hitler youth division of the Nazi Party, used to indoctrinate young people.

Hoax: A falsehood deliberately fabricated as the truth. Fake news; a malicious deception and distinguishable from an error.

Holocaust Denial: Proponents of the ideology that the Holocaust never occurred, that it is a ploy to create sympathy for Jews. That the Holocaust was merely customary casualties of war.

I

Idi Amin: Ugandan military officer who served as the president of Uganda from 1971 to 1979; the cruel despot known as the "Butcher of Uganda."

IDP: Internally displaced people in Afghanistan, approximately one million people.

IG Farben: One of the largest chemical companies in the world, located in Germany. Pro-Nazi in their ideology, they knowingly and willingly collaborated to produce enormous quantities of Zyklon-B gas used to murder millions of people in concentration camps.

ISIS: The Islamic State of Iraq and Syria; they promote religious fundamentalism, holding slaves, and are known for killing thousands through violent means.

Isolationism: The policy of isolating one's country from the affairs of other nations by declining to enter into agreements and avoiding foreign relationships or entanglements. This dogma severely restricted foreign nationals from immigrating.

Istjude: A category of Jew who had at least three ethnic Jewish grandparents.

J

Jewish Plots: Stereotypes that promulgate the belief that Jews control the news, banks, and media; all of which are conspiracy theories, circulated then and now.

Joseph Stalin: Dictator of the Soviet Union who ruled by terror. An Ally during World War II.

Juden: The Jews.

Judenfrei: Free of Jews, i.e. ethnically cleansed.

Judenfrei Gemacht: To make Germany and elsewhere free of any Jewish people, i.e. through murder.

Judenrat: A council representing the Jewish community. The Germans required Jews to form the *Judenrat* within the ghettos. Members of the *Judenrat* frequently had to carry out the Nazi "selections", choosing who should live or die, and control the ghetto.

Judenrein: To get rid of Jews.

Judeocide: Killing of Jews. One of the terms used to define the Holocaust, also genocide, Shoah. The term Judeocide is a more precise definition drawing attention to the Jews as the specific victims.

CAMPS:

- Janowska, eastern Poland.

K

Kabul, Afghanistan: Capital city of Afghanistan, much of it controlled by Taliban militants.

Kristallnacht: "Night of Broken Glass," November 9-10, 1938; SA paramilitary forces smashed Jewish businesses, synagogues, and buildings. Jewish homes, hospitals, and schools were ransacked. One thousand synagogues were burned and 7,000 Jewish business were destroyed. Hundreds of deaths occurred and 30,000 Jews were arrested and incarcerated in concentration camps.

Ku Klux Klan: A secret hate group that existed and continues in almost every Southern state in the US, founded in 1856. The oldest and most well-known American hate group. Their goal: to establish white supremacy. Known for wearing white pointed hoods, they denounce Black people, Jews, Muslims, immigrants, LGBTQ people, and Catholics using violent means.

Kurdish Genocide: Known as the Anfal operation, the 1988 genocide of thousands of Kurdish civilians during the Iran–Iraq War.

CAMPS:

- Kaufering/Landsberg, Germany.
- Koldichevo, Belarus.

L

Lagerbordell: Camp bordello; a camp's on-site brothel. Female forced sex workers were kept as a work incentive for some Kapos and other favored prisoners, as well as for servicing Nazis.

Lebensborn: Fountain of Life, program founded by Heinrich Himmler in Nazi Germany as a state-supported effort to increase the birth rate of Aryan and "racially pure" children. Himmler ordered SS officers to father children so as to create a superior race based on Nazi ideals. Young women who passed rigorous examination were granted admission to the program, the majority unwed mothers. The children born in Lebensborn nurseries were subsequently taken by the SS.

Lebensraum: Living space. Hitler determined Germans required more territory, i.e. colonialism; conquest of land.

Lebensunwertes Leben: Unworthy of Life.

Leichenkeller: Corpse cellars, or in other words, crematoriums.

Loser: Donald Trump's disparaging term. A person or thing that loses especially consistently. Incompetent; unable to succeed.

Lügenpresse: Volatile and defaming propaganda slogan and slur, used to foment hatred against communists and Jews. Explosive in nature, any critic of the Hitler regime was referred to as members of the "Lügenpresse apparatus," denoting hatred against journalists, mainstream press, and anyone who opposed the "will of the people." First emerging in a book in 1918, the term often prompted physical violence.

Lying Press: Pejorative and defamatory term appropriated from its explosive use by Germany during World War II. Alternative facts, fake news; in other words, propaganda. Today a common slogan used by xenophobic and right-wing groups.

CAMPS:

- Le Vernet, France—internment camp.

M

Mao Tse-tung: Also known as Chairman Mao, founder of the People's Republic of China. Although a Marxist–Leninist ideologically, his theories, military strategies, and politics are called Maoism. Responsible for the deaths of as many as 65 million Chinese citizens from mass starvation under his rule; creator of the Cultural Revolution; a repressor of the arts.

Mein Kampf: Hitler's autobiographical manifesto outlining his political ideology and antisemitic views.

Mischlinge: Mongrels; Jews of mixed blood, or those who had a non-Jewish spouse.

Misogynist: A person who hates or is strongly prejudiced against women.

Mulatto: Derogatory; from Spanish *mulato* meaning mule, a person of mixed race ancestry, offspring of one white and one Black parent.

CAMPS:

- Majdanek, Poland.
- Mauthausen, Austria.

N

Nacht und Nebel: Night and Fog; the codename for a 1941 decree by Hitler. Clandestine activities to abduct individuals who "undermined" or opposed the German regime.

Nasty Lady; *Nasty Woman:* Donald Trump's derogatory and misogynistic term.

Nebenlager: Subcamp; Buchenwald had over 100. Dachau also had many subcamps, including Kaufering.

Neo-Nazism: A militant social and political movement to revive the ideology of Nazism in our time.

Nigger: Slur for an African American, Black, or dark-skinned person.

NJA: Acronym meaning No Jews Allowed (US).

Nuremberg Laws: Racist and antisemitic laws enacted in 1935.

CAMPS:

- Nordhausen, Germany.
- Natzweiler-Struthof, France.

O

Obersturmführer: A senior Nazi part paramilitary military rank. The SS or SA "Senior storm or assault leader" had responsibilities as a Gestapo officer, concentration camp supervisor, and Waffen-SS commander.

Octoroon: Derogatory; a person who is one-eighth Black.

Operation Reinhard: The codename of the secretive German plan carried out in 1942 and 1943 to exterminate two million Polish Jews. Three killing centers were established: Belzec, Sobibor, and Treblinka. Evidence of mass murder was concealed. An unknown number of Poles, Roma, and Soviet prisoners of war were also murdered.

Organization Todt: A military engineering company, which supplied industry with forced labor, created by Hitler.

Osama Bin Laden: Founder of the Islamic militant terrorist group, al-Qaeda; a network of Islamic extremists.

Ostjuden: Eastern Jews; Yiddish-speaking Jews from Eastern European countries, some who'd immigrated to Germany and Austria.

CAMPS:

- Operation Reinhard Camps.
- Ohrdruf, Germany—a Buchenwald subcamp.

P

PLO: Palestine Liberation Organization; its purpose is to liberate Palestine through armed struggle.

Pogrom: An organized massacre of a particular ethnic group. Aimed at Jews and prevalent in Russia.

Pol Pot: Cambodian revolutionary and politician, who governed

Cambodia from 1975 to 1979. He led the Khmer Rouge and is responsible for the Cambodian Genocide.

Ponary Massacre: Also known as the Paneriai Massacre; the massmurder of up to 100,000 people, mostly Jews, as well as Poles opposed to the Nazi regime, and Soviet prisoners of war in Vilna (today Vilnius), Lithuania. From June 1941 until July 1944 over 75,000 victims were marched to the site and shot into deep pits and trenches located there. Later, Jews were recruited to burn the corpses, and hide evidence of mass murder.

Protocols of the Elders of Zion: Notorious and widely distributed, originally published in 1903 as a hoax, a fabricated antisemitic and racist text that describes a so-called Jewish plot of global domination.

CAMPS:

- Plaszow, Poland.

Q

Quadroon: Derogatory. A person who is one-quarter Black.

Queer: A sexual or gender identity label; an umbrella term for not being heterosexual and/or cisgender. Used at one time with disparaging intent.

Question, as in Jewish Question: Also known as the Jewish Problem; European and German writers, philosophers, and theologians claimed the presence of Jews in society was an issue that needed to be addressed, including whether they should be granted civil rights, equality, and whether or not they should be forced to adapt and to give up their traditions.

Quisling: A pejorative meaning “traitor” or collaborator during World War II.

R

Racist Skinheads: Dangerous radical right, violent groups whose members embody Neo-Nazi and white supremacist beliefs.

Rape of Nanking: The mass murder and mass rape committed by imperial Japanese troops against the people of Nanking, China, in 1937.

Reich: Realm, or kingdom.

Resettlement of Jews: Ostensibly sending Jews to live elsewhere, banishing them, but intending the murder of Jews.

Restricted: Exclusive; i.e., no Jews allowed (US).

Rohingya Genocide: An ongoing genocide of Rohingya Muslims in Myanmar.

Rwandan Genocide: During a period of 100 days, between April 7 and July 15, 1994, the Hutu-led Rwandan government killed an estimated 800,000 people, mostly members of the Tutsi ethnic group.

CAMPS:

- Ravensbrück, Germany—a concentration camp for women with at least ten subcamps. Also a training base for 3,500 SS Nazi guards.

S

Saddam Hussein: Iraqi president, despot; responsible for expelling 40,000 Shiite Muslims, a massacre in Dujail in 1982, the 1988 genocide of Kurdish people, and the 1990 invasion of Kuwait, which began the Persian Gulf War.

Schutzstaffel (SS): Protection squads, initially Hitler's bodyguard unit, eventually became the elite guard that controlled the German police and the concentration camp system without regard for the law.

Shoah: Hebrew meaning "catastrophe," the mass murder of Jewish people under the German Nazi regime; a term used interchangeably with Holocaust.

Sicherheitsdienst (SD): The intelligence agency of the SS in Nazi Germany.

Sonderaktionen and *Sonderbehandlung*: Special actions or treatment, which meant execution of Jews.

Sturmabteilung (SA): Storm Detachment, also Brownshirts; a paramilitary organization, founded in 1921, that was important in the rise of Hitler and carried out violence in the streets against Jews and Nazi opponents. Subordinate to the SS.

Sturmhauptführer: A Nazi Party paramilitary rank used by both the *Sturmabteilung* and the *Schutzstaffel.*

CAMPS:

- Sobibor, Poland.
- Sachsenhausen, Berlin, Germany.
- Stutthof, near Danzig, which became part of Poland.

T

Taliban: Afghan Sunni-Islamic fundamentalist military group, waging war in Afghanistan.

Tausendjähriges Reich: Thousand-Year Reich; popularly used by the Nazis to refer to the Nazi state, a connotation which suggested that the Reich society would last for 1,000 years.

CAMPS:

- Theresienstadt, or Terezin, close to Prague, Czechoslovakia.
- Treblinka, close to Warsaw, Poland.

U

Übermenschen: Superior men. Ideal features: with white skin, Germanic or related blood, blond hair, and blue eyes.

Umsiedlung: Resettlement; deportation to a death camp.

Untermenschen: Subhumans; all Jews, Semitic peoples, Roma, Slavs, LGBTQ and Black people are referred to as primitive animals, not worthy of life or of Geneva Convention protections. Impure, with polluted blood from racial intermixing.

V

Verbrennungs und Vernichtungs Kommando: Burning and Destruction Detachment.

Vergassungskeller: Gas cellars, or gasification cellar.

Vernichtungslager: Extermination camp.

W

Waffen-SS: The military branch of the Nazi SS.

Weimar Republic: Germany's government from 1919 to 1933, just prior to the rise of Nazi Germany.

CAMPS:

- Westerbork, the Netherlands.

X

Xenophobe: A person who fears or hates foreigners and strangers, their customs and their religions; bigoted, prejudiced, sexist, white supremacist, fanatic; antisemitic.

Y

Yellow Star: Star of David required to be worn as an armband or affixed to outer garments, or, as in Hungary, on apartment buildings.

Z

Zion: *see* Protocols of Zion.

Zivilcourage: Civil courage or moral courage of your convictions.

Zyklon B: Produced by IG Farber, the German chemicals company. A powerful pesticide used in Auschwitz to annihilate millions of people.

The dictionary is of necessity incomplete. The United States Holocaust Memorial Museum indicates that "Between 1933 and 1945 Nazi Germany and its allies established more than 44,000 camps and other incarceration sites (including ghettos) throughout Europe."

Today in the US, virtually every state in the country has established hate groups: 1,020 in 2018 (Southern Poverty Law Center).

ACKNOWLEDGMENTS

I wrote this book for my parents and the millions of others whose lives were uprooted and marked by the Holocaust. Although this story took a lifetime to unearth, there are still other stories to tell—more than six million, if we include the experiences of following generations.

The many people who helped me with the research and technical aspects of the book warrant thousands of thanks. Without the expertise and technical know-how of my son Harris Kleyman, the book would never have left my computer. Doug Lang was a tremendous help with the photos. Linda Levi at the American Jewish Joint Distribution Committee, Judith Cohen and Michlean Lowy Amir from the United States Holocaust Memorial Museum, and Esther Brumberg from the Museum of Jewish Heritage—A Living Memorial to the Holocaust, thank you for your assistance and patience while I burrowed through your archives. My deepest gratitude to the people who shared their stories with me and who took time to help me during my odysseys to Hungary and Germany.

This story would not have come to fruition without Sonia Beker, her book *Symphony on Fire: A Story of Music and Spiritual Resistance During the Holocaust*, her photographs, and our shared experiences. Indeed, the encouragement of her entire family, Rita Lerner, Abe Gurko, Vivian Reisman, and the inspiration of my dear shvesters whose parents were also survivors, Anat Bar-Cohen and Deb Filler, are deeply appreciated.

Walter Elias and András Koltai in Hungary were enormously helpful with genealogical research.

The guidance of my professors at Hamline University in St. Paul,

Minnesota—Larry Sutin, Deborah Keenan, Katrina Vandenberg, and Laura Flynn—is immeasurable.

Heartfelt thanks to Michael Dennis Browne, Stephen Paulus, Michael O'Connell, Martin Goldsmith, Marin Alsop, James A. Grymes, and Leonard Bernstein, and to all the musicians and artists who, despite all the odds, persevered.

Sincere appreciation to my first editors who believed in me: Jenniey Talman, Gwendolyn Freed, Barbara Elvecrog, and to early readers Bonnie Gainsley, Jennifer Hildebrandt, Melanie Heuiser-Hill, Pam and Cory Biladeau, Diane Tremaine, Walter and Ruth Elias, and Nora Shulman, who helped make this book sing. A special shout-out to my high school English professor, William Martyn, who always thought I should pursue writing, even then. He has been a lifelong mentor and an encouraging and critical reader.

And I am so eternally grateful to Liesbeth Heenk of Amsterdam Publishers for believing in me and for publishing this book.

Another thousand thanks to the tremendous encouragement and wise counsel of my brother Robert Horvath, my sister-in-law Sara Shiewitz, and my husband Howard Kleyman, who have supported me through the years of obsession with this story. Howie encouraged me to take classes, earn my MFA, travel to do research, and he never complained about the many months I've been tethered to my computer. No matter how firmly entrenched my mind and soul have been, he maintained a calm presence throughout, cheering me through the doubts, and celebrating the discoveries.

BOOKCLUB QUESTIONS

After discussing these family secrets and histories, does this story spur you to ask questions of your own family?

Are there parallel experiences in your life that especially resonated for you? How might you examine these further?

How much of this history were you aware of? What in particular will you discuss with your family, friends, co-workers, or community?

Bertrand Russell made the comment, "Man is a credulous animal and must believe in something. In the absence of good grounds for belief, he will be satisfied with bad ones." Could the perpetrators have all been evil? What behaviors are justified during war?

The callousness of bystanders made a profound and lifelong impact on Holocaust survivors and their families. How can we prevent this now and in the future? Do you have ideas about how you might make positive changes in society? How might you advocate today for refugees?

APPENDIX

Chicken Paprikás Extraordinaire

The paprikás sauce serves as the basis for many a Hungarian dish. Chicken is the perennial favorite but it's delicious with veal or with beef, potatoes, and carrots (which is the recipe for Goulash), or lots more bell peppers, potatoes, and a little sausage (spicy, vegetarian, or chicken sausage), and it's a meal in itself, called Lecso.

2 medium sized onions, *chopped*

2 TBs vegetable oil

1 plump chicken, *skinned*

(I use a three-legged fryer, washed and cut up into serving pieces)

2 large ripe tomatoes, *cut into pieces*

or 1 pint cherry or grape-seed tomatoes, *halved*

1 green bell pepper, *cut into 1-inch chunks*

½ red pepper, *cut into 1-inch chunks*

½ yellow pepper, *cut into 1-inch chunks*

1 heaping TB sweet Hungarian paprika (or if you prefer, it can be the spicy variety).

2 garlic cloves, *minced*

salt and pepper to taste

(optional: dollop of sour cream)

Instructions:

1. Use a Dutch oven with a lid. Line the pan with the oil, then heat the oil. When the oil is hot, add the onion and brown until it's almost caramelized, stirring frequently.
2. Add the bell peppers and tomatoes and sauté for 2 minutes. Remove pan from the heat and stir in the paprika, salt, pepper, and garlic.
3. Return the pan to the heat and add the chicken and enough water to just cover the meat. Put the lid on and simmer for one hour, stirring occasionally and adding a bit more water if needed.
4. Serve over rice or dumplings. If desired, top with a dollop of sour cream.

Serves 4–6, is tastier the next day, and freezes well.

Székely Kaposzta, or Székely Goulash

It is interesting to note that Hungary probably has more recipes for cabbage than any other country. The Hungarian recipes rarely indicate whether the intended ingredient is cabbage or the more popular sauerkraut, assuming that the true connoisseur would know (a little like performance practices for Baroque music—where and whether to embellish in the notation).

3 cans sauerkraut (German, if possible)
¼–⅓ cup vegetable oil
2 large onions, *chopped*
4 ripe tomatoes, *chopped*
or 2 containers sweet cherry or grape-seed tomatoes, *halved*
1 each red, green, and yellow bell peppers, *cut into chunks*
2–3 TBs paprika (Hungarian is best)
2 TBs garlic (or more, to taste)
a few Bay leaves
salt and pepper to taste
Caraway seeds (optional)

1 cup water or tomato juice

3 lbs cut-up beef for stew. Non-Jewish people might make this with pork.

(I sometimes add a smoked turkey leg or non-Jews might add a smoked pork hock, and once it's cooked, cut the meat off the bone and add it back into the stew for a smoky flavor)

1 container sour cream (for non-Jewish or non-kosher cooks)

Instructions: •

1. Rinse the sauerkraut in cold running water for several minutes (this is to reduce the sour taste). Drain well, and squeeze the water out of it.
2. Heat the oil in a large Dutch oven pan or deep pot. Add the chopped onions and sauté until brown but not caramelized.
3. Add the bell peppers and tomato and sauté for another five minutes, stirring frequently.
4. Remove the pot from the heat, add paprika and garlic. Stir well.
5. Add the meat and the water or tomato juice, just enough to cover the meat. Stir and add the other spices. Cover and simmer over low heat for two hours, stirring every so often.
6. Add the sauerkraut and season to taste. Stir well, until the sauerkraut is coated with the paprika mixture.
7. Sauté for another hour, stirring frequently to keep the sauerkraut from sticking. If it starts to stick, add more water or tomato juice.
8. If you used smoked meat on a bone, remove it and cut the meat off the bone, then add the meat back to the pot.
9. Serve over cooked rice or quinoa and (if you don't keep kosher) swirl in a large dollop of sour cream.

This dish is even tastier the next day and freezes well. If you freeze it, leave out the sour cream.

KL. Weimar - Buchenwald

Jude

Häftlings-Personal-Karte

97.587

Fam.-Name: H o r v a t
Vorname: Nandor
Geb. am: 13.7.86 in: Szentes
Stand: verh. Kinder: 2
Wohnort: Budapest VI
Strasse: Vörösmarty ut.60
Religion: mos. Staatsang.: Ungarn
Wohnort d. Angehörigen: Ehefrau: Irma H.g. Hirschfeld Budapest w.o.
Eingewiesen am: 19.11.44
durch: BDS Budapest
in KL.: Buchenwald
Grund: Polit.Ungar - Jude
Vorstrafen: keine

Überstellt
am: ... an KL.
am: ... an KL.
am: ... an KL.
am: ... an KL.
am: ... an KL.
am: ... an KL.

Entlassung:
am: ... durch KL.:
mit Verfügung v.:

Personen-Beschreibung:
Grösse: 158 cm
Gestalt: kräft.
Gesicht: oval
Augen: braun
Nase: geb.
Mund: gew.
Ohren: abste.
Zähne: lück.Proth.
Haare: grau
Sprache: ung.dtsch.,
Bes. Kennzeichen: keine
Charakt.-Eigenschaften:
Sicherheit b. Einsatz:
I.T.S. FOTO No.
Körperliche Verfassung:

Strafen im Lager:
Grund: Art: Bemerkung:
MIL. GOV. QUESTIONNAIRE EXISTS
LIBERATED BY US ARMY

1981

__Nándor detention personal card, "Jew" from Weimar—Buchenwald.__ The upper right corner is the number assigned to my grandfather, 97-587, the same number as on the Buchenwald ID document with my father's photo. Left side, personal details: my grandfather's name, birthdate, address, "briefed" or committed November 19, 1944. Right, physical details: weight 158, build (strong), face (oval) eyes (brown), nose, teeth, hair (gray) and language. Note the bottom stamped "LIBERATED BY US ARMY."

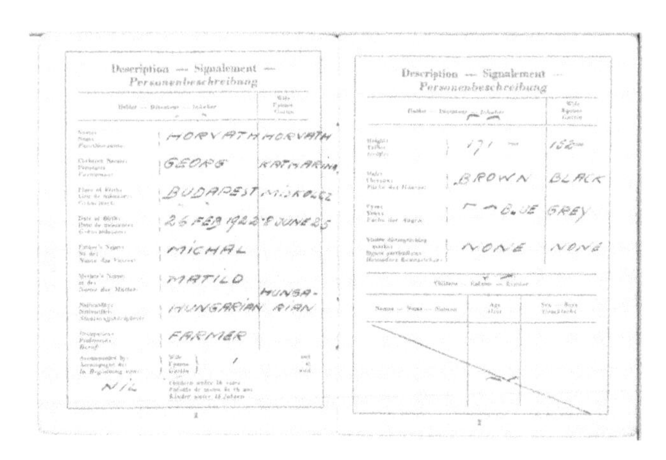

Description — Signalement — Personenbeschreibung

	Bearer	Wife
Name	HORVATH	HORVATH
Christian Name	GEORG	KATHARINA
Place of Birth	BUDAPEST	MISKOLCZ
Date of Birth	26 FEB 1922	8 JUNE 25
Father's Name	MICHAL	
Mother's Name	MATILD	
Nationality	HUNGARIAN	HUNGARIAN
Occupation	FARMER	
Accompanied by:	N/L	

Description — Signalement — Personenbeschreibung

	Bearer	Wife
Height	171	162
Hair	BROWN	BLACK
Eyes	BLUE	GREY
Visible distinguishing marks	NONE	NONE

Visa stating my father as a FARMER.

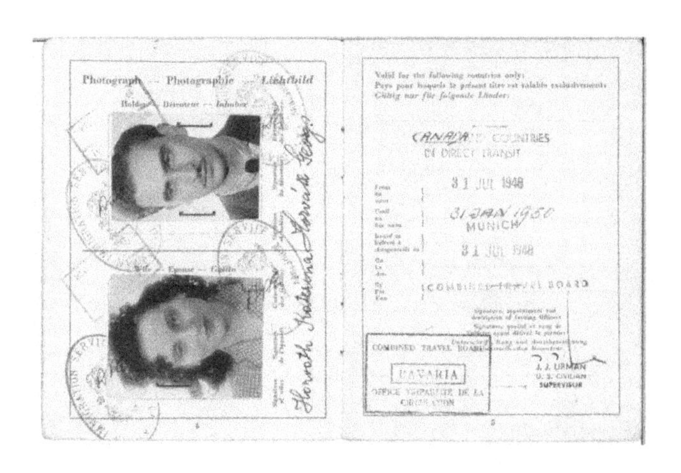

Photograph — Photographie — Lichtbild

Valid for the following countries only:
Pays pour lesquels le présent titre est valable exclusivement:
Gültig nur für folgende Länder:

CANADA & COUNTRIES
IN DIRECT TRANSIT

31 JUL 1948

31 JAN 1950
MUNICH

31 JUL 1948

COMBINED TRAVEL BOARD

COMBINED TRAVEL BOARD
BAVARIA

J. J. URMAN
U. S. CIVILIAN
SUPERVISOR

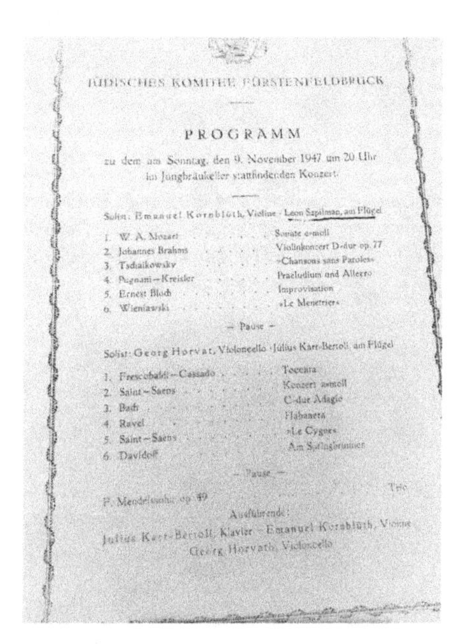

JÜDISCHES KOMITEE FÜRSTENFELDBRUCK

PROGRAMM

zu dem am Sonntag, den 9. November 1947 um 20 Uhr
im Jungbräukeller stattfindenden Konzert

Solist: Emanuel Kornblüth, Violine · Leon Szpilman, am Flügel

1. W. A. Mozart . . . . . . Sonate e-moll
2. Johannes Brahms . . . . . . Violinkonzert D-dur op. 77
3. Tschaikowsky . . . . . . »Chansons sans Paroles«
4. Pugnani – Kreisler . . . . . . Praeludium und Allegro
5. Ernest Bloch . . . . . . Improvisation
6. Wieniawski . . . . . . »Le Menetrier«

– Pause –

Solist: Georg Horvat, Violoncello · Julius Karr-Bertoli, am Flügel

1. Frescobaldi – Cassado . . . . . . Toccata
2. Saint – Saens . . . . . . Konzert a-moll
3. Bach . . . . . . C-dur Adagio
4. Ravel . . . . . . Habanera
5. Saint – Saens . . . . . . »Le Cygne«
6. Davidoff . . . . . . Am Springbrunnen

– Pause –

F. Mendelssohn op. 49 . . . . . . Trio

Ausführende:
Julius Karr-Bertoli, Klavier · Emanuel Kornblüth, Violine
Georg Horvath, Violoncello

My father's many performances. *November 1947:* Jüdisches Komitee Fürstenfeldbruck *(a town west of Munich). The pianist, Leo Szpilman, was a cousin of the protagonist in the Polanski film* The Pianist.

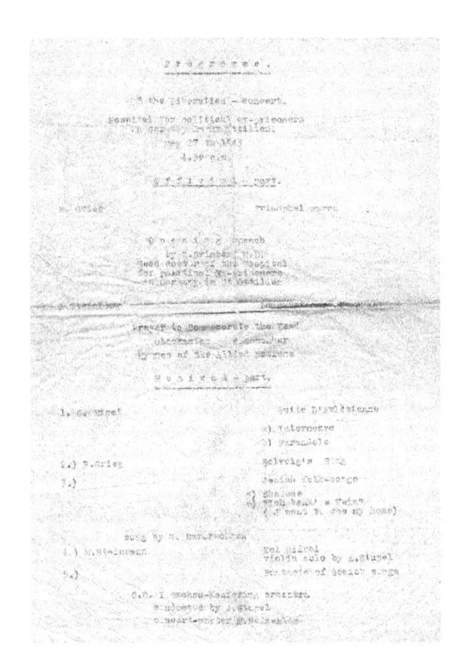

Programme.

the Liberation - Concert.

Official - part.

Opening Speech

Musical - part.

Suite L'Arlésienne

a) Intermezzo

b) Farandole

2.) E. Grieg — Solveig's Song

3.) Jewish folk-songs

Kol Nidrei
violin solo by A. Stupel

5.)

Liberation Concert Program on May 27, 1945. Kol Nidrei *was on this first performance of the St Ottilien Orchestra. Document kindly provided by Dr. Robert Hilliard and Cyrill Schaefer from the dphospital-ottilien.org.*

6 óp. után [illegible] mentünk a táborba, [illegible] és utána [illegible]
a [illegible] legényeinek a [illegible], Kint a [illegible] „[illegible]”
[illegible] végezni. Volt nekem egy új kabátom ami teljesen
[illegible] (Ezt azért jegyzem meg [illegible] nagy [illegible])
[illegible]
[illegible] és a [illegible]
[illegible]
[illegible]
[illegible]
[illegible]
[illegible]
[illegible]
[illegible]
[illegible]
[illegible] Tel. [illegible], ahol egy [illegible]
[illegible]
[illegible]
[illegible]
[illegible]
[illegible] és cipőt. [illegible] adtak [illegible]
[illegible]
[illegible] és az is [illegible] volt.
[illegible] egy [illegible]
Volt [illegible]
a [illegible] új szép ruhát, inget, cipőt adtak, [illegible]
[illegible] Budapest [illegible]
[illegible]

BAD-~~[illegible]~~
REICHENHALL

[illegible]

My father's handwritten testimony

ABOUT THE AUTHOR

Janet Horvath is a lifelong performing classical musician, soloist, speaker, educator, and author. The Minnesota Orchestra's associate principal cello from 1980 to 2012, she has appeared as soloist with orchestra, and in recital and chamber music throughout the United States, Canada, and Europe. She has appeared on national radio and television, including the BBC, CBC, and NPR and on podcasts.

A contributing writer for the online classical music e-magazine Interlude.HK, she has penned over 350 feature articles about music and musicians. Recent essays have appeared in national publications, including *The New York Times, The Atlantic, The Minneapolis Star Tribune* and international music publications *Musical America, Chamber Music America, Strings Magazine, The Brass Herald* and *Strad Magazine*.

The author of the award-winning book *Playing (Less) Hurt—an Injury Prevention Guide for Musicians*, she has worked with instrumentalists to establish a holistic approach to music making.

A pioneer and authority in the area of the medical problems of performing artists, and a passionate arts advocate, Janet is well-known among both amateur and professional musicians, teachers and students, and health care providers. Her masterclasses and seminars have been well received by orchestras including the San Francisco Symphony, Utah Symphony, Indianapolis Symphony, and Boston Symphony Orchestra, and at colleges, conservatories, and conferences from coast to coast.

Through her writing and musical performances, Janet creates restorative conversations, offers spiritual sustenance, and explores music's life-bringing and healing power. In the age of fast-moving news, despite our best efforts, uncertainty and divisiveness prevail. Janet hopes to counteract the consequences of intolerance and endeavors to stimulate dialogue about inequality and the ramifications of racism.

Ms. Horvath earned her master's degree in music performance from Indiana University and completed her MFA in creative writing at Hamline University in St. Paul, MN.

Look for her classical music articles which appear at www.interlude.hk. More information can be found on her website www.janethorvath.com.

AMSTERDAM PUBLISHERS HOLOCAUST LIBRARY

The series **Holocaust Survivor Memoirs World War II** consists of the following autobiographies of survivors:

Outcry. Holocaust Memoirs, by Manny Steinberg

Hank Brodt Holocaust Memoirs. A Candle and a Promise, by Deborah Donnelly

The Dead Years. Holocaust Memoirs, by Joseph Schupack

Rescued from the Ashes. The Diary of Leokadia Schmidt, Survivor of the Warsaw Ghetto, by Leokadia Schmidt

My Lvov. Holocaust Memoir of a twelve-year-old Girl, by Janina Hescheles

Remembering Ravensbrück. From Holocaust to Healing, by Natalie Hess

Wolf. A Story of Hate, by Zeev Scheinwald with Ella Scheinwald

Save my Children. An Astonishing Tale of Survival and its Unlikely Hero, by Leon Kleiner with Edwin Stepp

Holocaust Memoirs of a Bergen-Belsen Survivor & Classmate of Anne Frank, by Nanette Blitz Konig

Defiant German - Defiant Jew. A Holocaust Memoir from inside the Third Reich, by Walter Leopold with Les Leopold

In a Land of Forest and Darkness. The Holocaust Story of two Jewish Partisans, by Sara Lustigman Omelinski

Holocaust Memories. Annihilation and Survival in Slovakia, by Paul Davidovits

From Auschwitz with Love. The Inspiring Memoir of Two Sisters' Survival, Devotion and Triumph Told by Manci Grunberger Beran & Ruth Grunberger Mermelstein, by Daniel Seymour

Remetz. Resistance Fighter and Survivor of the Warsaw Ghetto, by Jan Yohay Remetz

My March Through Hell. A Young Girl's Terrifying Journey to Survival, by Halina Kleiner with Edwin Stepp

The series **Holocaust Survivor True Stories WWII** consists of the following biographies:

Among the Reeds. The true story of how a family survived the Holocaust, by Tammy Bottner

A Holocaust Memoir of Love & Resilience. Mama's Survival from Lithuania to America, by Ettie Zilber

Living among the Dead. My Grandmother's Holocaust Survival Story of Love and Strength, by Adena Bernstein Astrowsky

Heart Songs. A Holocaust Memoir, by Barbara Gilford

Shoes of the Shoah. The Tomorrow of Yesterday, by Dorothy Pierce

Hidden in Berlin. A Holocaust Memoir, by Evelyn Joseph Grossman

Separated Together. The Incredible True WWII Story of Soulmates Stranded an Ocean Apart, by Kenneth P. Price, Ph.D.

The Man Across the River. The incredible story of one man's will to survive the Holocaust, by Zvi Wiesenfeld

If Anyone Calls, Tell Them I Died. A Memoir, by Emanuel (Manu) Rosen

The House on Thrömerstrasse. A Story of Rebirth and Renewal in the Wake of the Holocaust, by Ron Vincent

Dancing with my Father. His hidden past. Her quest for truth. How Nazi Vienna shaped a family's identity, by Jo Sorochinsky

The Story Keeper. Weaving the Threads of Time and Memory - A Memoir, by Fred Feldman

Krisia's Silence. The Girl who was not on Schindler's List, by Ronny Hein

Defying Death on the Danube. A Holocaust Survival Story, by Debbie J. Callahan with Henry Stern

A Doorway to Heroism. A decorated German-Jewish Soldier who became an American Hero, by Rabbi W. Jack Romberg

The Shoemaker's Son. The Life of a Holocaust Resister, by Laura Beth Bakst

The Redhead of Auschwitz. A True Story, by Nechama Birnbaum

Land of Many Bridges. My Father's Story, by Bela Ruth Samuel Tenenholtz

Creating Beauty from the Abyss. The Amazing Story of Sam Herciger, Auschwitz Survivor and Artist, by Lesley Ann Richardson

On Sunny Days We Sang. A Holocaust Story of Survival and Resilience, by Jeannette Grunhaus de Gelman

Painful Joy. A Holocaust Family Memoir, by Max J. Friedman

I Give You My Heart. A True Story of Courage and Survival, by Wendy Holden

In the Time of Madmen, by Mark A. Prelas

Monsters and Miracles. Horror, Heroes and the Holocaust, by Ira Wesley Kitmacher

Flower of Vlora. Growing up Jewish in Communist Albania, by Anna Kohen

Aftermath: Coming of Age on Three Continents. A Memoir, by Annette Libeskind Berkovits

Not a real Enemy. The True Story of a Hungarian Jewish Man's Fight for Freedom, by Robert Wolf

Zaidy's War. Four Armies, Three Continents, Two Brothers. One Man's Impossible Story of Endurance, by Martin Bodek

The Glassmaker's Son. Looking for the World my Father left behind in Nazi Germany, by Peter Kupfer

The Apprentice of Buchenwald. The True Story of the Teenage Boy Who Sabotaged Hitler's War Machine, by Oren Schneider

The Cello Still Sings. A Generational Story of the Holocaust and of the Transformative Power of Music, by Janet Horvath

The series **Jewish Children in the Holocaust** consists of the following autobiographies of Jewish children hidden during WWII in the Netherlands:

Searching for Home. The Impact of WWII on a Hidden Child, by Joseph Gosler

See You Tonight and Promise to be a Good Boy! War memories, by Salo Muller

Sounds from Silence. Reflections of a Child Holocaust Survivor, Psychiatrist and Teacher, by Robert Krell

Sabine's Odyssey. A Hidden Child and her Dutch Rescuers, by Agnes Schipper

The Journey of a Hidden Child, by Harry Pila and Robin Black

The series **New Jewish Fiction** consists of the following novels, written by Jewish authors. All novels are set in the time during or after the Holocaust.

The Corset Maker. A Novel, by Annette Libeskind Berkovits

Escaping the Whale. The Holocaust is over. But is it ever over for the next generation? by Ruth Rotkowitz

When the Music Stopped. Willy Rosen's Holocaust, by Casey Hayes

Hands of Gold. One Man's Quest to Find the Silver Lining in Misfortune, by Roni Robbins

The Girl Who Counted Numbers. A Novel, by Roslyn Bernstein

There was a garden in Nuremberg. A Novel, by Navina Michal Clemerson

The Butterfly and the Axe, by Omer Bartov

Good for a Single Journey, by Helen Joyce

The series **Holocaust Books for Young Adults** consists of the following novels, based on true stories:

The Boy behind the Door. How Salomon Kool Escaped the Nazis. Inspired by a True Story, by David Tabatsky

Running for Shelter. A True Story, by Suzette Sheft

The Precious Few. An Inspirational Saga of Courage based on True Stories, by David Twain with Art Twain

Jacob's Courage: A Holocaust Love Story, by Charles S. Weinblatt

The series **WW2 Historical Fiction** consists of the following novels, some of which are based on true stories:

Mendelevski's Box. A Heartwarming and Heartbreaking Jewish Survivor's Story, by Roger Swindells

A Quiet Genocide. The Untold Holocaust of Disabled Children WW2 Germany, by Glenn Bryant

The Knife-Edge Path, by Patrick T. Leahy

Brave Face. The Inspiring WWII Memoir of a Dutch/German Child, by I. Caroline Crocker and Meta A. Evenly

When We Had Wings. The Gripping Story of an Orphan in Janusz Korczak's Orphanage. A Historical Novel, by Tami Shem-Tov

Want to be an AP book reviewer?

Reviews are very important in a world dominated by the social media and social proof. Please drop us a line if you want to join the *AP review team.* We will then add you to our list of advance reviewers. No strings attached. info@amsterdampublishers.com

CPSIA information can be obtained
at www.ICGtesting.com
Printed in the USA
BVHW032107160223
658656BV00001B/1